PAT BROWN, MBA

Financial Literacy For Pro Athletes

"Financial Strategies Every Pro Athlete Needs to Build, Protect, and Sustain Wealth"

AF811716

ABRAM 47 BROWN

First published by AbramBrown47 2025

Copyright © 2025 by Pat Brown, MBA

All rights reserved. No part of this publication may be reproduced, stored or transmitted in any form or by any means, electronic, mechanical, photocopying, recording, scanning, or otherwise without written permission from the publisher. It is illegal to copy this book, post it to a website, or distribute it by any other means without permission.

Pat Brown, MBA asserts the moral right to be identified as the author of this work.

Pat Brown, MBA has no responsibility for the persistence or accuracy of URLs for external or third-party Internet Websites referred to in this publication and does not guarantee that any content on such Websites is, or will remain, accurate or appropriate.

Designations used by companies to distinguish their products are often claimed as trademarks. All brand names and product names used in this book and on its cover are trade names, service marks, trademarks and registered trademarks of their respective owners. The publishers and the book are not associated with any product or vendor mentioned in this book. None of the companies referenced within the book have endorsed the book.

First edition

ISBN: 978-1-967737-22-2

This book was professionally typeset on Reedsy.
Find out more at reedsy.com

Contents

Preface

There are moments in life that change everything.

For athletes, one of those moments is the day you officially "make it" — the day your name gets called, your contract gets signed, or your dream finally crosses into reality.

It's a moment filled with pride, adrenaline, and gratitude. All the early mornings, late nights, injuries, sacrifices, and doubters — they were all worth it.

But there's something that almost nobody prepares you for: what happens next.

Because the truth is, *making it* and *keeping it* are two very different games.

And staying at the top — financially, professionally, and personally — requires a skill set most athletes were never taught.

That's why I wrote this book.

My Story: Why This Book Exists

My name is Pat Brown. I'm a former Division I football player, team captain at the University of Kansas, and a brief professional athlete myself. Today, I'm a wealth advisor and a fierce advocate for financial literacy, especially for athletes, entertainers, and high-achieving individuals stepping into the big leagues of life.

I've seen too much.

I've watched teammates sign life-changing deals... only to file for bankruptcy a few years later.

I've watched good people get manipulated by bad "friends," shady "advisors," and high-pressure "opportunities."

I've seen the pressure athletes face — the unspoken expectation to "save" their family, fund their friends' dreams, and live up to a lifestyle that often burns faster than the money coming in.

And I've seen the toll it takes when the money dries up — the shame, the silence, the "how did this happen to me?"

But I've also seen the other side: the athletes who take control, who learn, who build, who protect, who invest, who win the *long* game, not just the highlight reel.

That's who this book is for.

If you're reading this, you're not just an athlete.

You're a CEO. You're a business. You're a brand. You're a future success story — not just in your sport, but in your life.

This book exists to make sure you have the tools, the mindset, and the real-world knowledge to protect what you worked so hard to earn.

If You Read My Previous Books...

If you read *Financial Literacy for NIL*, *Financial Literacy for Student Athletes*, or *Financial Literacy for Parents of Student Athletes* while you were in college, congratulations.

You already have a strong foundation.

You know the basics of budgeting, credit, savings, insurance, and the importance of building the right financial team.

But let me be very clear:

The pro game is different.

Bigger money.

More people pulling at you.

More complex taxes.

More risk if you make mistakes.

This book is not just a repeat of what you learned in college. This is the graduate-level playbook — the full game plan for your professional career.

Everything we're about to cover is about *protecting, growing,* and *securing* your financial future, not just your financial present.

What's Different Now That You're Pro?

When you're in college, you're playing for your future.

When you're a pro, you're playing for your life.

The money starts flowing. So do the expectations.

You're not just managing yourself anymore — you're managing contracts, agents, taxes, marketing deals, endorsements, investment pitches, family pressures, social media demands, and the unknown length of your career.

One injury can change everything.

One bad decision can cost you millions.

One bad investment can erase everything you've built.

But one *smart decision*?

It can set you up for a lifetime.

How This Book Will Help You

This isn't a "how to get rich quick" book.

This isn't a lecture.

This isn't about fear or paranoia.

This is about **education**, **empowerment**, and **execution**.

Inside this book, we'll cover:

- How to set up your banking and budgeting systems as a pro
- How to read and truly understand your contract
- What to do with your signing bonus (spoiler alert: it's not all for spending)
- How to handle taxes in multiple states and cities
- Why you MUST keep your agent, manager, and financial advisor

separate

- How to deal with the pressure from family and friends
- The realities of building wealth as a Black, Latino, or international athlete
- How to protect your name, image, and brand
- How to create a financial foundation that lasts beyond your career
- How to avoid the "broke athlete" trap

And much more.

Think of this book as your financial playbook for the pros.

You wouldn't step onto the field, court, track, or ring without a game plan.

Don't step into your financial life without one either.

My Promise to You

I'm not here to sell you a fantasy.

I'm here to give you the real talk you deserve.

I'll break down complex financial ideas into simple, plain English.

I'll share real examples — the good, the bad, and the ugly — from athletes who've walked this path before you.

I'll give you action steps at every turn.

I'll tell you what to watch for, what to avoid, what to lean into, and what to question.

Most of all, I'll treat you with the respect you deserve.

You're not just another "athlete story." You're the author of your own future.

And that future can be *incredible* if you play it right.

How to Use This Book

You don't need to read this entire book in one sitting.

In fact, I encourage you not to.

Read what you need, when you need it.

Come back to chapters as situations arise: when you're signing a deal, when you're renegotiating, when you're thinking about real estate, when you're fielding business offers, when you're planning for retirement.

Use this book like a training manual.

- Highlight it.
- Tab it.
- Write in the margins.
- Bookmark key sections.
- Share it with your inner circle (the ones you trust).

This isn't just a book. It's a resource. It's your playbook for a long, successful, financially powerful life.

Final Thought Before We Dive In

You made it here because of your discipline, your vision, your grind, and your belief in yourself.

Those same qualities will serve you in your financial life.

It's easy to get overwhelmed.

It's tempting to delegate everything to "experts."

It's seductive to live in the moment and push off "adulting" until "later."

But later comes fast.

And trust me — it's much better to be prepared *now* than to try to play catch-up when things get m

Why I Write This Book

By Pat Brown, MBA

If you ask most people why they write a book, they might say it's because they had a story to tell, a message to share, or a goal to achieve.

For me, it's all of those things — but also something deeper.

I wrote *Financial Literacy For Pro Athletes* because I've lived this world.

I've been the athlete stepping into the unknown.

I've been the young man handed opportunities and challenges I wasn't financially prepared for.

I've seen teammates go from signing bonuses to bankruptcy.

I've sat across from friends who were once on top of the world, only to see them struggling once the lights faded.

And I've lived long enough to understand that while talent gets you in the door, wisdom keeps you in the game.

Financial literacy is that wisdom.

It's the difference between a career that builds a legacy and a career that ends in regret.

I wrote this book because athletes deserve better.

Better education.

Better preparation.

Better futures.

Growing Up Without Financial Literacy

I wasn't born understanding money.

I grew up in a world where financial conversations didn't happen at the dinner table.

Where money was a source of stress, not strategy.

Where dreams were big but the financial blueprint to achieve them was missing.

When I went off to college on a football scholarship, I was financially illiterate.

I could read defenses. I could outwork anyone in the weight room. I could lead a team.

But I couldn't tell you what a credit score was.

I didn't understand taxes, investing, saving, or budgeting.

And I was embarrassed by it.

That embarrassment turned into motivation.

I started reading, learning, asking questions.

And over time, I realized something:

Financial literacy isn't a talent. It's a skill.

A skill anyone can learn — if they're given the chance.

Most athletes are never given that chance.

Until now.

Watching Teammates Struggle

When you're part of a team, you see everything.

You see the guy who buys three new cars the day after he signs.

You see the guy who supports his entire extended family — until the money runs out.

You see the guy who signs every "business opportunity" that gets pitched his way — gyms, restaurants, record labels, fashion lines — and loses it all.

You see the marriages crumble under financial stress.

You see the friendships disappear when the money dries up.

You see the mental health struggles that come when the checks stop and the calls stop and the "love" stops.

And you start to realize:

Talent doesn't protect you from financial destruction.

Fame doesn't protect you.

Money alone doesn't protect you.

Only *wisdom* does.

Only *discipline* does.

Only *knowledge* and *preparation* do.

Building a Career in Financial Education

After my playing days, I pursued a career in finance.

Not because I dreamed of spreadsheets and suits.

But because I was driven by a mission: to make sure other athletes — other young men and women stepping into life-changing moments — had the tools I wish I had.

Over the years, I've worked with athletes, entertainers, entrepreneurs, doctors, lawyers, and everyday families.

And the lesson is always the same:

It's not how much you make. It's how much you keep, grow, and protect.

Financial literacy isn't just about numbers.

It's about freedom.

Freedom to choose your future.

Freedom to say "yes" when you want to.

Freedom to say "no" when you need to.

Freedom to retire when you want, not when you're forced to.

Freedom to help your family responsibly — not become their crutch.

Freedom to build a life that's about *more* than survival.

A life that's about *purpose*.

Seeing the Same Mistakes, Over and Over

Writing this book wasn't a "nice idea."

It was a *necessity*.

Because no matter how much changes in the sports world — bigger salaries, bigger endorsement deals, bigger platforms — the same financial mistakes keep happening.

- Signing contracts without understanding the terms
- Trusting the wrong people
- Overspending to "keep up" with an image
- Underestimating taxes
- Overcommitting to family and friends
- Investing in businesses without doing real due diligence
- Failing to build a real financial plan for life after sports

These mistakes are predictable.

Which means they're preventable — if you're educated.

If you're empowered.

If you're equipped.

Giving You the Playbook I Wish I Had

If someone had handed me a playbook like this when I was 21 years old, it would have changed my entire financial journey.

It would have saved me from mistakes.

It would have accelerated my growth.

It would have given me peace, confidence, and control much earlier in life.

That's what I want for you.

Not perfection.

Not "never making a mistake."

But *power.*

The power to make informed decisions.

The power to recover when you stumble.

The power to create a life that's about ownership, not regret.

Respecting Your Journey

You didn't get here by accident.

You've outworked, out-hustled, outlasted, and out-believed a million others who wanted what you have.

You deserve to be here.

You deserve to be successful — not just athletically, but financially.

And you deserve resources that treat you with respect, not condescension.

That's why this book is written the way it is:

- Plain English, not financial jargon
- Real-world examples, not textbook theories
- Action steps, not just advice
- Empathy for where you're starting
- Belief in where you can go

Honoring Your Legacy

Most athletes don't just play for themselves.

They play for their families.

Their communities.

Their cultures.

Their future kids.

Their future grandkids.

When you get financially literate, you're not just protecting your career.

You're protecting your *legacy*.

You're changing the trajectory of your family's future.

You're creating opportunities that ripple out far beyond your playing days.

You're proving that athletes can be more than headlines about "broke after retirement."

You're showing that athletes can be financial leaders, investors, entrepreneurs, philanthropists, and wealth-builders.

You're showing that you are more than a player. You are a CEO of your own life.

Because You Deserve Freedom

At the end of the day, that's what this is all about.

Freedom.

Freedom to live life on your terms.

Freedom to retire on your own schedule.

Freedom to say "no" to bad deals.

Freedom to say "yes" to dreams you haven't even dreamed yet.

Freedom to enjoy the fruits of your labor without fear.

Freedom to give back without going broke.

Freedom to inspire the next generation of athletes to do it smarter, better, stronger.

You didn't come this far just to lose.

You came this far to win — not just on the field, but in life.

And that's why I wrote this book.

Because you deserve every tool, every strategy, and every ounce of wisdom that will help you win the biggest game of all:

The game of building a life of stability, strength, and legacy.

Let's get it.

My Background: From College Athlete to Financial Advisor

When people look at my life today — financial advisor, educator, author, speaker — they often assume that I must have always had this knowledge.

But the truth is, my journey to financial literacy was not smooth, straight, or even intentional at the start.

It was born out of necessity.

It was shaped by experience.

And it was fueled by a deep desire to make sure others had a roadmap I didn't.

This chapter isn't just about my credentials. It's about context — so you understand where I come from, why I do this work, and why *you* can trust that I get it.

From Humble Beginnings

I wasn't born into wealth.

I wasn't raised with investment accounts, financial advisors, or trust funds.

I was raised in a family where money conversations were rare, usually stressful, and often centered around "making ends meet."

I grew up watching my parents work hard — very hard — just to provide the basics.

And even though love, discipline, and values were abundant, financial education wasn't.

When you grow up like that, money can feel like a mystery —

something you hope shows up when you need it, rather than something you learn how to manage, grow, and control.

That's the environment I came from.

And it shaped everything that followed.

Chasing the Dream: College Athletics

Sports were my ticket to something bigger.

I poured myself into football. It wasn't just a game — it was a lifeline.

My work ethic, discipline, and competitive drive earned me a scholarship to the University of Kansas, where I played Division I football.

I served as a team captain. I experienced the thrill of competing at the highest collegiate level.

And for a moment, it felt like all my dreams were coming true.

But behind the scenes?

Financially, I was still flying blind.

I didn't understand budgeting.

I didn't know how taxes worked.

I didn't understand credit scores, insurance, or investing.

I knew how to run routes, read defenses, and motivate a locker room.

But when it came to money? I was vulnerable.

And that vulnerability scared me.

A Brief Professional Career — and a Wake-Up Call

After college, I had a brief professional stint.

It was enough to get a taste of the "pro athlete life"... and enough to realize how unprepared I was for it.

I saw how quickly money could come — and how quickly it could go.

I saw how teammates could be surrounded by people who didn't have their best interests at heart.

I saw how the pressure to "look rich" could outpace actually *being* rich.

And I realized: if I didn't get serious about financial literacy, I'd end up another cautionary tale.

I didn't want that.

Not for me.

Not for the people I cared about.

And not for the next generation coming up behind me.

Pivoting Into Finance

That realization changed the course of my life.

I went back to school.

I earned my MBA.

I immersed myself in the world of finance, investments, insurance, estate planning, and wealth management.

I sought mentors.

I asked questions.

I studied not just the technical skills, but the emotional realities of money: fear, greed, insecurity, pride, hope.

And over time, I built a career as a financial advisor, specializing in working with athletes, entertainers, medical professionals, and other high-achieving individuals who needed real, relatable, trusted financial guidance.

Guidance that was clear, practical, and free of the usual financial jargon.

Guidance that treated them with respect.

Guidance that wasn't about selling products — but about building futures.

Why Athletes Are Different

Working with athletes is different.

The money often comes fast.

The careers are often short.

The public pressure is intense.

The family expectations are heavy.

The investment pitches are endless.

And the margin for error is razor-thin.

Most traditional financial planning advice doesn't account for that.

It assumes a steady, 40-year career with a predictable income.

That's not the reality for most athletes.

And that's why athletes need advice that's tailored to *their* reality — not recycled advice meant for a completely different life.

That's the advice I strive to provide.

Advice grounded in experience.

Advice grounded in respect.

Advice grounded in real-world understanding of what it's like to be in their cleats, their shoes, their jersey.

Full Circle: From Student to Teacher

Today, when I speak to athletes, I don't come at them like some outsider wagging a finger.

I come as someone who sat where they sit.

Someone who faced the same temptations, the same fears, the same hopes.

Someone who made mistakes.

Someone who learned.

Someone who rebuilt.

Someone who now dedicates his life to making sure *they* have a better path.

A clearer roadmap.

A stronger foundation.

Because every athlete deserves the chance to win the biggest game of all:

The game of life after sports.

Financially.

Emotionally.

Relationally.
And generationally.
That's my mission.
That's why I do this work.
That's why I wrote this book.
And that's why I'm honored you're reading it now.
Let's keep building — together.

My Passion for Financial Literacy in the Athletic Community

When you've lived inside the world of athletics — when you've sweated, bled, celebrated, and sacrificed alongside other athletes — you understand something that most outsiders never will:

Athletes are some of the most driven, disciplined, ambitious people on the planet.

But when it comes to financial literacy?

They've often been set up to fail.

That reality — that injustice — lights a fire inside me every single day.

It's why I wrote this book.

It's why I speak at colleges, professional teams, and training camps.

It's why I mentor young athletes long after their playing days are over.

It's why I've dedicated my career to making financial education relatable, accessible, and real for the athletic community.

Because the truth is, athletes don't need pity.

They need preparation.

They don't need lectures.

They need tools.

They don't need handouts.

They need empowerment.

And they deserve it.

They've earned it.

They've already proven that with the grit, resilience, and commitment it took to get where they are.

My passion for this work isn't academic.

It's personal.
It's lived.
It's real.

Why Athletes Are Often Left Out

Financial education is broken in this country.

Most people don't grow up learning how to budget, invest, protect themselves, or build wealth.

But athletes face an even more extreme version of that problem.

They're thrust into high-earning careers at a young age — often with no real preparation for what that money means, how to manage it, or how quickly it can disappear.

They're treated like superheroes — invincible, untouchable — when in reality, their financial lives are often as vulnerable as anyone else's.

They're surrounded by expectations — to spend, to save others, to live a certain lifestyle — without being taught how to create lasting financial security.

And when things go wrong?

They're judged harshly.

They're mocked.

They're used as cautionary tales.

It's unfair.

It's preventable.

And it's exactly why I'm passionate about being part of the solution.

Financial Literacy as a Form of Freedom

To me, financial literacy isn't just about math skills.

It's about freedom.

Freedom to:

- Walk away from bad deals.

- Say no to bad relationships.
- Protect yourself against predators.
- Retire on your own terms.
- Support your family without sacrificing your future.
- Create generational wealth.
- Build businesses, charities, and legacies that matter.

When an athlete understands money, they don't just survive — they thrive.

They don't just play the game — they own the game.

They move from being "managed" to being "in control."

And that shift? That empowerment?

It's one of the most beautiful things I've had the honor of witnessing.

Changing the Narrative

For too long, the dominant narrative around athletes and money has been one of failure.

"Athletes go broke."

"Athletes make dumb decisions."

"Athletes are irresponsible."

That narrative is lazy.

It ignores the systemic failures — the lack of education, the exploitation, the isolation.

It ignores the human side of the story.

My passion is about changing that narrative.

It's about showing that with the right education, the right tools, and the right mindset, athletes can be among the *best* financial stewards, leaders, investors, and wealth-builders in the world.

I've seen it happen.

I've helped it happen.

And I believe in it with every fiber of my being.

Why This Work Matters So Much

Because every athlete who gets financially literate changes the game for themselves.

And for their families.

And for their communities.

And for the generations that follow.

When an athlete takes control of their money, they model a new possibility for everyone watching:

- That success isn't just about highlights and contracts.
- That real wealth isn't about spending — it's about ownership.
- That smart is strong.
- That being financially prepared is being professionally prepared.
- That you can live free, not trapped.

This work matters because *you* matter.

Your story matters.

Your future matters.

And your impact — far beyond the field, court, track, or arena — matters.

A Personal Commitment

I'm not here to check a box.

I'm not here for clout.

I'm here because I know what it feels like to be talented, driven, ambitious — and financially underprepared.

I'm here because I believe in athletes — not just as players, but as people.

I'm here because I believe in *you*.

And I'm committed — fiercely, fully, and unapologetically — to making sure you have every tool, every strategy, and every advantage possible to win the biggest game of all:

The game of life after sports.

Financially strong.

Emotionally strong.

Generationally strong.

That's my passion.

That's my mission.

And that's why this book — and this movement toward athlete financial literacy — matters so much.

Let's build it together.

How This Book Is Different

If you've picked up financial books before, you might be expecting more of the same:

Charts. Graphs. Complicated formulas. Generic advice like "Spend less than you earn" or "Invest early and often."

That's not what you're going to find here.

Financial Literacy For Pro Athletes was written with a different mission, a different understanding, and a different level of respect for who you are and what you face.

This book was built specifically for the athlete experience.

Not just any athlete.

The professional athlete experience.

An experience where money comes fast, careers can be short, opportunities are enormous, and the risks are just as high.

An experience where the old "work for 40 years and retire at 65" playbook simply does not apply.

An experience that demands a different kind of financial thinking, strategy, and execution.

Here's how this book is different:

It's Written By Someone Who's Lived It

I'm not an outsider looking in.

I'm not a financial academic who studied athletes from a distance.

I'm someone who played at the highest collegiate level, had a brief professional career, transitioned into finance, and has spent two decades advising high-achieving individuals — including athletes like you.

I know the pressures.

I know the temptations.

I know the expectations.

I know how quickly the money can come — and how quickly it can go.

I'm not guessing at what you need.

I've lived it. I've seen it. I've helped others navigate it.

This book comes from real life, not theory.

It Respects Your Intelligence and Your Reality

Too many financial "experts" talk down to athletes.

They assume you can't understand complex concepts.

They assume you're reckless or irresponsible.

They assume that if you fail financially, it's because you didn't listen.

I don't believe that.

I believe that most athletes have incredible discipline, focus, and drive — they just haven't been given the right tools or the right education at the right time.

This book gives you those tools.

Clear. Straightforward. No jargon. No condescension. Just real information you can use immediately to build a stronger future.

It Addresses the Real Athlete Lifestyle

Traditional financial advice assumes you:

- Have a steady paycheck for 30-40 years.
- Live and work in the same city most of your life.
- Don't have to navigate multi-state taxes.
- Aren't a public figure with brand value.
- Aren't supporting multiple people financially.
- Aren't fielding daily "investment opportunities" from friends, family,

and strangers.

That's not your life.

Your life is unique.

Your financial strategy needs to be, too.

This book is built around:

- Seasonal income flows.
- Multi-state and multi-country tax realities.
- Brand building and protection.
- Wealth-building over a shorter earning window.
- Family dynamics and financial boundaries.
- Managing fame, expectations, and pressure.

It Focuses on Ownership, Not Just Earnings

Anyone can "make money."

The real power is in *keeping it, growing it, protecting it,* and *owning it.*

This book isn't just about getting the bag.

It's about securing it.

- Understanding contracts.
- Choosing the right professionals.
- Building investment portfolios.
- Protecting yourself with the right insurance.
- Setting up businesses (the right way).
- Creating estate plans that leave a legacy, not chaos.

You worked too hard to lose it all because you didn't know better.

This book makes sure you know better — and do better.

It's Built for the Long Game

Some people think an athlete's financial life ends when their playing days do.

Wrong.

That's when the real game begins.

The game of sustaining, growing, and multiplying your wealth.

The game of transitioning into business, entrepreneurship, philanthropy, or new careers.

The game of living life on your terms for decades to come.

This book isn't just about surviving your playing career.

It's about setting you up to thrive for the next 40, 50, 60 years.

Financial literacy isn't a one-time thing.

It's a lifestyle.

This book teaches you how to live it.

It Honors Your Whole Story

You are not just an athlete.

You are a person.

A son. A daughter. A sibling. A parent. A partner. A leader. A builder.

You carry the hopes and dreams of your family, your community, your younger self.

You are more than your stats.

You are more than your contract.

You are more than your playing career.

You are the architect of your future.

This book was written to honor all of that.

To honor *you*.

To help you build a future that reflects the full greatness of who you are — not just who you were on game day.

That's how this book is different.

It's real.

It's respectful.
It's practical.
It's empowering.
And it's here to serve you — at every stage of your journey.
Let's get started.

How to Use This Book

You're about to step into a financial playbook designed specifically for professional athletes.

Not fans. Not outsiders. Not armchair critics who have never lived the pressure, the spotlight, or the reality you're living.

This book is for you.

And like any great playbook, it's here to be *used* — not just read.

Not memorized.

Not tucked away on a shelf.

Used.

Over and over again. As your career grows. As your life evolves. As new financial challenges and opportunities come your way.

This book was built to move with you.

Here's how to make the most of it:

1. Take It One Chapter at a Time

You don't need to read this book cover to cover in one sitting.

In fact, I recommend you don't.

Some chapters will hit you right now — like how to handle your signing bonus, how to budget during the season, how to vet an agent or financial advisor.

Other chapters may not feel urgent until later — like estate planning, retirement strategies, or setting up charitable foundations.

That's okay.

Treat this book like a toolbox.

Come to the right tool when you need it.

Mark the chapters that matter to you today.

Then circle back when life calls for the next move.

2. Read Actively, Not Passively

This isn't a Netflix show you zone out to.

This is your life.

Highlight. Underline. Dog-ear pages. Take notes. Write questions in the margins.

Make this book messy with your engagement.

The more you interact with it, the more you'll own the information — and the better prepared you'll be when real decisions show up.

3. Apply As You Go

Knowledge without action is useless.

If you read a chapter about setting up automatic savings — go set up automatic savings.

If you learn about why you need an independent financial advisor — book some interviews with candidates.

If you read about multi-state tax issues — schedule a meeting with your CPA.

Don't just "know" this stuff.

Do it.

Your future self will thank you.

4. Keep This Book Nearby During Key Career Moments

This book will be especially useful during key career milestones:

- Signing your first pro contract
- Receiving your first signing bonus
- Entering free agency

- Renegotiating contracts
- Landing endorsement deals
- Dealing with injuries or forced retirement
- Transitioning out of sports entirely

When these moments come — and they will — pull this book back out.

Revisit the relevant sections.

Give yourself a financial refresh.

Prepare.

Protect.

Pivot wisely.

5. Share It with Your Trusted Circle

Not everyone in your life needs to read this book.

But your inner circle — the people you trust most — should.

Your family. Your agent. Your business manager. Your financial advisor.

If they understand these principles, they'll be better equipped to support you.

And you'll be better equipped to hold them accountable.

This book can be a common language.

A standard.

A shield.

Use it.

6. Understand This is a Living Playbook

The world changes.

Tax laws shift.

Markets rise and fall.

New opportunities emerge.

Your needs will evolve as your career and life evolve.

That's why financial literacy isn't something you "finish."

It's something you live.

This book gives you the foundation.

But your commitment to staying educated, staying humble, and staying proactive will make all the difference.

Stay curious.

Stay adaptable.

Stay in the game.

7. Come Back to the Mindset Lessons

This book isn't just about money.

It's about mindset.

Ownership.

Freedom.

Confidence.

Whenever you find yourself drifting back into old habits — spending for show, trusting without verifying, avoiding financial conversations — come back to the mindset chapters.

Recenter yourself.

Remember why you're doing this.

Not to be flashy.

Not to impress strangers.

To build a life of freedom, purpose, and stability for yourself and the people you love.

Final Reminder:

This is your career.

Your money.

Your future.

Nobody will care about it like you do.

Nobody will protect it like you can.

Use this book.

Use it boldly.

Use it relentlessly.
Use it proudly.
Because you deserve more than a few great seasons.
You deserve a great life.
Let's build it — one smart financial move at a time.

Mention of Other Works

Mention of Other Works

Before we dive into the heart of this book, I want to take a moment to acknowledge the larger journey that led us here.

Financial Literacy For Pro Athletes didn't come out of nowhere.

It's part of a much bigger mission — one that's been years in the making, built book by book, platform by platform, and athlete by athlete.

This book is part of a broader family of resources designed to support you not just at the professional level, but at every step of your athletic and financial journey.

If you've read any of my earlier works, you've already begun to build a strong foundation. Each book and platform was crafted to meet you exactly where you were — and to prepare you for where you're going.

Here's a quick overview of the other works and platforms that laid the groundwork for this moment:

Financial Literacy For NIL

Written for college athletes navigating the new and complex world of Name, Image, and Likeness (NIL) opportunities.

In *Financial Literacy for NIL,* I broke down:

- How to budget NIL earnings wisely
- How taxes affect NIL deals
- How to protect yourself legally and financially

- How to think of yourself as a business from day one

If you read this book while you were still in school, congratulations. You already have a head start on understanding the responsibilities that come with managing income, brand, and expectations.

Financial Literacy For College Coaches

A vital resource for college coaches who want to understand how financial literacy and NIL opportunities impact their athletes.

In *Financial Literacy For College Coaches,* I help coaches:

- Understand the financial pressures athletes face
- Guide athletes to trustworthy resources
- Navigate recruiting conversations around NIL
- Become advocates for the holistic development of their players

If your coaches have read this, they're better positioned to mentor you both on and off the field.

Financial Literacy For NIL for Parents of Student Athletes

Because athletes don't walk this journey alone — families are often in it too.

This book equips parents to:

- Understand NIL opportunities and challenges
- Ask the right questions of schools, agents, and advisors
- Help their children manage newfound income responsibly
- Avoid common financial pitfalls and family conflicts

If your parents read this, they're part of your financial support system — informed, prepared, and ready to protect your future.

Financial Literacy For NIL for International Student Athletes

International athletes face a whole different layer of complexity when it comes to NIL and finances.

In *Financial Literacy For NIL for International Student Athletes,* I cover:

- Visa issues and restrictions
- Tax responsibilities in multiple countries
- Currency exchange risks
- Building a brand while navigating international laws

If you're an international athlete or know one, this resource is crucial for staying legal, protected, and prosperous.

Financial Literacy For NIL for High School Student Athletes

The NIL era has reached high school.

Financial Literacy For NIL for High School Student Athletes prepares young athletes to:

- Understand NIL basics before college
- Build smart money habits early
- Navigate early endorsements and sponsorships
- Protect eligibility and long-term goals

If you started your journey here, you've been building financial literacy earlier than most — and you're setting yourself up for long-term success.

How This Book Builds on Those Foundations

Each of those previous works and platforms was designed to prepare you.

To teach you.

To empower you.

Financial Literacy For Pro Athletes is the next level.

This book is built for the professional stage.

It tackles the complexities of:

- Signing bonuses
- Rookie contracts
- Free agency
- Endorsements
- Multi-state and international tax laws
- Wealth protection
- Long-term financial independence

If you've been with me through the earlier books, you'll recognize some foundational principles.

If this is your first time picking up one of my works, welcome. You're starting at the perfect time.

Wherever you're beginning, know this:

You're not starting from scratch. You're starting from strength.

And this book — like the ones before it — is here to serve you, support you, and set you up for a future you can be proud of.

Let's get to work.

Synopsis: Part 1 - The Dream Becomes Real — Preparing Financially Before You Get Drafted

Making it to the professional level is every athlete's dream. The blood, sweat, and sacrifice finally pay off when you hear your name called, sign your first contract, or get the call that changes everything.

But while your physical game has been honed for years, your financial game needs to be just as sharp — and most athletes aren't given the tools to prepare.

Part 1: The Dream Becomes Real — Preparing Financially Before You Get Drafted is about getting ahead of the curve, making smart money moves before the big moment arrives, and laying the groundwork for lasting success.

In this section, we tackle the critical steps every athlete should take to be financially ready for the transition from amateur to professional life.

You'll learn:

- **Why financial literacy must start before the first paycheck hits**
- **How to build your financial dream team early — agent, financial advisor, CPA, and attorney**
- **Which banking and investment accounts to open now**
- **Why establishing good credit before you go pro matters more than you think**

- **How to create a pre-draft budget that prevents lifestyle creep**
- **The reality of draft systems across major leagues (NFL, NBA, MLB, NHL, MLS, WNBA, MMA, international soccer, and more)**
- **Common financial red flags during the pre-draft hype phase**

We'll break down why "getting drafted" isn't a guarantee of financial security — it's only the beginning.

You'll learn how to:

- Protect yourself from early mistakes that can cost millions later.
- Set up a foundation that allows you to capitalize on your talent — not squander it.
- Prepare mentally for the sudden changes in income, expectations, and pressure.

This part is about being proactive, not reactive.

You've been preparing physically for this moment your entire life.

Now it's time to prepare financially — with the same intensity, focus, and discipline.

Because the dream becoming real is just the beginning.

The real game is just starting.

And how you prepare today will determine how you live tomorrow.

Chapter 1: Why Financial Literacy Is Crucial for Pro Athletes

When you cross the threshold from amateur to professional athlete, you step into a world that looks very different from the one you came from. The arenas are bigger. The contracts are larger. The cameras are everywhere. And so is the pressure — not just to perform, but to manage a life that suddenly feels more complex than ever before.

It's easy to assume that because the checks are bigger, life automatically gets easier. But talk to any retired athlete who's been through it, and they'll tell you the truth: **the money amplifies everything** — your opportunities, your challenges, your vulnerabilities, and your risks.

Financial literacy — real, lived, applicable financial literacy — isn't just a "nice thing to have" when you go pro.

It's essential.

It's the difference between being rich for a season and being wealthy for life.

It's the difference between freedom and fear.

It's the difference between building a legacy and becoming a cautionary tale.

If you read my earlier books — *Financial Literacy For NIL, Financial Literacy For Student Athletes,* or *Financial Literacy For Parents of Student Athletes* — then you already have some of the foundation: budgeting, saving, credit, protecting your brand.

But now?

Now you're in the big leagues.

The stakes are higher.

The money is bigger.

The mistakes are more expensive.

And the opportunity to build generational wealth is right in front of you — if you're ready.

This chapter is about why financial literacy is no longer optional.

It's survival.

It's ownership.

It's the hidden game inside the game.

Let's talk about it.

The Money Is Big — But So Are the Risks

When the outside world sees an athlete sign a contract for millions, they assume that athlete is automatically set for life.

But those of us who have lived this life, who have walked alongside friends, teammates, and clients in the pro world, know the reality:

- Taxes take a massive bite. (40% or more depending on where you live and play)
- Agent fees, marketing fees, union dues, and trainers chip away at the rest.
- Injuries, roster moves, and trades can cut careers short with little warning.
- Family and friends often expect financial support — sometimes for years.
- The pressure to "live up" to an image can lead to reckless spending.
- Bad investments and scams target you more once you have wealth.

The math isn't automatic.

Yes, you might sign for millions.

But if you don't manage that money with discipline, education, and intention, it can — and will — evaporate faster than you think.

Just ask the countless athletes who made tens of millions and ended up bankrupt, depressed, and isolated within a few years of retirement.

Talent doesn't protect you from financial loss.

Fame doesn't protect you.

Big checks don't protect you.

Only wisdom, discipline, and financial literacy protect you.

The Career Window Is Short

Here's a hard truth:

- NFL average career length: 3.3 years
- NBA average career length: 4.5 years
- MLB average career length: 5.6 years
- NHL average career length: 5 years
- WNBA average career length: 3.5 years
- Professional soccer, MMA, boxing: varies widely, often less than 5 years

And those are averages — meaning many careers are even shorter.

When you're 22 and cashing big checks, it's easy to assume it will last forever.

But the reality is: **you may only have a few prime earning years.**

Your money needs to last not just for today — but for the 50, 60, or even 70 years after your playing days are over.

Financial literacy teaches you to think beyond the now.

It teaches you to plan for the whole game, not just the first quarter.

The Pressure Is Real

You didn't just make it.

You made it for your family.

You made it for your neighborhood.

You made it for every coach, every mentor, every friend who supported your dream.

And when the checks start coming, so do the calls.

"Can you help me with rent?"

"Can you invest in my business?"

"Can you pay for Mom's surgery?"

"Can you put my kid through school?"

It's real. It's emotional. It's human.

But without financial literacy, the generosity that comes from a good heart can destroy your financial future.

You can help others **only if you first build a strong foundation for yourself.**

Financial literacy teaches you how to say "yes" responsibly — and how to say "no" with wisdom and grace when needed.

The Business Pitches Never Stop

Once you make it, you become a magnet for "opportunities."

Restaurants.

Nightclubs.

Record labels.

Fashion brands.

Real estate deals.

Friends, cousins, old classmates, strangers — everyone has "an idea."

Some are legit.

Most are not.

Without financial literacy, you're flying blind.

You're trusting people instead of vetting opportunities.

You're risking everything on hope instead of due diligence.

Financial literacy teaches you to:

- Ask the right questions
- Demand transparency
- Bring in independent advisors
- Protect yourself legally and financially

You don't have to be paranoid.

You have to be prepared.

Real Trade-Offs You Will Face

Buying vs. Leasing a Car

- Buying can be smart if you keep the car for years; leasing can be a trap if you're chasing a new model every year.

Renting vs. Buying a Home

- Renting offers flexibility if you're traded or relocated; buying ties you to a location (and comes with hidden costs).

Gifting vs. Investing

- Gifting feels good in the short term; investing builds a future where you can give sustainably for decades.

Hiring vs. Firing Professionals

- Loyalty is great — but if someone isn't serving you well, you must be willing to make a change to protect yourself.

Financial literacy doesn't make decisions for you.

It gives you the tools to *make better decisions* for yourself.

Immediate Action Steps to Take

- Open a high-yield savings account for your emergency fund
- Set up automatic savings (even a small amount every paycheck)
- Create a simple budget based on "season" and "offseason" income
- Interview at least two financial advisors (get references)
- Interview at least two CPAs who understand athlete taxes
- Build a "Money Team" that includes separation of duties
- Protect yourself with proper insurance (disability, life, health)
- Draft a basic will and estate plan — now, not later

These are foundational moves — not "someday" tasks.

They're urgent.

They're essential.

They're doable.

Real-World Scenarios and Stories

Scenario: The Rookie and the Lambo

You're a first-round pick.

You cash your signing bonus.

You go buy a $250,000 Lamborghini.

What you didn't plan for:

- $8,000/year insurance premiums
- $1,500/month maintenance costs
- $20,000 in annual depreciation

Within two years, the car is worth half what you paid — and you're stuck with it.

Financial literacy helps you think long-term, not just short-term flex.

Scenario: The Family Loan

Your cousin wants a $50,000 "loan" to start a new gym.

They promise they'll pay you back within a year.

You feel torn: it's family.

Financial literacy helps you ask:

- Is there a formal business plan?
- Are there legal protections for repayment?
- If this goes to zero, am I okay with that?

Generosity without boundaries leads to regret.

Generosity with wisdom leads to lasting impact.

Sports Analogies That Matter

Football: You wouldn't step into a blitz without a protection plan. Financial literacy is your pocket protection.

Basketball: You don't force shots under pressure — you find the best opportunity. Financial literacy teaches you patience and shot selection.

Soccer: The best defense is often your best offense. Strong financial fundamentals protect you from bad deals and bad luck.

Baseball: Managing your pitch count protects your arm for the long haul. Managing your spending protects your wealth for decades.

MMA: Defense wins fights. Defense wins financial freedom.

Track and Field: It's not the sprinter who wins the financial race — it's the marathoner.

Golf: One bad hole doesn't ruin your round if you stay composed. One bad investment doesn't destroy your wealth if you stay disciplined.

Tennis: Unforced errors cost you championships. Unforced financial errors cost you your legacy.

Whatever your sport, the principles apply.

Preparation. Discipline. Patience. Execution.

Final Encouragement

I know this is a lot.

I know you didn't dream of being a money manager — you dreamed of playing at the highest level.

But now you're here.

And the reality is: your financial game must be as strong as your physical game.

Because talent alone won't protect you.

Charisma alone won't protect you.

Hard work alone won't protect you.

Only wisdom will.

You don't have to be perfect.

You don't have to figure it all out today.

But you do have to care.

You do have to learn.

You do have to own it.

Because your career won't last forever.

But your life will.

And the choices you make right now — the small ones, the boring ones, the disciplined ones — will build the future you get to live in for decades to come.

You are more than an athlete.

You are a CEO.

You are a brand.

You are a builder of generational wealth.

The game of financial literacy isn't played under bright lights.

It's played quietly, daily, steadily.

But it matters.

And you're ready for it.

Let's get to work.

Chapter 2: The True Odds of "Making It" — Know the Numbers

Every athlete who laces up their shoes, tightens their gloves, or pulls on their jersey dreams of "making it."

Making it to the league.

Making it to the big contracts.

Making it to the fame and fortune that most people only see on highlight reels and social media.

But before we can talk about managing your money once you make it, we have to get real about the journey itself.

The odds.

The reality.

The numbers.

This isn't meant to discourage you.

It's meant to empower you.

Because when you understand the reality of what you've accomplished — or are fighting to accomplish — you understand just how important it is to protect it.

You realize just how rare, valuable, and fragile this opportunity is.

You realize why smart financial moves are not optional — they're non-negotiable.

You didn't beat the odds just to blow the opportunity.

You're here to build something lasting.

And that starts with seeing the full picture.

Let's talk about it.

The Reality Check: Odds of Going Pro

Let's break it down by sport.

Football (NFL)

- About 1 million high school football players.
- About 73,000 play college football (all divisions).
- About 1.6% of NCAA players get drafted into the NFL.
- Fewer than 0.08% of high school players ever play in the NFL.

Basketball (NBA/WNBA)

- About 540,000 high school boys basketball players.
- About 18,000 play in the NCAA.
- About 1.2% of NCAA men's basketball players get drafted into the NBA.
- For women, the WNBA draft is even more selective — only 36 players total drafted each year.

Baseball (MLB)

- About 482,000 high school baseball players.
- About 36,000 play college baseball.
- About 10% of NCAA players get drafted.
- But making it to the major leagues from the minors? Still extremely rare.

Hockey (NHL)

- About 35,000 high school hockey players.
- About 4,300 play college hockey.

- About 1% of NCAA players make it to the NHL.

Soccer (MLS, NWSL, Overseas)

- Growing rapidly but still brutal odds.
- Roughly 1% of NCAA soccer players turn pro.
- Many players must go overseas to pursue professional careers.

MMA, Boxing, Combat Sports

- No "draft" system.
- Purely performance and promotion based.
- Less than 1% of fighters ever fight at the UFC or Bellator level.

Tennis, Golf, Track and Field, Swimming

- Individual sports.
- Professional success is even more brutally selective.
- Even "pro" status doesn't mean you earn livable money — prize money is heavily weighted toward the top few competitors.

eSports

- Growing but still extremely competitive.
- Top players earn millions; most earn little to nothing.

Women's Pro Sports

- WNBA, NWSL, women's golf (LPGA), women's tennis (WTA) have even fewer spots and often much lower salaries compared to men's leagues.

Bottom line: **the odds are brutal in every sport.**

And if you're here — reading this — you're already beating those odds.

You are a statistical miracle.

Now the goal is not just to survive — but to thrive.

Why Knowing the Odds Matters

Understanding how rare your position is changes your mindset.

It reminds you:

- You can't afford to be careless with this opportunity.
- You can't afford to assume it will last forever.
- You can't afford to "figure it out later."

You have to move like your window is precious.

Because it is.

The Myth of the "Automatic Riches"

Just because you made it doesn't mean you're set for life.

Remember:

- Rookie contracts are often modest compared to veteran deals.
- Taxes, agent fees, and living costs slice your net income dramatically.
- Injury or poor performance can end careers abruptly.
- Fame comes fast; financial ruin comes faster without discipline.

Getting drafted, signed, or called up is the beginning, not the finish line.

Financial literacy is how you protect the dream once it becomes reality.

Real Trade-Offs You Will Face

Flashy Now vs. Freedom Later

- Flashy now means expensive cars, big houses, constant vacations.
- Freedom later means strategic savings, smart investments, delayed gratification.

Friends' Dreams vs. Your Stability

- Funding friends' businesses can destroy your financial foundation.
- Investing carefully (and saying "no" when necessary) preserves your future.

Living Like a Star vs. Living Like a CEO

- Living like a star impresses outsiders.
- Living like a CEO builds generational wealth.

Every dollar has a direction.
You choose whether it moves you closer to freedom or to regret.

Immediate Action Steps

- Know your net income (after taxes and fees) — not just your gross salary.
- Create a "real cost of living" budget based on your actual take-home pay.
- Save at least 50% of every paycheck until you have $500,000 saved.
- Invest early — even small amounts compound over time.
- Hire independent professionals (CPA, financial advisor, attorney).
- Start learning the basics of wealth preservation (not just wealth creation).

Plain Language Breakdown: Financial Realities for Athletes

How Contracts Work

- Only the guaranteed portion is truly yours.
- Incentives are "if you hit X," not automatic.
- Signing bonuses are often taxed upfront.
- Roster bonuses can disappear if you're cut.

How Taxes Crush Bad Planning

- Play in California? Your state income tax could be 13%+.
- Play in Florida or Texas? No state income tax.
- Play games in multiple states? You owe taxes in every state you play.

How Agents, Advisors, and Managers Must Stay in Their Lanes

- Your agent negotiates contracts.
- Your financial advisor manages your investments.
- Your manager handles brand deals.
- Your CPA handles taxes.
- Never let one person wear multiple hats unchecked.

How to Build Wealth While You're Still Playing

- Save aggressively.
- Spend modestly.
- Invest wisely.
- Insure intelligently.
- Plan strategically.

Real-World Scenarios and Relatable Stories

Scenario: The "Millionaire Rookie" Mindset

You sign a $3 million contract.

You assume you're rich.

After taxes, agent fees, union dues, and living expenses?

You might only see $1.4 million.

If you spend like you're a multi-millionaire, you'll be broke in 3 years or less.

Financial literacy shifts your mindset from "spend" to "build."

Scenario: The Free Agent Hustle

You go unsigned for a season.

Suddenly there's no paycheck coming.

You're living off savings — if you have any.

If you built no financial cushion during the "good years," you're forced into panic mode.

Financial literacy gives you breathing room.

It buys you time.

It buys you choices.

Sports Analogies That Matter

Football: You can't win a championship in Week 1 — but you can lose it. Set the tone early with financial fundamentals.

Basketball: Championship teams play great defense. Financial defense (saving, protecting, insuring) is how you stay in the game.

Soccer: A team can dominate possession and still lose if they don't finish. Managing your income is like finishing your financial opportunities.

Baseball: You won't hit a home run every at-bat. But consistent singles (small savings and smart decisions) win games.

MMA: One wrong move can end a fight instantly. One bad financial decision can wreck your wealth instantly.

Track: It's not about how you start — it's about how you finish. The sprint is making it pro. The marathon is staying wealthy for life.

Golf: You can't win the tournament on Day 1 — but you can lose it with careless play. The same goes for your first contract.

Tennis: Each point matters. Each financial decision adds up.

eSports: One bad decision chain can throw the entire match. Protect your resources early.

Final Encouragement

You have already beaten the odds to get here.

You are the 1% of the 1%.

But staying here?

Winning here?

Building a life of freedom, wealth, impact, and peace?

That takes a different kind of discipline.

It's not the discipline of 5AM workouts or two-a-day practices.

It's the discipline of saying "no" to short-term flexing.

It's the discipline of thinking like a CEO, not just a player.

It's the discipline of building quietly while others burn loudly.

You don't owe anyone an explanation.

You don't owe anyone an apology for protecting your future.

You owe it to yourself — and the generations who come after you — to get this right.

You didn't beat the odds just to survive.

You beat the odds to thrive.

Let's build a future worthy of the miracle that is your journey.

Let's play the long game.

Let's win the game of life.

Chapter 3: What You Must Know Financially Before You Get Drafted

There's a moment that every young athlete dreams about — the moment your name is called.

Draft day.

The day everything changes.

But here's the truth most people won't tell you:

Draft day is not the finish line.

It's the starting line.

And if you're not financially prepared *before* you step across that stage, you're setting yourself up for stress, mistakes, and regrets that could follow you long after the cameras stop flashing.

This chapter is about getting ready.

Mentally.

Emotionally.

Financially.

It's about making sure you don't just get drafted — you *stay drafted* in the game of life.

If you've read *Financial Literacy For NIL, Financial Literacy For Student Athletes,* or *Financial Literacy For Parents of Student Athletes,* then you already know the basics of budgeting, saving, and protecting your brand.

Now it's time to take it to the next level.

This is Financial Literacy for the Big Leagues — literally.

Let's talk about what you must know *before* you hear your name called.

Why Preparation Matters Before You Get Paid

By the time the money hits your account, it's too late to start preparing.

You need systems in place *before* the money comes.

You need a strategy.

A plan.

A team.

Because when the money arrives, so does the chaos:

- People you barely know asking for "help"
- "Opportunities" flooding your DMs
- Friends expecting upgrades on their lifestyle
- Scammers targeting you because they know you're new
- Tax authorities tracking every penny you make

If you're not ready, you'll be reacting instead of deciding.

And in the world of money, *reacting* is how people lose it all.

What You Must Know About Money Before You Get Drafted

1. Gross Pay vs. Net Pay

Your contract might say $2 million.

But after taxes, agent fees, union dues, insurance, and living expenses?

You might actually see $1 million or less.

Understand your real take-home pay.

2. Taxes Are Non-Negotiable

Every dollar you earn is taxed.

If you live or play in multiple states, you might owe taxes in all of them.

Failing to plan for taxes leads to massive bills, penalties, and even legal trouble.

Set aside money for taxes before you spend anything.

3. Every Check Has a Purpose

Before you get your first paycheck, decide:

- What percent goes to savings
- What percent goes to investments
- What percent goes to living expenses
- What percent (if any) is "fun money"

If you don't give your money a job, someone else will.

4. Lifestyle Inflation Is the Silent Killer

Just because you make more doesn't mean you should spend more.

Lifestyle inflation is when your spending grows with your income — and it's how rich people end up broke.

Set a lifestyle budget and stick to it.

5. Protect Yourself Before You Flex

Insurance.

Legal protection.

Financial buffers.

These are boring compared to Lambos and jewelry.

But they're what keep you rich.

Protect first. Flex later — if ever.

Pros and Cons of Early Financial Decisions

Buying vs. Leasing a Car

- *Buying*: Pros include ownership and no mileage limits; cons include rapid depreciation.
- *Leasing*: Pros include lower upfront costs; cons include expensive over time with no ownership.

Renting vs. Buying a Home

- *Renting*: Pros include flexibility; cons include no equity built.

- *Buying*: Pros include investment potential; cons include responsibility for maintenance and possible relocation issues if traded.

Gifting vs. Investing

- *Gifting*: Feels good short-term; drains long-term financial stability.
- *Investing*: Grows wealth sustainably over time.

Every financial decision has trade-offs.

Financial literacy helps you make them wisely.

Action Steps to Take Before You Get Drafted

- Open a high-yield savings account at a reputable bank
- Set up automatic transfers to savings and investments
- Interview and hire an independent CPA who understands multi-state taxation
- Interview and hire an independent financial advisor who has no conflicts of interest
- Meet with an attorney to create basic legal protections (will, power of attorney)
- Draft a realistic "rookie budget" based on your projected net pay, not gross
- Create a "Family and Friends Policy" to set boundaries before the asks come
- Set clear goals: How much do you want saved by the end of Year 1?

Preparation is protection.

Plain Language Breakdown of Complex Concepts

How Rookie Contracts Are Structured

- Signing Bonus: Usually guaranteed; taxed immediately.
- Base Salary: Paid during the season; not always guaranteed beyond Year 1.
- Incentives: Only paid if you hit performance milestones (games played, stats achieved).

Always know which money is real (guaranteed) and which money is "maybe."

How Taxes Eat Up Contracts

Example: If you're drafted by a team in California (13.3% state tax) and you play away games in high-tax states like New York (10.9% state tax), your effective tax rate could easily hit 45% or more.

Ignoring taxes is financial suicide.

Why Agents, Advisors, and CPAs Must Stay in Their Lanes

No one person should control everything.

Your agent handles contracts.

Your financial advisor handles investments.

Your CPA handles taxes.

Each role needs clear boundaries to protect you from fraud, mismanagement, or simple mistakes.

Why Early Investing Matters

The earlier you start investing, the more your money grows thanks to compounding.

Even small amounts add up massively over 10-20 years.

Waiting "until you're rich" to invest is how athletes lose millions.

Real-World Scenarios and Relatable Stories

Scenario: The Pre-Draft Spending Spree

An athlete expects to be drafted in the first round.

Before the draft, he:

- Buys a $200,000 car
- Puts a $100,000 down payment on a mansion
- Takes out loans assuming "the money is coming"

He ends up drafted in the fourth round.

Smaller contract. Smaller signing bonus. Bigger debt.

Financial literacy would have taught him: *Nothing is real until the check clears — and even then, manage it like it's fragile.*

Scenario: The "Helper" Who Wasn't Helping

A cousin offers to "manage" an athlete's money "to keep it in the family."

No contracts. No credentials.

Within two years, hundreds of thousands disappear.

Financial literacy would have taught him: *Hire professionals. Get it in writing. Trust, but verify.*

Sports Analogies That Matter

Football: You don't wait until the blitz is coming to call the protection. You call it pre-snap. Financial literacy is your pre-snap read.

Basketball: You don't throw a full-court pass blindly. You read the defense first. Financial literacy is reading your financial defense.

Soccer: You don't chase the ball; you move into position to intercept. Financial literacy positions you ahead of problems.

Baseball: You don't swing at every pitch. You wait for your pitch. Financial literacy teaches you patience and discipline.

MMA: You don't throw haymakers with no defense. Financial literacy is protecting your financial chin.

Track and Field: You don't sprint at the start of a marathon. Financial literacy helps you pace yourself for the long haul.

Tennis: You win with consistency, not just flashy shots. Financial literacy wins with consistency.

Golf: One bad hole doesn't ruin the tournament if you recover smartly. One bad purchase doesn't ruin you if you stay disciplined.

eSports: You win by managing resources wisely, not by wasting them early. Financial literacy is resource management.

Final Encouragement

Draft day will be one of the greatest days of your life.

But the real wins happen quietly, behind the scenes, in the months and years that follow.

The win is:

- Having enough saved to weather a trade, an injury, or a bad season.
- Having peace of mind that your future is protected.
- Being able to say "no" to bad deals without fear.
- Retiring on your terms, not because you're broke.

You deserve that.

You worked for that.

And it starts with being ready.

Before the money hits.

Before the pressure starts.

Before the chaos comes.

Prepare now.

So when your name is called, you're not just ready to play.

You're ready to win.

In every sense of the word.

Let's get it.

Chapter 4: Building Your Financial Team Early (Agent, Financial Advisor, CPA, Attorney)

You may be the one putting in the work.

The one getting hit.

The one running the drills.

The one lifting the weights.

The one shooting the shots.

The one laying your body on the line.

But the truth is — you can't build lasting success by yourself.

Not in professional sports.

And definitely not in professional wealth.

You need a team.

Not just a team on the field, court, mat, track, or pool.

You need a financial team off it.

A *real* team.

A smart, disciplined, experienced, loyal team.

Because once you step into the world of professional athletics, you're not just competing against other players.

You're competing against bad advice.

You're competing against predators.

You're competing against your own instincts to trust people who may not deserve it.

This chapter is about building your off-the-field dream team early.

Not waiting until you're in trouble.
Not waiting until you've made a mistake.
Building it now.
Before the money hits.
Before the pressure starts.
So that when the chaos comes — and it will — you're already protected.
You're already positioned.
You're already playing to win.
Let's break it down.

The Core Financial Team You Need

Your basic off-the-field team should include:

- **Agent**
- **Financial Advisor**
- **Certified Public Accountant (CPA)**
- **Attorney**

Each one plays a crucial role.
Each one must stay in their lane.
Each one must serve *you,* not themselves.
And you must **separate their roles** to protect yourself.
No overlap.
No "one person does everything."
That's how mistakes — and theft — happen.

Why You Need Each Member

Agent

Your agent is your dealmaker.
They negotiate your playing contracts.
They negotiate your endorsement deals.

They fight to maximize your earning potential.

A great agent knows the landscape, knows the value of your skills, and protects your interests in negotiations.

Financial Advisor

Your financial advisor manages your money.

They help you save, invest, and grow your wealth.

They build a plan based on your real life, not just a fantasy spreadsheet.

They create systems that protect you from blowing through your money.

CPA (Certified Public Accountant)

Your CPA handles taxes.

They make sure you file correctly in every state and city you play.

They structure your finances to minimize taxes legally.

They protect you from audits, penalties, and surprises.

Attorney

Your attorney protects your contracts.

They review endorsement deals.

They draft legal documents (like a will or business agreements).

They protect you if disputes arise.

They make sure you're not signing your future away without realizing it.

Each role is separate.

Each role is critical.

And when they work together — but independently — you win.

Pros and Cons of Common Team Building Decisions

One-Stop Shop vs. Separate Professionals

- *One-Stop Shop*: Easier to manage. High risk of conflicts of interest.
- *Separate Professionals*: More work up front. Much safer long-term.

Hiring Friends/Family vs. Hiring Experts

- *Friends/Family*: Loyalty. But often lack expertise or objectivity.
- *Experts*: Professional skills and accountability. May feel less "comfortable" initially.

Waiting Until After You Get Paid vs. Building Team Early

- *Waiting*: Easy to justify. But leaves you vulnerable to early mistakes.
- *Building Early*: Requires effort before the money comes. But protects you when the stakes are highest.

Action Steps to Build Your Team

- Interview at least three candidates for each role
- Check their certifications, experience, and client list
- Ask about fees — make sure they're transparent
- Ask for references and actually call them
- Demand written contracts outlining responsibilities and expectations
- Make sure you can fire any team member easily if needed
- Never let loyalty override accountability

If someone is offended that you want to vet them thoroughly, **they are not the right person.**

You are the CEO.

You are the client.

You have the power.

Use it.

Plain Language Breakdown: Understanding Each Role in Detail

Agent Details

- Should be licensed.
- Should explain all commission structures clearly.
- Should have a track record of ethical, aggressive negotiation.
- Should never "manage" your money.

Financial Advisor Details

- Should be a fiduciary (legally required to act in your best interest).
- Should have transparent, written fee structures (not hidden commissions).
- Should focus on long-term planning, not quick gains.

CPA Details

- Should specialize in working with pro athletes or high-net-worth clients.
- Should understand multi-state tax filing.
- Should provide proactive advice, not just file paperwork.

Attorney Details

- Should specialize in sports/entertainment law, or contracts and estate planning.
- Should explain every document you sign in plain English.
- Should protect your interests, not just "close the deal."

Real-World Scenarios and Relatable Stories

Scenario: The One-Man Show Disaster

An athlete hires his cousin to be his agent, financial advisor, tax guy, and business manager.

No oversight.

No second opinions.

Five years later, the IRS shows up.

The money is gone.

The athlete trusted too much and verified too little.

Financial literacy teaches you: *Trust, but verify. And separate roles.*

Scenario: The Early Hiring Win

A rookie invests in hiring:

- A top agent
- An independent financial advisor
- A sports-specialist CPA
- A sharp entertainment lawyer

He saves 50% of every paycheck.

He minimizes taxes.

He protects himself from bad deals.

Ten years later, he retires with more money than he made playing.

Financial literacy wins in the end.

Sports Analogies That Matter

Football: A quarterback needs different teammates — blockers, receivers, coaches. You can't win with just one guy doing it all.

Basketball: You need a team with different skillsets — scorers, defenders, rebounders. Building wealth needs the same.

Soccer: Every position matters — you can't just have strikers. Your financial team needs specialists too.

Baseball: A good manager uses different pitchers for different situations. You need different advisors for different needs.

MMA: You train with striking coaches, grappling coaches, strength coaches. You build your financial game with different experts too.

Track and Field: You don't have one coach for sprints, hurdles, throws. Specialists make you better.

Tennis: Top players have hitting coaches, fitness trainers, mental coaches. You need a financial "support team."

Golf: You have a swing coach, a putting coach, a fitness trainer. Diversify your financial support too.

eSports: You have strategy coaches, mechanics coaches, team managers. Financial literacy requires building a smart "support staff."

Final Encouragement

You are not alone.

You are not expected to figure this all out by yourself.

That's not a weakness.

That's wisdom.

But you must build smart.

You must choose carefully.

You must stay in control.

Because nobody will care about your career, your money, and your future like *you* do.

Not your agent.

Not your advisor.

Not your CPA.

Not your lawyer.

You.

You are the CEO.

You are the franchise.

You are the dynasty.

Build your team accordingly.

Demand excellence.

Expect loyalty.

Require transparency.

And when in doubt, remember:

Your career is short. Your wealth should be forever.

Start building your dream team today.

Start protecting your future today.

Because you didn't come this far just to lose.

You came to dominate.

On the field. Off the field. In life.

Let's get to work.

Chapter 5: Accounts You Must Open Before You Sign (Banking, Roth IRA, Investment Accounts)

One of the biggest mistakes young professional athletes make is assuming that financial success starts when the checks start rolling in.

Wrong.

Financial success — real, lasting success — starts *before* the money hits your account.

It starts with preparation.

It starts with systems.

It starts with setting up the right accounts before you ever cash your first professional paycheck.

If you've read *Financial Literacy For NIL, Financial Literacy For Student Athletes,* or *Financial Literacy For Parents of Student Athletes,* you already know the basics of budgeting, saving, and protecting your brand.

Now we're stepping into the big leagues.

This is not just about managing "stipend money" or "summer job" income anymore.

This is about managing six, seven, or even eight-figure career earnings.

This chapter will give you the blueprint to build your financial foundation.

Before the chaos.

Before the headlines.

Before the pressure.

Because once the money hits, the world moves fast.

And if you're not ready, you'll be playing catch-up — and that's how mistakes get made.

Let's build it right from the start.

The Big Three Accounts You Must Set Up

Before you sign anything — before you play your first game — you must set up:

- A primary checking account
- A high-yield savings account
- An investment account (including a Roth IRA if possible)

Each one serves a specific, crucial purpose.

Each one is a tool to help you win financially.

Let's break it down.

Primary Checking Account

Purpose: Your "home base" for daily money management.

Why it matters:

- Direct deposit of your paychecks
- Bill payments
- Cash flow management
- Immediate access for living expenses

What to look for:

- FDIC insurance (federal protection up to $250,000)
- Minimal or no fees

- Mobile app access for easy management
- Ability to set up automatic bill pay

Pro Tip: Use this account only for spending and paying bills. **Do not treat it like your savings account.**

Separate your spending money from your saving money — or you will accidentally spend it all.

High-Yield Savings Account

Purpose: Your "defense account."

Why it matters:

- Emergency fund (injury, trades, lockouts, etc.)
- Tax savings account
- Peace of mind during the offseason

What to look for:

- High interest rates (look for online banks)
- FDIC insurance
- No monthly fees

Pro Tip: Treat this like your "do not touch" account.

This is your safety net.

You don't brag about it.

You don't show it off.

You protect it at all costs.

Target: 6-12 months of living expenses saved here ASAP.

Investment Account (Including Roth IRA)

Purpose: Your "offense account" for building long-term wealth.
Why it matters:

- Grow your money faster than inflation
- Build wealth for life after sports
- Take advantage of compound interest

What to look for:

- Reputable brokerage firms (Fidelity, Schwab, Vanguard, etc.)
- Low-fee index funds
- Clear account statements
- Easy automatic contributions

Pro Tip: Set up automatic monthly contributions — even if small.
Investing early matters way more than investing big later.
Time is your greatest asset.
Bonus: Roth IRA

- Funded with after-tax money.
- Grows tax-free.
- Withdrawals in retirement are tax-free.

Roth IRAs have income limits, but most rookies qualify.

Once you start making huge money, you may not be eligible anymore — so open and fund it early!

Other Accounts to Consider

Health Savings Account (HSA)

- If offered through your team/insurance plan
- Triple tax advantage (tax-deductible contributions, tax-free growth, tax-free withdrawals for medical expenses)
- Unused funds roll over year-to-year

Business Bank Account

- If you plan to launch a business, brand, or LLC
- Separates personal and business expenses
- Essential for endorsements, appearances, or camps

Charitable Giving Account

- If philanthropy is part of your plan
- Helps manage donations strategically
- May provide tax benefits

Starting small is better than waiting forever.
You don't have to fund every account immediately.
You just need to start the system.

Pros and Cons of Early Account Setup

Pros

- Immediate protection for incoming money
- Builds good habits early
- Allows compounding to start ASAP
- Reduces emotional spending mistakes

Cons

- Takes effort and planning upfront
- Might feel "boring" compared to celebrating success

Translation?

Zero real downsides.

Only upside if you're serious about winning off the field.

Action Steps to Take Immediately

- Open a checking account at a major bank or credit union
- Open a high-yield online savings account
- Open a basic brokerage account for investing
- Open a Roth IRA (fund it immediately if eligible)
- Set up automatic transfers from checking to savings
- Set up automatic transfers from checking to investments
- Choose low-cost index funds (S&P 500 index is a great starting point)

Set it.

Automate it.

Forget it.

Let time and discipline do the heavy lifting.

Plain Language Breakdown: How These Accounts Work Together

- **Checking Account** = Day-to-day transactions.
- **Savings Account** = Emergency protection.
- **Investment Account** = Long-term wealth.
- **Roth IRA** = Long-term, tax-free wealth.

Money flows from paycheck to checking.
From checking, it flows into savings and investing automatically.
You live on what's left after you pay your future self first.
Not the other way around.

Real-World Scenarios and Relatable Stories

Scenario: The Rookie Without a Plan
An athlete signs a $5 million contract.
No savings account.
No investment account.
No tax planning.
Spends freely.
Owes $2 million in taxes the next year — but already spent the money.
Has to sell assets, take out loans, and play catch-up for years.
Scenario: The Rookie With Systems
An athlete signs a $1.5 million contract.
Immediately:

- Opens checking, savings, investment, and Roth IRA accounts.
- Automates savings and investing.
- Sets aside 40% of each check for taxes.
- Lives modestly.

Within 3 years, even if his career ends early, he has:

- $750,000 saved.
- $200,000 invested.
- Zero debt.
- Options.

Sports Analogies That Matter

Football: You don't build your offensive line after the quarterback gets sacked. You build protection early. Savings accounts are your offensive line.

Basketball: You don't take shots without setting up your offense. Investment accounts set up your offense for long-term success.

Soccer: You don't wait for the opponent to score before defending. High-yield savings accounts are your goalie.

Baseball: You don't only swing for home runs. You win games with base hits. Small, regular contributions to savings and investing are your base hits.

MMA: You don't enter a fight with no defense. Emergency savings is your guard.

Track and Field: You pace yourself smartly to finish strong. Consistent saving and investing paces your financial race.

Tennis: You build points patiently. You build wealth patiently.

Golf: You don't win the Masters on Day 1. Financial security takes multiple "rounds" of smart decisions.

eSports: You don't blow all your resources in the first five minutes. Smart financial players build slowly and strategically.

Final Encouragement

I know it doesn't feel urgent.

I know it's easy to think:

"I'll set up my accounts after I sign."

"I'll figure it out once the checks come."

"I'm too busy training, preparing, grinding."

But let me tell you something:

Money moves fast.

And once it's gone, it's hard to get back.

Your financial future will not be built on good intentions.

It will be built on preparation.

On systems.

On discipline.

You will never regret setting up the right accounts early.

You will always regret waiting too long.

So set them up now.

Automate your protection.

Automate your wealth building.

Automate your peace of mind.

Because when the money hits, you won't have time to think.

You'll either have a system protecting you — or chaos exposing you.

You deserve better than chaos.

You deserve better than stress.

You deserve freedom.

Financial freedom.

And it starts with a few simple accounts, opened early, funded consistently, protected fiercely.

You are the CEO of your career.

You are the architect of your legacy.

You are the builder of your wealth.

Let's start building it — right now.

Chapter 6: Credit Matters — Why You Need Good Credit Before Turning Pro

When you're about to sign your first pro contract, it's easy to think that cash is king.

And it is—for a while.

Cash lets you move. Cash lets you flex. Cash lets you buy what you want, when you want.

But if you think cash alone will carry you through your career and beyond, you're playing the wrong game.

Credit matters.

Credit is your reputation with money.

Credit is your ticket to bigger opportunities.

Credit is your backup plan when cash runs tight.

And good credit? Good credit is leverage.

It's freedom.

It's power.

If you've read *Financial Literacy For NIL, Financial Literacy For Student Athletes,* or *Financial Literacy For Parents of Student Athletes,* you know we talked about starting to build your credit early.

Now that you're stepping into the big leagues, it's more important than ever.

Because bad credit can hold you back no matter how much cash you have in the bank.

Good credit can open doors you didn't even know existed.

Let's talk about it.

What Is Credit, Really?

Credit is your financial resume.

It tells banks, lenders, landlords, insurance companies, and even some employers how trustworthy you are with money.

It's not about how much you earn.

It's about how responsibly you manage what you have.

Your credit score is a number (between 300 and 850) that sums up your financial trustworthiness.

Higher = better.

Lower = problems.

Why Credit Matters Even When You're Rich

You might be thinking, "If I'm signing a multi-million dollar contract, why should I care about credit? I'll just pay cash for everything."

Here's why:

1. You May Still Need Financing

- Mortgages for homes
- Business loans
- Auto loans
- Investment property financing

Even rich people use loans strategically. Smart leverage can build even more wealth.

2. Better Credit = Lower Costs

- Lower interest rates on loans
- Lower insurance premiums
- Lower security deposits for housing

Bad credit makes everything more expensive.

3. Life Changes Fast

Careers end.

Incomes drop.

Cash dries up.

Good credit gives you options when circumstances change.

4. Protect Your Reputation

Bad credit doesn't just hurt financially.

It hurts your image.

Endorsers, sponsors, and teams want responsible representatives.

How Your Credit Score Is Built

Your credit score is made up of:

- **35% Payment History:** Did you pay your bills on time?
- **30% Credit Utilization:** How much of your available credit are you using?
- **15% Length of Credit History:** How long have your accounts been open?
- **10% New Credit Inquiries:** Have you applied for a lot of credit recently?
- **10% Credit Mix:** Do you have different types of accounts (credit cards, loans, etc.)?

Every move you make with money builds (or damages) your score.

Pros and Cons of Building Credit Early

Pros

- Higher scores by the time you hit your peak earning years
- Easier access to mortgages, business loans, and investment opportu-

nities

- Lower insurance premiums and better financial offers

Cons

- Requires discipline and consistency
- Easy to ruin if you're careless or impulsive

In other words, like everything else in your career: **the disciplined ones win.**

Immediate Action Steps to Build Credit Before You Sign

- Open a basic credit card (secured if needed)
- Use it for small, recurring expenses (Netflix, phone bill)
- Pay it off in full every month — never carry a balance
- Set up autopay to avoid late payments
- Check your credit score and report annually
- Freeze your credit if you're not applying for anything to prevent identity theft

Credit is a long game.
Start early.
Protect it fiercely.

Plain Language Breakdown: What Good and Bad Credit Really Mean

Good Credit = Freedom

- Lower interest rates
- Easier approvals
- Bigger opportunities
- Better financial reputation

Bad Credit = Barriers

- Higher costs
- Loan denials
- Higher insurance rates
- Damaged professional reputation

Real-World Scenarios and Relatable Stories

Scenario: The Rookie Who Ignored Credit

An athlete signs a $3 million deal.
Buys everything in cash.
Never builds credit.
Three years later, wants to buy a $5 million home.
Bank denies the mortgage because he has no credit history.
Cash runs low. No backup options.

Scenario: The Rookie Who Built Credit Early

Another athlete signs a $1 million deal.
Opens a credit card.
Pays it off every month.
Builds a 780+ credit score within two years.
Buys a house with a low-interest mortgage.
Uses savings to invest, not to tie up in cash purchases.

Grows wealth smartly and sustainably.

Sports Analogies That Matter

Football: Building credit is like staying in shape during the offseason. You don't notice the payoff every day, but it shows up when the game is on the line.

Basketball: Good credit is like free throws. Boring? Maybe. But championships are won at the line.

Soccer: Maintaining credit is like maintaining possession. It's not glamorous, but it controls the flow of the game.

Baseball: Good credit is like a strong bullpen. You don't realize how badly you need it until you're in a jam.

MMA: Protecting your credit is like protecting your chin. One bad hit can end the fight.

Track and Field: Credit building is a marathon, not a sprint.

Tennis: Winning financial matches requires steady, consistent strokes, not just highlight-reel shots.

Golf: Every hole matters. Every financial move impacts your credit.

eSports: Managing credit is like resource management. Spend too much early? You lose late.

Final Encouragement

You're stepping into a life most people can only dream about.

But dreams without preparation become nightmares.

Credit isn't exciting.

Credit isn't flashy.

Credit doesn't get likes on Instagram.

But credit is your shield.

Credit is your flexibility.

Credit is your key to playing the long game, not just the short hustle.

You are not just playing for today.

You are playing for your entire life.

You are building a legacy.

Good credit is one of the invisible forces that will either propel you or sabotage you.

You get to choose.

Choose discipline.

Choose preparation.

Choose freedom.

Because freedom is the real flex.

And financial freedom — protected by smart credit management — is the biggest win of all.

You're not just an athlete.

You're a CEO.

You're a brand.

You're a builder.

Start building today.

Chapter 7: Building a Financial Foundation: Budget, Save, Protect

Making it to the professional level is incredible.

You've beaten the odds.

You've stepped into a world few people will ever experience.

But stepping into that world is only part of the journey.

Staying there—and thriving long after your playing days are over—requires a different skill set.

It requires building a financial foundation that can withstand pressure, change, and even setbacks.

This chapter is about teaching you how to build that foundation.

Before the big headlines.

Before the temptations.

Before the noise.

Because once you're in the game, the pressure doesn't stop.

It amplifies.

And the only way to withstand that pressure is to have a solid financial game plan you believe in, trust, and stick to—no matter what.

If you read *Financial Literacy For NIL*, *Financial Literacy For Student Athletes*, or *Financial Literacy For Parents of Student Athletes*, you've already heard me say it:

Money without a plan is money that's already gone.

Let's talk about how to build your foundation right.

Not just for now.
For life.

The Three Pillars of a Strong Financial Foundation

Every successful athlete — every successful CEO, every successful entrepreneur — has mastered three things:

- Budgeting
- Saving
- Protecting

Simple?
Yes.
Easy?
Not without discipline.
But discipline is what got you here.
It's what will keep you here financially too.
Let's break it down.

Pillar 1: Budget — Control the Flow of Your Money

A budget isn't a punishment.
It's not a restriction.
A budget is a freedom plan.
It's you telling your money where to go, instead of wondering where it went.

Why Budgeting Matters:

- Controls lifestyle inflation
- Prepares you for income fluctuations (injuries, trades, cuts)
- Creates intentionality with spending
- Reduces financial anxiety

Basic Pro Athlete Budget Formula:

- 50% → Saving and investing
- 30% → Living expenses
- 10% → Taxes (on top of withholdings)
- 10% → Fun, family, charity

Action Steps:

- Create a monthly budget based on your *net income* (after taxes and fees)
- Categorize all expenses
- Track your spending weekly
- Adjust as needed, but stick to overall targets

Your budget is your playbook.
Without it, you're playing without a game plan.
And you know how that ends.

Pillar 2: Save — Pay Your Future Self First

Saving is not what's left over after spending.
Saving comes *first.*
You earn.
You save.
Then you spend.
Every paycheck.
Every deal.
Every bonus.
Why Saving Matters:

- Creates a safety net for emergencies
- Provides options if your career ends early

- Funds investments that grow wealth

Types of Saving Accounts You Should Have:

- Emergency Fund (6-12 months of expenses)
- Tax Savings Account
- Investment Accounts (brokerage, Roth IRA, SEP IRA)
- Short-Term Goals (house down payment, car, family needs)

Action Steps:

- Automate savings to pull money before you can spend it
- Open separate accounts for different goals
- Prioritize emergency fund before luxury spending

Saving is your insurance against bad seasons, bad investments, bad luck. Without it, you're one bad month away from panic.

Pillar 3: Protect — Guard Your Wealth Before You Build It Bigger

Protection is not optional.
It's non-negotiable.
The richer you get, the bigger your target becomes.
Everyone wants a piece.
Some are genuine.
Some are predators.

What You Must Protect Against:

- Taxes
- Lawsuits
- Scams
- Bad investments

- Family pressures
- Entourage drain

Protection Tools You Need:

- Insurance (health, disability, life, property, umbrella liability)
- Legal Structures (LLCs, trusts)
- Trusted Professionals (financial advisor, CPA, attorney)
- Written Contracts (always, no matter who you're dealing with)

Action Steps:

- Meet with a trusted insurance advisor to review policies annually
- Hire an attorney to review *every* deal before you sign
- Require transparency and written agreements from all professionals
- Separate your business from your personal life (separate accounts, separate structures)

If you don't protect what you build, someone will take it from you.

It's that simple.

Real-World Scenarios and Relatable Stories

Scenario 1: The Budgetless Rookie

Signs a $2 million contract.

Lives like he's making $10 million.

No budget.

No tracking.

Gone within three years.

Scenario 2: The Saver

Signs a $1 million contract.

Saves 50% of every check.

Lives modestly.

Invests wisely.

Has $500,000+ saved by year three — and options for the future.

Scenario 3: The Unprotected Star

Huge signing bonus.

No insurance.

Career-ending injury.

Medical bills and lawsuits cripple finances.

Sports Analogies That Matter

Football: You don't step on the field without pads. Budgeting is your helmet. Saving is your shoulder pads. Protection is your mouthguard.

Basketball: You don't win games without defense. Saving and protecting is your defensive strategy against financial ruin.

Soccer: Midfielders control the pace. Your budget controls the pace of your spending.

Baseball: You don't win championships swinging at everything. Smart savings are your smart pitches.

MMA: Protect your chin, protect your career. Protect your money, protect your legacy.

Track and Field: Pacing wins marathons. Consistent budgeting and saving win the financial race.

Tennis: Winning points consistently wins matches. Consistently saving small amounts wins wealth.

Golf: Every shot builds your round. Every financial decision builds your future.

eSports: Resource management wins championships. Budgeting and protecting resources win financial freedom.

Final Encouragement

Building your financial foundation isn't glamorous.

It doesn't get applause.

It doesn't go viral.

But it's what separates the highlights from the legends.

It's what separates the quick millionaires from the lifetime wealth builders.

You have a choice.

You can be a cautionary tale.

Or you can be a champion.

A champion in your career.

A champion in your finances.

A champion in your legacy.

It starts with the basics.

Budget.

Save.

Protect.

Every month.

Every deal.

Every year.

Because championships aren't won by talent alone.

They're won by discipline.

Consistency.

Preparation.

You already have the talent.

Now build the foundation.

Own your career.

Own your future.

Own your financial life.

You're not just playing for today.

You're playing for every day that comes after your final game.

Let's build it right — and let's start now.

Chapter 8: The First Contract: Rookie Deals Across Different Sports

Your first professional contract is a moment you'll never forget.

The celebration.

The validation.

The realization that all those years of hard work finally led to a payoff.

But what most rookies don't realize is that the first contract — across almost every professional sport — is structured very differently than the multimillion-dollar deals you see on ESPN.

Before you start mentally spending every dollar you think you're going to earn, you need to understand exactly how rookie deals work.

If you've read *Financial Literacy For NIL, Financial Literacy For Student Athletes,* or *Financial Literacy For Parents of Student Athletes,* you've already started thinking about money differently.

Now it's time to take it even deeper.

This isn't about theory anymore.

This is real life.

Real contracts.

Real stakes.

And the real risk of misunderstanding what's actually yours — and what isn't.

Let's break it all the way down.

Rookie Contracts: A Sport-by-Sport Breakdown

Every league is different.

Every sport has its own rules.

Understanding the differences matters because it shapes how you need to manage your money.

Let's go sport by sport.

NFL (National Football League)

How Rookie Deals Work:

- Slotted contracts based on draft position (CBA rules)
- 4-year deal for most players; first-rounders often have a 5th-year option
- Signing bonuses are guaranteed; base salaries usually are not
- Heavy taxes depending on where you play (state + city "jock tax")

Realities to Understand:

- If you're cut early, you don't get the full contract
- Injuries can wipe out future earnings quickly
- Roster bonuses can be tied to making the team each year

Key Point:

Your signing bonus is the only money you can count on being 100% yours from Day 1.

Manage it like it's your career.

NBA (National Basketball Association)

How Rookie Deals Work:

- 2-year guaranteed contracts with team options for years 3 and 4
- Salaries are slotted by draft position
- Signing bonuses are built into first-year salaries
- Endorsements can be a major income booster early

Realities to Understand:

- Even guaranteed contracts get taxed heavily
- Rookie scale salaries, while good, are nowhere near superstar deals
- Staying healthy and developing is key to earning the "big" second contract

Key Point:
Don't spend like you're on a max deal when you're still on a rookie scale.

MLB (Major League Baseball)

How Rookie Deals Work:

- Players start in the minors (often low salaries)
- 3 years of team control (pre-arbitration)
- Arbitration years (years 4-6) offer salary growth
- Free agency typically after 6 years

Realities to Understand:

- Huge signing bonuses for first-round draft picks
- Grinding in the minors can last years

- First real big money often doesn't come until second contract

Key Point:
Even top MLB prospects often live modestly early on — and you should too.

NHL (National Hockey League)

How Rookie Deals Work:

- Entry-level contracts (ELCs) are standard for first three years
- Salary cap on rookie earnings
- Signing bonuses possible but limited
- Two-way contracts (different pay if you're sent to AHL)

Realities to Understand:

- Only after ELC expires do bigger salaries arrive
- Injuries are a huge career risk

Key Point:
Manage your rookie money as if it's your only money.

MLS (Major League Soccer) and NWSL (National Women's Soccer League)

How Rookie Deals Work:

- Base salaries are often low by "pro athlete" standards
- Designated players can make millions, but rookies often don't
- Endorsements vary greatly depending on national team exposure

Realities to Understand:

- Financial discipline is crucial early
- Many players supplement income with endorsements or camps

Key Point:
You need a financial plan whether you're making $60,000 or $600,000.

Combat Sports (MMA, Boxing)

How Rookie Deals Work:

- No "draft" system; earnings are fight-by-fight
- Purse structures vary wildly
- Sponsorship deals crucial for income
- Management fees, gym fees, travel costs often self-funded

Realities to Understand:

- You pay coaches, trainers, agents from your purse
- Injuries can cancel fights — and paydays

Key Point:
Cash flow planning is life or death in combat sports.

Individual Sports (Tennis, Golf, Track, Swimming)

How Rookie Deals Work:

- No guaranteed salaries
- Income based entirely on performance and sponsorships

Realities to Understand:

- Travel, coaching, and training costs are massive

- Prize money is heavily taxed

Key Point:

You are your own business from Day 1.
Budget like an entrepreneur.

Pros and Cons of Rookie Contracts

Pros:

- Launches your professional career
- Provides financial security (at least temporarily)
- Opportunity to prove yourself and earn more

Cons:

- Often heavily taxed
- May not be fully guaranteed
- Career-ending risks before second contract
- Huge pressure to support family and friends early

Action Steps: Managing Your First Contract Wisely

- **Treat signing bonuses as your "career money," not "fun money."
- **Live like you're undrafted** until your second contract
- **Save at least 50%-70%** of net pay for the first three years
- **Set up automatic savings and investment accounts immediately**
- **Create a "Needs First, Wants Later" spending rule**
- **Hire a fiduciary financial advisor and CPA immediately**
- **Understand every line of your contract** (get legal help if needed)
- **Insure yourself properly** (disability insurance is key)

Plain Language Breakdowns: Rookie Contracts Are Not What They Seem

Not All Money Is Guaranteed

Just because you sign a $4 million contract doesn't mean you'll see $4 million.

Read the fine print.

Know what's real.

Taxes Take a Huge Bite

Federal income tax.

State income tax.

City taxes.

Agent fees.

Union dues.

Jock tax (for games played in other states).

It's real.

Plan for it.

Agent Fees Are Standard

Typically 3%-5% of contract and endorsement earnings.

Pay them, but make sure they earn it.

You Must Think Past Year One

Plan as if your career will be short.

Hope for the long run.

Prepare for the short one.

Real-World Scenarios and Relatable Stories

Scenario: The Rookie Who Lived Too Big

Drafted top 10.

Signed a $15 million contract.

After buying a mansion, luxury cars, jewelry, and "helping out" too many friends and family members, was broke within five years.

Scenario: The Rookie Who Played It Smart

Drafted in the second round.

Lived in a modest apartment.

Saved 70% of net pay.

By year four, had enough saved to retire comfortably if necessary.

Sports Analogies That Matter

Football: Rookie contracts are like your first playoff appearance. It's great, but it's just the beginning.

Basketball: First-round picks have to earn their second contracts. Just like winning Game 1 doesn't win you the series.

Soccer: Your first season is about adjusting and proving your worth. Manage your money the same way—steady and strategic.

Baseball: Minor league grind teaches patience. So does smart money management.

MMA: Every fight is a chance to move up—or move out. Same with your finances.

Tennis: Winning one major match is great. Building a career is the real goal.

Golf: Making your first cut is good. Consistently making cuts is how you build a future.

eSports: Winning one tournament doesn't mean you've "made it." You have to keep earning.

Final Encouragement

Your rookie contract is the key that unlocks the first door.

But there are many more doors to open.

How you manage this first deal will set the tone for everything that comes next.

Live smart.

Save aggressively.

Protect fiercely.

Play the long game.

You didn't beat the odds just to be broke in five years.

You beat the odds to build something lasting.

You beat the odds to create a life of freedom.

You beat the odds to win—on the field, off the field, and in life.

The first contract is just the beginning.

Play it smart.

Play it strong.

Play it forever.

Chapter 9: Understanding the Sports Draft Systems (NFL, NBA, MLB, NHL, MLS, WNBA, MMA Drafts/Recruiting, International Soccer, Tennis/Individual Sports Contracts)

Crossing the line from amateur to professional isn't just about talent.

It's about navigating systems.

Drafts.

Recruiting.

Agent negotiations.

International signings.

Every sport has its own system, rules, and traps.

Understanding how you get "in the game" financially is just as important as understanding how to play the game physically.

If you've read *Financial Literacy For NIL, Financial Literacy For Student Athletes,* or *Financial Literacy For Parents of Student Athletes,* you already know how important it is to prepare mentally and financially for life-changing opportunities.

Now that you're here, it's time to dig even deeper.

This isn't about waiting to get drafted and "hoping for the best."

This is about understanding how the system works so you can navigate it like a pro — because you are one.

Let's break it down.

NFL Draft System

How It Works:

- 7 rounds, 32 picks per round (plus compensatory picks)
- Slotted contracts based on draft position
- 4-year deals with a potential 5th-year option for first-round picks
- Signing bonuses are guaranteed; base salaries may not be

Realities:

- Top picks get big money; late-round picks have to grind for roster spots
- Undrafted free agents hustle for training camp invites and smaller deals
- Career length: Average NFL career is around 3.3 years

Key Point:

Being drafted is a door opening—not a guarantee of long-term wealth.

NBA Draft System

How It Works:

- 2 rounds, 60 picks total (some years fewer with forfeited picks)
- Rookie scale contracts: two guaranteed years, team options for years 3 and 4
- First-round picks get guaranteed money; second-rounders have less security

Realities:

- Lottery picks (top 14) command major endorsement attention
- G-League assignments can impact income for second-rounders

Key Point:
Guaranteed money is good, but you have to *earn* your second contract.

MLB Draft System

How It Works:

- 20 rounds (was previously 40 rounds)
- Huge signing bonuses for first-round picks
- Minor league contracts initially; major league minimum only after call-up
- Arbitration and free agency rules control earnings until year 6

Realities:

- Many players never make it out of the minors
- Living on minor league salaries can be brutal
- Big checks often come much later (or not at all)

Key Point:
Sign a smart deal early, live modestly, and focus on developing your game.

NHL Draft System

How It Works:

- 7 rounds, 32 picks per round

- Players often drafted as teenagers
- Entry-level contracts (ELCs) for three years, with salary caps on rookie pay

Realities:

- Players may spend years developing in junior leagues or AHL
- Injuries and physical wear-and-tear are significant risks

Key Point:

You are an investment for the team—act like a long-term asset.

MLS Draft System

How It Works:

- MLS SuperDraft for college players and Generation Adidas signees
- Base salaries vary widely
- Homegrown Player signings (through academies) often bypass the draft

Realities:

- Not all contracts are life-changing financially
- Many players need endorsements, camps, or second jobs early on

Key Point:

Focus on building value both on and off the field.

WNBA Draft System

How It Works:

- 3 rounds, 12 picks per round
- Rookie contracts set by a salary scale
- Top picks earn six-figure salaries; others earn much less

Realities:

- Many players play overseas in the offseason to supplement income
- Endorsements play a huge role in total earnings

Key Point:
Have a year-round financial strategy, not just a summer plan.

MMA and Combat Sports Recruiting

How It Works:

- No draft; contracts awarded based on amateur record, buzz, and management connections
- UFC, Bellator, PFL offer tiered contracts
- Fighters are often "independent contractors"

Realities:

- Fighters pay for coaches, gyms, managers out of their purse
- Injuries and lost fights can destroy earning potential

Key Point:
Cash flow management is life-or-death financially in combat sports.

International Soccer Signings

How It Works:

- No "draft" — players are scouted and signed by clubs
- Transfer fees paid by clubs for players under contract elsewhere
- Salaries vary enormously based on league and club

Realities:

- Contracts may include bonuses for goals, appearances, trophies
- Language, culture, and legal differences complicate negotiations

Key Point:
Hire international-savvy agents and attorneys—don't go it alone.

Tennis, Golf, Track, Swimming: Individual Sport Contracts

How It Works:

- No salary guarantees
- Prize money earned by performance
- Sponsorship deals vary widely

Realities:

- Travel, coaching, and training costs come out of your own pocket
- Prize money can be heavily taxed across countries

Key Point:
You are the business.
Treat yourself like a brand and a CEO from day one.

Pros and Cons of Draft Systems and Recruiting

Pros:

- Gives structure to entering the professional ranks
- Provides a clear, public platform
- Signing bonuses and contracts provide initial stability

Cons:

- Slotted earnings limit early financial upside
- Team control over your career for several years
- Financial gaps for lower-round picks and undrafted athletes

Action Steps to Prepare for Your Draft or Signing

- Hire a qualified agent and attorney before signing anything
- Understand slotting and salary expectations in your sport
- Prepare mentally for the business side of professional sports
- Build a budget assuming minimum earnings, not maximum dreams
- Start financial literacy education *before* you get paid
- Protect your future with insurance (disability, loss of value)

Plain Language Breakdown: What You Must Understand

- Not everyone makes life-changing money from Day 1.
- Not every contract guarantees financial security.
- Team needs and politics can affect your opportunities.
- Endorsements are never "guaranteed" even for first-rounders.
- Your career's financial success depends on *your decisions,* not your draft spot.

Real-World Scenarios and Relatable Stories

Scenario: The First-Rounder Who Didn't Plan

Drafted top 10.

Blew money assuming career longevity.

Injuries and underperformance shortened career to three years.

No savings.

Now struggling financially.

Scenario: The Undrafted Hustler

Signed as an undrafted free agent.

Lived humbly.

Saved 70% of earnings.

Built a brand slowly.

By year five, became a multimillionaire with real estate investments.

Sports Analogies That Matter

Football: Being drafted is like making the team — it's just the beginning.

Basketball: The draft is your ticket; how you play determines if you stay.

Soccer: Signing a contract is like being transferred to a new club. It's an opportunity, not a guarantee.

Baseball: Getting drafted is like being called up to AA—you're not in the majors yet.

MMA: Getting signed to the UFC is just the first fight.

Tennis: Getting your first sponsor doesn't mean you've made it—you still have to win matches.

Golf: Making the Tour doesn't mean you're financially set—you still have to make cuts.

eSports: Getting signed to an org is step one—performing and building your brand is step two.

Final Encouragement

Getting drafted, signed, or recruited is a dream come true.

But it's not the finish line.

It's the starting line.

It's your opportunity to build something real, something lasting, something powerful.

You have already done something 99% of people will never do.

Now finish the journey the right way.

With clarity.

With discipline.

With wisdom.

Because while the draft system gets you in the door, it's your decisions—financial, personal, and professional—that determine whether you stay, thrive, and build a legacy.

You are not just an athlete.

You are a brand.

You are a business.

You are a builder.

Own your career.

Own your money.

Own your future.

Let's go win.

Chapter 10: Financial Red Flags to Watch During Pre-Draft Hype

There's nothing quite like the energy around draft season.

You're being flown out for visits.

You're taking calls from agents.

You're seeing your name pop up on social media.

Everybody's telling you "you've made it"—before you've even signed a contract.

And that's exactly why this is one of the most dangerous financial periods of your life.

If you've read *Financial Literacy For NIL*, *Financial Literacy For Student Athletes*, or *Financial Literacy For Parents of Student Athletes*, you've already seen how quickly attention can shift your mindset.

Now that you're stepping into the pros, the spotlight is even brighter.

And so are the risks.

Because where there's hype, there's hustle.

Where there's excitement, there's exploitation.

You're about to learn how to spot the financial red flags that can wreck everything you've worked for.

Let's break it all the way down.

The Reality of Pre-Draft Hype

Everyone loves a rising star.

But not everyone has your best interests at heart.

During the pre-draft process, you will be flooded with:

- "Business opportunities"
- "Family investment ideas"
- "Management offers"
- "Can't-miss deals"
- "Financial advisors" who found you before you found them

And if you're not careful, your trust, your name, and your money will be taken before you even sign your first deal.

Pre-draft hype makes you vulnerable.

Because it's easy to start believing the hype yourself.

And when you believe you're untouchable, you stop doing the due diligence you did to get here.

Financial Red Flags to Watch Out For

1. Agents Promising "Guaranteed" Draft Spots

There are no guarantees.

Draft boards change daily.

Promising you'll "definitely" go first round is manipulation.

The best agents promise preparation—not placement.

2. Advisors Offering "Secret" Investment Deals Before You Get Paid

If someone pitches you an investment before you've even cashed a check, walk away.

If it's so "guaranteed," they wouldn't need your money.

Legitimate opportunities don't require rush decisions.

3. Family and Friends Asking for Money "Early"

"Once you get paid, you're going to take care of us, right?"

"We just need a little loan to start our business."

"You can trust us — we're family."

Emotions run high.

Boundaries must run higher.

If someone can't respect "not yet," they won't respect "never."

4. Early Endorsement Deals With Crazy Clauses

Some brands will try to lock you into long-term contracts before you establish your full value.

They offer upfront cash but hide:

- Ownership of your name/image/likeness for years
- Clauses that prevent you from signing better deals later

Get every contract reviewed by your attorney—not just your agent.

5. Management Groups Offering "Free" Services

If someone offers you "free":

- Training

- Housing
- Marketing

...they are getting paid somehow.

Usually by back-end cuts of your future earnings.

Nothing is free.

Everything costs something.

Demand transparency.

6. Financial Advisors Pushing You Into Complex Investments

If you don't understand it, don't invest in it.

Period.

You should not be buying:

- Restaurants
- Car washes
- Nightclubs
- Real estate syndicates
- Startups your "boy" wants to launch

...before you've even been paid once.

Keep it simple: save, protect, and invest conservatively.

7. Unlicensed "Money Managers"

Anyone giving financial advice must be licensed and registered.

Ask for their:

- FINRA registration (for brokers)
- SEC registration (for advisors)
- References (real ones, not just their cousin)

No credentials? No conversation.

8. Pressure to "Live Like a Star" Early

Luxury apartments.

Luxury cars.

Designer clothes.

VIP sections.

If you spend like a superstar before you are one, you'll be broke before you even arrive.

Pros and Cons of Pre-Draft Opportunities

Pros:

- Early brand building (when done right)
- Opportunities to network for life after sports
- The right advisors can set you up for success

Cons:

- Predatory financial schemes
- Manipulative contracts
- Emotional pressures from friends and family
- Distractions from training and focus

Action Steps to Protect Yourself During Pre-Draft Hype

- Hire an independent fiduciary financial advisor early
- Hire an independent sports attorney (not your agent's buddy)
- Set a policy: "I don't invest in anything until after my second contract"
- Create a "Family and Friends Fund" if you must — cap it early

- Vet every deal with a licensed attorney and advisor
- Remember: Saying "No" now protects your ability to say "Yes" later

Plain Language Breakdown: How to Spot the Hustles

- If it's too good to be true, it is.
- If they need you to sign today, say no.
- If they're offering you "secret" investment opportunities, walk away.
- If it makes you feel uncomfortable, trust your gut.
- If they don't want you to bring your own lawyer or advisor into the conversation, they're hiding something.

Real-World Scenarios and Relatable Stories

Scenario: The Pre-Draft Investment Trap

An athlete, projected to go top 20, gets pitched a "guaranteed" real estate investment.

Signs papers without legal review.

Ends up owing $500,000 before his first paycheck even clears.

Scenario: The Family Pressure Explosion

Draft buzz gets the family excited.

Everyone starts spending money they don't have, expecting to get "paid back" later.

When the athlete goes undrafted, family relationships are destroyed.

Sports Analogies That Matter

Football: Pre-draft hype is like pre-snap motion. Lots of movement, lots of noise—but don't jump offsides.

Basketball: Pre-draft buzz is like a full-court press. Stay calm. Break the pressure with smart decisions.

Soccer: Pre-draft hype is like a fake injury. Looks dramatic but doesn't mean anything real.

Baseball: Pre-draft promises are like a hanging curveball. Easy to swing at—and easy to miss badly.

MMA: Pre-draft deals are like a feint. If you react without thinking, you get knocked out.

Track and Field: Hype is the first 50 meters. The race is much longer.

Tennis: The pre-draft period is like the warmup. The real match hasn't even started.

Golf: Draft hype is like the driving range. Looks impressive, but the real game happens on the course.

eSports: Pre-draft business pitches are like early-game rushes. Defend first, counterattack later.

Final Encouragement

You are stepping into one of the most exciting, dangerous, powerful periods of your life.

The attention is real.

The opportunities are real.

But the traps are real, too.

You must stay grounded.

You must stay disciplined.

You must stay focused on the long game—not the quick win.

You worked too hard to blow it now.

You didn't grind all these years just to hand your future over to someone with a fancy pitch deck.

You are not a lottery ticket for others.

You are not a quick payday.

You are a builder.

You are a CEO.

You are the franchise.

Own it.

Protect it.

Respect it.

The draft is just the beginning.

The decisions you make during this pre-draft period will echo for years to come.

Choose wisely.

Move patiently.

Think long-term.

Because your career, your wealth, your peace, and your legacy are worth protecting.

Let's keep building.

Let's keep winning.

Let's stay ready.

Part 2: First Paycheck, First Big Mistakes — Handling Early Money

The first paycheck feels like a dream come true — and for many athletes, it's the biggest check they've ever seen. But with new money comes new temptations, new pressures, and new risks. Part 2 of this book is about what happens after the money hits your account. It's about why early mistakes are so common — and so costly — and how you can avoid becoming another cautionary tale.

This section walks you through the critical financial decisions you'll face once you start getting paid: how to set up your cash flow, how to avoid lifestyle creep, how to manage taxes, how to say no to bad deals, and how to protect your future while everyone around you may be living in the moment.

If you read *Financial Literacy For NIL* or *Financial Literacy For Student Athletes*, you learned how to set a financial foundation. Now, it's time to apply those lessons at a higher level, where the stakes are bigger, the mistakes are more expensive, and the consequences can last a lifetime.

Part 2 isn't just about making your first big money. It's about making sure it's not your last. It's about learning to think like a pro — not just on the field, but in every financial move you make off of it.

This is where careers are built — or broken.

This is where legends are made — or lost.

And it starts with how you handle your very first check.

Chapter 11: Understanding Your Rookie Contract — Every Clause Matters

Congratulations.

You made it.

You got drafted.

You signed.

You're officially a professional athlete.

But before you pop the champagne, before you start ordering custom chains or planning luxury vacations, you need to sit down and really understand what you just signed.

Because your rookie contract is not just a paycheck.

It's a map.

And if you don't know how to read it, you could end up lost—fast.

If you've read *Financial Literacy For NIL*, *Financial Literacy For Student Athletes*, or *Financial Literacy For Parents of Student Athletes*, you already know that details matter when it comes to money.

Now, the stakes are even higher.

This chapter will teach you how to read your rookie contract like a seasoned vet—so you protect yourself, build wisely, and move like the pro you are.

Let's get into it.

Why Every Clause Matters

A contract isn't just about how much money you make.
It's about:

- When you make it
- How you make it
- What can take it away
- What obligations you're agreeing to
- How you protect yourself if things go sideways

Every sentence, every clause, every line matters.
Because the details determine the dollars.
And the dollars determine the freedom you'll have later.

Breaking Down the Key Sections of a Rookie Contract

1. Signing Bonus

What It Is:

- A lump-sum payment you get for signing the contract
- Typically guaranteed

Things to Watch:

- When is it paid? (Immediately? In installments?)
- Are there conditions that could void it?

Pro Tip:
Save at least 50%-70% of your signing bonus.
Don't treat it like lottery winnings.
Treat it like career capital.

2. Base Salary

What It Is:

- Your yearly "regular" salary paid during the season

Things to Watch:

- Is it guaranteed?
- Is it split across game checks?
- Are there roster bonuses that could affect it?

Pro Tip:
Budget based on your *lowest guaranteed amount,* not your "on paper" salary.

3. Roster Bonuses

What It Is:

- Extra payments for making the active roster on specific dates

Things to Watch:

- What counts as "active"? Injured reserve? Practice squad?

Pro Tip:
Never assume you'll get every roster bonus.
Earn them—but don't spend them before you see them.

4. Workout Bonuses

What It Is:

- Bonuses for participating in offseason workouts

Things to Watch:

- Attendance requirements (specific days, mandatory events)

Pro Tip:
Show up, get paid.
Every dollar you stack early gives you options later.

5. Performance Bonuses

What It Is:

- Bonuses for hitting specific statistical or award-based goals

Things to Watch:

- Are the benchmarks realistic?
- Are there team-based contingencies?

Pro Tip:
Treat performance bonuses as "nice to have," not "must have."
Never build your budget around uncertain money.

6. Guarantees

What It Is:

- Money that's yours regardless of injury or being cut

Things to Watch:

- Is it full guarantee, injury-only, or roster bonus-based?

Pro Tip:

Your true contract value is the guaranteed money, not the headline number.

Agents love to hype "$40 million deals" — but if only $8 million is guaranteed, that's your real floor.

7. Offset Language

What It Is:

- Rules about what happens if you're cut and sign with another team

Things to Watch:

- Do offsets reduce your old team's obligations?

Pro Tip:

Fight for no-offset clauses when possible.

It preserves more guaranteed money if things go sideways.

8. Injury Clauses

What It Is:

- Defines how injuries affect your salary and bonuses

Things to Watch:

- Are there "failure to disclose" penalties?
- Does the team have broad discretion over "recovery" timelines?

Pro Tip:
Always disclose injuries properly.
And protect yourself with private disability insurance.

9. Conduct Clauses

What It Is:

- Defines behavior that can void parts of your contract

Things to Watch:

- Broad language ("conduct detrimental to the team") can be weaponized

Pro Tip:
Stay professional on and off the field.
Bad decisions can literally cost you millions overnight.

10. Representation and Fee Structures

What It Is:

- Details about agent fees and obligations

Things to Watch:

- Are agent fees capped appropriately (3%-5%)?
- Are there hidden "marketing" fees tucked in?

Pro Tip:
Understand every fee you're paying.
If it's not clear, it's a no-go.

Pros and Cons of Rookie Contracts

Pros:

- Launch your professional career
- Provide early financial security
- Set the stage for future endorsements and contracts

Cons:

- Teams often hold most of the power
- Slotted deals limit early negotiating leverage
- Non-guaranteed money creates career uncertainty

Action Steps to Master Your Rookie Deal

- Hire an independent attorney to review your contract before you sign
- Ask questions until you truly understand every clause
- Create two budgets: one based on guaranteed money, one on total contract value
- Protect your signing bonus aggressively
- Start estate planning immediately (wills, trusts, powers of attorney)

Plain Language Breakdown: Rookie Contracts Aren't as Simple as You Think

- The headline number is marketing.
- The real number is the guaranteed money.
- Every bonus has conditions.
- Every obligation matters.
- Every clause affects your financial freedom.

Real-World Scenarios and Relatable Stories

Scenario: The Rookie Who Only Looked at the Total Value

Signed a "$20 million" deal.
Only $6 million guaranteed.
Cut after Year 2.
Walked away with far less than expected.

Scenario: The Rookie Who Read Every Line

Negotiated strong guarantees.
Protected against offsets.
Saved signing bonus.
Built wealth steadily even after career-ending injury.

Sports Analogies That Matter

Football: Rookie contracts are like your first playbook. If you don't study it, you won't survive training camp.

Basketball: The rookie contract is like a two-way contract—opportunity and risk rolled into one.

Soccer: Rookie deals are like promotion to the first team. You're there—but your spot isn't guaranteed.

Baseball: Your rookie deal is your minor league contract. You're not "made" until you survive and thrive.

MMA: The first contract gets you in the cage—how you fight determines what comes next.

Track and Field: Signing your rookie deal is qualifying for the Olympics. It's not the medal yet.

Tennis: It's your first Grand Slam main draw—now you have to win matches.

Golf: Your rookie deal is like earning your Tour card. Now the real grind begins.

eSports: Signing with a team is just Phase 1—you still have to perform under the lights.

Final Encouragement

Your rookie contract is the first big test of your business career.

Pass it with flying colors.

Take it seriously.

Respect the details.

Protect yourself.

Because if you get the foundation right now, you set yourself up to:

- Stay in control
- Build real wealth
- Avoid unnecessary risk

- Maximize your opportunities

You're not just signing a deal.

You're signing a launchpad for your future.

And smart players know:

The smartest play is the one that sets you up to keep playing — long after the lights go out.

You're not here just to get drafted.

You're here to dominate.

Financially.

Professionally.

Personally.

Own your rookie deal.

Understand every word.

And build the future you deserve.

Chapter 12: Signing Bonuses: Blessing or Trap?

When you hear "signing bonus," it feels like you've already won.

A big check.

A big moment.

A big payoff after years of sacrifice.

And don't get it twisted—signing bonuses can be a huge blessing.

They're often the only guaranteed money in your rookie deal.

They can create security, freedom, and opportunity.

But...

Signing bonuses can also be a trap.

A fast ticket to financial stress if you don't manage them right.

If you've read *Financial Literacy For NIL, Financial Literacy For Student Athletes,* or *Financial Literacy For Parents of Student Athletes,* you've already learned how important it is to build a strong foundation.

Now, the stakes are even higher.

Your signing bonus isn't just a celebration.

It's your seed money for a lifetime of wealth.

Or it's your first financial mistake—if you're not careful.

Let's walk through it carefully, patiently, and smartly.

What a Signing Bonus Really Is

A signing bonus is a lump-sum payment you receive when you officially sign your rookie contract.

It's often paid upfront or split into installments.

In most leagues (NFL, NBA, MLB, NHL), signing bonuses are:

- Negotiated as part of your rookie deal
- Counted against salary caps (affecting team budgets)
- Sometimes the only fully guaranteed money you will see

Key point:

Your signing bonus is likely your most secure source of early money.

Blessing: Why Signing Bonuses Are Powerful

1. Immediate Liquidity

You get cash you can access and control — not just "theoretical" salary over years.

2. Career Insurance

If your career ends early, your bonus is money you already secured.

3. Financial Launchpad

Properly managed, your signing bonus can:

- Pay off debts
- Build emergency funds
- Start investment accounts
- Create generational wealth

4. Flexibility

You can start making choices based on freedom—not desperation.

Trap: How Signing Bonuses Create Financial Danger

1. Lifestyle Inflation

You suddenly feel "rich."

You start spending like you're on a $20 million deal—even if your guaranteed bonus is a fraction of that.

2. Misunderstanding Taxes

Uncle Sam is coming.

Depending on where you sign, state taxes are coming too.

Signing bonuses are heavily taxed at both federal and state levels.

If you don't plan ahead, your "big check" shrinks fast.

3. Pressure from Family and Friends

"Help me start a business."

"Buy me a house."

"Invest in this idea."

Suddenly, everyone has a "plan" for your money.

4. Predatory Pitches

- Bad investment deals
- Shady "financial advisors"
- "Can't miss" business opportunities

All of them see your signing bonus as their lottery ticket.

Not yours.

Pros and Cons of Signing Bonuses

Pros:

- Provides early financial security
- Protects against early career-ending injuries
- Allows you to build wealth faster

Cons:

- Creates pressure to spend immediately
- Exposes you to bad advice and financial predators
- Easy to underestimate taxes and hidden costs

Action Steps to Manage Your Signing Bonus Smartly

1. Build a "Hold Back" Plan

- Immediately set aside 40%-50% for taxes.
- Set aside 20% for emergency savings.
- Set aside 20% for investments.
- Live off the remaining 10%-20%.

2. Open Multiple Accounts

- Checking account for living expenses.
- High-yield savings account for emergency fund.
- Brokerage account for investments.
- Roth IRA if eligible.

3. Create a Cash Flow Map
Plan monthly cash flow based on needs, not wants.
4. Hire a Fiduciary Financial Advisor
Not a "friend."
Not a "family member."
A licensed, registered fiduciary who works in your best interests.
5. Say No Early and Often
You are not obligated to fund every dream and fix every problem.
6. Insure Your Wealth
Purchase:

- Disability insurance
- Umbrella liability insurance
- Health and life insurance

7. Pay Yourself First

Automate savings and investments before you spend anything.

Plain Language Breakdown: How to Handle Your Bonus

- Assume half is already gone to taxes.
- Pretend the bonus is half its actual size when planning.
- Set up "invisible" savings so you don't even feel the money disappearing.
- Protect your bonus like you protect your body.

Real-World Scenarios and Relatable Stories

Scenario: The Rookie Who Spent the Bonus Early

Signed a $1 million signing bonus.

Bought a $500,000 house.

Bought a $100,000 car.

Gave away $200,000 to friends and family.

Didn't save for taxes.

Owed $400,000 in taxes the next year.

Had to sell the house just to pay the IRS.

Scenario: The Rookie Who Built a Fortress

Signed a $750,000 signing bonus.

Saved 70%.

Lived on a modest $50,000/year budget.

Invested conservatively.

Within five years, had over $1 million saved and invested—regardless of career ups and downs.

Sports Analogies That Matter

Football: Your signing bonus is like your offensive line. If you protect it, it protects you.

Basketball: Your bonus is your first quarter lead. Protect it so you can finish strong.

Soccer: It's your early goal. Don't lose focus and give it right back.

Baseball: It's your early lead. Manage it wisely inning by inning.

MMA: It's your first-round knockdown. Stay calm. Finish the fight smart.

Track and Field: It's a strong first lap in the 400m. Pace yourself for the rest of the race.

Tennis: It's the first set win. Stay focused—the match isn't over.

Golf: It's your birdie on Hole 1. There's a long course ahead.

eSports: It's winning early map control. Now you need smart resource management.

Final Encouragement

Your signing bonus is a gift.

A blessing.

A once-in-a-lifetime opportunity to jump-start your future.

But it's only a blessing if you treat it with the respect it deserves.

Protect it.

Manage it.

Grow it.

Because if you blow it, you'll spend the rest of your career trying to chase what you already had.

And chasing is a dangerous financial game.

You have a chance right now to set yourself apart.

Not just by how you play on the field.

But by how you manage your blessings off the field.

You're not just an athlete.

You're an empire.

You're not just here for the highlights.

You're here for the legacy.

It starts with your first real check.

Your signing bonus.

Your launchpad.

Treat it right.

And let it work for you for the rest of your life.

Let's go.

Let's build.

Let's win the long game.

Chapter 13: What to Do with Your Signing Bonus

The moment your signing bonus hits your account, everything feels different.

For maybe the first time in your life, you see real money sitting there — numbers you used to dream about.

You earned it.

You worked for it.

You deserve it.

But now comes the most important play of your financial career so far:

What you *do* with that signing bonus will shape your future far more than how big the bonus actually is.

If you've read *Financial Literacy For NIL, Financial Literacy For Student Athletes,* or *Financial Literacy For Parents of Student Athletes,* you already know that quick money without a smart plan disappears even faster.

This chapter is about making sure your signing bonus doesn't just change your *today* — it changes your *tomorrow, next year, and next decade.*

Let's get into it.

First Things First: Slow Down

The first move after receiving your signing bonus isn't buying anything.

It's slowing down.

Taking a breath.

Creating space between the money hitting your account and you doing anything with it.

Because money makes noise.

Friends will call.

Family will hint.

"Businessmen" will appear out of nowhere.

Everybody will have an idea.

But you need a plan — not pressure.

The right first move with your signing bonus is silence.

Silence lets you hear your own thoughts.

Silence lets you think beyond today.

Step 1: Pay the Taxes First

Uncle Sam doesn't care that you're a rookie.

He doesn't care about your dreams.

He only cares about his cut.

Signing bonuses are taxed heavily — federal, state, sometimes city.

Depending on your state, taxes could take 40% or more of your bonus.

Action Step:

- Immediately move 40%-50% of your bonus into a high-yield savings account earmarked for taxes.

Pro Tip:

Over-save for taxes rather than under-saving.

Getting a refund beats owing the IRS.

Step 2: Build Your Emergency Fund

The next thing you do is protect yourself.

An emergency fund is the financial equivalent of health insurance for your wallet.

When — not if — unexpected things happen, your emergency fund keeps you from spiraling into panic or debt.

Action Step:

- Save 6 to 12 months' worth of living expenses in a separate high-yield savings account.

This is money you don't touch unless it's truly an emergency:

- Career-ending injury
- Family emergency
- Health crisis

Pro Tip:

This is not "vacation money." Lock it down.

Step 3: Pay Off Any High-Interest Debt

If you have any high-interest debt (credit cards, payday loans, personal loans), pay it off immediately.

Debt eats wealth faster than almost anything else.

Action Step:

- Prioritize paying off any debt with an interest rate higher than 6%-7%.

Pro Tip:

Clearing debt is an immediate guaranteed return on your money.

Step 4: Set Up "Invisible Savings"

Now you need to make saving automatic and invisible.

Invisible money is protected money.

If you don't see it, you don't spend it.

Action Step:

- Set up automatic transfers from your checking account to separate savings and investment accounts every month.

This way, saving isn't a decision you have to make over and over.

It just happens.

Step 5: Start Investing for the Long-Term

You're not playing for one season.

You're playing for life.

Investing wisely is how you turn today's bonus into tomorrow's freedom.

Where to Start:

- Open a Roth IRA (if eligible)
- Max out employer-sponsored plans (if offered)
- Open a simple, low-cost brokerage account for additional investing

Pro Tip:

Start with boring, proven investments:

- Index funds
- ETFs
- Target-date funds

Don't chase flashy "get rich quick" schemes.

Step 6: Protect Yourself with Insurance

You've just become a high-value target.

Financially.

Legally.

Personally.

You need protection.

Action Step:

- Purchase disability insurance
- Purchase umbrella liability insurance
- Purchase life insurance if you have dependents

Pro Tip:

The richer you get, the more important protection becomes.

Step 7: Create a "Fun Fund"

Life isn't just about saving.

You're allowed to celebrate.

But the celebration should be planned.

Action Step:

- Set aside 5%-10% of your after-tax signing bonus for fun.

Use it guilt-free.

Enjoy it.

But when it's gone, it's gone.

Pro Tip:

You're not "cheap" for being disciplined.

You're smart.

Step 8: Plan for Family and Friends

You will feel pressure.

Guilt.

Obligation.

You're human.

But you can't help everyone.

Especially not at the cost of your own future.

Action Step:

- Create a "family and friends" budget—a specific amount you're willing to gift.
- Set clear boundaries.
- Say "no" with love and firmness.

Pro Tip:

Helping responsibly is more powerful than enabling recklessly.

Step 9: Hire and Separate the Right Professionals

You need a team:

- Fiduciary financial advisor
- Licensed CPA
- Sports-savvy attorney

But they should all be separate people.

Checks and balances protect you.

No one person should control everything.

Pro Tip:

If a "professional" can't explain things to you simply, they don't respect you.

Fire them.

Immediately.

Step 10: Build a Season-Based Cash Flow Plan

Your salary isn't year-round.

It's seasonal.

You get paid during the season, not during the offseason.

Your money must last all year.

Action Step:

- Budget monthly cash flow as if you're only paid once a year.
- Stretch your money over 12 months, not just the season.

Pro Tip:

Offseason money mistakes kill careers.

Be smarter.

Pros and Cons of Big Signing Bonuses

Pros:

- Provides immediate financial opportunity
- Creates a foundation for long-term wealth
- Shields you from early career instability

Cons:

- Creates temptation to overspend
- Attracts financial predators
- Requires immediate discipline most people don't have

Real-World Scenarios and Relatable Stories

Scenario: The Rookie Who Saved First

Banked 70% of signing bonus.

Lived modestly.

Bought a condo with cash.

Invested early.

Was financially free by Year 5.

Scenario: The Rookie Who Gave It Away

Loaned money to family and friends.

Bought too many cars.

Ignored taxes.

Gone by Year 3.

Broke by Year 5.

Sports Analogies That Matter

Football: Your signing bonus is your first touchdown. Celebrate, but know there are four quarters left.

Basketball: It's like hitting the first 3-pointer—good start, but the game is long.

Soccer: It's scoring an early goal. Stay composed.

Baseball: It's getting on base in the first inning. Play smart for nine innings.

MMA: It's landing a clean shot early. Stay disciplined.

Track and Field: It's a good start out of the blocks. Don't burn out early.

Tennis: Winning the first game doesn't mean you win the match.

Golf: Birdieing the first hole feels good. But there's a full 18 ahead.

eSports: Early game dominance doesn't mean you've won yet—stay focused.

Final Encouragement

Your signing bonus isn't just a check.

It's a test.

It's a test of vision.

Of discipline.

Of maturity.

You're not here to live a highlight reel.

You're here to build a highlight career—and a highlight life.

What you do with this first money will echo for decades.

You have a chance to:

- Change your life
- Change your family's life
- Create freedom
- Build a legacy

Don't blow it on things that lose value the minute you drive them off the lot.

Invest in the one thing that always appreciates:

You.

Invest in your peace.

Invest in your freedom.

Invest in your future.

You earned this shot.

Now earn your freedom.

Let's build.

Let's protect it.

Let's own it.

This is your time.

This is your future.

Chapter 14: Avoiding Lifestyle Creep — Managing Newfound Wealth

You got the signing bonus.

You signed the contract.

You're finally living the dream you've been chasing for years.

But here's the reality: wealth doesn't just change your bank account — it changes your environment, your relationships, your expectations, and your temptations.

And one of the biggest threats to new money isn't bad investments or high taxes.

It's lifestyle creep.

If you've read *Financial Literacy For NIL*, *Financial Literacy For Student Athletes*, or *Financial Literacy For Parents of Student Athletes*, you know that managing sudden increases in income is a skill — not an accident.

This chapter will help you stay grounded, disciplined, and in control as your money grows.

Because true wealth isn't just about making money.

It's about keeping it, growing it, and living free.

Let's dive deep into how to avoid the trap of lifestyle creep and truly manage your newfound wealth like a champion.

What Is Lifestyle Creep?

Lifestyle creep happens when your spending rises as fast — or faster — than your income.

You get a raise? You upgrade your car.

You sign a contract? You buy a bigger house.

You land a new deal? You start flying private.

At first, it feels normal — "I earned this."

But slowly, without noticing, your "new normal" becomes expensive.

And suddenly, it takes *all* of your income — maybe even more — just to keep up with the life you've built.

No matter how much you make, it's never enough.

You're trapped.

Lifestyle creep is sneaky.

It's dangerous.

And it's everywhere in the world of pro sports.

Why Lifestyle Creep Is So Dangerous for Athletes

1. Short Career Windows

You might have 3 years.

Maybe 7.

If you're lucky, 10+.

Pro careers are short compared to the rest of your life.

If you build a life you can only afford while playing, what happens when you stop?

2. Taxes and Fees You Didn't Expect

Half your money is already gone to taxes, agents, and fees before you even touch it.

Lifestyle creep doesn't factor that in.

3. Fake Expectations from Others

People will start treating you like an ATM.

You're "expected" to:

- Pick up the tab.
- Buy your parents a house.
- Fund your friend's business idea.

4. Pressure to Flex

Social media.

Teammates.

Friends from back home.

You feel like you have to "prove" you're winning.

5. No Rewind Button

It's easy to scale up your lifestyle.

It's brutally hard to scale it back.

Once you're used to $10,000 weekends, $300,000 cars, and $50,000 vacations, "normal" feels like failure.

Pros and Cons of Lifestyle Inflation

Pros (when done smartly):

- Enjoying rewards for your hard work
- Upgrading areas that truly matter (health, safety, time)
- Investing in experiences over things

Cons (when unmanaged):

- Constant financial stress
- Limited savings and investing potential
- Risk of going broke after career ends
- Loss of real freedom and peace

Action Steps to Avoid Lifestyle Creep

1. Set a Baseline Budget

Before you touch a dollar, decide:

- How much you truly need to live well
- How much you will save and invest automatically

Use percentages, not dollar amounts.
Example:

- 50% saving/investing
- 30% living expenses
- 10% taxes (above initial withholdings)
- 10% fun money

2. Create "Financial Red Zones"

Identify behaviors that indicate you're slipping:

- Buying a car that costs more than 10%-15% of your annual income
- Buying a home that stretches your monthly payment over 25%-30% of your monthly income
- Carrying a credit card balance
- Financing luxury purchases

When you enter a "red zone," stop and reassess.

3. Separate Public Flex from Private Wealth

Ask yourself:
"Do I want to look rich or be rich?"
Looking rich burns cash.
Being rich builds peace.

Live below your means in public.
Stack quietly in private.

4. Automate the Good Habits

- Automatic savings
- Automatic investments
- Automatic charitable giving (if you choose)

Let good habits happen without emotional decisions.

5. Delay Big Purchases

Use the 30-day rule.
When you want something expensive:

- Write it down
- Wait 30 days
- If you still want it after 30 days, consider it

Impulse spending destroys empires.

6. Build a Team of Protectors

- A fiduciary financial advisor
- A second-opinion CPA
- A personal attorney

They're not there to say "yes" to every idea.
They're there to help you say "no" to bad ones.

7. Design Your "Freedom Lifestyle"

Ask yourself:

"What kind of life do I want when I'm 35, 45, 65?"

Design backward.

Build a life today that your future self will be proud of—and grateful for.

Plain Language Breakdown: How to Beat Lifestyle Creep

- Save first, spend second.
- Protect your future before you "flex" today.
- Invest in experiences over things.
- Say "no" more than you say "yes."
- Don't measure success by what you post.
- Measure success by what you can walk away from without stress.

Real-World Scenarios and Relatable Stories

Scenario: The Rookie Who Stayed Modest

Lived on 20% of income.

Saved 70%.

Invested early.

By end of career, had 5X net worth of higher-drafted teammates who spent big.

Scenario: The Star Who Flexed Too Hard

Bought multiple mansions.

Maintained massive "crew."

Every offseason was more lavish.

After retirement, faced bankruptcy within three years.

Sports Analogies That Matter

Football: Lifestyle creep is like letting the opposing team gain 5 yards at a time—you don't notice it until they're in your red zone.

Basketball: It's like giving up easy layups—each one seems small until you're down 20 points.

Soccer: It's a slow counterattack—if you're not disciplined, you're caught out of position.

Baseball: It's like swinging at bad pitches—one at-bat wasted at a time.

MMA: It's taking body shots early—you don't feel it until your legs give out.

Track and Field: It's going out too fast in a marathon—you're cooked by Mile 20.

Tennis: It's losing focus one game at a time until the match slips away.

Golf: It's missing easy putts—the mistakes that add up silently.

eSports: It's bad resource management—small losses that become irreversible.

Final Encouragement

You earned the right to live well.

But don't let "living well" turn into "living reckless."

Freedom isn't just about how much you make.

Freedom is about how much you *keep, protect,* and *grow.*

The private victories — stacking cash, building investments, creating peace of mind — will outshine any public flex.

Own your money.

Own your choices.

Own your future.

You're not just playing for this season.

You're playing for the life after the lights go out.

Protect it.

Respect it.

Build it.

Your legacy depends on it.

Your family depends on it.

You depend on it.

Let's be smart.

Let's be strategic.

Let's keep winning—on and off the field.

Chapter 15: State Taxes — How Where You Play Impacts Your Net Income

When you sign your rookie contract, the numbers look amazing.

Six figures.

Seven figures.

Maybe more.

But those big numbers are not the money you'll actually get to keep.

Because Uncle Sam takes his cut.

And if you're playing in certain states, their tax collectors want their share too.

If you've read *Financial Literacy For NIL*, *Financial Literacy For Student Athletes*, or *Financial Literacy For Parents of Student Athletes*, you've seen how taxes can sneak up and take a huge bite out of your earnings.

Now, at the professional level, the game gets even more complicated.

Understanding how state taxes work — and how the "jock tax" affects your net income — is crucial if you want to manage your money wisely.

This chapter will break it down clearly, patiently, and practically.

Let's go.

Why State Taxes Matter for Pro Athletes

Most people work and pay taxes in one place.

Athletes are different.

You earn income in multiple states — every time you play a road game, you might owe taxes in that state.

This is called the "jock tax."

It's real.

It's complicated.

And if you're not prepared, it can wreck your cash flow.

Breaking Down the Basics

Federal Taxes

Everyone pays federal income tax.

It's based on your total income, regardless of where you live.

Top federal rates can eat up 37% of your income.

State Taxes

Some states have no income tax (like Florida, Texas, Washington).

Some states have very high income taxes (like California, New York).

If you play for a team in a high-tax state, your net pay will be lower.

If you play for a team in a no-tax state, your net pay will be higher.

Simple, right?

Not so fast.

The "Jock Tax"

Here's where it gets tricky.

You pay state income taxes based on where you *earn* the money, not just where you *live.*

So when you:

- Play a road game in New York, you owe New York taxes on that portion of income.
- Play a road game in California, you owe California taxes.
- Play a road game in Texas, no state tax owed for that game.

Bottom Line:

Your pay gets sliced up by geography.
Your CPA better know what they're doing.

Pros and Cons of State Tax Structures

Pros of No-Tax States:

- Keep more of your paycheck
- Simpler financial planning
- Long-term benefits for wealth building

Cons of No-Tax States:

- You still owe jock taxes for away games
- Cost of living might still be high (Miami, for example)
- Property taxes can be higher

Pros of Playing in High-Tax States:

- Access to big media markets (endorsement opportunities)
- Living in major cities (lifestyle, connections)

Cons of Playing in High-Tax States:

- Lower net income

- Complicated tax planning
- Potential "double taxation" issues

Real-World Example

Imagine two rookies:

- Rookie A signs with a Florida team (no state income tax)
- Rookie B signs with a California team (13.3% top state tax rate)

Both rookies have a $5 million salary.

Rookie A (Florida):

- Federal taxes: ≈ 37%
- No state income tax
- Net after tax: ≈ $3.15 million

Rookie B (California):

- Federal taxes: ≈ 37%
- State taxes: 13.3%
- Net after tax: ≈ $2.35 million

That's an $800,000 difference.

Same contract.

Different take-home.

Massive impact.

How to Plan Around State Taxes

1. Know Your Home State Rules

Where you claim "domicile" (permanent home) affects your tax obligations.

If you sign with a team in a no-tax state, set up your true domicile there — not just a "mailing address."

Action Step:

- Register to vote in that state
- Change your driver's license
- Open a local bank account
- Spend significant time there

2. Work With a CPA Who Knows Athlete Taxation

Not all accountants understand the jock tax.

Hire one who has experience with pro athletes.

They can:

- File multiple state tax returns
- Avoid double-taxation
- Minimize total tax burden legally

3. Budget for Taxes Conservatively

Assume worst-case tax hit every year.

If you end up owing less, great.

But never get caught short.

Action Step:

- Set aside 45%-50% of all paychecks for taxes immediately.

4. Consider Offseason Residency Moves

If you're a free agent, choosing where to sign matters beyond just the money.

Sometimes taking a slightly lower deal in a no-tax state nets you more money long-term.

Run the real numbers before deciding.

5. Plan for Endorsement Income Taxes Too

Endorsements are taxed based on where services are performed.

- Shoot a commercial in California? Pay California taxes.
- Appearance in New York? Pay New York taxes.

Every check has tax implications.

Track them.

Plan ahead.

Common Mistakes Athletes Make with State Taxes

- Assuming "no state tax" means no taxes at all
- Forgetting to file tax returns in multiple states
- Letting agents or business managers guess instead of using CPAs
- Ignoring "jock taxes" until audit letters show up

Plain Language Breakdown: Key Takeaways

- You pay taxes everywhere you play, not just where you live.
- No state income tax states help your bottom line — but you still owe jock taxes.
- A smart CPA is your tax MVP.
- Budget conservatively and assume taxes are higher than you think.

- Signing bonuses, endorsements, and salaries all have state-specific rules.

Real-World Scenarios and Relatable Stories

Scenario: The Rookie Who Moved Smart

Signed with a team in Texas.

Established legal domicile there.

Saved millions over career by avoiding California's high tax rates on future earnings.

Scenario: The Veteran Who Didn't Plan

Bounced between teams.

Didn't properly set up domicile.

Owed back taxes in multiple states.

Faced penalties and audits.

Lost hundreds of thousands fixing the mistakes.

Sports Analogies That Matter

Football: State taxes are like defensive backs you didn't see—they pick off your paycheck if you're sloppy.

Basketball: Taxes are like hidden turnovers. One here, one there — next thing you know, you're down 10.

Soccer: It's like playing an away game on a field you don't know — you've got to adjust smart.

Baseball: It's like understanding different ballparks — every city has quirks you must navigate.

MMA: It's like checking leg kicks. If you ignore them, you're hobbled by the second round.

Track and Field: It's headwinds you can't see — but they slow you down just the same.

Tennis: Taxes are unforced errors. Avoid them and you win easier.

Golf: They're the bunkers and water hazards. If you're not paying attention, you're stuck.

eSports: State taxes are like resource leaks — they drain your advantage without you realizing it.

Final Encouragement

Where you live.

Where you play.

Where you earn.

It all matters.

Taxes aren't glamorous.

But ignoring them can turn your dream career into a financial nightmare.

You worked too hard to lose money you didn't have to lose.

You deserve better.

Be smart.

Plan ahead.

Surround yourself with pros who protect your money like it's their own.

You're not just signing contracts.

You're building an empire.

And empires don't fall because of enemies you can see.

They fall because of details ignored.

You're better than that.

You're smarter than that.

Let's protect every dollar.

Let's play chess, not checkers.

Own your taxes.

Own your career.

Own your future.

Let's build wealth—the smart way.

Chapter 16: Tax Strategies for Multi-State Athletes

Welcome to the big leagues.

Welcome to multi-state taxation.

Because when you're a professional athlete, your money doesn't just get taxed where you live — it gets taxed everywhere you earn.

If you've read *Financial Literacy For NIL*, *Financial Literacy For Student Athletes*, or *Financial Literacy For Parents of Student Athletes*, you already understand the basics of taxes.

But at the pro level, the tax game changes.

It gets more complicated.

It gets more expensive.

And it gets much easier to make mistakes if you're not prepared.

This chapter will help you:

- Understand the unique challenges of multi-state taxation
- Learn how to structure your financial life smartly
- Save as much money legally as possible

Let's go.

The Challenge: You Work in Multiple States

Unlike a normal job where you work in one state and pay taxes there, pro athletes work in many states.

Every away game.

Every tournament.

Every road trip.

Every endorsement deal in another city.

Each event potentially creates a new state tax obligation.

This is the "jock tax" reality.

You earn money in different states.

You owe money in different states.

Simple in theory.

Brutal in practice.

Why Multi-State Tax Planning Is Crucial

1. To Avoid Overpaying Taxes

If you don't coordinate your filings, you might pay taxes twice on the same money.

2. To Avoid Underpaying Taxes

Failing to pay the right states can trigger audits, penalties, and back taxes.

3. To Maximize Deductions and Credits

Good planning lets you offset taxes paid to one state against taxes owed to another.

4. To Reduce Stress and Protect Your Reputation

Tax troubles follow you.

Media loves a "pro athlete owes back taxes" headline.

Smart planning keeps your name clean and your wallet strong.

Pros and Cons of Multi-State Income

Pros:

- Opportunity to maximize earnings across national and international markets
- Exposure to larger endorsement opportunities
- Potential to leverage residency in no-tax states

Cons:

- Complex tax filings
- Higher accounting costs
- Risk of penalties if mishandled

Key Tax Strategies for Multi-State Athletes

1. Establish True Domicile in a No-Tax or Low-Tax State

Your "domicile" is your legal home.
Where you:

- Register to vote
- Have a driver's license
- Spend most of your offseason
- Maintain your primary residence

If you play in a high-tax state but legally reside in a no-tax state, you could save millions over your career.

Action Step:

- Work with an attorney to properly establish domicile in Florida, Texas, Tennessee, Washington, or another favorable state.

2. Track Your Workdays Accurately

Every day you work in a different state matters.
Teams often provide "duty day" reports — track them yourself too.
Keep your own record of:

- Games
- Practices
- Media appearances
- Endorsement shoots

Action Step:

- Keep a personal calendar of all work-related days and locations.

Pro Tip:
If you overreport, you overpay.
If you underreport, you risk audits.
Precision matters.

3. Maximize State Tax Credits

Most states give credit for taxes paid to another state.
For example:

- Play a game in New York.
- Pay New York state tax.
- Get a credit against your home state's income tax.

But you must:

- File correctly
- Document everything

- Use experienced tax professionals

Action Step:

- Hire a CPA firm that specializes in multi-state filings for pro athletes.

4. Defer Income Strategically

You can sometimes defer income into years when your tax rate will be lower.

For example:

- Backload contracts into years when you're playing in no-tax states.
- Defer endorsement income into lower-earning years.

Action Step:

- Negotiate contract structures with tax planning in mind.

5. Use Entity Structures Smartly

Some athletes set up LLCs, S Corps, or personal service corporations for endorsements and appearances.

Benefits:

- Potential tax deferral
- Expense deductions
- Better audit protection

But they must be set up correctly.

No "paper companies."

No shortcuts.

Action Step:

- Work with an attorney and CPA to structure business entities legally and smartly.

6. Understand Per Diem and Travel Deductions

Meal per diems, lodging costs, and other travel-related expenses can sometimes be deducted.

This reduces taxable income.

But rules are strict.

And tax laws change often.

Action Step:

- Keep detailed receipts.
- Consult your CPA annually about deductible expenses.

7. Plan for Endorsement and Appearance Income

Endorsements often create different tax obligations than salary.

You're taxed based on where you perform services.

Example:

- Commercial shoot in California = California income tax.
- Signing event in New Jersey = New Jersey income tax.

Action Step:

- Track endorsement-related travel separately.
- Plan endorsement shoots in no-tax states if possible.

8. Beware of Residency Challenges

High-tax states (like California and New York) sometimes aggressively challenge athlete residency claims.

They want to prove you're "really" living there to tax more of your income.

Red Flags:

- Owning multiple homes without clear primary residence
- Spending significant time in high-tax states without documentation
- Having family still living there

Action Step:

- Build a clear, documented case for your true residency.

9. Budget for Tax Payments Quarterly

You don't just pay taxes once a year.

You often must pay estimated taxes quarterly.

Missing deadlines triggers penalties and interest.

Action Step:

- Set calendar reminders.
- Work with your CPA to pay on time, every time.

10. File Every State Return Carefully

Even if you only earned $1,000 in a state, you may need to file there.

Filing late or missing returns can trigger audits.

Action Step:

- File a return in every state where you earned income.

- Don't skip.
- Don't assume it's too small to matter.

Plain Language Breakdown: Key Takeaways

- You earn money in multiple states.
- You owe taxes in multiple states.
- You can use credits to avoid double taxation — if you file correctly.
- Residency planning can save you millions.
- Good records + smart pros = tax peace of mind.

Real-World Scenarios and Relatable Stories

Scenario: The Rookie Who Nailed It

Tracked every road game.

Filed in every necessary state.

Maximized credits.

Saved $250,000 over three seasons compared to teammates who "guessed."

Scenario: The Star Who Got Burned

Assumed "no big deal."

Didn't file in small-market states.

Audited by California for back taxes.

Lost $1 million+ in taxes, penalties, and interest.

Sports Analogies That Matter

Football: Tax planning is like defensive reads. If you're not paying attention to the whole field, you get burned.

Basketball: It's like switching defenses—you've got to adjust every possession.

Soccer: It's playing both offense and defense—you have to manage both.

Baseball: It's managing a pitching staff—you can't just throw fastballs every inning.

MMA: It's protecting your chin—one mistake can end the fight.

Track and Field: It's running the curves smart—not just sprinting straightaways.

Tennis: It's playing different surfaces—you adjust or you lose.

Golf: It's managing every hole—not just crushing drives.

eSports: It's map control—win small battles to win the war.

Final Encouragement

Multi-state taxes aren't glamorous.

They're not sexy.

They're not fun.

But they're critical.

Because managing them smartly protects your money, your peace, and your future.

You've worked too hard to lose wealth over paperwork mistakes.

You're not just playing for now.

You're building for life.

Be smart.

Be disciplined.

Build your dream—and keep it.

Taxes are part of the game.

Play it better than anyone.

Own your income.

Own your taxes.

Own your future.

Let's keep building smart.

Chapter 17: Building a Realistic Budget as a Rookie

The first paycheck hits.

The first bonus clears.

The dreams start feeling real.

You're officially a professional athlete.

But here's the hard truth:

If you don't have a real budget in place from the very beginning, your money will disappear faster than you ever imagined.

Not because you're irresponsible.

Not because you're a bad person.

Because without a plan, lifestyle, taxes, people, and poor advice will eat it alive.

If you've read *Financial Literacy For NIL, Financial Literacy For Student Athletes,* or *Financial Literacy For Parents of Student Athletes,* you already know that discipline and planning are the real superpowers.

At the pro level, you have to level up those skills immediately.

This chapter will walk you through exactly how to build a rookie budget that protects you, respects your grind, and sets you up for real wealth—not just short-term flexes.

Let's get it.

Why You Need a Budget as a Rookie

1. Your Money Arrives in Big Chunks, Not a Weekly Paycheck

You might be paid:

- Per game
- Per appearance
- In a lump sum signing bonus

Managing large, irregular cash flows is way harder than managing a regular salary.

2. Your Career Could Be Shorter Than You Think

The average NFL career? About 3 years.

NBA? Maybe 4-5 years.

MLS? WNBA? MMA? All have brutal turnover.

Your prime earning years could be over before you're 30.

3. Everyone Wants a Piece

Family.

Friends.

Old coaches.

"Business partners."

If you don't have a clear plan, you'll bleed money on guilt, pressure, and bad deals.

4. Freedom Requires Discipline

Budgeting isn't about being "cheap."

It's about building a life where you aren't a slave to money.

The Rookie Budget Framework

Step 1: Know Your Real Net Income

Not your contract number.

Not what ESPN says.

Your real net after:

- Federal taxes
- State taxes
- Agent fees
- CPA fees
- Union dues

Action Step:

- Work with your CPA to create a "real income" number.

Pro Tip:

It's usually 45%-55% of your "headline" salary.

Step 2: Split It Into Buckets

The Rookie Rule of Thumb:

- 50% to saving and investing
- 30% to living expenses
- 10% to taxes (on top of what's withheld)
- 10% to "fun money"

Step 3: Budget Monthly

Even if you get paid seasonally, you live monthly.

Break down your annual net income into a 12-month budget.

Example:

If you net $600,000 a year:

- That's $50,000 a month.
- Budget based on that.
- Not on $600,000.

Step 4: Prioritize the Big 5 Expenses

1. Housing

- Rent if you're not sure about staying in a city.
- Keep mortgage payments under 25%-30% of monthly income.

2. Transportation

- Buy a car you can pay cash for.
- No $200,000 vehicles if you're making $600,000.

3. Food

- Reasonable grocery budget.
- No need for $1,000-a-night dinners regularly.

4. Insurance

- Disability
- Health
- Life (if you have dependents)

5. Family Support (If You Choose)

- Set a fixed amount.
- Not "whatever they ask."

Step 5: Automate the Right Moves

- Automatic transfers to savings and investment accounts.
- Automatic bill pay.
- Automatic tax set-asides.

Take emotion out of the equation.

Step 6: Cap the Lifestyle Creep

Every time you earn more, save more.

Don't raise your spending automatically.

Rule:

- For every $1 you earn above your base salary, save at least 50 cents.

Pros and Cons of Rookie Budgeting

Pros:

- Protects you from running out of money.
- Creates real financial freedom.
- Reduces stress.

Cons:

- Requires saying "no" to yourself and others.
- Might feel "boring" compared to others flexing.
- Requires constant discipline.

Real-World Scenarios and Relatable Stories

Scenario: The Rookie Who Budgeted

Saved 50% of net income from Day 1.

Lived off modest 30%.

Invested smartly.

By end of rookie contract, had over $1 million saved and invested.

Financially free before second contract negotiations even started.

Scenario: The Rookie Who Flexed Early

No budget.

- Bought two cars.
- Bought a $3 million house.
- Took 15 "yes men" on private trips.

Blew through signing bonus in 18 months.

Had to sign desperation contracts later.

Sports Analogies That Matter

Football: Budgeting is like clock management. Play smart now so you're not desperate at the two-minute warning.

Basketball: It's like setting the pace. Don't blow all your energy in the first quarter.

Soccer: It's about possession. Control the ball (your money) and you control the game.

Baseball: It's about working counts. Don't swing wildly at every pitch (every purchase).

MMA: It's about conserving energy for later rounds.

Track and Field: It's strategic pacing—build to finish strong.

Tennis: Budgeting is like shot selection—play smart, not reckless.

Golf: It's course management—don't take unnecessary risks early.

eSports: Budgeting is resource management—if you burn it early, you're exposed later.

Common Rookie Budget Mistakes

- Underestimating taxes
- Overestimating how long your career will last
- Letting friends or family "budget" for you
- Spending money you haven't earned yet (future contracts, endorsements)
- Comparing yourself to older veterans who have already "made it"

Plain Language Breakdown: Budgeting Basics

- Know your real take-home pay.
- Break it into buckets.
- Live monthly, not yearly.
- Keep big expenses reasonable.
- Automate smart habits.
- Save raises.
- Be ready to say "no."

Action Steps

- Schedule a meeting with your CPA and financial advisor to map real net income.
- Create a written monthly budget plan.
- Set up automatic savings and investment contributions.
- Decide on a family/friend assistance limit.
- Check your spending monthly.

Final Encouragement

Your budget is your first championship plan.

It's not punishment.

It's protection.

It's power.

It's peace of mind.

Every dollar you control today is a decision you own tomorrow.

You're not just an athlete anymore.

You're a business.

You're a brand.

You're a wealth builder.

Budgeting isn't about living small.

It's about thinking big.

Long-term.

Strategically.

Champions aren't made in front of crowds.

They're made in quiet, disciplined moments.

Build your rookie budget.

Master it.

And use it as the foundation for a lifetime of real wealth, real freedom, and real peace.

Let's build smarter.

Let's win off the field.

Let's own the future, one budget at a time.

Chapter 18: Insurance You Need: Disability, Health, Life, Umbrella Policies

Welcome to the side of money nobody talks about enough.

The unglamorous.

The unsexy.

But absolutely critical side.

Insurance.

If you've read *Financial Literacy For NIL*, *Financial Literacy For Student Athletes*, or *Financial Literacy For Parents of Student Athletes*, you've already dipped your toes into protecting what you earn.

Now, as a pro, it's time to fully armor up.

Because it's not just about how much money you make.

It's about how much you keep, protect, and pass on.

Let's break down every insurance policy you need to safeguard your career, your money, and your family's future.

Let's protect your empire.

Why Insurance Matters for Pro Athletes

1. Your Income Is Highly Specialized

Your body is your business.

One bad injury, one illness, one freak accident can end your career.

2. You Have High Visibility

You're a target.

Lawsuits, accidents, public mistakes — they come for people with money.

3. Your Family May Depend on You

If you're the main provider, you have a duty to protect them no matter what happens.

4. Wealth Without Protection Is Fragile

All the saving and investing in the world won't matter if one lawsuit or health event wipes you out.

The Four Insurance Policies Every Pro Athlete Needs

1. Disability Insurance

What It Is:

Replaces a portion of your income if you get injured or sick and can't play.

Why It Matters:

Your athletic career depends on your body.

No games = No pay.

Disability insurance is the safety net.

Key Features to Look For:

- "Own Occupation" coverage (pays if you can't perform your specific sport, not just any job)
- High benefit limits to match your salary
- Quick elimination periods (time before payments start)
- No offsets for other income

Pros:

- Protects future earnings
- Provides peace of mind

Cons:

- Can be expensive (but still cheaper than losing millions)

Action Step:

- Get a personal disability policy, not just team-provided.

2. Health Insurance

What It Is:

Covers medical expenses: doctor visits, hospital stays, surgeries, rehab.

Why It Matters:

Pro athletes get injured.

All the time.

Without good health insurance, medical bills can bury you.

Key Features to Look For:

- Low deductibles for high earners
- Broad network of sports medicine specialists
- Coverage for physical therapy and rehab

Pros:

- Shields you from massive medical costs
- Supports faster, better recovery

Cons:

- Monthly premiums can be pricey

Action Step:

- Confirm if your league/team provides coverage.
- If not, get a private plan immediately.

3. Life Insurance

What It Is:

Pays your beneficiaries (family, kids, spouse) if you die.

Why It Matters:

If people depend on you financially, you must protect them.

Key Features to Look For:

- Term life insurance (not whole life) for starters
- Coverage amount: At least 10x your annual income
- Riders for disability or critical illness (optional)

Pros:

- Extremely affordable when young and healthy
- Provides family financial security

Cons:

- Premiums must be paid every year to keep policy active

Action Step:

- Buy term life insurance early while you're healthy.
- Lock in low rates.

4. Umbrella Liability Insurance

What It Is:

Covers you if someone sues you and your basic auto/homeowners insurance isn't enough.

Why It Matters:

You're a high-net-worth target.

One accident. One lawsuit. Game over without umbrella coverage.

Key Features to Look For:

- $1 million minimum coverage (many athletes get $5 million+)
- Covers personal injury, property damage, defamation suits, etc.

Pros:

- Extremely cheap compared to coverage amount
- Fills big gaps your other insurance won't

Cons:

- Must maintain good basic auto/home coverage to qualify

Action Step:

- Add umbrella coverage to your personal insurance plan.

Pros and Cons of Being Fully Insured

Pros:

- Sleep at night knowing you're protected
- Career-ending injury doesn't bankrupt you
- Lawsuits can't destroy your family's future

- Medical emergencies don't wipe out savings

Cons:

- Insurance premiums add up
- Requires annual reviews to keep policies updated

Real-World Scenarios and Relatable Stories

Scenario: The Smart Rookie

Bought disability and umbrella insurance immediately.

Suffered an ACL tear in year two.

Disability insurance replaced salary while rehabbing.

Avoided financial ruin.

Scenario: The Veteran Who Didn't Insure

Ignored insurance advice.

Tore Achilles in final contract year.

No disability income.

Medical bills piled up.

Had to sell home and downsize dramatically.

Sports Analogies That Matter

Football: Insurance is like wearing pads and a helmet. You'd never go on the field without protection.

Basketball: It's like staying in defensive stance—protect the paint, protect your wealth.

Soccer: Insurance is your goalie—last line of defense when everything else goes wrong.

Baseball: It's the bullpen—you need backup ready even if your starter gets knocked out.

MMA: It's protecting your chin and body at all times.

Track and Field: It's the extra training that prevents injuries.

Tennis: Insurance is like unforced error prevention—smart, steady, protective.

Golf: It's playing for par when birdies aren't an option—protect your scorecard.

eSports: It's building defense structures so you're not wiped out by one surprise attack.

Plain Language Breakdown: Quick Insurance Musts

- Disability insurance: Protect your earning power.
- Health insurance: Protect against hospital bills.
- Life insurance: Protect your family's future.
- Umbrella insurance: Protect your wealth from lawsuits.

Common Rookie Insurance Mistakes

- Thinking "I'm healthy, I don't need insurance."
- Trusting team coverage only
- Buying bad insurance from shady agents
- Skipping umbrella coverage
- Forgetting to update beneficiaries after life changes (marriage, kids)

Action Steps

- Meet with a fiduciary financial advisor.
- Get disability, health, life, and umbrella policies in place immediately.
- Review annually or after any major life event.

Final Encouragement

Buying insurance isn't about being scared.

It's about being smart.

It's about respecting your own journey.

It's about loving your family enough to protect them even when you're not around.

It's about honoring the sacrifices you've made to get here.

You didn't grind your whole life just to lose it all over one bad break.

You're bigger than that.

You're smarter than that.

You're built for more than just today's game.

You're built for a lifetime of winning—on and off the field.

Protect your career.

Protect your family.

Protect your peace.

Insurance isn't a burden.

It's a blessing.

Own it.

Invest in it.

Use it to build the life you've worked for.

Let's keep building smart.

Let's stay protected.

Let's own the future, no matter what.

Chapter 19: Estate Planning Basics for Rookies

When you're just starting your professional career, estate planning might sound like something only old billionaires need.

Wrong.

If you're earning real money—even in your rookie year—you already need an estate plan.

It doesn't have to be complicated.

It doesn't have to be expensive.

But it absolutely must exist.

If you've read *Financial Literacy For NIL, Financial Literacy For Student Athletes,* or *Financial Literacy For Parents of Student Athletes,* you already understand the idea of protecting what you build.

Estate planning is simply the next level of protection.

It's about:

- Protecting your family
- Protecting your assets
- Protecting your legacy

Let's break it down clearly, calmly, and practically—so you can build your plan and move forward like the pro you are.

Why Estate Planning Matters for Pro Athletes

1. You Have Assets Worth Protecting

Even if you're young.

Even if you're "just getting started."

Money in the bank.

A car.

A house.

Endorsements.

Business interests.

Your name, image, and likeness.

All of it matters.

2. Life Happens Fast

Injury.

Illness.

Accidents.

No one plans for tragedy—but the smart ones plan around it.

3. Family Will Be Grieving — Don't Leave Them Guessing

If something happens to you, your family shouldn't have to guess what you wanted.

Estate planning gives them clarity.

Gives them peace.

4. Court Battles Are Expensive and Ugly

Without clear legal documents, your assets could get tied up for months—even years—in probate court.

Avoid it by planning now.

The Rookie Estate Planning Checklist

You don't need a million-dollar plan yet.

You need a strong, simple foundation.

1. Last Will and Testament

What It Is:

A legal document that says who gets your stuff if you die.

Key Points:

- Names your beneficiaries (who gets what)
- Names your executor (who manages everything)
- Can appoint guardians for minor children (if you have any)

Pros:

- Easy to set up
- Essential for everyone

Cons:

- Does not avoid probate by itself

Action Step:

- Work with an estate attorney to draft a basic will.

2. Power of Attorney (Financial)

What It Is:

Gives someone legal power to handle your finances if you can't.

Key Points:

- Only valid while you're alive
- Ends at death

Pros:

- Allows bills, contracts, business to continue if you're incapacitated

Cons:

- Must trust the person 100%

Action Step:

- Choose a financially responsible person.
- Sign a durable power of attorney form.

3. Health Care Power of Attorney (Medical Directive)

What It Is:

Gives someone power to make medical decisions for you if you can't.

Key Points:

- Includes end-of-life wishes (life support, organ donation)

Pros:

- Avoids family arguments
- Ensures your wishes are respected

Cons:

- Emotionally tough to choose someone

Action Step:

- Choose someone calm under pressure.
- Sign a health care directive.

4. Beneficiary Designations

What It Is:

The "pay-on-death" instructions for:

- Life insurance policies
- Retirement accounts (401(k), IRAs)
- Bank accounts (with POD/TOD features)

Key Points:

- Supersedes your will
- Easy to update anytime

Pros:

- Fast asset transfer
- Avoids probate

Cons:

- Must remember to update after major life events

Action Step:

- Review and update all beneficiary forms annually.

5. Basic Living Trust (Optional Early On)

What It Is:

A legal entity that holds your assets during your lifetime and distributes them after your death without probate.

Key Points:

- Can help manage assets if you become incapacitated
- Can shield some information from public court records

Pros:

- Avoids probate
- Provides privacy
- Greater control over asset distribution

Cons:

- More expensive to set up than a simple will

Action Step:

- Consider a trust if you have significant assets or expect a long career.

Pros and Cons of Early Estate Planning

Pros:

- Peace of mind
- Protection for family
- Control over your legacy
- Reduces court costs and family fights

Cons:

- Requires tough conversations
- Small upfront legal fees (worth it!)

Real-World Scenarios and Relatable Stories

Scenario: The Rookie Who Planned

Set up a basic will, powers of attorney, and beneficiary designations before his first season.

After an unexpected injury and temporary incapacity, his family was able to manage his finances smoothly, avoiding chaos.

Scenario: The Star Who Didn't Plan

Unexpected accident.

No will.

Multiple family members fought over assets.

Estate tied up in court for two years.

Legal fees and taxes ate up half the estate.

Pain on top of grief.

Sports Analogies That Matter

Football: Estate planning is like having a game plan before the snap—don't freestyle in a crisis.

Basketball: It's running a play—not just relying on a buzzer-beater.

Soccer: It's setting your defensive formation—proactive protection.

Baseball: It's having a bullpen ready—if the starter goes down.

MMA: It's defensive fundamentals—not just relying on your chin.

Track and Field: It's warming up properly—preventing injuries before they happen.

Tennis: It's having a second serve—safety net when the first one misses.

Golf: It's course management—thinking three shots ahead.

eSports: It's building shields—not just relying on pure firepower.

Plain Language Breakdown: Estate Planning Basics

- Will = Who gets what.
- Financial Power of Attorney = Who handles your money if you can't.
- Health Care Directive = Who makes medical choices if you can't.
- Beneficiary Forms = Direct asset transfer outside of court.
- Living Trust = Optional for greater control and privacy.

Common Rookie Estate Planning Mistakes

- Thinking "I'm too young for that."
- Forgetting to update documents after big life events.
- Naming irresponsible people as executors or agents.
- Not discussing plans with family.
- Believing a simple will is "good enough" for complex assets.

Action Steps

- Meet with an estate planning attorney.
- Set up a will, financial POA, medical POA, and beneficiary designations.
- Review your plan annually or after major changes (marriage, kids, moves).

Final Encouragement

Estate planning isn't about fear.

It's about love.

It's about respect.

It's about making sure the people you love aren't left confused, hurting, and fighting.

You didn't grind your whole life to leave a mess.

You grinded to leave a legacy.

To leave protection.

To leave peace.

Don't delay.

Don't dodge it.

Be the pro who plans ahead.

Be the teammate, spouse, son, daughter, parent, friend who makes things easier—not harder—if life ever goes sideways.

You're not just building wealth.

You're building wisdom.

You're building a future.

Own your legacy.

Own your protection.

Own your life's work—all the way through.

Let's build smarter.

Let's plan ahead.

Let's honor the gift we've been given to live, love, and lead—on and off the field.

Chapter 20: Understanding the Hidden Costs: Agent Fees, Union Dues, CPA Costs

When you hear about an athlete's contract—$5 million, $10 million, $100 million—it sounds massive.

But here's what you don't hear on SportsCenter:

How much of that money actually gets deposited into their bank account.

Because before you ever see a dime, there's a whole line of people and expenses taking a slice of your pie.

If you've read *Financial Literacy For NIL, Financial Literacy For Student Athletes,* or *Financial Literacy For Parents of Student Athletes,* you know the importance of protecting your earnings.

At the pro level, hidden costs are part of the game.

The more you understand them, the smarter you can play.

This chapter is about clarity.

Not fear.

Not paranoia.

Just real talk.

So you can build wealth—not just flex paychecks.

Why Hidden Costs Matter

1. They Shrink Your Real Income

You might think you're a millionaire.

But after agent fees, taxes, dues, and professional services?

Maybe you're a "half-millionaire" instead.

2. They Add Up Over Time

One small percentage here.

One annual fee there.

Over a 5-10 year career, we're talking hundreds of thousands—even millions—lost or saved.

3. You Can't Manage What You Don't See

Budgeting and planning start with real numbers—not "contract headline" numbers.

Major Hidden Costs Every Pro Athlete Faces

1. Agent Fees

What It Is:

Your sports agent negotiates contracts, endorsement deals, and sometimes helps with PR and appearances.

Typical Cost:

- 1% to 4% of your playing contract (NFL players, by rule, max at 3% agents' fee)
- Up to 10%-20% on endorsements

Example:

$5 million contract

- 3% agent fee = $150,000

Pros:

- Agents can negotiate better deals
- Open endorsement opportunities
- Handle contract complexities you don't want to touch

Cons:

- Some agents take more than they deliver
- Some may double-dip (represent you and team/brand—conflict of interest)

Action Step:

- Read your agent agreement carefully.
- Interview multiple agents before signing.
- Ensure your agent is properly licensed with your league's players' association.

2. Union Dues

What It Is:
Mandatory fees paid to your players' union (NFLPA, NBPA, MLBPA, WNBPA, etc.)
What It Covers:

- Collective bargaining
- Pension plans
- Health and safety advocacy
- Legal representation

Typical Cost:

- Often $10,000-$20,000+ annually depending on league

Pros:

- Protects your rights as a player
- Negotiates better overall pay and benefits

Cons:

- No opt-out; dues are mandatory whether you like it or not

Action Step:

- Budget for union dues from Day 1.
- Understand what your union offers (pensions, resources, career transition help).

3. CPA and Tax Professional Fees

What It Is:
Licensed accountants (CPAs) who handle your complex, multi-state and international tax situation.

Typical Cost:

- $5,000 to $25,000+ annually depending on income and number of states/countries filed

Pros:

- Helps you legally minimize taxes
- Protects you from audits and penalties
- Helps with estimated quarterly tax payments

Cons:

- Not all CPAs understand athlete-specific challenges

Action Step:

- Hire a CPA experienced with pro athletes.
- Pay for expertise—cheap advice is expensive in the long run.

4. Financial Advisor Fees

What It Is:
Investment management, financial planning, and wealth protection services.
Typical Fee Models:

- 1% of assets under management (AUM)
- Flat annual fees ($5,000-$50,000+)

Pros:

- Professional money management
- Big-picture planning (investing, retirement, estate, philanthropy)

Cons:

- Fee structures vary—some advisors sell products, others work for fees only
- You need to vet credentials carefully

Action Step:

- Choose fiduciary advisors (legally obligated to put your best interests first).

- Ask: "Are you a fiduciary? How are you compensated?"

5. Attorney Fees

What It Is:

Legal services for contracts, endorsements, lawsuits, estate planning, and business deals.

Typical Costs:

- $250/hour to $1,000/hour depending on experience
- Flat fees for specific services (like wills, trusts)

Pros:

- Protects you in high-stakes deals
- Reviews contracts for hidden risks

Cons:

- Quality varies widely

Action Step:

- Build a legal team early.
- Use specialists (entertainment law, estate law, business contracts) when needed.

Pros and Cons of Paying for Professional Help

Pros:

- You don't have to figure everything out alone

- Protects your money and career
- Saves massive headaches and penalties later

Cons:

- Not all professionals are equally trustworthy
- Costs can eat into income quickly

Real-World Scenarios and Relatable Stories

Scenario: The Rookie Who Budgeted for Hidden Costs

Before signing his rookie deal, met with:

- CPA
- Financial Advisor
- Attorney

Built professional fees into his budget from Day 1.

Outcome: No surprise tax bills, better investment planning, peace of mind.

Scenario: The Rookie Who Ignored Hidden Costs

Celebrated first paycheck.

Forgot to withhold agent fees, taxes, union dues.

At year-end, owed $350,000 more than expected.

Had to sell off assets to cover IRS demands.

Sports Analogies That Matter

Football: Agent fees are like offensive linemen. You pay them to protect your quarterback (career).

Basketball: Union dues are like the locker room—you pay to be part of a team that protects you.

Soccer: Your CPA is your sweeper—cleaning up financial messes before they turn into goals against.

Baseball: Your financial advisor is your catcher—seeing the whole field and calling the right pitches.

MMA: Legal protection is like a strong guard game—defense wins championships.

Track and Field: Budgeting for hidden costs is like training for every event—not just your specialty.

Tennis: A good lawyer is like a strong second serve—saves you when your first plan doesn't work.

Golf: Financial planning is your caddie—helps you pick the right shots, manage the course.

eSports: Hidden costs are like resource management—win the long game, not just the next match.

Plain Language Breakdown: The Hidden Cost Checklist

- **Agent**: 1%-4% of playing salary, 10%-20% of endorsements
- **Union dues**: $10,000-$20,000+/year
- **CPA fees**: $5,000-$25,000+/year
- **Financial advisor fees**: 1% of assets or flat fees
- **Attorney fees**: $250-$1,000/hour or flat fees

Common Rookie Mistakes

- Thinking "the team covers everything."
- Not budgeting for agent fees.
- Assuming taxes are automatically handled.
- Choosing professionals based only on lowest cost.
- Forgetting union dues until it's paycheck deduction day.

Action Steps

- Create a "hidden cost" budget category.
- Interview at least two CPAs, two financial advisors, and two attorneys before hiring.
- Build your team before your first contract—not after.
- Ask questions until you truly understand each professional's fee structure.
- Review professional costs annually.

Final Encouragement

The real pros?

They don't just focus on earning.

They focus on keeping.

And growing.

Every dollar lost to confusion, neglect, or bad advice is a dollar you can't use to:

- Build generational wealth
- Give your family opportunities
- Start businesses
- Launch foundations
- Create the legacy you dream of

You didn't grind your whole life just to flex a few years and fade.

You grinded to win the long game.

And winning the long game means:

- Knowing the costs
- Planning for them
- Managing them like a CEO

You're not just an athlete.

You're an enterprise.

Protect the business of YOU.

Budget for every hidden cost.

Own every financial decision.

Lead with your mind, not your ego.

Protect what you've built, protect what you're building, and most importantly—protect who you're becoming.

Let's build smart.

Let's play the whole field.

Let's stay winning, on and off the field, for decades to come.

Part 3: Contracts, Negotiations, and Agents — Protecting Your Career

When you make it to the professional level, the ballgame changes. It's no longer just about talent on the field, court, pitch, or rink — it's about mastering the business behind the scenes. Part 3 of *Financial Literacy For Pro Athletes* pulls back the curtain on one of the most critical — and misunderstood — aspects of your professional life: contracts, negotiations, and the team of agents and advisors who will either protect your career or put it at risk.

This section teaches you how to think like a CEO, not just an athlete. You'll learn how to truly understand every piece of paper you sign — from rookie contracts to endorsement deals — so you're not leaving money on the table or accidentally tying yourself to obligations that hurt your future. You'll get clear guidance on what makes a strong contract, what red flags to look for, and how to prepare for negotiations at every stage of your career, from rookie to veteran to free agent.

We'll dive deep into the real role of agents, financial advisors, attorneys, and managers — and most importantly, how to make sure each professional stays in their lane and serves your best interest. We'll also show you why it's dangerous to blur the lines between financial and contract advice, and why keeping your business team independent from each other protects you in the long run.

Whether you're negotiating your first pro deal, navigating extensions, endorsements, free agency, or preparing for your next chapter after sports, this part of the book will equip you with the practical knowledge, real-world strategies, and professional wisdom you need to own your career — on your terms.

Protect your contracts.

Protect your brand.

Protect your future.

Because talent gets you there — but smart business keeps you there.

Chapter 21: What's in a Contract? (Salary, Incentives, Clauses, Guarantees)

When you finally sign that first professional contract, it's one of the proudest moments of your life.

But make no mistake:

That contract is more than a handshake and a dream.

It's a detailed, binding agreement full of numbers, clauses, incentives, penalties, and protections.

If you've read *Financial Literacy for NIL*, *Financial Literacy for Student Athletes*, or *Financial Literacy for Parents of Student Athletes*, you already know the importance of understanding paperwork.

Now, the stakes are even higher.

In this chapter, we're going to slow it down.

Break it down.

And make sure you truly understand what you're signing—so you can protect yourself, your career, and your future.

Because once the ink is dry, excuses don't matter.

Why Understanding Contracts Matters

1. Contracts Define Your Money

Not just salary—but bonuses, incentives, fines, and guarantees.

2. Contracts Define Your Freedom

Waivers, trades, buyouts—your mobility depends on the fine print.

3. Contracts Define Your Security
Are you getting paid no matter what? Or only if you're active?
4. Contracts Define Your Leverage
Knowing your contract gives you power at renegotiation time.

The Big Pieces of a Professional Contract

Let's start with the core pillars:

1. Base Salary

What It Is:
The fixed amount you are paid for playing during a season.
Key Points:

- Usually paid in weekly or bi-weekly installments
- Subject to taxes, agent fees, union dues

Pros:

- Predictable income

Cons:

- Not always guaranteed (depends on the league and contract)

Action Step:

- Ask: "Is my salary fully guaranteed or only partially guaranteed?"

2. Signing Bonus

What It Is:

A one-time payment given when you sign the contract.

Key Points:

- Often taxed heavily
- Sometimes paid out in installments (not always all at once)

Pros:

- Immediate cash influx

Cons:

- Can create false sense of "I'm rich" if not managed wisely

Action Step:

- Set aside taxes immediately from your signing bonus.

3. Performance Incentives

What It Is:

Extra money if you hit specific achievements (ex: number of games played, awards, playoff appearances).

Key Points:

- Can be big money or small add-ons
- Not always easy to achieve

Pros:

- Motivating
- Allows upside if you outperform

Cons:

- Not guaranteed
- Sometimes teams control opportunity (ex: limiting your playing time)

Action Step:

- Understand exactly what triggers incentives—and if it's realistically attainable.

4. Roster Bonuses

What It Is:

Payment for being on the roster at a specific date (start of training camp, season opener, playoff rosters).

Key Points:

- Incentivizes teams to cut players before payment triggers

Pros:

- Adds extra cash opportunities

Cons:

- Creates roster insecurity if near bonus dates

Action Step:

- Know your roster bonus dates.

5. Workout Bonuses

What It Is:

Money for attending offseason training or workouts.

Key Points:

- Common in NFL contracts

Pros:

- Encourages offseason conditioning

Cons:

- Small compared to base salary

Action Step:

- Always meet workout requirements if financially beneficial.

6. Guarantees

What It Is:

Money you get even if you're cut, injured, or otherwise unable to play.

Key Points:

- "Fully guaranteed" means no matter what happens
- "Injury guaranteed" means only if hurt
- "Skill guarantees" mean protection if you get released for poor performance

Pros:

- Provides income security

Cons:

- Harder to negotiate full guarantees

Action Step:

- Fight for as much guaranteed money as possible.

7. Clauses

What It Is:
Specific conditions or rules built into your contract.
Common Clauses:

- **Injury Clauses**: Different pay if injured
- **Morality Clauses**: Conduct rules (public image, arrests, fines)
- **Trade Clauses**: Control over team trades
- **Non-Compete Clauses**: Restrict playing elsewhere
- **Offset Language**: Determines if a new salary can reduce old team's obligations

Pros:

- Can protect you

Cons:

- Can severely limit freedom

Action Step:

- Review every clause carefully with your agent and personal attorney.

8. Buyout Clauses

What It Is:

Terms under which the team can end your contract early.

Key Points:

- Defines how much they owe you if they cut you

Pros:

- Gives clear exit strategy

Cons:

- Sometimes structured heavily in team's favor

Action Step:

- Always know your buyout terms.

Pros and Cons of Signing Early vs Waiting

Pros of Signing Early:

- Security
- Immediate income
- Avoids injury risk pre-signing

Cons of Signing Early:

- May accept less favorable terms
- Limits ability to renegotiate later

Real-World Scenarios and Relatable Stories

Scenario: The Rookie Who Read the Fine Print

Understood his incentives and triggered a $250,000 bonus by playing 50% of snaps—where another rookie missed it by one snap because he didn't know.

Scenario: The Vet Who Ignored Clauses

Violating a morality clause voided $2 million guaranteed after a minor arrest that could've been avoided.

Sports Analogies That Matter

Football: Reading your contract is like studying the defensive coverage pre-snap.

Basketball: It's like knowing the playbook—not just winging it on offense.

Soccer: It's seeing the field—anticipating the next move, not just reacting.

Baseball: It's knowing the signs from the dugout—not just swinging for the fences.

MMA: It's understanding the rules of engagement before stepping into the cage.

Track and Field: It's knowing where the hurdles are before you sprint.

Tennis: It's knowing where the out-of-bounds lines are—so you don't play yourself.

Golf: It's reading the course layout—not just blasting drives blindly.

eSports: It's understanding character strengths and weaknesses—not just button-mashing.

Plain Language Breakdown: Key Questions to Ask

- What's guaranteed?
- What's performance-based?
- What's at risk if I'm injured?
- Are there trade restrictions?
- Are there morality clauses?
- Who gets final say on endorsement conflicts?
- What happens if I'm cut?

Common Rookie Contract Mistakes

- Trusting team reps to "explain" everything
- Ignoring the tax impact of bonuses
- Not negotiating roster and workout bonuses
- Overestimating guaranteed money
- Not planning for incentives to be "unreachable"

Action Steps

- Demand a plain-language version of your contract to review.
- Hire your own independent attorney to review before signing.
- Ask tough questions—even if it feels uncomfortable.
- Plan your budget around "guaranteed" money only—not best-case earnings.

Final Encouragement

Signing your first pro contract is a dream come true.

But dreams turn into nightmares when you sign things you don't understand.

You're not "difficult" for asking questions.

You're not "greedy" for wanting protections.

You're smart.

You're responsible.

You're protecting everything you've worked for.

You didn't grind your whole life to end up broke because you trusted the wrong words in the wrong clauses.

You grinded to win.

On the field.

And at the table.

This is your career.

This is your business.

This is your legacy.

Own your signature.

Own your contract.

Own your future.

Let's stay protected.

Let's stay powerful.

Let's keep building smarter—every deal, every chapter, every move.

Chapter 22: How Often You Can Renegotiate Contracts by Sport

When you sign your first pro contract, you're not just setting the tone for the next year or two — you're setting the foundation for how your career is going to unfold.

But here's the thing most rookies don't realize: that first deal isn't necessarily your last.

In fact, depending on your performance, health, leverage, and the sport you're in, you might renegotiate your contract several times during your career.

Or you might get stuck in a bad deal you can't touch for years.

If you've read *Financial Literacy For NIL, Financial Literacy For Student Athletes,* or *Financial Literacy For Parents of Student Athletes,* you already know how important it is to advocate for yourself. Now, it's time to take that mindset to the professional level.

This chapter is about knowing your window.

Knowing your leverage.

And knowing how—and when—you can take your shot at a better deal.

Why Understanding Renegotiation Rules Matters

1. It Impacts Your Money Timeline

You need to know when you can ask for a raise—and when you're stuck.

2. It Impacts Your Strategy

If you're locked into a low-paying deal, you may need to be more conservative with spending.

3. It Impacts Your Career Moves

Sometimes, waiting for free agency is smarter than forcing a renegotiation.

Major League Differences: How Often Can You Renegotiate?

Let's go sport-by-sport:

NFL (National Football League)

Typical Rookie Contract:

- 4 years (first-rounders may have 5th-year team option)

Renegotiation Rules:

- You can't renegotiate your rookie deal until after Year 3.
- Free agency comes after Year 4 (unless you're cut or franchised).

Why It Matters:

- No matter how well you play—Pro Bowler, MVP, etc.—you're stuck until after your third year.

Pros:

- Stability for developing players

Cons:

- Underpaid stars early (see: Dak Prescott, Russell Wilson early years)

Action Step:

- Budget assuming no renegotiation for 3 years.

NBA (National Basketball Association)

Typical Rookie Contract:

- 2 years guaranteed, team options for Years 3 and 4

Renegotiation Rules:

- Extension eligible after Year 3 (before free agency)
- Restricted free agency after rookie deal expires

Why It Matters:

- Strong early play can earn a big extension (think: Jayson Tatum, Ja Morant)

Pros:

- Big raise opportunities after Year 3

Cons:

- Team controls your early years tightly

Action Step:

- Focus on maximizing your third-year performance for extension leverage.

MLB (Major League Baseball)

Typical Rookie Contract:

- Minor League deal first
- MLB contracts after call-up
- Arbitration after 3 years of service
- Free agency after 6 years

Renegotiation Rules:

- Arbitration-eligible after 3 years (sometimes Super Two after 2 years)
- True free agent after 6 years

Why It Matters:

- Very long runway before major paydays

Pros:

- Arbitration can yield raises based on performance

Cons:

- Underpaid during early peak years

Action Step:

- Budget conservatively early; big paydays are delayed.

NHL (National Hockey League)

Typical Rookie Contract:

- 3 years (Entry-Level Contract)

Renegotiation Rules:

- Restricted free agent after Entry-Level
- Eligible for extensions during final year

Why It Matters:

- Perform early, secure the bag with an extension

Pros:

- Early opportunity to extend and lock in

Cons:

- RFA status limits free agency mobility

Action Step:

- Crush Year 2 to create leverage for Year 3 extension.

MLS (Major League Soccer)

Typical Rookie Contract:

- 2 to 4 years

Renegotiation Rules:

- Often renegotiated after 2 strong seasons

Why It Matters:

- Early performance can rapidly increase pay

Pros:

- MLS salaries are rising; more opportunities

Cons:

- League office has strong control over contracts

Action Step:

- Build your brand on and off the pitch to maximize renegotiation power.

WNBA (Women's National Basketball Association)

Typical Rookie Contract:

- 3 to 4 years

Renegotiation Rules:

- Extension after Year 3
- Restricted free agency after 4 years

Why It Matters:

- Lower pay scale overall; endorsements matter

Pros:

- Marketability helps bridge income gaps

Cons:

- Smaller contracts = smaller leverage margins

Action Step:

- Maximize visibility and endorsements early.

MMA (UFC/Bellator)

Typical Rookie Contract:

- Typically 4-fight or 6-fight deals

Renegotiation Rules:

- Often renegotiated after major win streaks or title contention

Why It Matters:

- Fighters live fight-to-fight; success reopens negotiations

Pros:

- Big wins can trigger rapid raises

Cons:

- Risky; one bad loss can tank leverage

Action Step:

- Invest in top training camps to maximize your early fight record.

International Soccer (EPL, La Liga, Serie A, MLS transfers)

Typical Rookie Contract:

- 3 to 5 years

Renegotiation Rules:

- Mid-contract renegotiations are common after breakout seasons

Why It Matters:

- Transfer fees create external leverage

Pros:

- Massive money potential

Cons:

- Clubs hold heavy negotiating power early

Action Step:

- Work with agent and club PR to raise your profile internationally.

Tennis, Golf, Individual Sports

Typical Deals:

- Endorsement contracts (Nike, Adidas, Titleist, Rolex, etc.)

Renegotiation Rules:

- Linked to rankings and tournament wins

Why It Matters:

- Your "contract" is your personal brand

Pros:

- Win = more deals

Cons:

- No guaranteed team salary safety net

Action Step:

- Build a sustainable brand, not just highlight-reel moments.

Real-World Scenarios and Relatable Stories

Scenario: NFL Player Waiting Patiently

Played three years on rookie minimum.

Exploded in Year 3.

Negotiated a $45 million extension before Year 4.

Scenario: NBA Player Who Bet on Himself

Declined early extension.

Played Year 4 without a safety net.

Earned a max contract as a free agent.

Scenario: MLB Player Stuck in Arbitration

Dominated early but trapped at $700k until arbitration.

Finally broke through with $12M+ settlement after.

Pros and Cons of Early Renegotiation

Pros:

- Lock in security sooner
- Protect against injury risk
- Increase cash flow

Cons:

- Sometimes leave money on table if you explode later
- Can create tension with current team

Action Steps for Smart Contract Timing

- **Know your league's rules** about renegotiations.
- **Work with your agent** to build a performance case.
- **Stay professional**—whining kills leverage.
- **Be willing to bet on yourself**—but only when smart.

- **Prioritize guarantees** over flashy totals.

Final Encouragement

You're not just playing a sport.

You're managing a business.

The business of YOU.

Knowing when—and how—you can renegotiate is like knowing when to strike in a game:

- A quarterback senses the perfect blitz pickup and launches a bomb.
- A point guard sees the defense cheat and attacks the rim.
- A striker notices a lazy backline and goes all-in on a run.
- A golfer reads the wind and changes clubs for a daring shot.

Same mentality here.

You have to read the field.

Study the rules.

Work your leverage.

Move when the timing is right—not just when you feel frustrated.

Protect your career.

Protect your income.

Protect your power.

Be patient.

Be prepared.

Be smart.

You're not just negotiating for today's paycheck.

You're negotiating for your long-term wealth.

And the best players?

They always think two steps ahead.

Let's stay ahead of the game.

Let's own every deal, every move, every season.

Because your career deserves nothing less.

Chapter 23: The Business Side of Free Agency — Signing Without Being Drafted

There's something romanticized about getting drafted. Your name called on national TV. Your family celebrating. The image of walking across a stage, jersey in hand, flashing lights in your eyes.

But real life? It's not always like that.

Many talented athletes don't hear their names called on draft day.

And here's the truth:

Going undrafted doesn't mean your dreams are dead.

It just means your path will be different — and if you handle it right, your career might end up stronger, longer, and wealthier than some players who "made it" on draft night.

In this chapter, we're going to break down everything you need to know about the business side of free agency. Whether you're a rookie undrafted free agent, a veteran trying to stick around, or a late bloomer finally getting your shot, this chapter will be your blueprint for turning uncertainty into opportunity.

Let's dive deep.

Why Free Agency Knowledge Matters

1. Timing Is Everything

- Free agency moves fast.
- Hesitation can cost you opportunities.

2. Leverage Is Different

- You might have to sell yourself harder.
- The money, perks, and security won't come automatically.

3. You're a Business From Day One

- No draft slot money.
- You have to negotiate everything.

4. Relationships Matter More

- Agents, coaches, scouts, and GMs become critical.
- Who vouches for you might matter as much as your stat line.

How Signing as an Undrafted Free Agent (UDFA) Works

NFL

- Teams immediately call players once the draft ends.
- Signing bonuses range from $0 to $100,000+ (very rare)
- You may have multiple offers; timing matters.

NBA

- Summer League invites first.
- Two-way contracts (G League + NBA) are common.
- Exhibit 10 contracts (training camp invites with bonuses) exist.

MLB

- After 20 rounds, teams can still sign undrafted players.
- Bonuses capped at $20,000 for UDFAs.
- Path is longer through the minor leagues.

NHL

- College and junior hockey players can sign as free agents.
- Often need strong relationships with scouts and minor league affiliates.

MLS

- Supplemental and reserve roster contracts available.
- College players can sign even if not drafted through the SuperDraft.

WNBA

- Extremely limited roster spots.
- Training camp contracts are common.

MMA/Boxing

- Every fighter is technically a "free agent" until signed by a promotion.
- Early fights and tournament wins are your resume.

International Soccer, Tennis, Golf, Track and Field

- Agents must build market opportunities.
- Visibility and highlight reels are critical.

The Pros and Cons of Free Agency

Pros:

- You choose your fit (team, system, coach, city).
- You can negotiate better bonuses if multiple teams want you.
- You often enter with a chip on your shoulder (proven winners' mentality).

Cons:

- Less financial security.
- No draft prestige buffer (teams cut faster).
- You must prove yourself every single day.

What to Watch Out For as an Undrafted Player

- **Lowball contracts:** Know your worth.
- **Unwritten expectations:** Free agents often work harder for fewer chances.
- **Tax consequences:** Signing bonuses are taxed immediately.
- **Pressure from family/friends:** Manage expectations wisely.

Action Steps Before You Sign

1. Work With Your Agent

- Target teams with real opportunity, not just brand name.

2. Prioritize Fit Over Flash

- Where can you play? Where can you earn reps? Where will you be developed?

3. Understand the Deal Terms

- What's guaranteed?
- What bonuses are available?
- What are the cut dates?

4. Prepare Financially

- You may need to live lean for a year or two.
- Open a high-interest savings account.
- Set up a basic emergency fund immediately.

5. Stay Healthy

- Your body is your business.
- Invest in physical therapy, nutrition, training.

Understanding Contract Terms for Free Agents

- **Base salary** (League minimum or negotiated rate)
- **Signing bonus** (Negotiated up front)
- **Workout bonuses** (Conditioning goals)
- **Roster bonuses** (If you make opening day)
- **Incentives** (Performance-based money)
- **Split contracts** (Different pay if sent to minors/G-League/Practice Squad)

Real-World Scenarios: Undrafted Players Who Became Legends

NFL: Kurt Warner, Tony Romo, Wes Welker

NBA: Ben Wallace, Fred VanVleet, Udonis Haslem

MLB: Kevin Pillar, Josh Harrison

NHL: Tyler Bozak, Artemi Panarin

Soccer: Jamie Vardy (started in non-league soccer)

Tennis: Multiple ATP/WTA players outside top 200 rankings early in careers

MMA: Francis Ngannou started fighting homeless

How to Build Your Leverage as an Undrafted Player

1. Become Obsessed with the Details

- Special teams, rebounding, defensive positioning, footwork, hustle—teams notice effort.

2. Dominate Every Opportunity

- Every practice, every workout, every meeting—you're being evaluated.

3. Build Relationships with Coaches and Staff

- Coaches advocate for players they trust and respect.

4. Be a Pro Every Day

- Show up early. Stay late. Study film. Take care of your body.

5. Handle Setbacks Like a Pro

- Cut? Waived? Reassigned? Stay ready. Stay positive. The next call can change everything.

Financial Tips for Undrafted Players

- **Live Like a Rookie:** Not a rock star.
- **Save Signing Bonus:** Don't blow it on material things.
- **Insure Yourself:** Disability policies are smart early.
- **Stay Disciplined:** Long careers are built on short-term sacrifices.

Sports Analogies That Apply

Football:

- Being undrafted is like being a walk-on. Hustle beats talent when talent doesn't hustle.

Basketball:

- You're the sixth man trying to earn starter minutes—maximize every possession.

Baseball:

- You're the utility player—be ready to play any position when called.

Soccer:

- You're the super-sub—changing the game with energy and impact.

Track:

- You're the lane 8 runner—underrated, but dangerous if underestimated.

Golf/Tennis:

- You're qualifying round material—one good tournament changes your ranking.

MMA:

- You're the late replacement fighter—one upset win can change your life.

Final Encouragement

You are not your draft status.

You are your work ethic.

You are your consistency.

You are your resilience.

Plenty of guys with big draft nights never live up to it.

Plenty of guys who never got a call end up with Hall of Fame careers.

It's not about how you start.

It's about how you build.

It's about how you fight.

It's about how you invest—in yourself, in your craft, in your future.

Undrafted doesn't mean unwanted.

Undrafted means unleashed.

You control the narrative now.

Go write a legacy that no one can deny.

Own your journey.

Own your opportunity.

Own your financial future.

You're not just trying to survive.

You're building something bigger than the draft ever could have promised.

Let's stay locked in.

Let's stay hungry.

Let's go turn "undrafted" into "unstoppable."

Chapter 24: How to Evaluate and Vet an Agent

When you enter the professional world, one of the most important hires you'll make — maybe the most important early on — is your agent.

Your agent isn't just the person who "gets you paid." They're your first line of defense. Your negotiator. Your gatekeeper. Your advocate.

Or, if you pick wrong, your first regret.

Choosing the right agent isn't just about who has the flashiest Instagram account or who promises the biggest signing bonus.

It's about choosing someone who sees you not as a commission check, but as a career. As a legacy.

If you've read my other books — *Financial Literacy For NIL, Financial Literacy For Student Athletes, Financial Literacy For Parents of Student Athletes* — you already know the warning signs to look for.

Now? We're taking it up a level.

Let's talk about how to really vet an agent like a pro.

Why Agent Selection Matters More Than You Think

1. Contracts are only one part of your career.

An agent needs to manage your career arc — not just your first deal.

2. Bad agents can cost you millions — literally.

Negotiating poorly. Missing clauses. Creating bad blood with teams.

3. Your agent shapes your reputation.
How your agent behaves reflects on you.
4. Long-term wealth starts with short-term decisions.
Good agents build sustainable careers, not just cash grabs.

Red Flags When Choosing an Agent

1. Overpromising

- "I'll make you a millionaire overnight"
- "Every team wants you"

2. Lack of Transparency

- Dodging questions about fees or processes

3. No Plan Beyond Year 1

- Great agents think in 3, 5, 10-year windows

4. Poor Reputation

- Check how teams, players, and execs talk about them

5. Aggressive Recruitment Tactics

- Gifts, pressure, guilt-tripping

Key Questions to Ask a Prospective Agent

1. How many clients do you personally represent?

- Too many = you're just another file

2. What's your communication style?

- Weekly updates? Monthly check-ins? Text-only?

3. What's your approach to contract negotiations?

- Aggressive? Strategic? Collaborative?

4. Who else is on your team (lawyers, marketing, etc.)?

- Good agents are backed by strong support.

5. How do you handle conflicts of interest?

- What if they represent someone in your same position group?

6. Can I talk to a few of your current clients?

- Real agents have real references.

Vetting an Agent: Step-by-Step

Step 1: Research

- Google them.
- Check league certifications.
- Look at public client lists.

Step 2: Interview at least 3 agents.

- Compare styles, visions, fees.

Step 3: Talk to Players.

- DM players they've represented.
- Ask about responsiveness, negotiating power, honesty.

Step 4: Understand the Fee Structure.

- NFL: max 3%
- NBA: max 4%
- MLB: varies (consultation + commissions)
- MMA: often higher (up to 20% in small shows)

Step 5: Check for Lawsuits, Scandals, Suspensions.

- No drama allowed in your corner.

Pros and Cons of Different Types of Agents

Big Agency Agents (CAA, Wasserman, Octagon)
Pros:

- Big connections
- Access to endorsement deals

Cons:

- Might be treated like a number
- Less personalized attention

Boutique Agents (Small Firms)
Pros:

- Highly personalized
- Hungry to grow with you

Cons:

- Less muscle in major negotiations
- Limited brand resources

Real-World Stories: Agent Choices That Changed Careers

Success:

- Steph Curry stayed loyal to a small agent who truly understood him, despite bigger agencies circling early.

Failure:

- Countless athletes lost millions through shady agents who mismanaged money or missed contract deadlines.

Plain Language Breakdowns

Certification Matters:

- NFLPA, NBPA, MLBPA, NHLPA, WNBAPA all have certification requirements.
- Only certified agents can legally negotiate player contracts.

Negotiation Styles:

- **Aggressive agents** sometimes blow up deals.
- **Strategic agents** build long-term goodwill.

Marketing Arm:

- Agents sometimes have a marketing "wing" — separate fees apply.

- Clarify this upfront.

Action Steps You Can Take Today

- Build a short list of agents you admire.
- Read articles about contract disputes and lessons learned.
- Write down your career goals for the next 10 years.
- Make a checklist for vetting agents.

Sports Analogies for Choosing an Agent

Football:

- You don't just pick a quarterback because he throws hard — you pick the one who reads defenses and protects the ball.

Basketball:

- You don't draft a flashy dunker with no fundamentals — you pick the two-way player who gets buckets AND plays defense.

Baseball:

- You don't sign a home run hitter who strikes out 200 times a year — you want consistent contact and good glove work.

Soccer:

- You don't just sign the flashy dribbler — you want someone who tracks back on defense, too.

Tennis/Golf:

- You pick a coach who works on footwork, conditioning, AND mental strength — not just serves or drives.

Final Encouragement

Choosing your agent isn't a popularity contest.

It's a business decision.

It's a wealth decision.

It's a legacy decision.

Your agent isn't just the person who negotiates your next paycheck.

They're the person who helps you protect your future.

They help you:

- Maximize every opportunity
- Avoid hidden traps
- Build a brand that lasts beyond your playing days

Take your time.

Ask smart questions.

Trust your gut—but verify everything.

You're not just hiring an agent.

You're building your board of directors.

You're hiring your first CEO of Brand You.

Make it count.

Because when the lights are brightest and the contracts are biggest, you'll want the right person in your corner.

Not just someone who wants to get paid.

Someone who wants to see you win—in every sense of the word.

Let's choose wisely.

Let's stay smart.

Let's stay legendary.

You're building more than a career.

You're building generational wealth.

And it starts with who you trust on Day 1.

Chapter 25: What a Good Agent Should (and Shouldn't) Do

Choosing your agent is one of the first major business decisions of your professional career. And it isn't just about who can get you signed. It's about who will set you up for success, protect your interests, and help you build a long, sustainable career—on and off the field, court, octagon, or pitch.

Let's break it down clearly: What a good agent should do, what a good agent shouldn't do, and how to spot the difference early.

What a Good Agent Should Do

1. Prioritize Your Long-Term Career, Not Just a Fast Check

- A good agent sees the 10-year picture.
- They don't chase flashy but short-lived deals.
- They think about your health, reputation, earnings, and life after sports.

2. Negotiate with Precision and Patience

- Good agents know when to push and when to hold.
- They understand salary caps, incentives, bonuses, and how to frame your value.

3. Communicate Clearly and Often

- You should never wonder where you stand.
- Weekly updates during free agency.
- Clear explanation of offers and contracts.

4. Be Transparent About Fees and Services

- No hidden charges.
- No surprise deductions.
- Everything spelled out in writing.

5. Protect Your Reputation

- Agents who trash talk teams, leak false stories, or act like divas can hurt your brand.
- Good agents are respected in front offices and locker rooms.

6. Build Relationships, Not Just Transactions

- With GMs, scouts, owners, brands, media.
- They know that relationships win opportunities.

7. Educate You, Not Just Represent You

- Good agents explain contracts, clauses, and endorsement opportunities.
- They don't keep you in the dark.

8. Stay in Their Lane

- Agents negotiate contracts.
- Financial advisors manage investments.

- CPAs handle taxes.
- Lawyers review legal documents.
- Good agents respect the boundaries.

9. Advocate Without Alienating

- It's a balance: strong for you without burning bridges.
- Emotional intelligence matters.

10. Look Out for Your Well-Being Beyond Sports

- Mental health resources.
- Career development after playing days.
- Helping you build your life, not just your stats.

What a Good Agent Shouldn't Do

1. Make You Feel Pressured to Sign Immediately

- You should feel confident, not rushed.

2. Overpromise and Underdeliver

- "First-round pick, guaranteed" promises are a red flag.

3. Take Bigger Cuts Than Allowed

- League caps exist for a reason.

4. Push You Toward Risky Endorsements

- Crypto schemes, shady energy drinks, random startups.
- Protect your image.

5. Act Like They Own You

- You are the client.
- They work for you.

6. Get Too Personally Involved

- It's a business relationship first.
- Boundaries matter.

7. Ignore Your Priorities

- If you want to prioritize staying close to family, education, or certain markets, they need to respect that.

8. Keep You Out of Conversations

- You should be informed.
- Every major move should involve your input.

9. Mix Roles Unprofessionally

- Your agent should not double as your financial planner or tax preparer.
- Checks and balances are healthy.

10. Disappear After You Sign

- Good agents stay involved.
- They're not "done" once your rookie contract is inked.

Pros and Cons of Agent Styles

Aggressive Negotiators

Pros:

- Squeeze maximum money.

Cons:

- Can alienate teams, limit future deals.

Collaborative Negotiators

Pros:

- Build long-term relationships.

Cons:

- Might leave a little money on the table initially.

Big Agency Agents

Pros:

- Deep brand networks.
- Resources for endorsements.

Cons:

- You could be one client among hundreds.

Boutique Agents

Pros:

- Personalized attention.
- Nurtured career management.

Cons:

- Less reach nationally.

Real-World Examples

- *Good Agent:* Drew Brees stayed with Tom Condon throughout his NFL career. Long-term trust = long-term success.
- *Bad Agent:* Numerous pro athletes sued agents for stealing money, cutting backdoor endorsement deals, or failing to disclose conflicts of interest.

Lesson: Loyalty matters—but it must be earned by results and transparency.

Action Steps for Athletes

- Make a checklist for evaluating your agent's behavior.
- Schedule regular sit-downs (at least quarterly).
- Insist on written reports of negotiations and deals.
- Review your contract yourself (with a lawyer) even after your agent explains it.

Sports Analogies for Choosing Good Agents

Football:

- A good offensive coordinator adapts to your strengths—not just calls plays from a dusty old book.

Basketball:

- A good point guard doesn't just score—they make everyone around them better.

Soccer:

- The best midfielders control the flow of the game—not just chase the ball.

MMA:

- Your corner coach's advice between rounds can make the difference between winning and getting knocked out.

Golf/Tennis:

- Your swing coach isn't just there for big tournaments—they're there in the offseason, building your fundamentals.

Same thing with your agent.

Final Encouragement

If you're reading this, it means you're serious about your career.

And being serious means being smart about who represents you.

Never forget:

- You're the CEO of your career.
- Your agent is an executive you hire, not the boss.

Hire wisely.

Communicate clearly.

Hold them accountable.

Your career — your livelihood, your family's future, your legacy — deserves nothing less.

You've worked too hard to hand the keys to someone who doesn't truly have your best interests at heart.

Stay focused.

Stay sharp.

Stay powerful.

The world may see you as just another athlete.

But you? You're building an empire.

And empires are built one smart decision at a time.

Choosing the right agent is one of the first.

Let's get it right.

Let's keep climbing.

Let's stay legendary.

Chapter 26: The Role of a Manager — How They Differ from Agents

When you're stepping into the professional world of sports, the term "management team" gets thrown around a lot. But what does it really mean? And more importantly, how is a manager different from an agent?

In this chapter, we're going to pull back the curtain and break it all the way down — no jargon, no confusion, just real talk about what managers do, what they don't do, and how to make sure you're building a team around you that actually works for YOU.

What a Manager Actually Does

1. Big Picture Career Management

- Managers help oversee your ENTIRE career, not just a contract or a one-time deal.
- They're your career quarterbacks — helping coordinate the team (agent, financial advisor, CPA, marketing rep, PR firm) so everything moves in harmony.

2. Brand Development

- Managers help you build your brand: securing endorsements, arranging speaking engagements, developing your public image, social media presence, and partnerships.

3. Scheduling and Logistics

- Appearance schedules, charity events, photo shoots, brand meetings — they handle the daily moving parts.

4. Crisis Management

- If a controversy or emergency happens, managers are often the ones putting out fires and protecting your reputation.

5. Life Organization

- They're often the ones making sure your business, personal appearances, and brand commitments don't conflict with your athletic priorities.

6. Long-Term Planning

- Retirement planning, second careers, business ventures, media opportunities.
- They help strategize for life AFTER sports.

What a Manager Does NOT Do

1. Negotiate Playing Contracts

- That's the agent's job, period.

2. Give Financial Advice

- They should not be touching your money or investments.

3. File Your Taxes

- That's your CPA's responsibility.

4. Act as Your Lawyer

- Managers are not legal experts. They help coordinate with your legal team, but they don't replace it.

5. Make Decisions Without You

- They suggest, recommend, and coordinate. You decide.

Pros and Cons of Having a Manager

Pros:

- Full-time career guidance.
- Coordination across your brand, business, and appearances.
- Proactive planning for life after your sport.

Cons:

- Cost: Managers typically charge either a flat fee, a percentage of off-field earnings (5-15%), or a monthly retainer.
- Risk of overreliance: If you're not paying attention, you might become too dependent.

Action Steps Before Hiring a Manager

1. Define What You Need

- Are you getting so many endorsement opportunities you need help managing them?
- Are your speaking and charity events getting complicated?
- Is your social media blowing up?

If not, you might not need a manager yet. (Or you might just need a marketing rep.)

2. Vet Candidates Thoroughly

- Background checks.
- References from other athletes.
- Detailed understanding of their prior work and client list.

3. Get Everything in Writing

- What's their role?
- What's their pay structure?
- What's their non-compete and non-disclosure agreement?

4. Maintain Ultimate Control

- No manager should make major decisions without your clear, written approval.

5. Keep Your Money Separate

- Managers don't touch your money.
- They help you organize your business life, not own it.

Real-World Stories

- *Good Management:* Serena Williams' career has been carefully managed beyond tennis — fashion brands, media deals, investment firms. It didn't happen by accident.
- *Bad Management:* Countless athletes have trusted "managers" who had no real experience and lost money or reputation because of it.

Sports Analogies for Understanding Managers

Football:

- Your manager is like the head coach. They don't throw the ball — they organize the game plan.

Basketball:

- Like a point guard setting up plays but not taking every shot.

Soccer:

- Like a team captain who coordinates but isn't the only one scoring goals.

MMA:

- Like your camp coach, preparing your fight plan — but YOU still step into the cage.

Baseball:

- Like a team manager setting the lineup — but you've still got to hit the ball.

Golf/Tennis:

- Like a swing coach setting strategy — but you're swinging the club or racquet.

Bottom line: Managers support — they don't substitute for you.

Red Flags When Hiring a Manager

- They can't clearly explain their experience.
- They promise the world without showing how.
- They want control of your money.
- They refuse to put expectations in writing.
- They pressure you to hire their "friends" for other roles (lawyers, agents, financial advisors) without you meeting them first.

Final Encouragement

You've come too far to fumble the bag because you trusted the wrong people.

You're not just an athlete — you're a business, a brand, and a future Hall of Famer in life.

So build your team like a championship roster:

- Agent.
- CPA.
- Financial Advisor.
- Manager (if and when needed).
- Attorney.

Every person should have a clear role.

Every person should be vetted.

Every person should be accountable.

And YOU are the GM.

Protect your name.

Protect your game.

Protect your future.

You deserve a team that sees your vision and helps you achieve it — not one that distracts, derails, or drains you.

The world will know your name.

Make sure you're building a legacy that lasts.

Let's keep building.

Let's keep winning.

Let's keep owning it.

Chapter 27: Why Your Agent and Financial Advisor Should Remain Separate

When you're a pro athlete, your entire world moves fast. Contracts. Endorsements. Travel. Appearances. Training. Recovery. Repeat.

It's tempting to think you should make your financial life "easier" by letting one person handle everything for you. Sometimes your agent — who negotiated your deal — will offer to "handle your money too." They'll say it's "convenient." They'll say it's "efficient." They'll promise to "manage everything" so you can focus on your sport.

It sounds great.

It's not.

Let's have a real conversation about why you must keep your agent and your financial advisor separate — for your protection, your wealth, your sanity, and your future.

Understanding the Roles

What an Agent Does:

- Negotiate contracts with teams, leagues, and organizations.
- Pursue endorsement deals.
- Advocate for you in salary negotiations.

- Handle matters related to your employment and playing career.

What a Financial Advisor Does:

- Help you budget your income.
- Help you save and invest wisely.
- Build wealth plans for your future.
- Navigate tax strategies, insurance, estate planning, and risk management.

THESE ARE DIFFERENT SKILL SETS.

One negotiates deals. One manages wealth.

Trying to have one person do both is like asking your wide receiver coach to also be your orthopedic surgeon.

Pros and Cons of Keeping Them Separate

Pros:

- Checks and balances: One professional can't cover for another's mistakes.
- Specialized expertise: Each professional focuses 100% on what they're trained to do.
- Reduced conflict of interest.
- Transparency: You know exactly who's advising you on what.

Cons:

- More people to coordinate.
- Slightly more time needed for meetings.

But you're running a multi-million-dollar career. Taking a little extra time to do it right is what CEOs do. And YOU are the CEO of your life.

Why You Need Checks and Balances

1. Prevent Conflict of Interest

- An agent who manages your money could steer you toward decisions that benefit them (like faster deals or high-risk opportunities) instead of what's best for your long-term financial health.

2. Protect Against Mismanagement or Theft

- It's easier to steal from someone when they're the only one looking at the books.
- Separation creates a natural layer of accountability.

3. Specialized Expertise Matters

- Good agents are experts at contracts.
- Good financial advisors are experts at money.
- You want the BEST at both — not a jack-of-all-trades.

4. You Stay Informed

- With two advisors, you hear two perspectives.
- This forces you to learn, think critically, and OWN your financial life — instead of handing it away.

5. Long-Term Planning Requires a Different Mindset

- Agents think short-term (securing deals).
- Financial advisors think long-term (building wealth for 30, 40, 50 years).

You need both views — but from different people.

Real-World Scenarios

Best Case:

- Your agent lands you a solid contract.
- Your financial advisor builds a conservative, smart plan around your earnings.
- They work together (with you in the middle) to maximize your income AND security.

Worst Case:

- Your agent pressures you to sign deals quickly.
- Your "advisor" (who is really your agent in disguise) suggests risky investments.
- Your money gets lost, wasted, or stolen.
- You're left broke and betrayed.

We've seen both outcomes. Choose the first.

Action Steps

1. Hire an Independent Financial Advisor

- Not connected to your agent's firm.
- No hidden relationships.
- Completely separate.

2. Ask About Fiduciary Duty

- A fiduciary MUST put your interests ahead of theirs.
- Ask directly: "Are you a fiduciary?"

3. Set Up Regular Check-Ins

- Quarterly meetings with both your agent and your financial advisor — separately.
- Annual joint meetings where you're the boss in the room.

4. Keep Separate Contracts

- Separate agreements for agent services and financial advisory services.

5. Trust but Verify

- Always get second opinions.
- Always review statements.
- Always ask questions.

Sports Analogies

Football:

- Your agent is your offensive coordinator.
- Your financial advisor is your strength coach.
- They BOTH matter — but their jobs are completely different.

Basketball:

- Your agent draws up the play.
- Your financial advisor builds your conditioning program to last 7-game series.

Soccer:

- Your agent negotiates your contract with the club.
- Your financial advisor ensures you're protected after your playing days.

Tennis:

- Your agent schedules tournaments.
- Your financial advisor manages winnings and endorsements.

Golf:

- Your agent lines up sponsors.
- Your financial advisor manages tour winnings and business ventures.

Different fields. Different expertise.

Red Flags If They're Too Close

- Your agent "recommends" only one financial advisor — who's at the same firm.
- Your agent wants "to be able to move your money for you."
- Your financial advisor says you don't need to review your portfolio.
- Your agent says, "Don't worry about it — I'll handle everything."

Wrong.

You're smart. You're capable. You're building generational wealth.

No one should be "handling everything" without your full understanding and approval.

Final Encouragement

You're not a kid anymore. You're not a "client" on paper. You're the CEO of a major business: your life.

You've worked too hard to hand the keys to your financial future to one person — no matter how "nice" or "loyal" they seem.

Checks and balances protect you.

Clear roles protect you.

Independent professionals protect you.

This is how you stay in the league. This is how you stay wealthy. This is how you win for decades — not just seasons.

You've already started the journey by investing in your financial literacy.

You've already proven that you're willing to do the work.

Now protect that work.

Play the long game.

Build your empire — brick by brick, decision by decision.

Separate your agent and your financial advisor.

Be the boss you were born to be.

Let's keep going.

Let's keep winning.

Let's keep OWNING it.

Chapter 28: Why You Still Need an Independent Financial Advisor

When you step into the professional world as an athlete, it can feel like the entire universe opens up around you. Opportunities, money, fame, responsibility, and pressure flood in all at once. It can be exhilarating—but it can also be overwhelming.

And one of the most critical, most overlooked, and most important moves you will make in your financial life is choosing to have an **independent financial advisor** at your side.

Not just "a" financial advisor.

Not just whoever your agent recommends.

Not just a family friend who "knows a little about investing."

An **independent, credentialed, conflict-free financial advisor** whose only loyalty is to **you**.

Let's break down why this matters so much, and why it could be one of the biggest long-term difference makers in your career and your life.

Why Independence Matters

Imagine you're playing basketball, and you're down by two points with five seconds left. Would you want your coach drawing up the final play—or a guy from the stands who knows the referee?

Exactly.

An independent advisor is like a trusted coach. They work only for **your best outcome**, not for anyone else's cut of the action.

Here's what true independence gives you:

- **No hidden agendas.**
- **No behind-the-scenes commissions.**
- **No "friends of friends" cutting side deals with your agent.**
- **No pressure to buy products you don't need.**
- **No distractions from YOUR goals.**

An independent advisor sits on your side of the table. Not the team's table. Not the agent's table. Not the endorsement deal's table.

Your table.

And in the world of pro sports, where everyone thinks they should have a say in how you handle your money, you need someone who's fiercely loyal to **you** and only **you**.

What an Independent Financial Advisor Should Actually Do

Let's keep it simple.

An independent financial advisor should help you:

- Build a custom budget (not a cookie-cutter plan).
- Set up a savings strategy that actually matches your career arc.
- Protect you against career-ending injuries and the financial disaster that can follow.
- Help you understand taxes, investments, insurance, and estate planning—without talking over your head.
- Keep your long-term future (not just your next endorsement) in mind.
- Hold you accountable in the right ways—no "yes men" allowed.

They are your strategist. Your shield. Your sounding board. Your reality check. Your advocate.

They aren't just trying to "sell you stuff" or "get you hyped up." They're here to quietly, steadily, consistently guide you—through the highs and lows of your career, and into the life you want after the cheering fades.

What to Watch Out for When Picking an Advisor

Look... not all "advisors" are created equal.

Just like not all coaches know how to build a championship team. Just like not all managers know how to set up a career that lasts longer than a hot minute.

Here's what you want to avoid:

- Advisors who work **only** on commission.
- Advisors who **push certain products** (insurance, annuities, private investments) without a full plan.
- Advisors who **"team up" with your agent** and don't make it clear who's paying who.
- Advisors who **brag about "big-name clients"** but don't show real care for you.
- Advisors who **don't take the time to teach you** — they just tell you to "trust them."

Trust is earned. Not demanded.

If you feel pressure? If it feels rushed? If you can't understand what they're saying?

Walk away.

Pros and Cons of Hiring an Independent Advisor

Pros:

- True fiduciary duty (they are legally required to act in your best interest).

- No product pushing.
- Personalized game plan based on your goals.
- Full access to budgeting, investing, insurance, and legacy strategies.
- You're in the driver's seat—not them.

Cons:

- You'll pay a fee for their advice (but good advice is worth 10x the cost).
- It takes a little time upfront to find the right fit.
- You'll need to stay engaged—this isn't "set it and forget it."

But believe me: those "cons" are nothing compared to the problems you'll face if you don't have a true pro helping you.

This is the cost of protection.

Think of it like hiring a great personal trainer. Yeah, it costs a little money. But without it? You could tear an ACL because you lifted wrong.

Same thing here—except we're talking about your financial muscles.

Action Steps: How to Hire an Independent Advisor

Here's your starter playbook:

1. **Start Early**: Don't wait until you get your first paycheck.
2. **Ask About Fiduciary Status**: Only hire someone who is legally obligated to put your interests first.
3. **Check Certifications**: CFP, CFA, CPA—letters that actually matter.
4. **Interview at Least Three Advisors**: Get a feel for different personalities and approaches.
5. **Ask for References**: Real clients, not just hype.
6. **Demand Transparency**: How they get paid. What they do. What

they don't do.

7. **Trust Your Gut**: If you feel "off" about someone? Move on.

Remember: **this is your career, your future, and your money**.

You're not hiring a buddy. You're hiring a professional to help you win a much bigger game than the one you play on the field or court.

Real-Life Scenario

Let's break it down with a quick analogy.

Football: Imagine you're the quarterback. You have your offensive coordinator (agent) designing plays for you. But who's your QB coach?

Your financial advisor is your QB coach. Quietly in the background. Watching your technique. Keeping you sharp. Making sure you don't throw picks when the money blitz comes.

Basketball: You're a star point guard. You have your agent locking down your next shoe deal. But who's helping you read the defense when the double team comes off the pick?

Your financial advisor.

Baseball: You're in your first big league season. The endorsement checks start rolling in. Who's helping you set up your long-term batting average—financially?

Your financial advisor.

In every sport, you need that steady hand.

Why Independence Gives You the Power

When you have an independent advisor:

- You control your financial future.
- You don't get stuck with hidden fees.
- You don't wake up one day wondering where your money went.
- You have someone to call when the world gets noisy.

- You have a professional advocate when everyone else wants a piece of your pie.

You take the power back.

You stay in control of the game.

And the best part?

You build real wealth.

Not just for your playing days. Not just for your highlight reel. Not just for the next five years.

For the rest of your life.

That's the real win.

Final Thought

Look, the world isn't short on people who will "advise" you.

But an independent financial advisor is different. They don't chase your money. They don't chase your fame. They don't chase your shine.

They are there to make sure that when your cleats, sneakers, or gloves are finally hung up, you walk away with something **far more valuable** than stats or rings:

Financial security. Freedom. Dignity. Peace.

And **you deserve that**.

You worked too hard. You sacrificed too much. You fought too long.

Protect your future the way you protect the ball, the puck, the shot, the swing.

Get yourself an independent financial advisor.

Own your future.

Because this isn't just about money.

It's about building a legacy.

And if you've read my previous books? You already know:

Your legacy is worth fighting for.

Chapter 29: Negotiating Endorsements and Sponsorships Smartly

Negotiating endorsements and sponsorships is one of the most exciting, rewarding, and risky parts of a pro athlete's financial journey. It's where your name, image, and brand go to work for you beyond the field, court, track, or arena. But just like negotiating contracts, the way you handle endorsements can either elevate your career and bank account or create headaches that follow you for years.

This chapter will walk you through everything you need to know to negotiate endorsement deals smartly, confidently, and with your long-term best interests in mind.

Understanding the Landscape: What Are Endorsements and Sponsorships?

An endorsement is when you allow a company to use your name, image, or likeness (NIL) to promote their product or service. You might shoot commercials, post about their product on social media, or make appearances at their events.

A sponsorship often involves a longer-term relationship where a brand supports your career, pays you a fee, and sometimes covers costs like travel or training, in exchange for visibility and promotion.

In the pro sports world, the lines between endorsements and sponsorships often blur. Sometimes you'll have hybrid deals that include elements of both.

Pros and Cons of Endorsements and Sponsorships

Pros:

- Additional revenue streams outside your playing contract.
- Opportunities to build your personal brand and visibility.
- Partnerships with companies you truly believe in.
- Potential stepping stones for post-playing career opportunities.

Cons:

- Time commitments that can conflict with your training or recovery.
- Risk of attaching your name to a company that faces scandal or bankruptcy.
- Complex tax implications, especially if travel, gifts, or stock options are involved.
- Damage to your brand if a product or partnership goes sideways.

Action Step: Before signing any deal, ask yourself: "Will this partnership enhance or dilute my brand over the next 5-10 years?"

Plain Language Breakdown: How Endorsement Deals Are Structured

A standard endorsement agreement might include:

- **Scope of Services:** What exactly are you required to do?
- **Term:** How long is the deal for? 6 months? 1 year? 3 years?
- **Exclusivity:** Are you prevented from working with competitors?
- **Compensation:** Flat fee? Bonuses for social media engagement?
- **Termination Clauses:** What happens if you get injured, cut, or the company gets bought?
- **Morality Clause:** If you do something "unbecoming," can they cancel the deal and claw back your money?

Real-World Scenario: Imagine you're a rookie wide receiver who just signed a deal with an upstart energy drink company. A few months in, the company gets hit with lawsuits over contaminated products. Because of the morality clause, your contract is terminated, and you lose not only future payments but also part of the signing bonus you already spent.

Lesson: Always have a trusted attorney and agent review endorsement contracts.

The Power of Saying No

Not every deal is worth it.

Early in your career, you might be tempted to say "yes" to every opportunity. It's flattering. It's income. It's validation. But the wrong deal can damage your brand and your future earning potential.

Just like you wouldn't wear mismatched shoes on game day, you shouldn't mismatch your brand with companies that don't align with who you are.

Action Step: Create a "Brand Filter" list. Write down your personal values, goals, and what you want to be known for. Evaluate every opportunity against that filter.

Vetting the Company: Due Diligence Matters

Before you endorse:

- Research the company's financial health.
- Look at the CEO and leadership team's backgrounds.
- Google past lawsuits, scandals, controversies.
- Ask yourself: "Would I still endorse this company if I wasn't getting paid?"

Negotiation Tips for Endorsement Deals

1. **Know Your Value:** Don't just rely on Instagram followers or jersey sales. Your value also comes from your story, authenticity, performance, and character.
2. **Get Performance Bonuses:** Negotiate bonuses for things like Pro Bowl selections, All-Star appearances, MVP awards, etc.
3. **Limit Exclusivity:** Don't let one deal block you from future

opportunities unless the payday is truly worth it.

4. **Get Paid Upfront When Possible:** Especially with newer or unproven companies.
5. **Negotiate "Out" Clauses:** Protect yourself if the company fails or your circumstances change.

Tax Implications of Endorsements

Yes, Uncle Sam wants a piece of your endorsement money too.

- Endorsement income is taxable.
- If you do appearances, travel expenses might be deductible, but only if structured properly.
- You may owe taxes in multiple states if you promote products across state lines.

Action Step: Have your CPA set up a separate "Endorsement Income" account for tax withholdings.

Real-World Scenario: A rising tennis star accepted payments in "product" instead of cash to avoid taxes. A few years later, she owed taxes on the value of the products and penalties for underreporting income.

Lesson: Always report all income and consult tax professionals early.

Social Media Endorsements: Read the Fine Print

Influencer marketing is booming. Companies may want you to:

- Post a certain number of times per month.
- Tag specific handles.
- Write captions using provided language.

Warning: The FTC (Federal Trade Commission) requires clear disclosures like #ad or #sponsored. Failing to disclose can lead to fines for both you and the brand.

Action Step: Hire a social media manager or agent who understands FTC guidelines.

Negotiating Endorsements: A Playbook from Different Sports

- **NFL Players:** Short career windows mean locking in larger upfront payments is critical.
- **NBA Players:** Personal brands are massive. Strategic partnerships can build lifetime brands.
- **Soccer Players (MLS and International):** Global markets matter. Think beyond the U.S.
- **MMA Fighters:** Endorsements can make up a huge part of total income; negotiate aggressively for "fight week" bonuses.
- **WNBA Players:** Community impact and empowerment brands are key niches.
- **Tennis Players:** Long careers mean playing the long game with endorsements tied to legacy and personal brand.

Avoid Common Endorsement Traps

- Endorsing "Get Rich Quick" products.
- Endorsing unproven cryptocurrencies.
- Jumping into "equity for services" deals without cash flow.
- Getting locked into multi-year deals with no performance bonuses.

Action Step: For any "equity for services" deal, negotiate:

- A cash retainer.
- Clear vesting schedules.
- Board observer rights if appropriate.

Protecting Your Image: More Than a Contract

Remember: Once you post it, wear it, or say it publicly, it's part of your brand forever. Choose carefully.

Education, Empowerment, Engagement

- **Education:** Learn what endorsement deals really mean legally and financially.
- **Empowerment:** Feel confident saying "no" to protect your brand.
- **Engagement:** Build relationships with brands that fit your vision, not just your paycheck.

Final Encouragement

You are more than an athlete. You are a brand. A CEO. A future legend. Every deal you sign is a brick in the empire you're building. Lay each one carefully, intentionally, and with pride.

Final Note

This chapter wasn't just about money. It was about protecting the opportunity you've worked your whole life for. About maximizing the rewards without losing your peace or purpose.

Own your career. Own your future. Own your financial life.

If you read my previous books, you already started that journey. Now it's time to keep building.

Chapter 30: Red Flags in Endorsement Contracts

When you sign your name to a contract, you're not just committing to show up and smile for a photo shoot or post about a brand on your social media. You're entering into a legal agreement that can either set you up for success—or trap you in obligations you didn't fully understand. Endorsement deals can be great opportunities to build your brand and increase your earnings, but they can also be a minefield if you aren't careful.

Let's slow it down and really unpack this. Imagine you're a rookie athlete who just lit up the draft boards. Brands are calling. Your agent is excited. It feels like the moment you've dreamed of. But before you sign anything—before you agree to be the "face" of anything—you need to know what to look for between the lines.

Exclusivity Clauses: The Silent Handcuffs

Exclusivity clauses are common in endorsement deals. They usually mean you can't work with competing brands in the same category. Makes sense, right? You wouldn't expect to endorse both Nike and Adidas at the same time. But here's the red flag: sometimes the language is written so broadly that it locks you out of opportunities you didn't even realize.

An exclusivity clause that says "no sports apparel" sounds fair, but what if it also includes sneakers, accessories, watches, or even fitness apps? Suddenly you've boxed yourself into a tiny corner with one brand—while countless other deals are off-limits.

Action Step: Always ask for narrowly defined exclusivity. Specify exactly what categories you're agreeing not to promote—and for how long.

Term Length and Auto-Renewals: When the Deal Never Ends

Some endorsement contracts sneak in auto-renewal clauses. That means if you don't formally cancel the agreement within a tight window—maybe 30 or 60 days before the end—the deal automatically extends for another full term.

Imagine you sign a three-year deal. You think you're free at the end of three years. But because you missed the 60-day cancellation window, the brand locks you in for another three.

Action Step: Push to remove auto-renewals or make renewal optional—not automatic. Always calendar contract milestones.

Payment Traps: Front-Loaded or Back-Loaded Payouts

Some brands promise big numbers, but the payout is structured in a way that doesn't really benefit you. They may front-load a small check to hook you, then delay the bulk of the payment with complicated conditions:

- Hitting a certain number of social media impressions.
- Participating in multiple mandatory appearances.
- Remaining on an active roster.

If you get injured or released, you might lose a big portion of the money you thought you secured.

Action Step: Ask for a clear, guaranteed payment schedule—not "maybe money."

Image Rights and Usage: Where Your Face Ends Up

Endorsement contracts often include language that lets the brand use your image, name, likeness, and even quotes. But how long? And for what?

You don't want a situation where a brand can keep running ads using your face—long after you've moved on or even if your relationship with that brand sours.

Action Step: Put clear limits on how long they can use your image and for what specific purposes.

Moral Clauses: One Mistake, One Post, One Career Shift

Almost every major endorsement contract has a "morals clause." It allows the brand to terminate the deal if you "bring disrepute" to yourself or them. That's fair—brands don't want their ambassadors caught up in scandals.

But some moral clauses are worded so loosely that almost anything—even a controversial tweet—could be considered a breach.

Action Step: Negotiate language that requires "material harm" to the brand's reputation, not just "any disrepute."

Bonus Structures and Incentives: Promises That Depend on Fine Print

Brands love to dangle bonuses—if you make an All-Star team, win a championship, or hit a certain number of appearances. But look carefully at how achievable these incentives really are.

Some bonuses are tied to factors outside your control, like your team's success or your coach's decisions. Others have hidden requirements you aren't even aware of.

Action Step: Get every bonus requirement in writing. Ask: "What exact conditions must I meet—and who verifies it?"

Expenses and Taxes: Who Covers What?

Traveling to an event for a brand? Shooting a commercial? Doing a media tour? Who pays for your flights, hotels, food, and ground transportation?

Don't assume it's the brand. Some contracts stick you with the bill—eating into your endorsement earnings. Worse, some deals pay you as a 1099 contractor, meaning you owe taxes you weren't planning for.

Action Step: Spell out who covers travel, lodging, and per diem. Plan for taxes.

Intellectual Property: Can They Own Your Ideas?

Sometimes an endorsement deal involves more than just appearances. Maybe you collaborate on a product line, design a jersey, or invent a slogan. Watch out—some contracts state that anything you create while working with them belongs to the brand.

Action Step: Protect your intellectual property rights. If you create something valuable, you deserve ownership or shared rights.

Liquidated Damages: Huge Penalties for Small Slip-Ups

Some endorsement contracts have liquidated damages clauses—basically, predetermined fines if you breach the contract.

The problem? Sometimes the penalties are wildly out of proportion to the mistake. Missing one appearance could cost you more than the fee you were paid.

Action Step: Negotiate reasonable damages, or better yet, limit damages to actual harm, not arbitrary amounts.

Representation and Approval Rights: Who Has the Final Say?

Sometimes contracts require you to get approval from the brand before you do anything else—even outside of your relationship with them. Like taking another endorsement, joining a new team, or collaborating with a charity.

That's too much control over your life.

Action Step: Make sure your personal and professional freedom are protected.

Ending Contracts: Termination Rights

Can you exit if things go south? Does the brand have all the power to end things—but you don't?

Action Step: Negotiate mutual termination rights—especially if there are major changes in leadership, strategy, or brand values.

Final Note

Contracts are not about trusting or distrusting people. They're about clarity. Protecting yourself now protects your future.

You've worked too hard to build your career. Your talent is your asset. Your brand is your asset. Your future earnings are your asset.

Every endorsement is a partnership—and partnerships must be built on respect, transparency, and fairness.

If you see red flags? Don't ignore them.

Bring in your independent financial advisor, attorney, and agent (separate people!) to review everything carefully.

When in doubt, remember this:

You are the prize.

They need you more than you need them.

Own your career. Own your future. Own your financial life.

Part 4: Banking, Budgeting, and Building Wealth

You made it. You signed the contract. You earned the paycheck. Now the real work begins.

Part 4 of this book is where we shift from chasing opportunity to protecting and growing it. This section is all about the *everyday moves* that set elite athletes apart financially—not because they signed the biggest contract, but because they made the smartest choices with what they earned.

In this part, we'll dig deep into the fundamentals that seem basic but separate the wealthy from the broke — banking smarter, budgeting wisely, and building wealth that lasts beyond your playing days. We'll break down how to organize your accounts, automate your savings, and create a budget that fits a pro athlete's unpredictable, feast-or-famine lifestyle. We'll show you how to use banking tools to your advantage, not as traps. We'll tackle how to think about your money in *seasons, cycles,* and *windows* of opportunity.

We'll also talk about the emotional side of money — because it's not just math. It's pressure, pride, family expectations, and personal dreams. We'll teach you how to avoid lifestyle creep (that slow financial drift that catches so many athletes off guard) and instead, lock in a foundation that gives you freedom, security, and peace of mind.

Whether you just signed your rookie deal, you're riding the bench fighting for a roster spot, or you're a few years into your career realizing you need a financial reboot, this section will meet you where you are.

Part 4 is the playbook for taking control off the field — and making sure your money keeps winning for you, long after the stadium lights fade.

Chapter 31: Banking 101 for Pro Athletes

Let's have a real conversation.

You're stepping into the professional arena. You've earned your shot. Maybe it's a rookie contract. Maybe it's a free agent deal. Maybe it's the second or third team you've been with already. Wherever you are, one thing is clear: **money is about to move through your life faster than ever before**.

The question is, **will you control it — or will it control you?**

One of the first steps to taking control is setting up your **banking** correctly. It's not glamorous. It's not flashy. No one's handing out trophies for opening a checking account. But here's the truth: **if you get sloppy with your banking, everything else falls apart**.

This chapter is going to teach you, in plain English, **how to set up your financial house so it doesn't collapse under the pressure of fame, money, family, and life.**

Let's go.

Why Banking Matters for Athletes

Picture this: You're a wide receiver who just caught the game-winning touchdown. Fans are screaming your name. Sponsors are calling. Your bank account just got a $1 million signing bonus deposit.

Now imagine that you don't even know **which account that money**

is sitting in.

Imagine not knowing:

- How much of it belongs to taxes
- How much needs to be saved
- How much you can actually spend
- How much is exposed to fraud

Imagine waking up one morning to a **zero balance** because someone got access to your card and drained it while you were sleeping.

It happens. All the time.

Banking isn't just about convenience. **It's about defense.** It's the equivalent of having a good offensive line — **you don't always notice it when it's working, but the second it breaks down, you're getting blindsided.**

The Core Accounts Every Pro Athlete Needs

Before the ink dries on your first contract, you need to have these accounts open:

1. Primary Checking Account

This is your operational account — your "**pay bills, buy groceries, get cash at the ATM" account**.

- Keep only **1–2 months of living expenses** here at all times.
- Everything else should be moved **out** to savings or investments.
- This protects you from overspending and fraud.

Tip: Use a major, nationally recognized bank that has good security, mobile apps, and 24/7 customer service.

2. High-Interest Savings Account

This is your **"hold and protect" account**.

- Where you put money for **taxes, off-season living expenses, emergency fund**.
- Should pay **higher interest** than your checking account (even if it's small).

Action Step: Open a savings account **at a different bank** than your checking account if you're worried about being tempted to dip into it. Make it a little harder to transfer casually.

3. Investment Account

This is your **wealth-building account**.

- It's where you invest your signing bonus, endorsement earnings, and extra income **for the future**.
- Opened with a trusted independent financial advisor or reputable investment firm — **NOT your cousin's "friend" who's "learning to day trade."**

Rule: No investing until your checking and savings foundations are fully set up.

4. Retirement Account (Roth IRA, SEP IRA, 401(k))

Athletes have **short windows to earn** but **long lives to live**.

- If you start saving for retirement at 21, you have decades for compound interest to work its magic.
- If you wait until 31 or 36, you lose millions of dollars of potential

growth.

Strategy Tip: Set up automatic monthly contributions into retirement accounts even during your rookie year. Future You will send you a thank-you card someday.

5. Trust Account (Optional for Larger Contracts)

If your first contract is huge — say, first-round NFL money, top-10 NBA pick, or guaranteed international soccer cash — your financial advisor might recommend setting up a **trust** immediately to protect assets, limit taxes, and set up multi-generational wealth.

This is a move you make **early if you're smart**, not later when you're scrambling.

Action Step: Your First Week of Being Signed

Within 7 days of signing:

- Open a primary checking account.
- Open a high-interest savings account.
- Sit down with a **fiduciary** financial advisor to plan your investment and retirement accounts.

This is **non-negotiable**.

Would you show up to your first pro camp without your cleats, skates, or sneakers? No way.

You shouldn't step into professional sports without your financial cleats on either.

Protecting Your Accounts: Don't Get Blitzed

You have more to lose now. Period.

Some quick "**must-dos**" to protect your banking life:

- **Use two-factor authentication** on every account.
- **Never share your password** with friends or family — no exceptions.
- **Get alerts** for every withdrawal, deposit, and large transaction.
- **Review your statements monthly** — like watching game tape.
- **Freeze your debit card** when you're traveling internationally if needed.

Fraud is like a defensive back looking to pick-six you — **one moment of laziness and you're cooked**.

Real Talk: Beware the "Money Manager" Red Flag

You'll hear from people offering to "manage your money" — sometimes before you even get drafted.

If someone tells you:

- "Just give me control of your accounts and I'll handle everything for you..."
- "You don't need to check your balances — I got you..."
- "You're too busy to deal with money stuff..."

Run. Fast.

Nobody cares about your money more than you do. **Banking is your personal responsibility, forever.**

You can have advisors. You can have teams. But **your name is the one on the bank account.**

Own it.

Common Mistakes Athletes Make With Banking (And How to Dodge Them)

Mistake 1: Keeping all your money in one checking account.

Why it's dangerous: You lose track of what's for taxes, savings, or spending. One swipe-happy week and half your year's earnings could vanish.

Better Move: Split money into specific accounts with specific purposes.

Mistake 2: Using debit cards for everything.

Why it's dangerous: Debit cards pull money **directly** from your account. If a fraudster gets your info, it's gone. Credit cards have more protection.

Better Move: Use a credit card for large purchases. Pay it off in full every month. Build your credit. Protect your cash.

Mistake 3: Letting someone else "own" your banking relationships.

Why it's dangerous: If something goes wrong, you're left holding the bag — legally and financially.

Better Move: You are the primary contact. **You** have logins. **You** get the alerts. Every dollar that moves, you should know about it.

Banking as a Pro Athlete = Playing Offense and Defense

- Checking account = short-yardage plays
- Savings account = long-term clock management
- Investment account = deep-ball shots downfield
- Retirement account = building a dynasty
- Trust account = protecting your family like a franchise quarterback protects the ball

You need **all parts of the playbook** working together to win.

A Few More Advanced Moves (Once You're Stable)

After you get your basics down, you can start thinking about:

- **Separate accounts** for different life goals (like home down payment, kid's college, business investment)
- **Dedicated accounts** for taxes (saving ahead avoids scrambling during tax season)
- **Treasury accounts** for big cash if you're sitting on millions (for safety and returns)

But don't get cute until you master the basics.

Banking isn't about being fancy. It's about being solid.

Final Words: Build a Banking System You Can Trust

You're not playing college ball anymore.

You're not playing for NIL money anymore.

You're **a professional** now — on the field, and **in your bank account**.

Professionalism in banking looks like:

- Stability
- Predictability
- Security
- Growth

It doesn't matter if you're hitting home runs, scoring hat tricks, draining threes, or knocking people out in the cage.

Every athlete at the highest level needs a professional banking setup.

In Closing: You're the CEO of Your Career

Think of yourself as a business.

Your body is the product.

Your brand is the marketing.

Your contract is the revenue stream.

And your **banking system** is the treasury department.

If you don't have a strong treasury, the whole company — **YOU, INC.** — collapses.

You've worked too hard to get here. Don't fumble the bag now.

Open your accounts. Set your boundaries. Watch your cash. Build your wealth. Protect your future.

It's not just about money.

It's about ownership. Leadership. Freedom.

Let's keep building.

Building Smart Banking Habits Early — Why Systems Matter More Than "Willpower"

Look — even the most disciplined athletes in the world don't try to "wing it" when it comes to training.

You have routines.

You have schedules.

You have practice plans.

You don't just show up on Sunday or game night and hope your muscles "remember" how to perform.

It's the **systems** — the plays you run every day — that make you great.

Banking is the same way.

It's not about "being good with money." It's about building systems so that **you don't have to think about it every day.**

Example of a Rookie Financial System:

1. **Direct Deposit** all paychecks into your primary checking account.
2. **Automatic Transfer** every week:

- 30% into a savings account for taxes.
- 20% into a high-yield savings account for off-season living.
- 20% into your investment account.
- 5% into your charitable giving account if that's important to you.

1. **Set Spending Limits** on your checking account.
2. **Use Alerts** so you know when big withdrawals or deposits happen.

No guessing. No scrambling. No emotional spending.

It just runs. Like clockwork.

How to Choose the Right Bank for You

Not all banks are created equal.

Some banks are set up for regular folks.

Some banks are set up for **high-net-worth individuals** — which, guess what, you might suddenly become when you sign your deal.

When choosing a bank, here's what you should be looking for:

Must-Haves:

- **FDIC insurance** for deposits (up to $250,000 per account).
- **Robust fraud protection** and customer service.
- **Mobile app access** for quick monitoring.
- **Branches near you** (or excellent online banking if you're always traveling).

Nice-to-Haves for Pro Athletes:

- **Private banking** services (for bigger contracts — they assign you a personal banker).
- **Wire transfer services** (sometimes you'll need to wire money quickly).
- **International banking features** (especially important if you're playing abroad).

Tip: Don't be so dazzled by a bank offering "exclusive VIP treatment" that you forget to ask about fees, restrictions, and hidden costs. **Being fancy doesn't always mean being smart.**

Banking for the Off-Season and Career Transitions

What happens when the checks stop coming every two weeks?

When the season ends?

When you get cut?

When your playing days end?

That's when bad banking setups get exposed.

If you don't have money in the right buckets early, you're going to struggle later.

Smart athletes bank with two seasons in mind:

- **In-season** (money coming in)
- **Off-season** (money mostly going out)

Pro Move: Create an "Off-Season Account" — and every in-season paycheck, put a chunk into it **as if you're already paying your future self.**

That's how veterans survive lean years, transition seasons, and even unexpected retirements.

Red Flags to Watch Out for With Banking

Not everything that glitters is gold. Especially in banking.

Here's what you need to **watch out for**:

- **Banks pushing "investment products" too soon.** (They want your fees, not necessarily your best interest.)
- **Banks trying to get you to take out huge loans.** (Be very careful — debt is dangerous early.)
- **People offering to "combine" your checking, savings, investments, and taxes into one "easy" account.** (Convenience can mean confusion later.)

Remember: **simple is strong** when it comes to banking.

If you don't understand how your money is being held, moved, or invested — don't agree to it.

Period.

Sports Analogy: Banking is Your Game Plan for Cash

In football, you don't just run random plays.

In basketball, you don't just jack up shots from half-court.

In baseball, you don't just swing at every pitch.

You have a game plan.

You scout.

You prepare.

You execute.

Banking is your cash game plan.

- Checking account = your everyday offense.
- Savings account = your backup QB — there when you need it.
- Investment account = your long ball — setting up future wins.
- Retirement account = your final season — making sure you go out

on top.

Banking might not be sexy — but it's championship-level work.

Real-World Scenario: The Cautionary Tale

Meet Marcus.

Marcus was a first-round draft pick in the NBA.

Signed for $4 million.

Got a $1.5 million signing bonus.

He had one checking account. One debit card. That's it.

Within the first year:

- His cousin convinced him to invest $200,000 into a bad restaurant deal.
- His girlfriend had access to his debit card and spent over $100,000 on luxury shopping.
- His "manager" withdrew $500,000 for "marketing expenses" — but never showed receipts.

Marcus didn't realize anything was wrong until his checking account hit $10,000.

By then it was too late.

The saddest part?

Marcus wasn't stupid.

He was just unprotected.

His banking setup was a **defensive liability**, and it cost him the game.

Real-World Scenario: The Smart Setup

Meet Aisha.

Aisha was a track & field athlete who went pro after the Olympics.

She set up:

- Checking for daily life.
- Savings for taxes.
- Separate savings for her off-season.
- Investment account for the future.
- Retirement account even though she was only 23.

She limited her debit card to $2,000 per week.

She had alerts set for any transactions over $500.

Result?

By 28, Aisha had no debt, owned a home outright, and had over $1 million invested.

She didn't have a "magic financial gift."

She just had a **system**.

You can too.

Step-by-Step: Setting Up Your Pro Banking Playbook

Here's exactly what you should do, step-by-step, before you ever touch your first pro check:

1. **Meet with a fiduciary financial advisor.** (Get real, independent advice.)
2. **Open your primary checking account** — ONLY for paying bills and spending.
3. **Open a high-yield savings account** — for taxes, emergencies, and off-season.
4. **Open your investment and retirement accounts** — set automatic monthly deposits.
5. **Turn on alerts** for every major transaction.
6. **Freeze your debit card** when not traveling or using it.
7. **Separate accounts**:

- Never mix "spending money" with "wealth building money."

1. **Monthly check-ins**: Review your accounts just like you review game film.

No exceptions. No shortcuts.

In Closing: Win the Banking Game, Win the Wealth Game

If you handle your banking business like a true professional from Day 1:

- You'll avoid rookie mistakes that cost millions.
- You'll have cash flow freedom even when your career ends.
- You'll build real wealth, not just flashy moments.

You're not just playing for the next season.

You're building a dynasty.

It starts with smart, disciplined, **boring banking habits** that nobody cheers for — but that win championships in life.

Just like the best teams in every sport, **the ones who dominate the fundamentals dominate the future.**

And now, you know how to run that play.

Chapter 32: Budgeting When You're Paid Seasonally (NFL, NBA, MLB, NHL, WNBA, etc.)

Let's start with a real-world reality check.

You sign your first pro contract.

You get your first paycheck during the season.

It's bigger than any check you've ever seen.

You feel like you're set.

But what you don't realize yet is that this check isn't coming every two weeks forever.

It's coming during the season.

Off-season? Different story.

No games, no game checks.

And that's where a lot of athletes—rookies, vets, even some seasoned pros—get themselves into real trouble.

Because when you're paid seasonally, you have to think *differently* about your money.

You're not just managing a paycheck.

You're managing a whole year's life expenses… on a partial year's income.

Let's break it down, real talk style.

The Truth About Seasonal Paychecks

In most major leagues—NFL, NBA, MLB, NHL, WNBA—you don't get paid year-round.

You get game checks during the season.

- NFL players get paid once a week during the regular season (typically 18 weeks, covering 17 games plus a bye week).
- NBA players usually get paid twice a month during the season (though contracts can vary slightly).
- MLB players get paid from April through September — six months of checks for a 12-month life.
- NHL players are paid biweekly during the season.
- WNBA players are often paid semi-monthly across the shorter WNBA season.

No matter the league, the reality is the same:

You are earning a full year's worth of living expenses...

...in about half a year's time.

If you don't adjust for that, your financial game plan is already broken before it even starts.

Why It Feels Different When the Money Hits

When your season starts and those checks start dropping, it feels *fast.*

Big checks, week after week.

It's easy to think:

"This is my normal now."

"This is how it's always going to feel."

But then the season ends.

And if you didn't prepare, it's like falling off a financial cliff.

Suddenly the money stops, but your rent doesn't.

Your mortgage doesn't.

Your car note doesn't.

Your family's needs don't.

Imagine running full speed down the court, and then the floor just ends.

That's what seasonal paychecks feel like if you don't plan.

Budgeting Like a Pro (Literally)

When you're a pro athlete, budgeting isn't just about "saving a little money."

It's about *managing your cash flow across a full calendar year,* even though you're only getting paid during part of it.

Here's the mindset shift you have to make:

Your *in-season pay* has to stretch across your *off-season life.*

You have to learn to:

- Set aside money *now* for expenses *later.*
- Think about your career not just in seasons, but in years.
- Know exactly what your monthly "life cost" is—whether you're in-season or not.

This is a discipline that separates athletes who *build wealth* from those who *burn through it.*

Step-by-Step: How to Budget for Seasonal Income

Here's a game plan you can start following today:

Step 1: Know Your Take-Home Pay, Not Just Your Contract Number

Your "contract" says you're making $2 million?

Cool.

But after taxes, agent fees, union dues, mandatory league deductions, and benefits?

Maybe you're really taking home $1.1 million.

Know that real number.

Step 2: Calculate Your Monthly Expenses for the Entire Year

Rent, utilities, groceries, insurance, car payments, family support, personal trainer fees, cell phone, travel — write down every bill.

Multiply your monthly cost by 12.

(Yes, 12 — even if you only work for 6 or 8 months.)

Step 3: Divide Your Seasonal Earnings Over 12 Months

Whatever you're taking home during the season, budget it as if it has to last *all year.*

You made $1.1 million take-home during your 6-month season?

Pretend you're living off $91,666 a month ($1.1 million ÷ 12).

Not $183,000 a month.

$91,000.

That's your real monthly "salary."

Step 4: Create Two Bank Accounts

- **Operating Account** — The account you use for bills, rent, everyday spending.
- **Reserve Account** — The account you "pay yourself" into each month to even out income during the off-season.

During season:

Pay your bills from the operating account.

Dump the rest into the reserve account.

Off-season:

Pay yourself from the reserve account.

Step 5: Automate It

Set up automatic transfers between your accounts.

Force yourself to "live on a salary" all year.

Don't trust yourself to remember it.

Automate the discipline.

Why It's Hard for Athletes (and Why You Can Beat It)

Most people who earn seasonal income struggle at first.

It's normal.

You're going from a broke college student one year...

...to a millionaire (on paper) the next.

It's like jumping from a YMCA game to the Super Bowl with no practices in between.

But you have an advantage:

You're used to discipline.

You're used to following a plan.

You're used to working on your craft every day even when nobody's watching.

Budgeting is just another form of that discipline.

Real-World Example: Rookie Season in the NFL

Let's say you're an NFL rookie.

You signed a four-year, $4 million deal.

Sounds huge, right?

But after taxes (say 37%), agent fees (3%), union dues (~$15,000), and other deductions, your first-year take-home might be around $450,000–$500,000.

And you only get paid for 18 weeks.

Let's say you take home $25,000 per week.

Over 18 weeks, that's about $450,000 total.

If you spend like you're making $25,000 every week all year long, you'll crash.

Instead:

Budget like you're living on $37,500 a month ($450,000 ÷ 12 months).

Big difference.

Sports Analogy: Playing the Full Season, Not Just the First Quarter

Budgeting when you're paid seasonally is like playing a full basketball game.

You can't blow all your energy (or points) in the first quarter.

If you do, you'll have nothing left when the game's on the line.

You pace yourself.

You distribute your energy.

You adjust your strategy as the game unfolds.

Same thing with your money.

First check?

Cool.

Celebrate responsibly.

Then settle in.

Play for the whole season...and beyond.

The Off-Season Trap: Why So Many Athletes Struggle

The off-season sounds like a dream.

You've got free time, no practices, no games.

Maybe you travel, maybe you go back home, maybe you work out and rest.

But financially?

The off-season is where dreams can turn into nightmares.

Here's why:

- No steady paychecks are coming in.
- Bills are still coming in — every month like clockwork.
- You're bored, and spending money becomes a "fun" activity.
- People around you expect handouts or expensive trips.
- You tell yourself, "I'll make it back next season" — but there are no

guarantees.

When you're paid seasonally, your *off-season mindset* can make or break your entire career financially.

If you don't treat off-season money management like in-season game planning, you will *always* feel broke by the time camp starts again.

Build a Season-Based Cash Flow Plan

A real pro doesn't wing it.

You need a cash flow plan that covers:

- **Season Earnings**: How much you'll actually receive, after deductions.
- **Off-Season Draw**: How much you'll "pay yourself" monthly during the off-season.
- **Big One-Time Expenses**: Training, travel, housing, car payments, insurance renewals, etc.
- **Emergency Fund**: Money set aside for unexpected injuries, surgeries, or surprise opportunities.
- **Savings and Investing**: Money you put away immediately to build long-term wealth.

Treat yourself like a business.

Because guess what?

You are one.

If you want to survive and thrive as a pro athlete, your money can't just work during the season.

It needs to work year-round.

Pros and Cons of Different Budgeting Strategies

Let's be real — there are a few different ways athletes try to handle seasonal paychecks.

Each has its pros and cons.

Option 1: Save All In-Season, Live Off Savings Off-Season

Pros:

- Simple.
- No monthly accounting stress during the season.

Cons:

- Easy to dip into savings too quickly.
- Requires major discipline.

Option 2: Pay Yourself a Salary Year-Round

Pros:

- Smooth, predictable lifestyle.
- You feel like a "normal" working professional.

Cons:

- Requires automatic systems.
- Requires good advisors or personal discipline to manage.

Option 3: Splurge During Season, Hustle Off-Season

Pros:

- You feel rich for a few months.

Cons:

- Terrible plan.
- Unsustainable.
- Leads to regret, embarrassment, debt, and pressure.

Guess which one the smartest pros pick?

Yeah.

Option 2.

Set your life up like you're an employee of *yourself,* not the league.

Real Talk: Rookies Who Got It Right (and Wrong)

Let me give you two real-world examples (names changed, but true stories).

Marcus (NFL Rookie):

Signed a 4th-round contract.

Immediately bought a luxury car, paid rent on a luxury apartment, bought jewelry, and flew his family around to games every week.

He lived like he was making $10 million a year.

By March?

He was taking out cash advances from his agent just to pay rent.

Jamal (NBA Rookie):

Signed a modest rookie deal.

Bought a used car cash.

Lived in a reasonable condo near the practice facility.

Set up auto-transfers to a savings account every time he got paid.

By year three?

He had enough money saved for a down payment on a second property he turned into a rental.

Marcus looked rich for a year.

Jamal *became* rich for life.

Big difference.

How to Mentally Prepare for Off-Season Financial Life

This part is bigger than just setting up bank accounts.

It's mental.

You have to:

- Accept that you are not "broke" just because the checks stop.
- Remind yourself: "My money is working even when I'm not."
- Shift your dopamine — instead of chasing big purchases, chase *big savings numbers* and *net worth goals.*
- Understand that short-term sacrifice equals long-term domination.

You have to *fall in love* with living under your means.

The same way you fell in love with practice, lifting, conditioning, drills —

you have to fall in love with financial training too.

Dealing with Pressure From Friends and Family During the Off-Season

Here's the thing about the off-season:

The pressure doesn't just stop because you're not playing.

Friends and family will:

- Ask for money.
- Invite you on expensive trips.
- Expect you to "cover it" because "you got it now."

And because you don't have fresh checks coming in every week?

Every dollar you give away *hurts even more* during the off-season.

You must:

- Set firm boundaries.

- Stick to your financial plan.
- Remember: Helping people isn't about buying things—it's about staying strong so you can help them for *decades,* not just one summer.

Bonus Tip: Build "Off-Season Buckets"

One smart move?

Create small sub-savings accounts for:

- Rent/Mortgage Bucket
- Bills/Utilities Bucket
- Travel Bucket
- Fun/Miscellaneous Spending Bucket

Name them.

Fund them during the season.

Then spend only what's in the bucket during the off-season.

It's like giving your money a playbook — and sticking to it.

Action Steps: Build Your Seasonal Budget Like a Pro

Here's what you can do today:

1. Get Your True Take-Home Pay Number

Ask your agent, CPA, or financial advisor to run it for you after deductions.

2. Write Out Your Monthly Expenses

Be honest.

Use a spreadsheet, notebook, or app.

3. Create a 12-Month Cash Flow Plan

Even if you're paid for 6 months, plan expenses for 12.

4. Set Up Two Accounts

One for daily spending, one for savings.

5. Automate Transfers

Treat yourself like your own employer.

6. Set an Off-Season "Paycheck" for Yourself

Give yourself a set monthly amount to spend.

7. Stick to It Even When It's Tempting Not To

Financial fitness is like physical fitness.

Consistency wins.

Final Encouragement

Let's keep it all the way real:

Money is emotional.

Seasonal paychecks add pressure.

But you didn't make it this far by folding under pressure.

You made it by preparing, training, adjusting, and executing under fire.

Budgeting with seasonal pay is just another opponent to scout, game plan against, and dominate.

Every great career — in sports or in money — is about consistency, not just big moments.

Handle your seasonal money right, and you won't just survive between seasons.

You'll thrive between seasons.

And before you know it?

You'll be looking back years later thinking:

"Damn, I'm glad I treated my rookie year like a vet."

Chapter 33: Saving and Investing — Rules of Thumb for Athletes

Introduction: Playing the Long Game

Think about the greatest athletes you know.

The legends.

The ones who left their mark on the game.

What do they all have in common?

Consistency.

Longevity.

Discipline.

They didn't just have one great game.

They strung great games together, season after season, year after year.

Saving and investing work the same way.

It's not about one big move.

It's about consistent, smart moves stacked up over time — until one day, you look up and realize you've built a legacy that lasts long after your playing days are over.

That's the mindset we're going to bring to your money starting today.

Why Saving and Investing Is Different for Pro Athletes

If you're a pro athlete, you live in a financial world that 99% of people will never understand:

- You make more money in your 20s than most people make in a lifetime.
- Your career might only last a few years.
- Your "retirement" could start at 30 instead of 65.
- Everyone around you thinks you're rich already — even before you are.

Because of that, saving and investing isn't optional.

It's essential.

Saving and investing isn't just about growing your money.

It's about **buying freedom**:

- Freedom from bad contracts.
- Freedom from needing to take bad deals.
- Freedom to walk away when it's time.

Saving = Survival.

Investing = Thriving.

Rule of Thumb #1: Pay Yourself First

You've heard this before, but let's make it real:

Every time you get paid, you should save a percentage before you spend a dime.

How much?

Aim for **at least 25%-50%** of every check.

If that sounds crazy high, good.

You're not living like a regular worker.

You're living like an athlete — where careers are shorter and money has to last longer.

Think of it like this:

- If you save 50% of your money while you're playing, you're setting yourself up to live free for decades.
- If you spend it all while you're hot, you'll struggle when the cheering stops.

Just like conditioning — the reps you put in now show up later when it matters most.

Action Step:

Every contract, every endorsement check — pay yourself first automatically.

Rule of Thumb #2: Protect the Downside First

Saving is your defense.

Before you start thinking about growing your money, you need to protect it.

That means:

- Build an emergency fund (at least 6-12 months of living expenses).
- Get disability insurance.
- Get health insurance.
- Get liability insurance.
- Get your legal paperwork right (wills, trusts, powers of attorney).

It's like playing football without pads if you don't protect the downside.

Sure, you might be fine for a while.

But one wrong hit — financially or physically — and it's game over.

Action Step:

Before you invest a single dollar, make sure your "financial pads" are strapped on tight.

Rule of Thumb #3: Don't Invest in What You Don't Understand

Real talk:

If you don't understand it, don't put your money in it.

No matter how good it sounds.

No matter who is pitching it.

No matter how much money other people say they're making.

This applies to:

- Private equity
- Startups
- Crypto
- Real estate flips
- Restaurants
- Record labels
- Nightclubs
- Anything that sounds "guaranteed" but isn't a basic savings account

The quickest way to go broke in pro sports?

Trusting people with your money who are smarter about *their* pockets than yours.

If it's too complicated for you to explain to your little brother in 60 seconds, you don't understand it.

Action Step:

Before investing, ask three questions:

1. How does this make money?
2. What could go wrong?
3. Can I afford to lose this money?

Rule of Thumb #4: Think in Seasons, Not Weeks

Athletes are used to thinking week to week — game to game.

When it comes to money?

You have to think in **seasons** — even decades.

- How much will I need if my career ends tomorrow?
- How much do I need to live for 30, 40, 50 years after I retire?
- How do I build income streams that last longer than my playing days?

The average NFL career lasts 3.3 years.

The average NBA career lasts 4.5 years.

The average MLB career lasts 5.6 years.

The average NHL career? 5 years.

You might play 5 seasons.

But you've got 50 seasons of life to fund afterward.

That's the real math.

Action Step:

Project out 40-50 years of life expenses with your advisor.

Then reverse-engineer how much you need to save now.

Rule of Thumb #5: Diversify Like a Champion

You wouldn't walk onto a basketball court and only know how to shoot free throws.

You wouldn't line up at wide receiver and only run one route.

Being great in sports means having a full skill set.

Investing is no different.

You need a **diverse portfolio**:

- Stocks
- Bonds

- Real estate
- Index funds
- Retirement accounts
- Maybe some small, smart alternative investments

If everything you own is in one basket?

You're gambling, not investing.

Diversification is how pros protect their wealth from market crashes, bad breaks, and bad years.

Action Step:

Work with your financial advisor to build a diversified, long-term investment portfolio.

Common Investing Mistakes Athletes Make (and How to Dodge Them)

Let's be honest:

Athletes get targeted.

Hard.

Some common traps:

Mistake 1: "Get Rich Quick" Deals

If someone says you'll double your money fast?

Walk away.

Mistake 2: Putting Friends and Family in Charge of Money

Business and personal life must stay separate.

Hire pros, not cousins.

Mistake 3: No Exit Strategy

Every investment should have a plan for when you want out — not just how you get in.

Mistake 4: Chasing Trends

By the time you hear about a "hot" investment, it's usually too late.

Mistake 5: Overleveraging

Never borrow money to invest — you're doubling your risk.

Action Step:

Commit to being boring with your investing.

Boring gets rich.

Flashy gets broke.

Real World Story: The Power of Slow Growth

Let's take two examples.

Player A:

Made $10 million over his career.

Blew it all trying to "flip" money fast.

Player B:

Made $5 million over his career.

Invested $100,000 every year into basic index funds.

At retirement, Player A was broke.

Player B had $6 million growing for him tax-efficiently.

Slow and steady wins.

Every. Single. Time.

Sports Analogies for Saving and Investing

Let's tie it back to your world:

- **Basketball:** Think of investing like free throws — boring, repetitive, but the foundation of championships.
- **Football:** Building wealth is like running the ball — 3 yards, 4 yards, 5 yards... it doesn't look flashy, but it wins games.
- **Baseball:** It's not about swinging for the fences every at-bat. It's about hitting singles, getting on base, moving the runner over.
- **Soccer:** Defense wins championships — protecting your downside is as important as scoring.
- **Tennis:** You can't just ace every serve. You have to rally, wear your opponent down. Same with building wealth — it's the rallies that

matter.

You don't win wealth with one play.

You win it with smart plays over and over.

Final Action Steps: Saving and Investing Starter Kit

1. Emergency Fund:

6-12 months of expenses in savings.

2. Retirement Accounts:

Max out IRAs, Roth IRAs, or 401(k)s if available.

3. Diversified Investment Portfolio:

Mix of stocks, bonds, real estate, and other assets.

4. Pay Yourself First:

Set automatic transfers to savings and investments.

5. Vet All Investments:

If you don't understand it, don't invest.

6. Build Your Money Team:

Financial advisor, CPA, estate planner — not just your agent.

Final Encouragement

Saving and investing isn't just for when you're old.

It's for *right now.*

It's about buying yourself choices.

Freedom.

Security.

Peace.

It's about making sure that *you* — not luck, not circumstances, not bad advice — control your destiny.

You've already proven you can handle pressure on the field, court, ice, or pitch.

Now it's time to prove you can handle it with your money.

Stack your savings.
Invest smart.
Stay consistent.
Your future self will thank you every single day.

Why Athletes Feel Pressure to Spend Instead of Save

Before we go any deeper into strategy, let's call out the emotional side of this game:

- You made it.
- You beat the odds.
- You want to enjoy it — and you should.
- You want to reward the people who helped you — and you should.
- You want to live a life that feels different than when you were broke — and you should.

But here's the problem:

If you're not careful, spending becomes a full-time sport too.

The pressure to spend doesn't just come from you:

- Family asking for help
- Friends expecting you to pick up the tab
- Social media making it seem like everyone's ballin' but you
- Teammates rolling up in six-figure cars and posting it

It's real.

And it's heavy.

But here's the truth:

The real flex isn't what you show.

The real flex is what you own.

It's having money 10, 20, 30 years from now when nobody's watching.

It's your kids never worrying about tuition.

It's your family never worrying about bills.

It's you waking up and deciding what you want to do — not what you *have* to do.

Saving and investing is the ultimate flex.

You just have to flip the switch in your mind.

Building Your Financial Playbook: How to Save and Invest in Phases

Think of your financial life like a sports career — it happens in phases.

Phase 1: Rookie Year - Build Your Base

- Save aggressively (50% if you can).
- Get the boring stuff done: Emergency fund, insurance, basic retirement accounts.
- Keep expenses low. (Just because you can buy it doesn't mean you should.)

Phase 2: Prime Earning Years - Grow Smart

- Keep living below your means — even when your checks get bigger.
- Start investing more heavily: brokerage accounts, real estate, business ownership.
- Keep working with your financial team to fine-tune your strategy.

Phase 3: Late Career - Preserve and Protect

- Shift more into income-generating and conservative investments.
- Lock in wealth preservation strategies.
- Start thinking legacy: family trusts, charitable giving, wealth transfer.

Phase 4: Retirement - Live Off the Field

- Live off the assets you built, not just past income.
- Stay engaged — managing money is still part of your life's work.

Action Step:

Sit down with your advisor and map out which phase you're in right now — and what your next move should be.

The "Seasons of Wealth" Mindset

Here's a mindset that will change your life:

Every season has a different financial focus.

- Offseason = Review your finances. Reset your goals.
- Preseason = Lock in your budget. Prepare for taxes.
- In-season = Stick to your cash flow plan. Don't overspend.
- Playoffs = Get ready for bonuses or big performance incentives.
- Postseason = Evaluate investments, plan for charity if you want.

You already live your athletic life by seasons.

Start living your financial life by seasons too.

Understanding Different Types of Investments (Plain English)

Let's break some options down without any Wall Street jargon:

1. Stocks

- Buying tiny pieces of companies like Nike, Apple, Amazon.
- They go up and down — sometimes fast.
- Good for long-term growth (5+ years).

2. Bonds

- Loaning money to companies or governments.
- They pay you interest.
- Usually safer than stocks but grow slower.

3. Index Funds

- Groups of stocks bundled together.
- Instead of betting on one company, you bet on lots at once.
- Lower fees, steady growth over time.

4. Real Estate

- Buying houses, apartments, land.
- Can create rental income and property value growth.
- But it's work — don't jump in without a plan.

5. Business Investments

- Investing in companies or startups.
- High risk, high reward.
- Only do it with money you can afford to lose.

6. Cash/Cash Equivalents

- Savings accounts, CDs, money markets.
- Safe but grow slow.
- Good for emergencies, not long-term growth.

Setting a Simple Investing Strategy

If you want something simple but powerful:

- **50% Index Funds (stocks for growth)**
- **20% Bonds (stability)**
- **20% Real Estate (income and appreciation)**
- **10% Cash (opportunity fund/emergencies)**

Customize based on your goals — but **keep it simple**.
Simple wins. Fancy often fails.

Quick "Golden Rules" to Remember

- If it sounds too good to be true, it is.
- If you can't explain it simply, don't invest in it.
- If everyone's doing it, you're probably too late.
- If you're getting emotional about it (greedy, scared, hyped), slow down.
- If your gut feels funny, listen.

The Power of Compound Interest (Magic for Athletes)

Let's say you invest $100,000 when you're 22.
You leave it alone, and it grows at 7% per year.
By the time you're 42?
That $100,000 could grow to around **$400,000** — even if you never add another dollar.
If you keep adding money each year?
You could become a **multi-millionaire** — quietly, patiently.
That's the real cheat code.
That's the real "generational wealth" plan.

Real Talk About Endorsements and Investment Opportunities

When the endorsement checks start rolling in:

- Don't just spend them. Invest them.
- Don't let brands "pay you" in product instead of money — unless it's part of a clear plan.
- Don't let people "talk you into" reinvesting your fee back into their company — that's riskier than you think.

If it's a partnership? Cool.

But make sure you get **paid first** — and protect yourself legally and financially.

Final Locker Room Speech on Saving and Investing

Saving and investing aren't for when you're old and boring.

Saving and investing are how you:

- Stay in control
- Build real wealth
- Create options your whole life
- Become the CEO of your future

It's just like your sport:

- You can't win if you don't practice.
- You can't succeed if you don't show up every day.
- You can't be great if you don't make the little smart decisions nobody else sees.

Money is no different.

Start small.

Stay steady.

Keep growing.

You've already beaten the odds by making it this far.

Now let's make sure you beat the odds financially too.

Chapter 34: Roth IRA, Traditional IRA, SEP IRA, 401(k): Which Ones Should You Use?

You finally have money to invest — not just spend.

You're looking past this season, this year, and even your playing career.

You're thinking about your future — and that's a beautiful thing.

But here's the deal:

You can't just stack cash under your mattress and call it a retirement plan.

You've got to put your money somewhere it can work for you.

And one of the best places to start?

Retirement accounts — like Roth IRAs, Traditional IRAs, SEP IRAs, and 401(k)s.

Each one has different rules.

Each one has different advantages.

Each one fits a different playbook depending on where you are in your career.

Let's walk through it — no jargon, no confusion.

Just real talk — like we're teammates game-planning for a championship.

Why Retirement Accounts Matter — Even If You're Young and Rich

I get it — retirement feels a million miles away.

You just got your first big check.

You're focused on today — not 30 years from now.

But here's why you should care:

- Retirement accounts give you **massive tax advantages** — either today or tomorrow.
- They grow your money **faster** because of tax deferral or tax-free compounding.
- They force you to **think long-term** — and that's where real wealth is built.

If you invest in your 20s or 30s?

You're giving your money decades to grow without the IRS snatching a big chunk every year.

It's the easiest, smartest money move you'll ever make.

First Things First: Understand the Two Big Leagues of Retirement Accounts

There are two main leagues when it comes to retirement accounts:

1. Tax-Deferred Accounts:

You don't pay taxes now. You pay later — when you withdraw the money in retirement.

Examples: Traditional IRA, 401(k), SEP IRA

2. Tax-Free Growth Accounts:

You pay taxes now. You never pay taxes again on the growth.

Example: Roth IRA

Different seasons of your career might make one better than the other.

Roth IRA — The Young Superstar's Secret Weapon

Think of a Roth IRA like a young rookie with unlimited upside:

- You put in **after-tax dollars** (money you've already paid taxes on).
- Your money grows **tax-free** forever.
- When you pull it out in retirement, you pay **zero** taxes on the gains.

Pros:

- Tax-free growth forever.
- You can pull out your contributions anytime (not the gains, unless you qualify).
- No required minimum distributions at 73 like traditional retirement accounts.
- Awesome for young athletes who are early in their career and in lower tax brackets.

Cons:

- Income limits apply (you can't contribute directly if you make too much — but there are strategies like the "Backdoor Roth").
- Contribution limit is relatively low ($7,000/year for 2024 if you're under 50).

Simple Rule of Thumb:

If you're young and your tax bracket is relatively low right now? **Max your Roth IRA every year.**

Action Step:

Open a Roth IRA and automate monthly contributions — treat it like another bill you have to pay.

Traditional IRA — The Veteran Grinder's Quiet Move

A Traditional IRA works like this:

- You put in **pre-tax dollars** if you qualify (based on income and whether you have a retirement plan at work).
- The money grows **tax-deferred** — no taxes on the growth each year.
- You pay **ordinary income taxes** when you withdraw the money in retirement.

Pros:

- Immediate tax deduction if you qualify.
- Defers taxes until later — when your income may be lower.
- Grows faster without yearly taxes slowing it down.

Cons:

- You eventually pay taxes when you pull the money out.
- Required Minimum Distributions (RMDs) start at age 73.

Simple Rule of Thumb:

If you want a **tax break today** and you qualify? A Traditional IRA can help.

401(k) — The League's Team Plan

If your team or employer offers a 401(k)?

It's like having a team bus that takes you straight toward wealth — you just have to hop on.

How it works:

- You contribute pre-tax dollars (lowers your taxable income today).
- Money grows tax-deferred.
- Some teams match your contributions (free money!).

Pros:

- High contribution limit ($23,000 for 2024 if under 50; $30,500 if 50+).
- Team match = instant 100% return.
- Automated — easy to stay consistent.

Cons:

- Limited investment choices (depends on your plan).
- Pay taxes later when you withdraw.

Simple Rule of Thumb:

If your team matches your 401(k) contributions, **contribute at least enough to get the full match.** Always.

SEP IRA — The Entrepreneur's Secret Play

If you do endorsement deals, run camps, or have side business income?

You're not just an athlete anymore — you're an entrepreneur.

And that means you can use a SEP IRA.

How it works:

- You can contribute up to 25% of your business earnings (up to $69,000 for 2024).
- Massive tax deduction.
- Great for freelance or self-employed income.

Pros:

- High contribution limits — perfect for athletes with side hustles.
- Easy to set up.
- Big tax deductions to offset your business income.

Cons:

- No Roth (tax-free) version — it's all tax-deferred.
- Have to treat employees fairly if you have them.

Simple Rule of Thumb:

If you have side income? **Open a SEP IRA. Save aggressively while your side money is flowing.**

Real-World Example: Rookie Contract vs. Veteran Star

Scenario 1: Rookie NFL player, $800,000 salary

- Max Roth IRA every year.
- Use the team's 401(k) to get the match.
- Save 10–20% of salary for investments outside retirement accounts too.
- Focus: Tax-free growth now because tax bracket is still manageable.

Scenario 2: Veteran NBA player, $20 million salary

- Max 401(k).
- Backdoor Roth if possible.
- Set up SEP IRA for side business income.
- Work with CPA to layer strategies (charitable giving, trusts, deferred comp).

Focus: Minimize taxes today + build diversified streams of tax-free and tax-deferred assets.

How to Actually Make It Happen

Step 1: Meet with a Fiduciary Advisor.

- Someone who legally works in YOUR best interest — not selling you stuff.

Step 2: Open the Right Accounts.

- Roth IRA: For young players or lower-tax years.
- Traditional IRA: If you want today's tax break.
- 401(k): Through team or employer.
- SEP IRA: For side hustle/self-employed income.

Step 3: Automate Contributions.

- Set it and forget it — just like your automatic workouts.

Step 4: Review Annually.

- As your career and income change, adjust your strategy.

Common Mistakes Athletes Make with Retirement Accounts

- Only saving in cash — not investing it to grow.
- Missing out on team 401(k) matches (free money).
- Waiting too late to start (and missing years of compound growth).
- Not having an independent advisor to help map it out.
- Forgetting about SEP IRA options for endorsements and side income.
- Believing they'll "figure it out later" — when the best time to start was yesterday.

Locker Room Talk: Why This Matters More Than You Think

Here's the truth nobody tells you:

It's not how much you make.

It's how much you keep — and grow.

The league minimum player who saves and invests can end up with more long-term wealth than the All-Star who spends it all.

Your earning window is short.

The game moves fast.

The spotlight eventually fades.

But your future — and your family's future — is forever.

Advanced Moves: Leveling Up Your Retirement Strategy

Once you've mastered the basics — Roth IRA, 401(k), SEP IRA — it's time to think bigger.

You're not just trying to retire.

You're trying to **retire wealthy.**

Here's how pro athletes can level up their retirement savings game:

Roth Conversions — Turning Tax-Deferred into Tax-Free

A Roth conversion is when you take money from a Traditional IRA or 401(k) (where it grows tax-deferred) and **move it into a Roth IRA** (where it grows tax-free).

But there's a catch:

You have to pay taxes on the amount you convert — *that year.*

Why would you do that?

- If you're in a low-income year (due to injury, free agency, or early retirement).

- If you expect taxes to go up in the future.
- If you want to build tax-free money for retirement flexibility.

Simple example:

Say you retire at 32. You don't have big paychecks anymore.

You have a window where your income (and tax rate) is lower before you start other businesses or take endorsement deals.

That's the perfect time to slowly convert some money to a Roth IRA — and build a big bucket of tax-free money for your 50s, 60s, and beyond.

The "Mega Backdoor Roth" — The Supercharger Move

If your employer's 401(k) plan allows after-tax contributions (NOT the same as Roth 401(k) contributions), you could supercharge your Roth savings through a Mega Backdoor Roth.

Here's how it works:

- You contribute AFTER-tax dollars into the 401(k) **beyond the $23,000 employee limit.**
- You immediately roll it into a Roth IRA or Roth 401(k).
- You get huge amounts into Roth accounts, tax-free forever.

Warning:

This only works if your plan allows it.

Ask your team or company's HR department or your financial advisor.

Solo 401(k) — For Athletes with Side Hustles

A Solo 401(k) is a beast if you have endorsement money, business income, or any 1099 earnings.

It lets you:

- Contribute as the **employee** ($23,000 for 2024).

- Contribute as the **employer** (up to 25% of net earnings).

Total possible contribution?

Up to $69,000 if you're crushing it.

Way bigger than just a normal 401(k) or SEP IRA.

If you're running camps, doing private coaching, endorsement deals, public appearances, podcasts — ANY side money — a Solo 401(k) lets you shelter way more of it.

Real-Life Athlete Scenarios

Let's break it down with some *real-world* setups:

Case Study 1: WNBA Star with Lower Seasonal Pay

- Max out Roth IRA early.
- Use a simple Traditional IRA if income gets high.
- SEP IRA for camps and clinics.
- Hustle endorsements to maximize off-season revenue.
- Use high-interest savings account for short-term needs between seasons.

Case Study 2: MLB Minor League Player (Big Upside, Small Pay Today)

- Roth IRA is #1 priority (since income is modest now).
- Save cash for emergencies (baseball seasons are unpredictable).
- Get financial coaching BEFORE signing first big major league deal.
- Avoid lifestyle creep now — future self will thank you.

Case Study 3: NFL Rookie (Practice Squad to Starter)

- Max Roth IRA first year (while salary is low).
- As income grows (starter deal), pivot to maxing 401(k).

- Open SEP IRA if doing camps, marketing appearances.
- Hire independent financial advisor early — don't wait for a "big mistake" first.

Common Myths About Retirement Accounts Athletes Believe

Myth 1: "I'm too young to think about retirement."

Reality: You're the perfect age. More time = more compound growth.

Myth 2: "I'll just save when my career is stable."

Reality: Most careers are short. Less than 5 years average in most leagues.

Myth 3: "I'll just live off endorsements later."

Reality: Endorsements fade fast — you need savings that are bullet-proof.

Myth 4: "I'll figure it out when I'm done playing."

Reality: You want the *freedom to walk away* when YOU want — not when your bank account forces you.

Tax Talk: Why the Government Wants You to Save

Here's a secret nobody talks about:

The IRS rewards people who think long-term.

When you use retirement accounts correctly:

- You lower your taxable income.
- You grow your money tax-deferred or tax-free.
- You reduce your future tax burden.
- You gain options for strategic withdrawals later.

The earlier you start?

The more these advantages snowball.

Action Plan: Your Playbook for the Next 30 Days

Week 1:

Open a Roth IRA or Traditional IRA (if not already open).

Week 2:

Review your team or employer's 401(k) plan.

Start contributing at least enough to get the full match.

Week 3:

If you have side business income, talk to your CPA about opening a SEP IRA or Solo 401(k).

Week 4:

Automate contributions.

Set a recurring transfer from your bank account every month.

Bonus:

Meet with a fiduciary financial advisor.

(Not your agent's buddy. Someone truly independent.)

Encouragement: You're Building Legacy Money

You're not just making money for today.

You're planting seeds that will feed your future family, your future dreams, and your future freedom.

Saving and investing isn't just about piling up cash.

It's about creating options.

- The option to retire when you want.
- The option to help your parents, your kids, your community.
- The option to walk away from bad deals.
- The option to chase passion projects without worrying about a paycheck.

That's real power.

That's real wealth.

Mistakes Pro Athletes Make With Retirement Accounts (And How to Avoid Them)

Let's be real for a second:

The financial graveyard is filled with athletes who **thought** they had it all handled.

You're smarter than that — and reading this already puts you ahead of the game.

But let's walk through some of the **most common mistakes** anyway:

Mistake 1: Not Using Retirement Accounts Early Enough

It's easy to think:

"I'm young. I'll max out when I'm older."

Here's why that's dangerous:

- You miss **compound growth** (your greatest weapon).
- You miss **tax savings** in your highest earning years.
- You create bad habits of spending everything you earn.

How to Avoid It:

Even if you only invest $100 a month at first, start immediately.

Treat retirement savings like your training — part of the daily grind.

Mistake 2: Only Saving in One Type of Account

Too many athletes put all their eggs in one basket:

- All Roth.
- Or all Traditional.
- Or only SEP IRAs.

Here's the problem:

Tax flexibility matters later.

If all your money is taxed the same way when you retire, you have fewer moves.

How to Avoid It:

Balance your buckets:

- Some tax-free (Roth).
- Some tax-deferred (Traditional).
- Some taxable brokerage accounts (for maximum flexibility).

Think like a coach:

You want multiple plays you can call — not just one.

Mistake 3: Forgetting About Vesting Schedules

Some 401(k) plans have **vesting schedules.**

That means you have to stay with the team or employer a certain number of years before you get all the matching money they gave you.

Example:

- 0% vesting year 1
- 50% vesting year 2
- 100% vesting year 3

If you leave early? You could lose some of that "free" money.

How to Avoid It:

Ask about the vesting schedule **before** you rely on employer matches. Plan accordingly if you think you might switch teams or careers soon.

Mistake 4: Listening to the Wrong People

Some agents, marketing managers, or even old teammates will give you financial "advice."

Problem is, they aren't fiduciaries.

They aren't legally required to put your interests first.

And sometimes?

They're just plain wrong.

How to Avoid It:

Only take retirement advice from:

- Certified financial planners (CFP®)
- CPAs with wealth management backgrounds
- Registered investment advisors (RIAs) acting as fiduciaries

Not the guy at your barbershop.

Not your agent's cousin.

Not random "wealth managers" who are really just salespeople.

How Different Career Lengths Affect Retirement Planning

Athletes have some of the **shortest earning windows** of any profession.

And that totally changes the strategy.

Here's how:

Short Career (2–5 Years)

Priority:

Save aggressively while you can.

Max everything.

Strategy:

- Roth IRA every year.

- Max 401(k) if available.
- SEP IRA if side income.
- Build massive emergency fund (2+ years expenses).
- Invest conservatively until your next career move is clear.

Medium Career (5–10 Years)

Priority:

Balance living well now with building future wealth.

Strategy:

- Still max Roth IRA or 401(k).
- Start mixing in taxable brokerage accounts for flexibility.
- Consider real estate investing cautiously.
- Protect yourself with strong disability and life insurance.

Long Career (10+ Years)

Priority:

Focus on diversification and future cash flow.

Strategy:

- Build up Roth, 401(k), SEP IRAs.
- Own multiple types of assets (stocks, bonds, real estate, business investments).
- Plan for tax diversification across retirement.
- Build an exit strategy (because no one plays forever).

The "Save and Invest Blueprint" for Pro Athletes (Sample Year-by-Year)

Here's what a rock-solid plan could look like:

Year 1: Rookie Year

- Open Roth IRA ($7,000 max).
- Open high-interest savings account.
- Save 20% of every paycheck.

Year 2: Second Season

- Increase 401(k) contributions.
- Open taxable brokerage account.
- Build cash reserve to cover next off-season.

Year 3: Breakout Year

- Max 401(k) and Roth IRA.
- Meet with CPA to start tax planning.
- Explore basic real estate if ready.

Year 4–6: Prime Earning Years

- Mega Backdoor Roth if available.
- Solo 401(k) for endorsements/side income.
- Diversify investments across stocks, bonds, real estate.

Year 7+: Preparing for Transition

- Maintain max contributions.
- Dial up real estate, passive income projects.
- Meet with estate planner.

- Start thinking about career after sports.

Banking vs. Investing: How They Work Together

Think of banking as **your defense.**
It's where you protect money you might need soon.
Think of investing as **your offense.**
It's how you move the ball down the field and score long-term points.
You need both.

- Checking account = everyday expenses
- High-yield savings = short-term goals (off-season survival, vacations)
- Investing = long-term wealth (retirement, freedom)

If you only save? You fall behind inflation.
If you only invest? You risk needing cash and having to sell low.
Balance = winning seasons, year after year.

Advanced Retirement Moves Athletes Should Know

1. Deferred Compensation Plans

Some teams offer **deferred comp** — they'll hold back part of your salary and pay it to you later (often at lower tax rates).
Pros:

- Tax deferral
- Steady income after retirement

Cons:

- Risk if the team faces financial problems

- Less flexibility

Ask your financial team to analyze any deferred comp offers carefully.

2. Non-Qualified Plans

Big endorsement contracts sometimes offer non-qualified deferred compensation.

These don't follow normal IRS retirement rules — so they offer different risks and rewards.

Important:

You MUST know the rules before signing anything.

3. Annuities (Carefully)

Some athletes use part of their money to buy annuities that guarantee income later.

But be careful:

- Only work with fee-only fiduciaries when considering annuities.
- Avoid high-commission annuity salesmen.

Annuities can make sense **in small doses** — not as your entire strategy.

Final Encouragement: You Are the CEO of Your Future

Here's the mindset shift you need to lock in:

You are not just an athlete.

You are not just a highlight reel.

You are the **CEO of You, Inc.**

And the smartest CEOs?

- Build cash reserves.

- Invest aggressively but wisely.
- Use every available tool to lower taxes.
- Play both defense and offense with their money.
- Think about decades, not days.

You worked too hard for this opportunity to let it slip away.

Start your retirement plan like a professional — because you are one.

Not someday.

Right now.

Chapter 35: Investment Strategies for Different Career Lengths

Why Investment Strategies Must Match Your Career Timeline

When it comes to investing, one-size-fits-all advice doesn't work — especially for pro athletes.

Because here's the truth:

You are not like the typical 9-to-5 worker.

- Most workers have 40+ years to earn and save.
- You might have 3… 5… maybe 10–15 years if you're lucky.
- And your highest income might hit when you're still in your 20s — not your 50s.

That's a completely different ball game.

And it requires a completely different game plan.

Just like you wouldn't use the same offensive scheme for a football team as you would for a basketball team, you can't blindly copy how "regular people" invest.

You need to **design your financial playbook** around the career you actually have — not the career you wish you had.

Let's break it all the way down.

Step One: Know Your Career Type

Before you make a single investment move, you have to figure out **what kind of career** you're likely to have.

Here are the three main categories for athletes:

Short Career (0–5 years)

- Think: NFL players, MMA fighters, fringe NBA or WNBA players, minor league baseball players.
- Reality: You may only get a few contracts, or you might even bounce in and out of active rosters.
- Financial Strategy: **Preserve capital. Prioritize liquidity. Limit big risks.** Save like crazy, because you might be living off those savings soon.

Medium Career (5–10 years)

- Think: Established NBA or NFL starters, mid-level MLB players, NHL players who carve out a role.
- Reality: You'll have more time to build wealth, but the clock is still ticking.
- Financial Strategy: **Balance growth with safety.** Aggressively invest early, but gradually de-risk as your career progresses.

Long Career (10–20+ years)

- Think: Star athletes, franchise players, GOAT-level talents.
- Reality: You have the rare chance to generate massive wealth over a longer period.
- Financial Strategy: **Think dynasty building.** Layer your investments. Diversify aggressively. Plan for legacy and succession.

Step Two: Match Investment Strategy to Career Type

Let's walk through what investment strategies should actually look like for each type.

Short Career: "Cash is King and Safety First"

You are sprinting a short race — not running a marathon.

So your investment game plan has to reflect that.

Goals:

- Build a strong savings base.
- Avoid losing money with risky or illiquid investments.
- Preserve flexibility to pivot careers or launch businesses later.

How to Invest:

- **Maximize emergency savings.** (12–24 months of living expenses.)
- **Contribute to Roth IRA.** (You may qualify due to lower income.)
- **Consider simple index funds.** (Low-cost S&P 500 or total market ETFs.)
- **Avoid complex private deals.** (No startups, no risky real estate syndications, no high-commission annuities.)

Example:

You earn $400,000 over three years.

- Save at least 40–50% of after-tax income.
- Max out Roth IRA each year.
- Keep 60–70% of your savings in conservative investments like bonds, CDs, and high-yield savings.
- Keep only 30–40% in the stock market.

Think defense first — not offense.

You're the shutdown cornerback in this stage — not the gunslinger quarterback.

Medium Career: "Balanced Attack — Offense and Defense"

Now you've got a little breathing room.

You still need to protect yourself — but you can start swinging for bigger plays too.

Goals:

- Grow your wealth while you still have earning power.
- Start building multiple income streams.
- Prepare for life after sports gradually — not all at once.

How to Invest:

- **Split your strategy: 60% stocks, 40% bonds/cash.**
- **Open brokerage accounts** for flexibility (not just retirement accounts).
- **Buy real estate carefully.** (Primary residence first; investment properties second.)
- **Explore private deals cautiously.** (Startups, franchises, business opportunities — but only a small %.)

Example:

You earn $8 million over 7 years.

- Save/invest at least 30–40% of each year's after-tax income.
- Max out 401(k) or SEP IRA contributions annually.
- Buy a moderate home — not a mansion — and pay it off quickly if possible.
- Allocate 5–10% to "alternative" investments (but no more).

You're running a balanced offense.

You've got passing plays (growth) and running plays (safety).

You're methodically moving down the field, not chucking Hail Marys.

Long Career: "Dynasty Building Mode"

Now you're in rare air — and the stakes are even higher.

It's not just about you anymore.

It's about your kids.

Your future businesses.

Your brand.

Your legacy.

Goals:

- Protect wealth.
- Grow it responsibly.
- Avoid catastrophic losses.
- Plan for generational wealth transfer.

How to Invest:

- **Diversify like a pro.** (Stocks, bonds, real estate, businesses, private equity, venture capital.)
- **Use trusts and estate planning.** (Minimize taxes, maximize control.)
- **Work with a professional team.** (Financial advisor, CPA, attorney.)
- **Invest internationally too.** (Currency diversification is real.)

Example:

You earn $80 million over 15 years.

- Save/invest 50–60% of net income after taxes.

- Own multiple homes — but make sure they are cash flow neutral or positive if possible.
- Build a personal family office or virtual family office.
- Fund charitable foundations or endowments.
- Set up dynasty trusts for your children and grandchildren.

You are now an owner — not just a player.

Think like Magic Johnson, Serena Williams, LeBron James, or Tom Brady.

You're not just playing the game — you're owning pieces of it.

Step Three: Real-World Examples

Scenario 1: NFL Player With a 3-Year Career

- Rookie contract: $750,000 signing bonus + $1.5M over three years.
- Taxes, agent fees, and union dues reduce net earnings to about $1 million.
- Strategy:
- Max Roth IRA each year.
- Live on $100,000/year or less.
- Save the rest in conservative index funds, savings accounts.
- Build skills for post-sports career immediately.

Scenario 2: MLB Player With a 7-Year Career

- Arbitration years + 2 free agent contracts: $15M total career earnings.
- Strategy:
- Max 401(k) every year.
- Use brokerage accounts for flexibility.
- Buy real estate rental properties slowly and carefully.
- Invest 5–10% into business ventures with due diligence.

Scenario 3: NBA Franchise Star With a 15-Year Career

- Supermax contracts + endorsements = $250M total earnings.
- Strategy:
- Diversify across public markets, private markets, real estate, and operating businesses.
- Create LLCs for investments.
- Build a team of professionals.
- Set up foundations and trusts for tax planning and legacy building.

Biggest Investment Mistakes Athletes Make and How to Avoid Them

Even if you have a great strategy on paper, one bad decision can derail everything.

Let's talk about the common pitfalls — and how to sidestep them like a seasoned pro.

1. Trying to "Catch Up" with Risky Investments

Sometimes players think:

> *"I lost time. I have to make it up with a big investment."*

Wrong move.

Trying to double your money overnight usually means you **lose it overnight**.

Lesson:

Play the long game.

Safe, consistent growth beats wild swings.

Just like in baseball — you win more games hitting singles and doubles consistently than swinging for the fences every time.

2. Investing Without an Exit Plan

Before you put money into anything — a business, real estate, a stock — ask:

- **How do I get my money back?**
- **Under what conditions can I sell or cash out?**
- **What are the penalties or risks if I need cash fast?**

If you can't answer those questions, **don't invest yet**.

Lesson:

Have a clear exit strategy.

Think of it like a playbook: know your plan for 1st down, 2nd down, 3rd down — and worst-case scenarios.

3. Letting Family and Friends Manage Your Money

This is one of the biggest landmines.

They love you. You love them.

But love doesn't mean financial competence.

Would you let your cousin run your NFL offense?

Would you let your high school buddy be your NBA point guard?

Lesson:

You need trained, professional advisors — not amateurs — to manage your career off the field.

4. Overleveraging

Debt can kill you faster than a torn ACL.

Buying houses you can't afford.

Using loans to "invest" in businesses you don't understand.

Taking advances against future earnings that might never materialize.

That's like playing defense with a 6-man roster — you're always a step behind.

Lesson:

Use debt carefully, sparingly, and only with a clear repayment plan.

5. Ignoring Taxes

You might be earning $1 million, but if you're spending like you have $1 million after-tax — you're in trouble.

Depending on where you live and play, taxes could slice off **40%–50%** of your gross income.

Lesson:

Always project income **after taxes**.

Work with a real sports CPA who understands multi-state filing, jock taxes, and deductions for pro athletes.

6. Believing Your Career Will Last Forever

It won't.

Even if you're a Hall of Famer.

Even if you feel invincible today.

Even if the checks are rolling in like clockwork right now.

Father Time is undefeated.

Every athlete — **every** athlete — eventually retires.

Lesson:

Prepare for life after the game from day one.

You wouldn't walk onto the field without knowing the clock was ticking down.

Treat your financial life the same way.

Action Steps to Build Wealth While You Play

Here's how to start building a real, lasting financial legacy while you're still active.

1. Set a Real Savings Target

Aim to save at least:

- **50% of your net income** if you're in a short career sport (like NFL).
- **30–40%** if you have a more stable career path (like MLB or NBA starters).

Make saving automatic — not optional.

Set up direct transfers from your checking account into investment accounts **every paycheck**.

2. Create a Season-Based Budget

Instead of thinking "monthly," think "seasonally."

- Budget around your actual pay periods.
- Plan for **no new income** during the off-season.

Create a "salary" for yourself that you live off year-round — even when you're earning millions during the season.

This is how pros stretch an 8-month salary over 12 months — without stress.

3. Use Buckets for Different Financial Goals

Separate your money into clear "buckets":

- **Short-Term Needs** (0–2 years): emergency fund, living expenses.
- **Medium-Term Goals** (2–7 years): business startup funds, buying a home.
- **Long-Term Wealth** (7+ years): retirement accounts, brokerage accounts, private investments.

Just like you train different muscle groups in the gym, train different "financial muscles" with your money.

4. Review Investments Annually

Once a year, sit down with your financial team and ask:

- Are we still on track for my career goals?
- Should we rebalance my investments?
- Has anything in my life or the economy changed that requires adjustments?

Think of it like your annual physical or team physical.
You want to catch problems early — not once it's too late.

Sports Analogies for Saving and Investing

Since you're an athlete, let's break it down even simpler — sports style.
Football:
Saving is your offensive line.
Investing is your quarterback.
Without protection, even the best QB gets sacked.
Basketball:

Saving is your defense.

Investing is your transition offense.

Both win championships — not just one or the other.

Baseball:

Saving is your bullpen.

Investing is your starting pitcher.

You need both to close out the game.

Hockey:

Saving is your goaltender.

Investing is your forward line.

Defense wins cups — but you still need to score.

Soccer:

Saving is your back line.

Investing is your striker.

Solid foundation first, flashy wins second.

In Closing: You're the CEO of Your Financial Life

You're not just a player anymore.

You're the CEO of **You, Inc.**

You have the opportunity to create generational wealth — not just for you, but for your family and community.

But it won't happen by accident.

It will happen because you took deliberate, thoughtful, consistent steps.

Here's the mindset I want you to remember:

- Save like you might retire tomorrow.
- Invest like you might live forever.
- Protect yourself like you're your own most valuable asset — because you are.

Chapter 36: Real Estate: Home Buying Versus Renting When You Play

When you sign that first contract, when that first real check hits, when you realize you're actually living your dream — it's natural to think about buying a house. Owning your own place feels like the ultimate symbol of "I made it."

But let's slow the game down a little bit.

Just because you *can* buy a house right away doesn't always mean you *should*.

Today, we're going to break down — patiently, step by step — the decision between **buying** versus **renting** when you're a professional athlete. This isn't just about flexing with a big mansion or playing it safe in an apartment. It's about understanding your career arc, your cash flow, your risk, and your freedom — and making a smart play based on *your* situation.

This is the conversation you deserve to have — the one that looks beyond the Instagram posts and the TV shows — and really sets you up for success, peace, and power.

First, Understand This: Your Career is a Sprint and a Marathon

A lot of people will tell you your career is short. And they're right — compared to most jobs, pro sports careers are short.

But inside that short career, you've got to run a long, smart marathon with your money. Every decision — like buying or renting a home — either fuels your long game or chips away at it.

Think of it like managing your minutes in a big game. Go too hard too fast, and you gas out early. Play smart, stay steady, and you give yourself a chance to finish strong — and win.

Renting: The Pros and Cons

Let's start with renting. A lot of players hear the word "rent" and think it's throwing money away. Not true — not if you're strategic.

Pros of Renting:

- **Flexibility**: You can move easily if you get traded, cut, or signed by another team.
- **Lower upfront costs**: No down payment, no big closing costs, no property taxes.
- **No maintenance headaches**: If the water heater breaks, it's not your $5,000 problem.
- **Freedom to live close to team facilities**: Renting gives you options to be 10 minutes from the stadium instead of 45.

Cons of Renting:

- **No equity build-up**: You're paying to live there, but you're not owning the property.
- **Landlord rules**: You can't always remodel, upgrade, or even hang

stuff on the walls without permission.
- **Rent increases**: Your landlord can hike the rent when your lease is up.

Renting makes a lot of sense when you're early in your career, your roster spot isn't guaranteed yet, or you're still feeling out the city and your future.

Buying: The Pros and Cons

Now let's look at buying. It's a big move, but it's not just about the flex.

Pros of Buying:

- **Building equity**: Every payment you make is slowly building ownership.
- **Stability**: You control the property — no landlord.
- **Tax benefits**: Mortgage interest deductions can save you on taxes.
- **Pride of ownership**: It feels good to say, "This is mine."

Cons of Buying:

- **Big upfront costs**: Down payment (often 20%+), closing costs, inspections.
- **Maintenance costs**: You break it, you bought it. Roof leaks, water damage, broken HVAC — that's your tab.
- **Tied down**: If you get traded or cut, it's a lot harder and slower to sell a home than it is to end a lease.
- **Market risk**: If the real estate market dips, you could owe more than your home is worth.

Buying makes more sense when you have **stability**:

- You've signed a multi-year contract.
- You've locked in a roster spot.
- You know you want to live in that city long-term.

Real-World Scenario: The Rookie Mansion Trap

Picture this:

You just got drafted. Signing bonus cleared. First paycheck hits. Your family is proud. Your friends are calling you "the man."

You drive past this incredible mansion — five bedrooms, a theater room, pool, gated driveway — and think, "I can afford that."

So you buy it. Full flex.

But then...you get cut after year two.

No second contract.

Now you're stuck with a \$2 million house, a \$15,000 a month mortgage, \$2,500 in monthly maintenance, property taxes, insurance, utilities — and no NFL salary.

You have to sell it fast...but the market's slow. Buyers are picky.

And you end up taking a loss.

That's not building wealth. That's building stress.

Rule of Thumb: If You Wouldn't Live There Five Years, Don't Buy It

Buying a home makes sense **only** if you can see yourself living there for at least **five years** — or longer.

If you're likely to get traded, released, injured, or simply decide you want to live somewhere else soon... **rent**.

Five years minimum — that's the play.

Action Steps: What You Should Do Right Now

1. **Meet with a real estate advisor** — Someone independent, not just a friend trying to make a commission.
2. **Understand your contract** — How secure is your future with this team? How much guaranteed money do you have?
3. **Run the numbers** — Budget out everything: mortgage, taxes, insurance, maintenance. Not just the sticker price.
4. **Plan for the worst** — Could you carry the mortgage if you got cut?
5. **Be patient** — You don't have to buy a house this year just because you can.

Hidden Costs of Homeownership Players Overlook

- **Property taxes**: These aren't optional, and they vary wildly by city and state.
- **HOA fees**: Gated communities often have hefty fees you have to pay every month.
- **Maintenance reserve**: You should budget at least 1%-2% of your home's value each year for maintenance.
- **Utilities**: Bigger homes = bigger electric, gas, and water bills.
- **Insurance**: Homeowner's insurance (and flood insurance in some areas) can be pricey.
- **Security**: You may need a more serious security system, not just a Ring doorbell.

The Emotional Side of Buying

Let's keep it real.

Buying a home feels emotional. It feels personal.

It feels like "arrival."

It feels like you made it.

And you have.

But don't let emotions make decisions that money has to pay for later.

The goal isn't just to buy a home.

The goal is to build a life you can sustain and enjoy.

Sometimes the best flex isn't the biggest house.

Sometimes the best flex is having no financial stress.

Sports Analogy: Homeownership and Coaching Changes

Imagine you're a college quarterback who signs at a big program because of the head coach.

But two years later, the coach leaves. New staff, new system, new expectations.

Suddenly your situation isn't as perfect as it seemed.

Same thing with buying a house early.

You think you're signing up for one thing — but life can change fast.

Flexibility is your friend when your career is unpredictable.

Quick Tips for Players Who Do Want to Buy:

- **Buy modest**: Just because you can buy a mansion doesn't mean you should.
- **Buy for you, not your Instagram**: You're the one paying that mortgage. Not your followers.
- **Stay liquid**: Don't drain all your cash for a down payment. Keep cash reserves strong.
- **Think resale**: If you had to sell it tomorrow, would anyone want to buy it?

Closing Real Talk

Buying a home is one of the biggest financial moves you'll make.

But it's not a trophy.

It's not a race.

It's a *responsibility*.

Whether you rent or buy, the goal is the same:

Live well, build wealth, and protect your career while it's still paying you.

You have options.

You have time.

And you have the power to make choices today that will make your future self proud.

Stay patient.

Stay smart.

Stay steady.

The house can wait.

Your future can't.

What Happens When Players Buy Too Early?

Let's not sugarcoat it — real estate mistakes are one of the fastest ways to fumble a good financial start.

Buying a huge house after your rookie deal but getting cut before you see a second contract is a story that plays out every single year in every single league.

Sometimes it's not even the player's fault.

The team's GM gets fired.

A new coach comes in with a new system.

A bad injury changes your career path overnight.

The economy crashes and housing prices drop 20%.

And suddenly, that $2 million house you bought because "you were supposed to" becomes an anchor.

You're paying for it whether you're playing or not.

You're paying for it whether you love the city or not.

You're paying for it whether your life fits it or not.

Flexibility = survival early in your career.

Locking yourself into a massive mortgage too soon kills flexibility.

Renting: The Veteran Move (Not the Rookie Mistake)

Here's something that doesn't get said enough:

Veteran players who have been around 5, 8, 10+ years — many of them **still rent**.

Why?

Because they understand this game.

They know that even if they're a starter this season, it can change fast.

They've seen friends get traded, injured, or even quietly blackballed from the league.

They know renting isn't "wasting money."

It's buying **flexibility** and **mental freedom**.

Real talk: The smartest thing you can sometimes do in Year 1 or Year 2 is to rent a simple, nice, but affordable place close to the facility.

Focus on your career.

Stack your money.

Wait until the dust settles.

Then *if* you're still with the team in a few years?

Then you can buy — and buy smart.

Red Flags Before Buying

Before you even *think* about buying a home during your playing career, run through this checklist:

- Am I guaranteed a roster spot for the next three seasons?

- Is my contract mostly guaranteed, or am I week-to-week?
- Am I emotionally buying just because it "looks good"?
- Do I have enough liquid savings to cover 6-12 months of mortgage, taxes, and living expenses if my income stopped?
- Have I factored in maintenance, property taxes, HOA fees, insurance, and utilities — not just the mortgage payment?

If you answer "no" or "I don't know" to any of those questions, **press pause**.

Rent for now.

Buy when you're ready — not when people expect you to be ready.

Advanced Strategy: Buying Investment Properties (Not Just Mansions)

Here's a way to flip the script:

Instead of buying a huge house for yourself right away...

What about buying a **small rental property** in a growing market?

For example:

- A 3-bedroom house near a college town.
- A duplex where you rent out one side.
- A small single-family home in a city with rising job growth.

You don't have to live there.

It can quietly collect rent checks while you play.

That's how you start building **real wealth** — not by showing off, but by letting your money work while you work.

Sports Analogy: Buying a House is Like Signing a Long-Term Contract

Imagine you're a free agent.

You're looking at teams.

One team offers you a three-year deal, but they have a new coaching staff that might not be around next season.

Another team offers a two-year deal, but it's a better fit and a more stable organization.

Where do you sign?

Smart players know — it's not just about the size of the deal.

It's about the stability, the system, the fit, and the likelihood of success.

Buying a house is the same.

It's not just about the size of the home.

It's about whether it fits your *real* life and career situation.

Myth-Busting: "Real Estate Always Goes Up"

Let's be clear:

Real estate does NOT always go up.

Especially if:

- You're forced to sell quickly (fire sale pricing).
- The market crashes (like 2008).
- You overpaid at the top of the market because you weren't patient.
- Your neighborhood starts declining instead of improving.

Real estate is **a good investment when done patiently and smartly** — not when done emotionally and recklessly.

Buying just because your teammates are buying is like running someone else's race — you'll never win your own that way.

The Emotional Traps Around Real Estate

Let's break down some of the emotional traps athletes fall into:

- **Keeping up with the locker room**: "He bought a mansion, so I need to, too."
- **Trying to impress family and friends**: "I want to show everyone back home that I made it."
- **Feeling rushed**: "I'm supposed to have a big house by now, right?"
- **Confusing 'things' with 'success'**: "If I don't own a house, does that mean I'm not successful?"

The truth?

Success is freedom.

Not debt.

Not stress.

Not trying to look like you're winning while quietly drowning inside.

Renting Wisely: How to Do It Right

If you decide renting is your best move for now, here are some pro tips:

- **Get a short-term lease**: 6 or 12 months at a time — max flexibility.
- **Rent close to the facility**: Save time, gas, and your mental energy.
- **Keep rent reasonable**: 10%-20% of your after-tax monthly income — not half your check.
- **Treat it like a home**: Stay professional. Pay on time. Maintain the place. You're representing yourself.
- **Stay low-key**: You don't have to live in the flashiest high-rise or the hottest zip code.

Buying Smart: What to Look For If You Do Buy

If you're **truly ready** to buy, here's your game plan:

- **Resale value**: Will other people want to buy this house later?
- **Location, location, location**: Proximity to good schools, highways, and basic amenities matter even if you don't have kids.
- **Low maintenance**: Simpler houses = fewer headaches.
- **Affordability**: Can you easily afford it on your *base salary* alone — not counting bonuses or endorsements?
- **Personal connection**: Do you *love* it for yourself, or are you buying it to impress others?

Final Word: Play the Long Game

You've already beaten the odds by making it this far.

Now beat the odds by making smart, patient decisions with your money.

Whether it's real estate, investing, endorsements, or lifestyle choices —

Play the long game.

Renting early in your career isn't a failure.

It's a flex.

Buying later when you're truly stable isn't luck.

It's strategy.

You are your own biggest asset.

Protect yourself.

Move smart.

Live free.

Your future deserves that much.

Chapter 37: Avoiding "Business Deals" Your Friends Suggest

Introduction: The First Call After You Make It

The moment your name flashes across ESPN...

The moment you sign your contract...

The moment you deposit that first big check...

It starts.

The phone calls.

The DMs.

The texts that say "Hey bro, I got this crazy idea..."

The people who never answered your calls before now calling you every week.

Business deals, investment opportunities, "can't miss" ideas, family projects, dreams, visions — all of it starts flowing your way.

And every single one of them sounds like it's wrapped in love, loyalty, and destiny.

They'll say things like:

- "This is bigger than just you — it's for the whole community."
- "We're family. We gotta build something together."
- "You can make double your money in six months!"
- "This is the move. Trust me."

But here's the reality most people won't tell you:

These "business deals" are the single biggest financial landmine pro athletes face.

And if you don't slow down, protect yourself, and move wisely, they can blow up everything you worked so hard to build.

Why This Happens: The Psychological Side

Before we even break down the financial mistakes, let's talk about the emotional side — because that's what they prey on.

- **Guilt**: You feel guilty for having more money than the people you grew up with.
- **Loyalty**: You want to help the people who supported you when you had nothing.
- **Survivor's Remorse**: You wonder why you made it when others didn't, and feel like you owe it to them to share.
- **Pride**: You want to show your people that you didn't forget where you came from.
- **Fear**: You worry they'll think you changed if you say no.

These emotions make you vulnerable — **even when the business deal makes no sense.**

And that's how a lot of great athletes, smart people, and good-hearted human beings end up broke.

A Real Talk Reality Check: You Are Not a Venture Capitalist

Let's just keep it real:

You're a professional athlete.

You worked for years to master your sport.

You are the CEO of your body, your career, and your brand.

But you are not a professional investor, venture capitalist, or private equity shark.

And you shouldn't be pretending to be one just because someone you know pitches you a business idea.

Even the best venture capitalists — the people who do this full time, professionally, with a team of researchers — lose money on **most** of their investments.

Think about that.

The pros, with millions of dollars and armies of accountants and analysts, still strike out **more than they hit**.

If they can get it wrong, what do you think your high school buddy with no business experience, no financial plan, and a dream of opening a car wash knows?

The 5 Most Common "Friend Business Pitches" (and Why You Should Say No)

1. The Restaurant or Bar Deal

Pitch: "We'll open the hottest sports bar in town! Everyone will come because you're famous!"

Reality:

Restaurants and bars have a **75%-80% failure rate** within the first five years.

Your name might fill the tables for a month.

After that, it's about management, marketing, margins — things your friends probably don't know.

Lesson: If you want a restaurant, be a silent investor once you're retired — not during your career.

2. The Clothing Line or Brand

Pitch: "Let's start a clothing line! You wear it, people will buy it!"

Reality:

The fashion industry is brutally competitive.

Building a brand from scratch takes **millions**, relentless work, and marketing genius.

Celebrity alone is not enough — not even for actual celebrities.

Lesson: If you're serious about branding, hire a professional team and do it right.

3. The Record Label or Studio

Pitch: "We'll launch a label! Everyone's got talent, we just need backing!"

Reality:

The music industry is full of heartbreak.

Talent is common.

Hits are rare.

And throwing money at a few mixtapes isn't a business plan.

Lesson: If you love music, support local artists — but don't dump six figures into your cousin's mixtape dreams.

4. The Real Estate "Flip" Deal

Pitch: "We buy a house, fix it up, flip it for double!"

Reality:

Good flips are hard to find.

Renovations cost way more than you think.

Markets change fast.

Most flips lose money without experienced contractors, realtors, and project managers.

Lesson: Real estate can be great — but not through your buddy's "YouTube-certified" flipping plan.

5. The Cryptocurrency/Scheme/Hot New Thing

Pitch: "Bro, crypto/NFTs/forex trading/sports gambling is where the money's at!"

Reality:

If they truly had a can't-miss strategy, they wouldn't need your money.

Hot new things are usually **hot because they're about to burn out**.

Lesson: Build slow. Build steady. Build for the long haul.

10 Red Flags That a "Business Opportunity" Is a Bad Idea

1. There's no formal written business plan.
2. They can't show you real financial projections.
3. They say "Trust me" instead of "Here's the data."
4. They want you to fund 90%-100% of it.
5. They have no experience in the industry.
6. They promise returns that sound too good to be true.
7. They get defensive when you ask hard questions.
8. They have no legal documents drawn up by a real attorney.
9. They want you to sign something immediately, no time to review.
10. They tie your friendship or loyalty to whether you invest.

If you see even **one** of these red flags?

Walk away.

No explanation needed.

Protect your peace.

Action Steps: How to Handle It Without Burning Bridges

You don't have to be rude.

You don't have to blow up relationships.

You just need to stand firm.

Here's what you can say:

> *"Hey, I appreciate you thinking of me. I'm flattered you trust me. But right now, I'm staying focused on my career and my long-term financial security. I'm not investing in outside businesses at this time. Hope you understand."*

That's it.

No apologies.

No debates.

No loopholes.

If they get mad?

That tells you everything you need to know.

Real friends respect boundaries.

Users get mad when you stop letting them use you.

Sports Analogy: Protecting Your Locker Room

Think of your financial life like a championship locker room.

You worked for years to build a winning culture around yourself.

Coaches. Teammates. Training staff.

Every person in that locker room has to earn their spot.

Everyone has to pull their weight.

Would you let someone who never trained, never practiced, and didn't even know the playbook show up and start calling plays?

Of course not.

So why would you let someone who has no financial track record control your money?

Protect your locker room.

Protect your circle.

Protect your money.

Closing: You Don't Owe Anyone a Shortcut

You can love people without funding their dreams.

You can honor your past without sinking your future.

You can support your community without risking everything you've worked for.

Here's the truth no one tells you:

You don't owe anyone your money.

Not your cousin.

Not your neighbor.

Not your old teammate.

Not even your childhood best friend.

What you owe — to yourself, to your family, and to your future — is to be wise.

To be steady.

To protect the opportunity you earned.

Because here's the final play:

You are not just a player.

You are a business.

You are a brand.

You are an empire in progress.

Move like it.

Decide like it.

Protect it like it.

That's how you build wealth that lasts long after the crowd stops cheering.

What If You Really Want to Help Someone?

Let's be real: sometimes it's not just random people hitting you up.

Sometimes it's people you *love.*

People who *really were* there for you.

Maybe it's your best friend who used to give you rides to practice when you didn't have a car.

Maybe it's your uncle who bought you cleats when your family couldn't afford them.

Maybe it's your brother who took care of things while you were away at school.

You *want* to help. You *feel* like you owe them.

So how do you do it **without blowing yourself up**?

Here's the key:

Help responsibly.

Support smartly.

Give — without giving away your foundation.

And here's how.

3 Safer Ways to Help Without Risking Everything

1. Give Small, One-Time Gifts — Not Investments

If you want to thank someone, **give a gift.**

A one-time, no-strings-attached check.

- "Hey, here's $10,000. No payback needed."
- "Here's a car paid in full."
- "Here's a scholarship to go back to school."

That's generosity. That's love.

But it's **contained**.

You know what you're giving.

You control the size.

You know it's gone and you're fine with that.

You're not tying yourself to a risky business for years to come.

2. Create Boundaries Early

You need to decide, **before** the phone calls start, how much you're willing to give.

Set a personal "giving budget."

Maybe it's:

- 5% of your signing bonus
- $50,000 total
- One-time help only, not ongoing support

Decide early — not when you're emotional.

Otherwise, the "asks" will keep growing until it drains you.

3. Invest in Your People's Education, Not Their Business Idea

If you really want to help someone build a business?

Pay for them to take a business class first.

Pay for them to meet with a real financial advisor.

Pay for them to work with a business coach.

If they won't invest the time to learn?

They have no business managing your money.

If they do?

Maybe down the road you can revisit it.

But education always comes first.

Not "good vibes."

Not promises.

Not childhood memories.

Financial Landmines: Business + Family = Disaster

Here's why mixing business with friends and family is so dangerous:

1. **Emotions make you ignore red flags.**
2. **You lose your leverage — you can't fire them easily.**
3. **If the business fails, you don't just lose money. You lose the relationship.**
4. **It becomes a loyalty test — and loyalty should never be tied to money.**

Money should **never** be what defines your family ties.

It should **never** be what determines your friendships.

And yet, once money enters the picture — it *does,* unless you protect yourself up front.

The "Yes Trap" Athletes Fall Into (And How to Escape It)

The "yes trap" looks like this:

- First you say yes to one thing ("small" favor).
- Then another.
- Then another.
- Then suddenly you're on the hook for someone else's entire dream.

And every time you try to pull back, they guilt trip you:

"You helped him, why not me?"

"You changed."

"You forgot where you came from."

Here's your play:

Expect the guilt.

Prepare for it.

Stand firm anyway.

You are not their bank.

You are not their lottery ticket.

You are not their backup plan.

Real Athlete Stories: The Warning Signs Are Always There

You don't hear about them in the media much.

But every locker room has them.

Athletes who lost it all — not because they were reckless — but because they were *too trusting*.

- The NFL player who funded his cousin's trucking company. $1.2 million — gone.
- The NBA player who invested in a nightclub in his hometown. It shut down after 18 months. He lost $800,000 and his relationship with his brother.
- The WNBA star who co-signed a business loan for a "friend" — and got stuck repaying $350,000 after the business failed.
- The MLB pitcher who trusted his uncle to "flip houses" — and wound up with three foreclosed properties and a broken family.

It's real.

It's painful.

It's preventable.

The signs were there.

They just didn't know how to say no.

Script for Saying No — Without Starting Drama

When someone approaches you with a business deal, here's what you can say:

> *"I appreciate you thinking of me. I really do. But I made a*

commitment to myself, my family, and my advisors that I'm not investing in businesses right now. I'm focused on building a stable financial future first."

Simple. Respectful. Clear.

If they push back?

Just repeat it.

You don't have to debate.

You don't have to explain.

You don't have to defend yourself.

You are the CEO of your financial future.

You set the policy.

You enforce it.

Period.

In Closing: You're Playing for Legacy, Not Likes

At the end of the day, you didn't work this hard just to buy fancy cars, post on Instagram, or make everyone else rich.

You worked for:

- Freedom
- Security
- Generational wealth
- Purpose

You're building a legacy.

You are playing a much bigger game than they realize.

And sometimes — as painful as it feels — the smartest thing you can do for your future, your family, and your community is **to say no.**

Because every no you say to a bad deal is a yes to:

- Your future kids' college education

- Your parents' peace of mind
- Your own retirement dreams
- The causes you actually care about

Stay focused.

Stay disciplined.

Stay true to the bigger mission.

You are not just here to make it.

You're here to last.

Chapter 38: Saying "No" to Family Without Guilt

The Hardest Defense You'll Ever Play

You've battled for every inch of your dream.

You've put in the work nobody sees — early mornings, injuries, setbacks, sacrifice.

And now, you've made it.

Not just to the league — but to a level of financial opportunity few people ever touch.

And here comes your next opponent.

Not an opponent on the court, the field, or the ice.

An opponent standing right in your own kitchen.

Family.

It's not an enemy. It's love. It's loyalty. It's guilt. It's expectations.

And if you don't learn to **defend your financial future with wisdom and compassion**,

you can lose everything you fought for — faster than you ever thought possible.

Why This Chapter Matters So Much

Let's get real.

The average pro career is short.

Way shorter than anyone expects.

NFL: about 3.3 years.

NBA: about 4.5 years.

MLB: about 5.6 years.

WNBA: even shorter.

That's it.

That's your window.

That's your earning prime.

The time to build generational wealth is **now**.

If you spend those years letting family obligations, guilt, and emotional decisions drain your resources?

You're setting yourself up for a post-career struggle.

No matter how much you love them.

No matter how much you feel you "owe" them.

You cannot save everyone.

You must protect yourself first —

because **if you don't**,

there won't be anything left to protect anyone else with later.

Why Family Asks Feel Different (and Hurt More)

When a business partner or an agent crosses you, you can cut them off.

Business is business.

When a cousin, a sibling, or a parent asks for money?

It feels personal.

It hits your soul.

Because it's not just about money.

It's about:

- Loyalty
- Love
- Shared history
- Survivor's guilt
- Cultural expectations
- The belief that "if one of us makes it, we all make it"

The pressure is **real**.

Especially if you come from a community that didn't have wealth before you.

Sports analogies apply here too.

It's like being the starting quarterback — everyone expects you to carry the whole team,

even when your shoulder's about to give out.

The Myth of the Endless Bank Account

Let's kill a lie right now:

Just because you're a pro athlete,

does **not** mean you can afford to pay everyone's bills forever.

Here's the math they don't see:

- Your contract isn't all yours — taxes, agent fees, union dues, expenses
- Your career isn't guaranteed — injuries, trades, cuts happen fast
- Your future isn't cheap — lifestyle, family, retirement, health care

You're not "selfish" for saying no.

You're being **smart**.

You're being **responsible**.

You're being the adult your family actually needs — even if they don't realize it yet.

Why You Need a "No" Game Plan (Before They Ask)

You would never walk onto the field without a defensive scheme.

You need one for money, too.

Here's how you build it.

Step 1: Set Your Personal Rules Before the Season Starts

Decide your giving rules **before** the calls come in:

- Will you help at all?
- Who will you help?
- How much will you help?
- Under what conditions?
- How many times?

Example:

"I will give one-time $5,000 gifts to immediate family only — no ongoing support — and only after I meet my personal savings targets."

Clear.

Simple.

Non-negotiable.

Step 2: Separate Love from Money

Here's the truth:

- You can love people deeply and still say no.
- You can honor your roots without funding every idea.
- You can stay connected without staying broke.

Love is not proven through checks.

It's proven through presence, respect, and healthy boundaries.

Step 3: Practice Saying "No" Out Loud

It sounds silly — but **practice it**.
Because when the emotions hit,
you'll freeze if you haven't rehearsed.
Practice phrases like:

- "I'm not in a position to fund that right now."
- "I've made a commitment to my long-term goals and can't invest in outside ventures."
- "I love you, but I can't take this on financially."

Say it in the mirror.
Say it in the car.
Get comfortable hearing yourself say it.

Step 4: Use Trusted Advisors As Your "Bad Cop"

Sometimes it's easier to say:
"My financial advisor said I can't do that."
Blame them.
That's part of what you pay them for.
It lets you stay loving and relational — while still holding the line.
Coaches do it all the time.
They take the heat so the players can keep playing.
Same idea here.

Step 5: Build a Legacy, Not a Leash

When you say no to bad money requests, you say yes to:

- Sending your future kids to college debt-free
- Owning your own businesses on your terms

- Funding scholarships for your community one day
- Taking care of your parents long-term, not just short-term

You're not turning your back on your people.
You're building a real foundation for them.

What Happens If You Keep Saying Yes

If you always say yes to every request, here's what's coming:

- Requests will **grow bigger, not smaller.**
- Respect for you will **decrease, not increase.**
- Dependence will **increase, not decrease.**
- Resentment will **build quietly** — both yours and theirs.

Eventually you'll either:

- Go broke trying to keep up
- Feel trapped and bitter
- Break relationships anyway — but with financial wreckage attached

What Happens If You Learn to Say No

If you learn to say no with grace and firmness, here's what can happen:

- You'll earn real respect over time
- You'll teach others financial boundaries
- You'll create space for real independence and growth
- You'll build something lasting for your family

It won't always be pretty at first.
Some people will be mad.
Some will guilt-trip you.

Some might even stop speaking to you for a while.

But the right people — the ones who truly love you — will eventually understand.

And you will have protected the future God, fate, or hard work blessed you with.

Final Words: You Are Not a Checkbook. You Are a Chainbreaker.

You were not put on this earth to be a walking ATM.

You are more than your contract.

You are more than your income.

You are a pioneer.

You are a first-generation wealth builder.

You are changing your family's future —

and sometimes the price of real change

is disappointing people who want the old patterns to continue.

Stand tall.

Stay humble.

But stay strong.

Because you're not just playing for now.

You're playing for forever.

And saying "no" — with love, with respect, and with firmness — is one of the most powerful, courageous, leadership moves you'll ever make.

10 Quick Ways to Say No Without Feeling Guilty

When the request comes in — and it **will** — you don't have to panic, freeze, or feel trapped.

Here are 10 go-to ways to respectfully but firmly protect your future:

1. **"I'm on a strict financial plan right now, and I can't take on**

any extra commitments."

2. **"I'm focused on building long-term stability. Right now, that means saying no to outside requests."**
3. **"I'm working with a financial advisor who has me on a tight structure. I have to stick to it."**
4. **"That's not something I can do, but I'm wishing you all the best with it."**
5. **"I love you, but financially, I have to stay in my lane to reach my goals."**
6. **"My future commitments are already set. I can't add anything new right now."**
7. **"I'm choosing to invest in my financial security so I can support my family long-term, not just short-term."**
8. **"Right now, my priority is saving and protecting what I've worked for."**
9. **"I'm not in a position to fund that, but I'm cheering you on."**
10. **"This doesn't fit into the boundaries I've set for my financial life. I hope you understand."**

Quick Reminder

You are not being selfish.

You are being strategic.

You are not abandoning your family.

You are building something that could bless them for generations — if you protect it now.

Saying "no" **today** means saying "yes" to security, opportunity, and freedom **tomorrow**.

You've got this.

Financial Red Flags When Family Asks for Money

Not every ask is a crisis you have to solve.

Not every request is healthy.

Not every opportunity is real.

Watch for these warning signs before you say yes:

1. **They expect a fast answer and pressure you to decide immediately.**
2. **They downplay the amount — "It's just a small favor" — but have no clear repayment plan.**
3. **They bring guilt into the conversation — "After everything I've done for you..."**
4. **They want a *gift* but are talking like it's a *loan* (with no intention of paying it back).**
5. **They have asked multiple times before without honoring previous agreements.**
6. **They have no written plan, no budget, and no accountability for the money they're asking for.**
7. **They refuse to let you consult your financial advisor or agent before answering.**
8. **They use your success as justification — "You make millions, what's $20,000 to you?"**
9. **They threaten the relationship if you say no — "You forgot where you came from."**
10. **You feel anxious, resentful, or trapped even *thinking* about saying yes.**

Quick Real Talk

Family is important.

But saving them **today** at the expense of your financial future could mean **both** of you drown later.

Love doesn't mean giving money you can't afford to lose.

Real love is protecting yourself *and* building a strong enough foundation to truly help when the time is right.

Protect your career.

Protect your future.

Protect your peace.

If You Must Say Yes Checklist

Sometimes, even with all the red flags, you may still decide — in your heart — that you want to help.

If you do, protect yourself and your future by following these steps:

1. Decide the amount you're willing to lose — and expect not to get it back.

Treat it like a *gift*, even if they call it a loan. If you can't afford to lose it and still stay financially strong, don't do it.

2. Put the agreement in writing.

No matter how close you are.

Simple. Clear. Signed by both sides.

Include how much is being given, whether it's a gift or loan, repayment terms if any, and consequences if not honored.

3. Use a third party when possible.

Have your financial advisor, CPA, or attorney help draft the document.

This removes emotion and makes it a business decision, not just a family favor.

4. Set clear expectations — and stick to them.

If it's a gift, say it's a one-time gift.

If it's a loan, make sure they understand the terms — and you are comfortable enforcing them if needed.

5. Never co-sign loans or mortgages.

Never.

You are tying your financial future to someone else's choices.

If they default, *you* pay — financially *and* emotionally.

6. Keep it separate from your core financial plan.

This should not affect your retirement savings, emergency fund, or core investments.

If helping them forces you to weaken your own future, the answer needs to be no.

7. Set a firm boundary going forward.

Helping once doesn't mean you have to help forever.

Be clear: "This is a one-time gift based on where I am right now. In the future, I need to focus on my long-term family stability."

8. Avoid becoming the family ATM.

If multiple family members hear you helped once, others may come asking.

Prepare a standard, polite response:

"I'm working with a financial advisor now. All my budgets and charitable plans are already set."

9. Remember that you are not selfish — you are being smart.

Taking care of your own financial security *first* means you'll be in a better place to help others *later* — if and when it makes sense.

10. Trust your gut.

If something feels off — even if you can't explain why — pause.

Say, "I need some time to think about it."

Pressure and guilt are not good reasons to give away your hard-earned wealth.

Real Talk Wrap-Up

Helping family can be beautiful — when it's done wisely, intentionally, and without jeopardizing your own future.

But no matter what, **your first responsibility is to protect the opportunity you fought for** — because if you lose it, you can't help anybody.

Remember:

Strong boundaries are not a betrayal.

Strong boundaries are love with wisdom.

Sample Script: How to Say No (or Yes With Limits)

You don't have to be mean.

You don't have to explain your entire budget.

You *do* have to protect yourself.

Here's a few real-world ways you can say it, depending on the situation:

If You're Saying "No" Politely but Firmly:

> ***"I love you, but right now I'm focused on building my long-term financial security. I'm not in a position to give or loan money right now. I hope you can understand."***

If You Need to Delay the Answer (Buying Time):

> ***"I appreciate you thinking of me. Let me talk to my financial team and get back to you."***
>
> (Then use that time to actually decide — with no pressure.)

If You're Giving a One-Time Gift and Want to Set a Boundary:

> ***"I'm willing to give [this specific amount] as a one-time gift to help out. But I want to be clear that this isn't something I can continue doing in the future. My focus has to stay on long-term financial stability."***

If You're Saying "No" After They Keep Pressuring You:

> ***"I've made my decision, and I need you to respect it. I'm working with a financial team, and all my financial plans are locked in. Please know it's not personal — it's about protecting my future."***

If You're Feeling Guilty and Want to Acknowledge It Without Giving In:

> ***"I understand why you're asking, and it's hard for me to say no. But I have to be responsible with what I've worked so hard to build. I can't say yes, even though I care about you."***

Key Phrases to Remember

When you're in the moment and it's emotional, here are simple phrases you can keep in your back pocket:

- **"I have a financial plan I'm committed to."**
- **"My budget doesn't allow for that."**
- **"I'm not able to do that, but I wish you the best."**
- **"I have to stick to my priorities."**
- **"This is not something I can support financially."**

Final Thought

Setting financial boundaries doesn't make you a bad person.

It makes you a responsible one.

You are not just protecting your money — you are protecting your future family, your peace of mind, and your ability to thrive beyond your playing days.

The people who truly love you will understand — even if it takes time.

The ones who don't?

That's not about you.

That's about them.

Own your future.

Own your financial life.

And remember: saying "no" today can often mean saying "yes" to a stronger, freer, more powerful life tomorrow.

Chapter 39: Gifting vs. Enabling — How to Help Smartly

When you finally sign your first big contract, everything changes — not just for you, but for everyone around you.

Suddenly, people see you differently.

Suddenly, people treat you differently.

Suddenly, people *expect* things from you.

Some of those people love you.

Some of them just love what they think you can give them.

And sometimes, even the people who truly love you can unintentionally start leaning on you in unhealthy ways.

Here's the reality no one tells you early enough:

There's a massive difference between gifting and enabling.

One builds love, freedom, and dignity.

The other builds resentment, dependence, and dysfunction.

You have to know the difference — or you could spend your whole career working hard for everyone else's peace while losing your own.

Let's break it all the way down.

What Is Gifting?

Gifting is when you choose — freely, joyfully, intentionally — to give something to someone without strings attached, because you want to.

It's an act of generosity.

It's planned.

It fits within your budget.

It's given without expectation of repayment, loyalty, or "owed favors" down the road.

It's like when a quarterback throws a perfect pass — and doesn't expect the wide receiver to hand it back at the 30-yard line.

It's clean.

It's complete.

It moves the game forward.

A gift is given from a place of abundance and security — not from fear, guilt, pressure, or manipulation.

What Is Enabling?

Enabling is very different.

Enabling happens when you *give* — but it doesn't actually help the person.

It props up bad habits.

It removes consequences.

It delays their growth.

And most dangerously?

It creates emotional chains between you and them.

Chains made of guilt.

Chains made of obligation.

Chains that eventually weigh you both down.

If you've ever felt resentful after giving money to someone you love, chances are it wasn't really a gift — it was enabling.

It's like constantly bailing out a teammate who refuses to practice.

At first, you think you're helping.

But after a while, you realize:

You're just delaying the inevitable — and exhausting yourself in the process.

Signs You're Gifting

- You feel good about it — not guilty, obligated, or resentful.
- You've budgeted for it and planned it ahead of time.
- You're not risking your own financial future.
- You're not expecting anything back (money, loyalty, favors, credit).
- You would still make the gift even if no one else ever knew about it.

Signs You're Enabling

- You feel pressure, guilt, or fear when saying yes.
- You're giving because you're afraid of disappointing someone.
- You keep rescuing the same person from the same problems over and over.
- You're risking your own stability to solve someone else's repeated crisis.
- You feel resentment afterward, but you don't feel free to say so.

Why Athletes Are Especially Vulnerable to This

You already know.

Because your family saw the grind.

They saw the practices.

The injuries.

The sacrifices.

The long bus rides.

The meals you couldn't afford.

The dreams they believed in with you.

Now that the checks are real, some family members and friends feel like they *deserve* a piece of it.

And if you're like a lot of athletes, you might feel like you owe them, too.

That's a heavy emotional weight to carry — especially when you're

21, 22, 23 years old, standing on the cusp of a career you worked your whole life to build.

But here's the truth:

You don't owe anyone your future.

You can be grateful.

You can be generous.

You can be loving.

But you cannot afford to sacrifice your financial peace because you're scared to disappoint people.

How to Help Without Hurting (Yourself or Them)

If you want to give — do it *smartly.*

Here's how:

1. Set an Annual Family Gift Budget

Create a line item in your budget for family support, just like you would for training, housing, taxes, or investing.

Example:

> *"Every year, I'm allocating $20,000 for family gifting — total."*

If you use it up?

That's it for the year.

No guilt.

No exceptions.

No explanations.

2. Never Give More Than You Can Afford to Lose

If you're going to give someone money, treat it like a permanent goodbye.

No expectations of repayment.

No bitterness if it doesn't work out.

If you can't afford to lose it without hurting yourself — you can't afford to give it.

Period.

3. Make It Clear: Gifts Are Gifts, Not Loans

Don't call it a loan unless you're truly structuring it like a loan — with signed agreements, clear repayment terms, and legal backing.

Otherwise, it's a gift — and you need to treat it like one.

Blurred lines create broken relationships.

4. Give in Ways That Empower, Not Enable

Instead of just handing over cash, consider these smarter ways to help:

- Pay directly for education (tuition, books).
- Fund professional training programs.
- Offer business seed money — but with accountability, contracts, and performance benchmarks.
- Buy essential needs (groceries, medical expenses) instead of handing out blank checks.

Remember: You want your money to *build people up*, not *bail people out*.

The Gifting Decision Checklist

Before you give, run through this quick gut-check:

- Am I giving out of love, not guilt?
- Is this amount budgeted and affordable?
- Will this truly help them long-term, or just solve a short-term problem?
- Would I still give this even if no one else knew?
- Can I walk away without expecting anything in return?

If you can answer yes to all of these?

Gift freely.

If not?

Pause.

Re-evaluate.

The Enabling Danger Zone

Here's the harsh truth:

If you enable people financially, it *will* eventually hurt your relationships.

At first, they'll feel grateful.

Then they'll start expecting.

Then they'll start resenting — because dependence breeds resentment over time.

You can either love people *with boundaries* now…

Or risk losing them completely later.

Real-Life Story: Two Paths

Let's say two rookies get drafted.

Rookie A decides he'll say yes to every family request.

He buys mom a house.

Puts cousins on payroll.

Pays off everyone's car loans.

Funds business ideas with no accountability.

Five years later?

The money runs dry.

The family falls apart in bitterness, accusations, and broken trust.

Rookie B sets boundaries early.

Gives small, planned gifts.

Says no to handouts but yes to support that builds independence.

Five years later?

His family relationships are strong.

His finances are stable.

And everyone respects the boundaries he built.

Which path do you want?

Final Encouragement

Being generous is beautiful.

Being wise is essential.

You can — and should — do both.

Remember:

You are not just building wealth for today.

You are building a legacy for the next 40, 50, 60 years.

Protect it.

Nurture it.

Grow it.

Gifting should be a blessing — not a burden.

Choose wisely.

And don't forget:

Saying "no" today doesn't make you a bad person.

It makes you a good steward of the future you fought so hard to earn.

Sample Scripts for Smart Gifting and Saying No

Sometimes, the hardest part isn't knowing *what* to do — it's knowing *how* to say it.

Especially when it's someone you love.

Especially when you don't want to sound selfish or stingy.

You're not just managing money here — you're managing emotions, history, family dynamics, and expectations.

That's heavy.

Having the right words ready can take a huge weight off your shoulders.

Here are some real-life scripts you can use or adapt to fit your situation.

If You Want to Say "Yes" to a Smart Gift

Script 1: Tuition Support

> *"I believe in you and your future. I can contribute $5,000 toward your college tuition this year. I'll send it directly to the school."*

Why it works:

It's specific, it's a one-time gift (not an open-ended checkbook), and it keeps you in control of how the money is used.

Script 2: Helping With Essentials

> *"I know things are tight. I'd be happy to cover your next two months of groceries. I'll send you a prepaid grocery card this week."*

Why it works:

You're offering tangible, temporary support — not setting up an endless ATM relationship.

If You Need to Say "No" (Without Guilt)

Script 3: Polite but Firm

> *"Right now, my financial plan is completely locked in for the year. I'm not able to help with that, but I'm rooting for you."*

Why it works:

It's kind but clear. You're not inviting negotiation.

Script 4: Redirecting to Empower

> *"I'm not in a position to fund that right now, but I'd be happy to help brainstorm other ways you could make it happen."*

Why it works:

You're offering support — emotional, not financial.

If You're Getting Pressured After Saying No

Script 5: Boundary Reinforcement

> *"I understand it's disappointing. But I have to stick to my financial boundaries. It's not personal — it's about protecting my future and making sure I can be there long-term for the people I love."*

Why it works:

It reframes the conversation. Boundaries = love and protection, not rejection.

If Someone Tries to Guilt-Trip You

Script 6: Calm Deflection

> *"I appreciate everything you've done for me. That doesn't change my need to make careful financial decisions today. I hope you can respect that."*

Why it works:
It acknowledges their feelings but doesn't crumble under emotional pressure.

Quick Reminders When Saying "No"

- You don't have to justify, argue, or overexplain.
- Short and kind is better than long and defensive.
- "No" is a full sentence.
- You're not selfish — you're being smart.

The "If You Must Say Yes" Checklist (Expanded)

If you are considering saying yes — run through this checklist before pulling the trigger:

- **Have I budgeted for this?**
- **Can I afford to lose this money permanently?**
- **Is this a one-time gift — not an ongoing obligation?**
- **Does this help the person grow, not just survive another month?**
- **Have I made the terms crystal clear?**
- **Would I feel peaceful even if I never got thanked?**
- **Am I giving from a place of strength, not fear or guilt?**

If the answer to all these is YES?

Go ahead — gift freely.

If not?

You need to pause.

Maybe even say no.

Sports Analogy: Gifting Is Like Training; Enabling Is Like Spotting Too Much

Think about lifting weights.

When a coach *spots* you on the bench press, they don't lift the bar for you.

They give just enough help to keep you from getting crushed — but you're doing the work.

That's gifting.

Now imagine if every time you tried to lift, the coach grabbed the bar and did all the lifting.

You'd get weaker, not stronger.

That's enabling.

Helping smartly means letting people grow their own strength — not carrying all their weight for them.

A Real-Life NFL Story (No Names)

There was a first-round draft pick — huge money, instant fame.

He loved his family deeply.

He promised his mom she'd never have to work again.

He bought houses for multiple siblings.

He gave cash to cousins to start "businesses" that never materialized.

Fast forward five years?

He was broke.

Not because he wasn't generous — but because he had no system.

No plan.

No boundaries.

He thought saying "yes" would keep everyone happy forever.

Instead, it broke everything.

Tough Love: Your Future Family Matters, Too

If you one day want to have a spouse, kids, or build generational wealth — you have to think long-term.

Every dollar you hand out today is a dollar that isn't available tomorrow for:

- Buying your first home
- Starting a business you own
- Investing in real estate
- Setting up college funds for your kids
- Building your retirement

Short-term emotional relief cannot come at the expense of long-term freedom.

Gifting Philosophy for Pro Athletes

Give from your overflow — not your foundation.

If your basic financial future isn't locked in yet — you're not ready to start giving big.

Secure your castle first.

Then send gifts from the extra.

Not before.

Final Encouragement

Learning to give smartly is part of growing into true leadership.

You're not just a professional athlete now.

You're a CEO.

You're a brand.

You're a builder of a legacy.

Leaders don't panic when people are disappointed.

Leaders make wise, principled, loving decisions — even when it's hard in the moment.

You're not cold.

You're not selfish.

You're not abandoning anyone.

You are building something bigger, something better, something that lasts.

Be the one who changes the game for your family — not just for today, but for generations.

You've got this.

And when you stay strong?

You don't just win financially —

you win at life.

Chapter 40: Maintaining Financial Independence Post-Career

There's a moment every pro athlete faces, whether they're ready or not.

The lights dim.

The crowds fade.

The last whistle blows.

And the world that once cheered every move starts to move on.

It's not personal.

It's just reality.

And here's the truth most people won't tell you:

The biggest financial game of your life doesn't happen on the field, the court, the rink, or the track.

It happens **after** you walk away.

After the contracts stop.

After the endorsement deals dry up.

After the regular paychecks disappear.

That's when you either stay free and independent — or you end up struggling like too many athletes before you.

This chapter is about preparing you for that next season of your life.

Not with fear.

Not with desperation.

But with **strategy**, **wisdom**, and **power**.

Let's talk about how to protect everything you worked so hard to build

— and keep winning long after the crowds are gone.

Why Post-Career Planning Matters Even When You're "On Top"

When you're at the top of your game, it feels like the money will never stop.

Big checks.

Bonuses.

Appearance fees.

Endorsements.

Business offers.

It's a flood.

But even the biggest rivers eventually dry up if you don't manage them right.

Sports careers are *short*.

Even in the most physically forgiving sports, you're lucky to play a decade.

In contact sports like football or hockey?

The average career is **less than four years**.

And yet — your life after sports could easily last **50 years or more**.

Think about that.

You might spend **10%** of your life as a pro athlete... and **90%** living off what you built during those years.

That's why you have to play the long game.

Not just the next contract.

Not just the next season.

The next *half-century*.

Pros and Cons of Post-Career Financial Life

Pros of Good Planning:

- True financial freedom — work because you want to, not because you have to
- Legacy building — set your family up for generations
- Mental peace — no fear about the next bill or emergency
- Flexibility — pursue passion projects, travel, start businesses, give back
- Stability — weather economic storms without panicking

Cons of Poor Planning:

- Burned through savings before 40
- Forced to take any job — even ones you hate — just to survive
- Strained relationships with family and friends
- Embarrassment or shame over losing your fortune
- Mental stress, depression, and regret about "what could have been"

Action Steps to Stay Financially Independent for Life

Let's break this down into real moves you can start making today — no matter where you are in your career.

Step 1: Treat Your Playing Career as Your Startup Capital

Imagine your sports career is like hitting the jackpot early.

You've got a head start most people dream about.

But it's not infinite.

It's a lump sum.

It's your seed money for the rest of your life.

You have two choices:

- Spend it like it's endless — and eventually run out.
- Plant it, grow it, and live off the fruit forever.

Think like an entrepreneur.
You're not just an athlete — you're the CEO of your future.

Step 2: Know Your True Burn Rate

Your **burn rate** = how much money you spend each year.
If you don't know your burn rate — you're flying blind.
Create a post-career budget now.
Think about:

- Housing
- Cars
- Health insurance (this gets expensive after you leave a team)
- Travel
- Food
- Kids' expenses
- Taxes
- Entertainment
- Business investments
- Emergency funds

Goal:
Figure out what it costs to live comfortably, not extravagantly.
Rule of thumb:
Try to live on **4-5%** of your invested net worth per year.
If you have $5 million invested smartly?
That's about $200,000–$250,000 a year without touching the principal.
Play defense first.
Stay in the game forever.

Step 3: Understand the 3 Financial Seasons of a Pro Athlete

Season 1: Accumulation (Playing Years)

- Maximize savings.
- Avoid lifestyle creep.
- Stay disciplined.

Season 2: Transition (1–5 Years After Retirement)

- Major identity shift.
- Resist impulse investments.
- Adjust spending habits fast.

Season 3: Preservation and Growth (The Rest of Life)

- Conservative investing.
- Smart income streams.
- Legacy and estate planning.

Most mistakes happen during the Transition Season.

You will be tempted.

You will be emotional.

Prepare now.

Have a plan ready before the last game.

Step 4: Build Multiple Streams of Income Before You Retire

You can't rely on one paycheck forever.

Set up multiple streams:

- Investments (stocks, bonds, real estate)
- Business ownership

- Speaking engagements
- Endorsements that fit your brand
- Coaching or consulting (if you want)

Start while you're still playing.

Rule of thumb:

The more income streams you have, the less vulnerable you are when one dries up.

Basketball analogy:

You don't win a championship with just one star player.

You need a deep bench.

Same with your money.

Step 5: Protect Your Downside — Always

This isn't just about growing money.

It's about **protecting** money.

Must-haves:

- Health insurance
- Disability insurance
- Life insurance
- Umbrella liability insurance
- Estate plan (will, power of attorney, healthcare proxy)
- Trusted CPA and financial advisor (independent!)

Defense wins championships.

Don't let one accident, lawsuit, or bad investment sink you.

Step 6: Stay Humble — and Stay Hungry

The biggest trap?

Feeling like you "made it" because you had a big first contract.

Plenty of athletes went broke **after** making $50M, $100M, even $200M.

Money doesn't protect itself.

Stay a student.

Stay hungry.

Keep asking questions.

Surround yourself with people who tell you the truth, not just what you want to hear.

Soccer analogy:

Even when you're up 3-0 at halftime, you still have to play smart in the second half.

Or you could lose it all.

Real-World Scenarios

Scenario 1: The Early Retiree

You tear your ACL your second year in the league.

Career's over.

Because you saved 60% of your salary and lived modestly, you're set for life.

You take a year to heal, then start a business you're passionate about.

You're not stressed.

You're free.

Scenario 2: The Over-Spender

You sign a $30M deal, buy a $10M mansion, 10 cars, fly private every weekend.

Three years later — after taxes, agent fees, and expenses — you have almost nothing left.

You're scrambling to land a reality show just to pay your bills.

You're bitter.

You're exhausted.

Scenario 3: The Smart Planner

You invest wisely while you play.

You own rental properties that cash-flow every month.

You have a diversified investment portfolio.

You build a speaking brand around leadership.

You retire from sports — and your *real* wealth-building begins.

You're growing faster now than you were when you played.

The Mental Shift You Must Make

Your value is not just your athletic ability.

Your value is:

- Your mind
- Your leadership
- Your discipline
- Your brand
- Your experience

Sports were just the platform.

You are the product.

And you have much more to offer the world.

Never forget that.

Final Encouragement

The second half of your life can be even greater than the first.

More impact.

More growth.

More freedom.

But only if you choose it.

Protect your money.
Protect your mind.
Protect your future.
The game is not over.
It's just beginning.
And trust me — you're ready.
You have what it takes to not just survive after sports —
but to thrive.
Let's go.

How Taxes Change After You Retire from Pro Sports

Most athletes underestimate how dramatically their tax situation changes once they stop playing.

When you're earning a salary, it's somewhat predictable.

When you stop?

- You might have irregular income.
- You might start realizing capital gains from investments.
- You might have passive income from rental properties.
- You might move states — which triggers new tax rules.
- You might owe self-employment taxes if you start consulting, speaking, or doing business deals.

Action Step:

Sit down with a CPA **every year** after you retire.
Not just in March or April when taxes are due.
Plan ahead.
Ask:

- Should I set up an LLC for speaking gigs or consulting?
- Should I move my investments to more tax-efficient accounts?

- Should I relocate to a no-income-tax state?

The tax code wasn't written with athletes in mind.

It was written for the government to win unless you know how to legally play defense.

Good tax planning = financial survival.

Building a New Purpose After the Games End

One of the biggest hidden dangers for athletes after retirement isn't financial.

It's emotional.

You spent your whole life being "the athlete."

The competitor.

The star.

The grinder.

When that ends, it can feel like a piece of your identity disappears.

That's when bad financial decisions start creeping in:

- **Overspending** to fill the void.
- **Bad business deals** to chase the old adrenaline rush.
- **Trusting the wrong people** out of loneliness or insecurity.
- **Lavish gifts** to stay "important" to others.

You must fill that emotional gap **with purpose**, not just with purchases.

Ask yourself:

- What causes do I care about?
- Who can I mentor?
- What can I build that's bigger than me?

Money can support that purpose — but it can't *be* your purpose.

You are more than a stat line.

You are more than your highlights.

You have *so much* more to offer.

Own that.

Pitfalls Athletes Commonly Fall Into After Retirement (And How to Avoid Them)

Here's a quick scouting report on the traps you need to watch for:

Trap #1: Buying a Mansion You Don't Need

A lot of athletes think retiring means buying their "forever home" — 15 bedrooms, 20 bathrooms, movie theater, indoor pool.

Then reality hits:

- Property taxes
- Maintenance costs
- Utilities
- Security
- Landscaping
- Repairs

All while your income has dropped dramatically.

Strategy:

Buy only what fits your new budget — not your old paycheck.

Better yet?

Rent first.

Test out the area.

Ease into it.

Golf analogy:

You don't pull out your driver on a tricky par-3.

Play smart.

Trap #2: Starting a Business Without a Real Plan

"I'll open a restaurant!"

"I'll launch a clothing line!"

"I'll start a record label!"

It sounds exciting — but 80% of new businesses fail within 5 years.

Athletes often get pitched *horrible* ideas by friends, family, and strangers.

Strategy:

If you want to invest, invest in yourself first.

- Take business courses.
- Find a real mentor.
- Start small.
- Stay patient.

Think like an owner — not just a dreamer.

Trap #3: Being the Family ATM

This one hurts the most.

You love your people.

You want to help.

But if you become the financial crutch for everyone you know?

- You'll run out of money.
- They'll never learn to stand on their own.
- You'll resent them — and they'll resent you when the money dries up.

Strategy:

Set clear, firm financial boundaries.

You are not a lottery ticket.

You are not a lifeboat.

You are a leader.

Leaders don't just hand out fish — they teach others how to fish.

The Power of Financial Simplicity

One major key to post-career success?

Keep it simple.

The more complicated your money life is, the easier it is to lose control.

Simple systems = less stress.

Examples:

- Auto-transfer money into savings every month.
- Have one trusted financial advisor (not 10 random ones).
- Invest in boring, steady growth — not flashy get-rich-quick schemes.
- Keep personal budgets lean and realistic.
- Avoid massive lifestyle inflation every time an investment pays off.

Tennis analogy:

You don't have to hit 140 mph aces every time.

You just have to put the ball in play, over and over again.

Consistency wins.

The New Game Plan: Financial Freedom Beyond Sports

Let's create a visual:

Imagine you're coaching a new team — "Team Future."

Here's your roster:

- **You** = Head Coach and Star Player
- **Financial Advisor** = Offensive Coordinator (building wealth plays)
- **CPA** = Defensive Coordinator (tax defense)
- **Attorney** = General Manager (contracts, protections)
- **Family** = Support Squad (not owners of the team)

You're not playing **for** others anymore.

You're playing **with** them — but *you* still call the shots.

Build your team wisely.
Lead with humility and strength.
Trust, but verify.
And always, always, always protect the jersey: **Your Name.**

Real Talk: How To Emotionally Handle the Transition

Nobody talks enough about the emotions behind financial decisions.

You're going to feel:

- **Lonely** sometimes.
- **Left out** when other guys keep living the "flashy" life.
- **Tempted** to flex again when you see younger players sign huge deals.
- **Unsure** if you're making the right moves.

It's normal.

You are not weak for feeling this way.
The strongest thing you can do is stay rooted.
Stay disciplined.
Stay true to the foundation you've built.
And remember:
Money is not the scoreboard.
Character is.
Peace of mind is.
Freedom is.

Key Rules to Live By Post-Career

Here are some quick truths to tape to your mental locker:

- **If it sounds too good to be true, it is.**
- **If you don't understand it, don't invest in it.**
- **If someone pressures you, walk away.**

- **If you wouldn't buy it at half your net worth, don't buy it now.**
- **If you have to hide it from your advisor or spouse, it's a bad move.**
- **If you stay humble, you'll stay rich.**

Simple.

Not easy.

But life-changing.

Closing Message for Chapter 40

You've worked too hard, sacrificed too much, and overcome too many odds to let poor planning steal your freedom.

You are not just a highlight reel.

You are not just your last contract.

You are a builder now.

A protector.

A visionary.

Play the long game.

Own your future.

And remember:

The greatest comeback stories aren't just about returning to the game.

They're about mastering life after the game.

And yours is just getting started.

Let's go.

Part 5: Career Longevity, Pensions, and Life After Sports

When you're living the dream of being a professional athlete, it's easy to feel like the ride will never end. But every athlete — no matter how talented, hardworking, or iconic — eventually faces the same reality: the playing days don't last forever. Part 5 is about getting ready for that next season of life while you're still winning on the field, court, or ice.

This section digs deep into the practical, emotional, and financial strategies that help athletes extend their careers wisely, transition into retirement with confidence, and protect the wealth they've worked so hard to earn. We'll cover what many athletes overlook until it's too late — like understanding your league's pension plan, making smart decisions about your benefits, knowing when and how to pivot professionally, and how to create a life of purpose, security, and freedom after your final game.

Whether you play for 3 years or 15, the real flex isn't just lasting longer in the league — it's thriving long after the crowds stop cheering.

In Part 5, you'll learn:

- How to think about your **career arc** like a smart GM would: with both the short game and long game in mind
- The differences between **league pension plans**, **retirement benefits**, and **how to maximize them**

- How to prepare mentally and financially for **retirement**, **transition periods**, and **second careers**
- Smart moves to **protect your body**, **your brand**, and **your bank account** during the high-earning years
- How to invest early, create multiple income streams, and build a **long runway of financial independence**
- Emotional and practical strategies for **life after sports** — from building businesses to giving back to simply enjoying freedom on your own terms

You'll also hear the honest truth about the dangers that end athletes' careers — and their financial freedom — way too soon: injuries, ego, overspending, bad investments, bad influences, and lack of planning.

We're not just talking theory.

We're drawing the real playbook — the one built for **longevity, leadership, legacy**, and a life you can be proud of both during and after your playing days.

This part of the journey isn't just important — it's everything.

Chapter 41: How Career Length Varies by Sport (Average Years for NFL, NBA, MLB, NHL, WNBA, etc.)

When you finally step into the world you've been dreaming about your whole life — walking into that first professional locker room, slipping on that jersey, hearing your name on TV — it feels invincible. Like the start of a dynasty.

And it *is* the start of something special.

But here's the part no one tells you on draft night, at training camp, or at your first big press conference:

The professional clock starts ticking the second you sign that first deal.

You have a window. A real window. It might be bigger or smaller than you think, but it's not forever. And what you do inside that window financially — not just athletically — will define your life after the game.

Today, we're going to talk about that window, sport by sport, so you can see exactly what you're up against. No scare tactics. No false promises. Just the truth — because you deserve the truth.

Average Career Lengths by Major Sport

NFL (National Football League)

- **Average career length:** About **3.3 years**.
- **Reality:**
- Brutal. Football is a violent, high-turnover sport. Even superstars feel the grind. One bad tackle, one wrong turn, one new draft pick coming for your spot — and you're out.
- **Most vulnerable positions:**
- Running backs often have the shortest lifespans, usually under **3 years**.
- Linemen and special teams players tend to stretch a little longer.

What this means:

In the NFL, if you're not planning your financial future immediately — like in your rookie year — you're already late.

NBA (National Basketball Association)

- **Average career length:** Around **4.5 years**.
- **Reality:**
- NBA players can have longer careers because the game is less physically punishing compared to football, but it's still incredibly competitive. Roster spots are limited. Teams constantly refresh with younger, cheaper talent.
- **Exceptions:**
- Superstar talent (think LeBron, Steph Curry) can play 15-20 years. But role players and journeymen? 3-5 years is common.

What this means:

Even if you're a lottery pick, you can't assume you'll have a 15-year run. Get the right team around you early.

MLB (Major League Baseball)

- **Average career length:** About **5.6 years**.
- **Reality:**
- Baseball careers tend to be longer, but it's harder to break in at the top level. Minor leagues chew up years, and once you hit the bigs, you have to perform constantly to stay.
- **Important factor:**
- MLB contracts are often fully guaranteed, meaning if you secure a good deal, it can be *golden* — but only if you manage it wisely.

What this means:

Baseball can create some of the highest earners in sports — but it also creates big spenders who flame out fast. Stability is key.

NHL (National Hockey League)

- **Average career length:** About **5 years**.
- **Reality:**
- Like football, hockey is a physical, demanding sport. Injuries are common. The grind is real. Even great players can be sidelined quickly.
- **Strong union support:**
- The NHLPA helps players secure pensions, benefits, and protections.

What this means:

You must budget for potential injuries and short stints — even if you're a top-six forward or starting goalie.

WNBA (Women's National Basketball Association)

- **Average career length:** Around **3 to 5 years**.
- **Reality:**
- The WNBA has fewer teams (12), fewer roster spots (12 players per team), and lower pay scales compared to male counterparts.
- Many players extend their careers by playing overseas in the offseason.
- **Double careers:**
- Many WNBA athletes simultaneously juggle overseas contracts, endorsements, and side businesses to build financial security.

What this means:

If you're in the W, you're likely hustling *year-round*. You must master budgeting across dual seasons (WNBA + overseas), understand taxes in two countries, and plan for early career transitions into coaching, broadcasting, or entrepreneurship.

Special Note:

Because WNBA players often face a huge pay gap compared to NBA players, building wealth early and diversifying income streams isn't optional — it's critical.

Other Sports Overview

MLS (Major League Soccer):

- **Average:** 3.2 years.
- Less financial security compared to Europe's top leagues.
- Massive gap between stars and average players.

Tennis:

- Top players (Serena, Federer) = 10-20 years.

- Average pro = 3-5 years struggling on tour.
- Earnings heavily tilted to the top 1%.

Golf (PGA/LPGA):

- If you're good, you can play for decades.
- But consistent money is only for elite earners who make cuts.

Olympic Sports (Track and Field, Swimming, etc.):

- 1 Olympic cycle (4 years) is common.
- Sponsorships disappear quickly without medals.

Combat Sports (Boxing, MMA):

- Often only 1-3 major fights.
- Brutal physically, financially volatile.

Why Understanding These Career Windows Matters

You don't want to wake up one day — after the team cuts you, after the next draft class replaces you, after an injury ends it all — and realize you were only thinking one season at a time.

The real professionals think differently.

The best mindset?

You assume your career is short.

You plan for it to be short.

You grind like you want it to be long.

If it turns out longer? Great.

If it turns out short? You survive — and thrive.

Action Steps to Prepare for a Short Career

- **Save at least 50-70% of your net pay immediately.**
- This is extreme — and necessary.
- **Invest early — not just late.**
- Compound growth needs time. Start ASAP.
- **Create offseason income strategies.**
- Endorsements. Clinics. Broadcasting. Mentoring. Coaching.
- **Have a Plan B before you ever need it.**
- Don't wait until you're waived or injured to figure out what's next.
- **Protect yourself with insurance.**
- Disability. Health. Umbrella policies.
- **Learn financial literacy as seriously as you learned your playbook.**
- Your future deserves it.

Sports Analogies for Career Planning

- **Basketball:**
- You might get hot from three one night — but you better have a full offensive game for when the threes stop falling.
- **Football:**
- Build your financial defense first. Great defenses (savings, investments) win championships (long-term wealth).
- **Soccer:**
- You can't just sprint for 90 minutes. You have to pace yourself. Career management is about pacing your financial moves too.
- **Tennis:**
- You can't win every point. But you can control your unforced errors. Don't make dumb financial mistakes.
- **Track:**
- Some careers are the 100m dash. Some are the 800m grind. Either way — run smart.

In Closing: Short Careers, Long Wealth

You might play 3 years. You might play 30.

But you *control* how prepared you are for life beyond the game.

Don't just be remembered as a great player for a few years.

Be remembered as someone who **built a legacy** — financially, personally, and professionally.

Your career is a chapter.

Your wealth is the book.

Own it.

Career Lengths by Sport (Expanded Real-World Breakdown)

NFL – Brutal, Beautiful, and Unforgiving

The NFL is the king of quick careers.

Let's be honest: football will chew you up if you're not ready.

Real-world examples:

- **Terrell Davis** – Hall of Fame RB, but played only 7 seasons due to knee injuries.
- **Andrew Luck** – Walked away at 29 years old, despite being a franchise quarterback.
- **Ryan Shazier** – Career ended in his prime due to spinal injury.

On the flip side:

- **Tom Brady** – Played 23 seasons by defying normal timelines — but he's the exception, not the rule.

Football truth:

You're one hit away from done.

Financial mindset needed:

Plan like your next season might be your last.

NBA – Flash vs. Foundation

The NBA often feels like the land of dreams:

Shoe deals. All-Star weekends. Flashy contracts.

But the reality?

Most NBA players don't last beyond their rookie contracts.

Real-world examples:

- **Greg Oden** – #1 pick, played only 3 seasons because of injuries.
- **Brandon Roy** – Rising superstar. Career derailed after 6 seasons by knee issues.

On the flip side:

- **Udonis Haslem** – 20-year career without being a superstar, because he knew his role and protected his finances.

Basketball truth:

Hype doesn't equal longevity.

Financial mindset needed:

Stay humble. Build wealth even in your first two years.

MLB – The Marathon

Baseball offers longer averages, but the grind to *stay* is intense.

Real-world examples:

- **Rick Ankiel** – Rocket arm, massive potential… lasted only a few seasons as a pitcher, had to reinvent as an outfielder.

- **Chris Davis** – Had a few superstar seasons, then declined sharply — yet still collected on a big guaranteed contract.

On the flip side:

- **Albert Pujols** – A 20+ year career, smart off-field investments, and longevity.

Baseball truth:

The minor leagues build callouses — but if you make it, you must respect the money.

Financial mindset needed:

Don't let long contracts fool you into overspending early.

NHL – Blood, Ice, and Pensions

Hockey players are warriors.

Their careers are longer on average because they start younger — but injuries are constant.

Real-world examples:

- **Bobby Orr** – Career cut short at 30 due to chronic knee problems, despite being a generational talent.

On the flip side:

- **Jaromír Jágr** – Played into his 40s, even after leaving and returning to the NHL.

Hockey truth:

Toughness buys time, but toughness doesn't guarantee contracts.

Financial mindset needed:

Plan for injuries. Respect every check you cash.

WNBA – Hustle on Two Courts

WNBA players are the definition of hustle.

They often work **year-round**, splitting time between WNBA seasons and overseas leagues.

Real-world examples:

- **Maya Moore** – Took time off from basketball to focus on criminal justice work.
- **Sue Bird** – Longevity icon, but she's the rare exception playing into her 40s.

Typical player experience:

WNBA contract in summer.

Overseas contract in winter.

WNBA truth:

Your brand is your real asset. Build it early.

Financial mindset needed:

Maximize endorsements, manage international taxes, and protect your body.

How Different Sports Impact Your Wealth Timeline

Sport Average Career Financial Focus Unique Challenge

NFL

3.3 years

Immediate cash flow control

High injury risk

NBA

4.5 years

Endorsements + early investments

Lifestyle creep

MLB

5.6 years
Long-term wealth planning
Slow earnings start
NHL
5 years
Pension and insurance protection
Injury and physical wear
WNBA
3-5 years
Dual income management
Overseas taxes and fatigue

The Invisible Clock: Psychological Pressure

Here's what happens when you don't recognize your career window:

- You think you have time.
- You spend like the checks will never stop.
- You make promises you can't keep to friends and family.
- You say yes to too many business "opportunities."
- You don't save early enough, so compound interest doesn't work for you.

Financial danger:

You'll feel rich while your earning window is wide open —
but if you're not careful, the second it closes, reality slams into you like a linebacker.

Real Talk: Why Rookie Mistakes Are So Common

1. Lifestyle inflation.

Your first $500K check feels like winning the lottery.

You start living like it's $50 million.

2. Trusting the wrong people.

Family. Friends. Fake advisors.

They smell your success and want a piece.

3. No plan for "life after the league."

Most athletes wait until it's too late to think about a second act.

4. Ego.

Everyone thinks they're going to be the exception.

Until they're not.

Action Plan: Preparing From Day One

Step 1: Reality Check

Look at your sport's average career length — and assume yours will be even shorter.

Step 2: Set a Career-End Financial Goal

What number would make you feel secure if you retired tomorrow?

Step 3: Play the Long Game Early

Invest, save, and build outside of your sport while you're still in it.

Step 4: Build Skills for Life After Sports

Public speaking. Business investing. Coaching. Entrepreneurship.

Step 5: Protect Your Brand

The way you carry yourself now impacts future endorsement deals, business partnerships, and post-career opportunities.

Bonus Real-World Mini Case Studies

Player A – NFL Rookie, 2-Year Career:

- Made $2 million total.
- Spent $1.6 million by Year 3.
- No degree, no plan, back home, depressed.

Player B – WNBA All-Star, 7-Year Career:

- Saved 40% of each overseas and WNBA check.
- Built a nonprofit.
- Bought rental properties.
- Retired at 30 with $750K invested and $3,000/mo in passive rental income.

Player C – MLB Utility Player, 8-Year Career:

- Made $5 million total.
- Bought dumb investments (restaurant, nightclub).
- Lost everything within 3 years of retiring.

Player D – NBA Benchwarmer, 4-Year Career:

- Lived on 20% of his salary.
- Saved 80%.
- Now owns part of 2 startups and never stresses about money.

Final Encouragement: Don't Fear the End — Fear Not Being Ready

The end of your career will come — guaranteed.
How you greet it depends on how you prepared.

- Some athletes retire **broke** and **bitter**.
- Some retire **stable** and **grateful**.
- Some retire **wealthy** and **free** — because they respected the clock.

Which one will you be?
You get to decide — today.
Own your career.
Own your money.
Own your future.

Chapter 42: Understanding League Pensions and Benefits (NFLPA, NBPA, MLBPA, WNBPA, etc.)

Chapter 42: Understanding League Pensions and Benefits (NFLPA, NBPA, MLBPA, WNBPA, etc.)

Why This Chapter Matters

You fight your whole life to make it to the league.

You lift.

You run.

You study film.

You push through injuries nobody else sees.

And then one day you're there:

Drafted. Signed. On a roster.

It's easy to get caught up in the moment.

The game. The lifestyle. The pressure.

You think about next week's opponent, not next decade's bills.

You think about next season's contract, not retirement.

But here's the real truth —

If you don't understand your pension, benefits, and long-term financial rights as a professional athlete, you are leaving money on the table you *already earned*.

This is part of your compensation package.

Not understanding it is like leaving cash, healthcare, and long-term security just sitting on the bench.

And if you've ever been benched — you know that's the worst feeling in the world.

This chapter is about making sure that **you never bench yourself financially**.

Let's get it.

The Big Picture: What Are League Pensions and Benefits?

When you make it to the league — whether it's the NFL, NBA, MLB, NHL, or WNBA — you don't just get a paycheck.

You're entitled to things like:

Pension benefits (money when you retire)

Health insurance (sometimes for life, depending on the league)

Post-career transition services

Disability benefits

401(k) or defined contribution plans

Access to special funds for education or second careers

In other words:

It's like your team is putting you on a scholarship for life — but only if you *understand* how to claim it.

Understanding Each League's System (Real-World Breakdown)

NFLPA (National Football League Players Association)

Career Length Reality:

Average career = 3.3 years

You need at least 3 credited seasons to qualify for a pension.

A "credited season" generally means you were on the roster (active, IR, or PUP list) for at least 3 regular season games.

Key NFL Pension Benefits:

Monthly retirement income beginning at age 55.

Health reimbursement accounts after 3+ seasons.

Severance pay based on credited seasons.

401(k) with matching contributions.

Real Talk Warning:

Many NFL players barely make it past Year 3.

If you flame out in Year 2 — you might walk away with nothing.

Get to that third season any way you can.

Practice squad. Special teams. Be a "glue guy."

Football Analogy:

Think of every season like a yard marker.

You don't win by Hail Marys.

You win by moving the chains, getting first downs, one at a time.

NBPA (National Basketball Players Association)

Career Length Reality:

Average NBA career = 4.5 years

You qualify for the pension after 3 years of service.

Key NBA Pension Benefits:

Monthly payments starting at 45 years old if you want — or bigger checks if you delay until 62.

Health insurance through the league and post-career options.

Annuity fund contributions.

401(k) matching program.

Real Talk Warning:

It's easier to last three years in the NBA than the NFL, but injuries, bad fits, and trades kill momentum fast.

Basketball Analogy:

Getting to your pension is like getting your rookie contract guaranteed money.

You don't take bad shots early. You play the long game.

MLBPA (Major League Baseball Players Association)

Career Length Reality:

Average MLB career = 5.6 years

Only 43 days of service time gets you a partial pension.

10 years gets you the full maximum benefit.

Key MLB Pension Benefits:

One of the richest pension systems in sports.

Fully vested after 43 days of service.

Health insurance for life after one day of service.

Annuity benefits and 401(k) savings plans.

Real Talk Warning:

Minor league guys grind for years — and many never get to that 43-day threshold.

Baseball Analogy:

It's like being a September call-up — even a cup of coffee in the Bigs can set you up for life, if you understand the rules.

WNBPA (Women's National Basketball Players Association)

Career Length Reality:

Average WNBA career = 3-5 years

Benefits depend on your years of service and collective bargaining agreements.

Key WNBA Pension Benefits:

401(k) retirement savings plans.

Health insurance during playing years, and health reimbursement accounts after.

Tuition reimbursement programs.

Post-career transition support.

Real Talk Warning:

WNBA players often must go overseas in the off-season — risking injury without guaranteed WNBA pension protections.

Basketball Analogy:

In the WNBA, managing your money is like managing your minutes:

Every single opportunity counts double.

Why Your Pension Is the Most Underrated Part of Your Contract

Your pension isn't flashy.

Nobody cheers for it on draft night.

But it's the only part of your career guaranteed to pay you 10, 20, even 40 years after you stop playing.

It's the **silent MVP** of your financial future.

And if you ignore it?

It's like voluntarily leaving your best teammate sitting on the bench.

Action Plan: Maximizing Your League Benefits Starting Today

Step 1: Know Your Vesting Rules

Find out exactly how many years, games, or service days you need for full benefits.

Step 2: Track Your Service Time Like a Stat

Every week you survive, every game you suit up, every day you're active — it matters.

Step 3: Contribute to League Retirement Accounts

Max out your 401(k) options if they match contributions.
It's free money.

Step 4: Stay Insured

Protect your health while you're healthy.
Use all team or union-offered health programs.

Step 5: Stay Informed

CBAs (Collective Bargaining Agreements) change.
Know when updates happen — benefits improve or deadlines shift.

Real-World Example

Player A – NFL Rookie

1 year on the roster.

Cut before reaching 3 credited seasons.

No pension. No post-career health benefits.

Now working a 9-5 trying to restart.

Player B – 7th-Round Pick Who Made It 4 Years

Reached 4 credited seasons.

Qualified for NFL pension and health benefits.

Used severance to pay off mortgage.

Now coaching and getting monthly pension checks starting at 55.

Pros and Cons of League Benefits

Pros:

Provides lifetime security if you qualify.

Helps cover health care when private insurance costs skyrocket.

Protects your family.

Cons:

You must survive long enough to qualify.

Some benefits aren't automatic — you have to apply or opt-in.

Not understanding your benefits = losing thousands or millions over time.

Final Encouragement: Respect the Opportunity

Fight for every credited season.

Save like you won't play next year.

Learn the pension system like you study a playbook.

The game won't last forever.

But if you play it right — your money, your benefits, and your future will.

Own your career.

Own your benefits.

Own your future.

The Dangerous Myths Athletes Believe About Pensions and Benefits

Let's clear something up right now:

Myth #1: "I'll figure it out later."

Wrong.

Later comes faster than you think. An injury, a trade, a waived contract — it can happen overnight. If you're not tracking it now, you might not have a "later."

Myth #2: "My agent is handling it."

Wrong.

Your agent negotiates your contracts. They don't file your pension paperwork, make sure you're vested, or tell you when to enroll in post-career benefits. That's YOUR job — or your financial advisor's.

Myth #3: "If I'm a star, it won't matter."

Wrong.

Big checks don't make up for missed benefits.

In fact, **the bigger your money, the more expensive it is to cover your own retirement without league benefits.**

Myth #4: "It's free money, it'll just show up."

Wrong again.

Pensions often require you to **apply** or **elect** certain benefits when you become eligible. If you don't file the paperwork, you don't get the check.

How the Payout Works: From Playing Field to Pension Check

Vesting

Vesting = Earning the right to benefits.

It's like unlocking a contract bonus.

You must "vest" by completing a certain number of credited seasons, days, or years.

Each league has different rules — know yours.

Benefit Start Age

Most league pensions don't pay immediately after you retire.

Instead, they start paying at a designated retirement age:

- **NFL:** 55
- **NBA:** 45 (optional early retirement) or bigger checks at 62
- **MLB:** Varies depending on service time
- **WNBA:** Post-career account access starts based on plan terms

Think of it like this:

You're setting up Future You for a second win — financial stability *long after* you hang up the jersey.

How Big Are the Checks?

Short answer: It depends.

Factors include:

- How many seasons you played.
- When you choose to start taking benefits.
- Whether the league changed benefit formulas.
- Your election of lump sum versus monthly payout (where available).

General Rule:

More service time = bigger pension.

Waiting longer to collect = bigger monthly checks.

Inside Look: What Happens If You Don't Qualify?

Let's say you play two NFL seasons but get cut before your third.

No third credited season =

No pension.

No retiree health benefits.

No severance bonus.

You're out.

It's brutal.

But it's reality.

This is why **every game**, **every practice**, **every roster day** matters.

And why you MUST have an off-the-field plan for career survival too — financially, mentally, emotionally.

Real Life "Benefit Recovery" Playbook (If You Get Cut)

If you find yourself off a roster and haven't vested yet, here's the play:

1. **Stay In Playing Shape**

- You might get a second shot — 10-day contract, late-season call-up, preseason roster.
- Even one more credited season could unlock lifetime benefits.

1. **Work With Your Union**

- Players Associations offer resources for free agent players.
- Job boards, workout invites, even alternative leagues.

1. **Use Transition Programs**

- Many leagues offer career transition grants, education reimbursements, and networking events to help you land back on your feet.

1. **Protect Your Health Insurance**

- If you're about to lose coverage, ask about COBRA continuation or find private insurance fast.

1. **Financial Triage**

- Slash expenses.
- Preserve cash.
- Consult a financial advisor immediately to adjust your plan.

Pension Mistakes You Must Avoid

Mistake #1: Not Tracking Your Credited Seasons

You need to know the exact number — don't trust rumors or memory.

Mistake #2: Missing Filing Deadlines

Some benefits require elections within **30 to 90 days** after retirement or vesting.

Mistake #3: Taking Early Payouts Without a Plan

Taking a reduced pension early can lock you into smaller checks forever.

Mistake #4: Overestimating Health Benefits

Not every player gets lifetime coverage — it often depends on how many years you played.

Example Checklist: Year-by-Year

Rookie Year:

- Confirm your credited season status with the union.
- Enroll in 401(k) plans and maximize matching.

Year 2:

- Review your vesting progress.
- Update your health insurance options if cut or waived.

Year 3+:

- Fight to stay on rosters to vest benefits.
- Meet with a financial advisor to build a long-term pension and cash flow plan.

Retirement Transition:

- File pension election forms with the union.
- Set a pension withdrawal strategy with your advisor.

Empowerment Talk: You Deserve the Full Reward

You earned your place.

You paid your dues.

You put your body, mind, and life on the line to compete.

Your benefits are not charity.

They are not a bonus.

They are compensation you fought for.

You owe it to yourself, your future family, and your legacy to collect **every dime, every dollar, every bit**.

This isn't about pride.

It's about power.

Your power to create a life you control — long after the lights go out.

Closing Pep Talk: Own Your Legacy

You don't want to be the cautionary tale.

The headline.

The "where are they now" tragedy.

You want to be the champion —

on the field and off.

Understanding your pensions and benefits isn't boring paperwork.

It's your **real-life championship ring**.

It's the ring you wear when the jerseys come off.

When nobody's cheering.
When nobody's watching.
It's the ring that matters most.
Own it.
Protect it.
Collect it.
Wear it with pride.

Bonus Section: Pension Strategies for Players Who Went International (EuroLeague, Overseas Baseball, Etc.)

Not every career stays in the U.S.

Sometimes, your best or only opportunity is overseas — and that comes with a **whole new set of pension challenges**.

Here's what you need to know:

1. Most International Leagues Have No Pension Plan

Unlike the NFL, NBA, MLB, or WNBA, most international leagues do not offer:

- Structured pension benefits
- Lifetime health coverage
- Player retirement accounts

Translation:

You are responsible for building your own pension.

2. Treat Your Overseas Salary Like "Pension Replacement"

If you're playing overseas:

- Take **at least 25-50%** of every paycheck and put it into your own investment accounts (IRA, SEP IRA, brokerage account).
- Pretend you are "paying into a pension" — even if the team isn't.

Simple Rule:

If you're not automatically building retirement while playing, you must manually build it yourself.

3. Work With a U.S.-Based Financial Advisor

International income can create:

- Tax headaches
- Currency exchange risks
- Investment access problems

You want a U.S.-based advisor who understands **global income** and **domestic asset protection**.

Even if you're living in Istanbul, Shanghai, or Paris, your long-term wealth should live somewhere safe — like New York, Kansas City, or San Diego.

4. Protect Your Money from Hyperinflation and Currency Risk

If you're getting paid in foreign currency:

- Set up periodic automatic transfers back to a U.S. bank account.
- Avoid keeping your entire net worth tied to one unstable currency.

Example:
If you played soccer in Argentina during a peso crash, your earnings could lose half their value in months if not moved to a safer currency.

Bonus Section: "Second Career" Checklist (Tied to Your Pension Start Date)

Whether you're 26 or 46, here's the blueprint:

3-5 Years Before Pension Eligibility

- Start building a second career identity: coaching, media, business, entrepreneurship, mentoring, real estate, financial services, etc.
- Begin networking *outside* of sports — LinkedIn, alumni events, executive education programs.
- Hire a career coach if you feel stuck.
- Update your resume and portfolio — even if it's mostly sports accomplishments for now.

1-2 Years Before Pension Eligibility

Meet with a financial advisor to model pension income into your future monthly budget.

- Explore part-time work or "passion projects" you could turn into full-time careers.
- Understand your healthcare options post-retirement (Medicare, COBRA, private insurance).
- Plan how you'll replace your paycheck when the game checks stop.

6-12 Months Before Pension Eligibility

Confirm with your union:

- Vesting credit
- Application deadlines
- Health benefit enrollments
- Set up automatic deposits for your pension checks — direct to a high-yield account or investment account.
- Create a new "post-retirement" budget based on new income streams.
- Decide: Will you work full-time? Part-time? Consult? Coach? Invest? Volunteer?

Bonus Section: Common League Benefit Upgrades to Watch For in CBA Renewals

When leagues renegotiate CBAs (Collective Bargaining Agreements), pensions and benefits **often change**.

You must pay attention.

Here's what to watch for:

1. Changes to Vesting Rules

Sometimes CBAs lower or raise the number of credited seasons needed to qualify for pensions.

Example:

The NFL shortened vesting from 4 years to 3 years for pension eligibility after 2020 CBA talks.

2. Increased Pension Multipliers

Some CBAs raise how much you earn per season played.

Example:

The MLB pension multiplier increased after the last CBA — boosting payouts for veteran players.

3. Expansion of Health Benefits

New deals may add:

- Free health insurance years after retirement
- Vision, dental, mental health services
- Long-term disability protections

These benefits are GOLD — and often overlooked.

4. Retirement Account Matching Programs

Some CBAs add (or improve) 401(k) matching programs for players.

Even if you don't stay long enough to fully vest in the pension, you could walk away with **thousands** from retirement savings matches.

5. Enhanced Disability and Injury Protection

Updated CBAs often improve post-career injury protection.

Example:

If you suffer long-term injury consequences, newer CBA terms may offer better settlements, medical support, or insurance payouts.

Final Power Statement to Close This Expanded Chapter

You didn't come this far to leave money on the table.

You didn't work this hard, suffer these injuries, fight through these battles — just to be broke at 40 or stressed at 60.

Your benefits, pensions, and second careers are part of the championship you keep winning for the rest of your life.

It's not just about finishing your career.

It's about finishing it **with freedom, dignity, and power.**

Play smart.

Think long-term.

Own it all.

Real-World Examples: How Athletes Handled Pensions and Life After the Game

Case Study #1: The NFL Player Who Didn't Vest

"Marcus" was a promising defensive back drafted in the 5th round.

He bounced around practice squads and played in 18 regular-season games over three seasons.

His career ended suddenly after an Achilles tear.

The Problem:

He thought he had "plenty of time" to qualify for the NFL pension (which used to require 4 credited seasons — now it's 3).

But because practice squad time doesn't always fully count, he was **half a season short**.

When he retired, he was eligible for very little — no pension, no lifetime health benefits.

The Lesson:

Know your vesting rules down to the letter.

Don't guess.

Don't hope.

Confirm.

If Marcus had understood he needed to be on the active roster for just 6 more games, he could have worked with his agent differently, delayed retirement for a few more weeks, or negotiated a practice squad bump to the main roster.

One season can be the difference between zero and six figures for life.

Case Study #2: The WNBA Player Who Made a Second Career Shine

"Jasmine" played seven seasons in the WNBA and three seasons overseas (EuroLeague, Australia).

She was never an All-Star, but she was solid, respected, and smart.

What She Did Right:

- She maxed her WNBA 401(k) contributions every year, taking full advantage of team matches.
- She invested 40% of her overseas salary each year into her own Roth IRA and brokerage account.
- She earned vested years in the WNBA pension plan (which kicks in at age 50).
- She used offseasons to earn her Master's degree in Sports Management.
- She stayed connected to players' unions, so when CBA upgrades happened (like expanded health benefits for retired players), she was first to enroll.

The Result:

By the time she officially retired at 30, Jasmine had:

- A six-figure investment portfolio
- An education
- Pension payments that will start at age 50
- Zero debt
- Two career options ready: coaching or athletic administration

The Lesson:

You don't have to be a superstar to build superstar-level freedom after retirement.

Smart beats flashy, every time.

Case Study #3: The MLB Player Who Ignored Pension Planning

"Tony" was a late bloomer — got called up to the Majors at 27 after toiling in Triple-A.

He played 6 years in the MLB but lived like he was Derek Jeter.

Big houses. Fancy cars. Lots of dinners for the whole crew.

When he was released at 33, he still owed:

- $700,000 on a second home
- $200,000 in taxes
- $150,000 in business losses (bad investments with friends)

He didn't even know he had a pension coming.

What Went Wrong:

- He never met with the MLBPA to understand his benefits.
- He never set up a second career while he was still playing.
- He lived paycheck-to-paycheck despite earning $4M+ total.
- Now?

His pension of about $40,000 a year at 62 will help... but it won't erase

20+ years of financial stress and rebuilding.

The Lesson:

The game ends faster than you think. Plan now. Act now. Protect yourself now.

Quick Takeaways From These Examples:

- **Vesting is everything** — one missed season can cost you lifetime benefits.
- **401(k)s and IRAs matter** even if you have a pension.
- **Education and second-career prep** are essential, not optional.
- **Cash flow discipline** while playing = options and freedom later.
- **Union updates and CBA changes** can be hidden gold if you stay plugged in.

Final Pep Talk

Your pension, your investments, your benefits — they are not "extra bonuses" for later.

They are part of **your championship strategy right now.**

Being smart today isn't about being paranoid.

It's about making sure the blood, sweat, and sacrifice you're pouring into your sport now **pay you back for the rest of your life.**

Play your career like a Hall of Famer.

Play your money game like a Hall of Famer.

Play your life like a Hall of Famer.

You deserve that.

And you have what it takes to own it.

Chapter 43: Preparing for a Second Career During Your Playing Days

Let's get one thing straight: your playing career will end.

It might end when you're ready.

It might end before you're ready.

It might end in a blaze of glory — or it might end quietly, without a headline.

But it *will* end.

That's not negativity.

That's reality.

And the smartest athletes — the ones who go on to be legends in life, not just in sports — are the ones who start preparing for their second career **while they're still in the middle of their first**.

Today we're going to talk about how you do that. Step by step.

No fluff. No wishful thinking.

Just real talk from someone who believes in you.

Why You Can't Afford to Wait

When you're still playing, it's easy to think you've got all the time in the world.

You're young. You're strong. You're living the dream.

But the same way Father Time catches up with every point guard's first step or every pitcher's fastball, it catches up with careers too.

You don't want to be figuring out your second act **after** you're already out of the game.

You want to start **while you still have the jersey on your back.**

Because while you're active, you have three priceless advantages:

- Visibility
- Access
- Financial Resources

Once you're out, those start to fade.

Visibility dries up.

Access closes down.

Financial resources start getting spent.

You have to capitalize **now**.

Step 1: Shift Your Mindset From "Athlete" to "Entrepreneur"

Right now, your product is your body. Your skillset. Your game.

But long term, your product will be your brain. Your relationships. Your leadership. Your brand.

You have to stop seeing yourself only as a player — and start seeing yourself as the CEO of **Your Life, Inc.**

Every decision you make from here on out needs to answer this question:

> *"Is this helping me build my post-career life?"*

If the answer is yes — lean in.

If the answer is no — pump the brakes.

Step 2: Educate Yourself (Quietly)

You don't have to announce to the world that you're thinking about life after sports.

In fact, it's better if you don't.

Move quietly.

Learn aggressively.

Start small:

- Take online business classes.
- Read books on entrepreneurship, leadership, and investing.
- Listen to podcasts about industries that interest you.
- Attend a seminar or conference in the offseason.

If your league offers career development programs (and most do), **use them.**

If your agent, team, or union offers tuition reimbursement for college courses or certificates, **use it.**

Learning doesn't mean you're giving up on your athletic career.

It means you're **setting yourself up** so when the playing days end, you're not starting from zero.

Step 3: Build Real Relationships Outside of Sports

While you're active, people want to meet you.

Take advantage of it.

Not to party.

Not to ask for favors.

Not to hand out business cards you don't really understand yet.

Meet people to **learn.**

Connect with business owners. CEOs. Leaders in industries you're curious about.

Ask them about their journey. How they got started. What lessons they learned the hard way.

Most successful people **love** mentoring athletes — because they respect the hustle it took to get where you are.

But they're not going to chase you down.

You have to reach out.

You have to be curious.

You have to be humble.

The relationships you start building now could turn into partnerships, job opportunities, investments, or mentorships when you hang up your cleats.

Step 4: Explore Interests Without Pressure

Don't force it.

You don't have to know today exactly what you'll do post-career.

But you do need to explore.

Love fashion? Learn about the business of retail.

Love gaming? Understand how the esports industry works.

Love helping others? Research non-profits, foundations, and community work.

The more you explore **now**, the less lost you'll feel **later.**

Second careers don't magically appear the day you retire.

They grow from seeds you plant **years before.**

Step 5: Create a Personal Development Plan

Write it down.

Not just in your head — on paper.

Map it out like you would a training program:

- Year 1: Shadow a business leader. Take a finance course.
- Year 2: Launch a small side project. Get a mentor in my second-career field.

- Year 3: Attend a major industry conference. Invest in a business coaching program.

Give yourself goals that have nothing to do with stats, championships, or contracts.

Train your second-career muscles **just like you train your body** — consistently, intentionally, and with purpose.

Step 6: Protect Your Brand

Everything you do today affects your opportunities tomorrow.

- Social media posts.
- Interview comments.
- How you treat fans, teammates, reporters, and staff.

Brands, companies, and partners want to work with people they can trust — on and off the field.

Remember: **Character compounds.**

Protect your reputation like it's a valuable asset — because it is.

Step 7: Save Like Your Career Could End Tomorrow

You can't chase your second-career dreams if you're broke.

It's simple:

- Save aggressively.
- Live beneath your means.
- Build an emergency fund that can last at least 2–5 years after retirement.

If you're smart with your money now, you'll have the freedom to be **strategic** about your second act — not **desperate**.

There's nothing worse than rushing into a bad business deal because you need cash.

Money equals freedom.

Freedom equals power.

Protect it.

Step 8: Avoid the "Fake Hustle" Trap

You're going to get pitched on all kinds of "business opportunities" while you're still playing.

- Record labels.
- Clothing brands.
- Nightclubs.
- Energy drinks.
- Startups that sound like the next Amazon.

Be careful.

Not every business idea is a real business.

Not every friend with an idea is a future CEO.

Ask questions.

Get second opinions.

Move slowly.

Protect your energy — and your bank account.

Step 9: Visualize the Transition

Close your eyes and picture it:

The moment you know your playing career is over.

Where are you?

What are you feeling?

What happens next?

If your only emotion is panic — you've got work to do.

If you can see a clear path forward — even if it's just the first few steps — you're on the right track.

Transition is hard.

But it's a lot harder when you haven't even thought about it.

Start picturing your second act now.

Step 10: Remember — You Are More Than Your Sport

You are not just a football player, basketball player, baseball player, hockey player, tennis player, or fighter.

You are a leader.

You are a brand.

You are a business.

You are a future CEO, entrepreneur, coach, investor, community builder — whatever you choose to be.

But only if you start preparing now.

You worked too hard, sacrificed too much, and overcame too many odds to let your story end when the final whistle blows.

Your second career is your chance to write the second chapter of your greatness.

Start writing it today.

Chapter 44: Continuing Education and Certification Options for Athletes

Let's talk real.

At some point in your career — whether it's your rookie year, your fifth year, or your final year — you're going to realize something:

You have the time, money, access, and influence to build a foundation for the next 40+ years of your life.

And one of the smartest ways you can do that is through **education.**

Not just college degrees.

Not just MBAs.

Not just the traditional classroom.

I'm talking about **strategic, flexible, real-world education and certifications** that can open doors, build credibility, and give you options — no matter what you choose to do after sports.

Education is power.

And you're already sitting in the driver's seat.

You just have to decide which roads you want to travel.

Why Continuing Education Matters for Athletes

The truth is, your athletic prime is short.

But your professional prime?

That can last the rest of your life.

When you invest in continuing education now, you are buying yourself options for the next 20, 30, 40 years.

You're not just preparing to survive after retirement — you're preparing to **thrive.**

It's not about putting "student" next to "athlete."

It's about putting "CEO," "founder," "investor," "coach," "analyst," "broadcaster," "agent," "author," or "business owner" next to your name once the final whistle blows.

You're stacking the deck in your favor.

And the earlier you start, the stronger your foundation will be.

Step 1: Understand the Different Types of Education Paths Available to You

You don't have to go back and sit in a classroom full of 18-year-olds to keep learning.

Today, there are **multiple educational paths** that fit your playing schedule, travel demands, and off-season time:

1. **Online Degree Programs** (Bachelor's or Master's)
2. **Professional Certifications**
3. **Business Certificate Programs**
4. **Executive Education Courses**
5. **Trade and Technical Schools**
6. **Real Estate Licensing Courses**
7. **Coaching Licenses and Certifications**
8. **Financial Certifications**
9. **Entrepreneurship Workshops**
10. **Media, Broadcasting, and Public Speaking Programs**

Each one is a tool.

You just have to pick the right one for the career you want after the game.

Step 2: Start With Your Interests

Don't just chase what sounds prestigious.

Chase what fits your real interests and talents.

- Love talking about sports? Broadcasting and media courses make sense.
- Fascinated by real estate? Get licensed as an agent or investor.
- Interested in helping others with money? Financial planning certification could be your lane.
- Passionate about fitness? Strength and conditioning or coaching certifications could lead to new careers.

Your interests now are clues to your second career later.

Pay attention.

Step 3: Explore Online Degree Programs

Today's online degrees are not the "diploma mills" they used to be.

Top universities now offer **fully online bachelor's and master's programs** that carry serious credibility.

You can knock out a degree during your playing years — at your own pace — without ever setting foot in a classroom.

Degrees to consider depending on your interests:

- Business Administration (BBA or MBA)
- Communications
- Sports Management
- Psychology
- Finance
- Marketing
- Nonprofit Management

If you already have some college credits, many programs will accept transfer credits — saving you time and money.

You're not starting over.

You're finishing stronger.

Step 4: Look Into Professional Certifications

Certifications are fast, targeted, and powerful.

Instead of spending years getting a new degree, you can earn certifications that position you for second careers quickly.

Some examples:

- **Certified Financial Planner (CFP)** – if you want to move into financial services
- **Certified Personal Trainer (CPT)** – if you want to stay in the fitness world
- **Project Management Professional (PMP)** – if you want to run businesses or manage big projects
- **Real Estate Agent/Broker Licenses** – if you love the real estate game
- **Certified Sports Agent** – if you want to represent athletes yourself
- **Strength and Conditioning Coach (CSCS)** – if you love training athletes

Certifications don't just add letters to your name — they add **value** to your brand.

Step 5: Maximize Business Certificate Programs

Not ready for a full MBA?

No problem.

Many universities offer **Business Certificate Programs** — short-term, highly focused classes in areas like:

- Entrepreneurship
- Negotiation and Leadership
- Strategic Management
- Branding and Marketing
- Real Estate Investment

Some are six weeks long. Some are six months.

You can finish during an offseason.

You get Ivy League-level education — without the four-year commitment.

Step 6: Executive Education for Athletes

Some schools even have programs specifically designed for athletes and entertainers who want to transition into business careers.

Examples:

- Harvard Business School's "Crossover into Business" program
- University of Miami's "Athlete Development" courses
- Wharton School of Business executive education programs

These programs understand your schedule, your brand, and your goals.

They're designed to help you build your second-career skills **while you're still playing.**

And trust me — when you say you completed coursework at a school like Harvard or Wharton, people listen.

Step 7: Technical and Trade Skills

Not every second career requires a suit and a corner office.

Some of the most financially successful ex-athletes went into industries like:

- Construction management
- Electrical contracting
- Carpentry and design
- Automotive restoration
- Aviation (private pilot training)

If you love building, fixing, engineering, or creating with your hands — technical education can set you up for a second career where you're in high demand and control your own schedule.

Step 8: Coaching Licenses and Certifications

Maybe you can't imagine life without the game.

That's fine — the game still needs you.

But coaching isn't just about passion.

You need credentials.

Depending on your sport, you may need:

- Coaching certifications (NCAA, FIFA, USA Basketball, USA Track & Field, etc.)
- First Aid/CPR certification
- Strength and conditioning licenses
- Athlete development coursework

You already know the game.

Now you need the paperwork and credibility to coach it at the next level.

Start early. Build your resume now.

Step 9: Financial Literacy and Advisor Programs

If you're passionate about money, investing, and helping others build wealth, consider certifications like:

- Certified Financial Planner (CFP)
- Chartered Financial Analyst (CFA)
- Registered Investment Advisor (RIA)

Athletes who become licensed advisors bring a rare, powerful combination: credibility in the sports world and knowledge of finance.

You could end up managing portfolios for other athletes — and protecting them from the money mistakes you learned to avoid.

Step 10: Entrepreneurship and Business Owner Workshops

A lot of athletes want to own businesses.

But owning a business is **not the same thing** as throwing money at a "good idea."

Learn how to:

- Write business plans
- Understand profit and loss statements
- Hire and manage employees
- Raise capital smartly

Workshops and bootcamps in entrepreneurship can help you avoid the "lost everything in a bad investment" horror stories that too many retired athletes face.

Get educated before you open that restaurant, gym, agency, or apparel line.

Your dream deserves better than guesswork.

Chapter 45: Transitioning from Pro to Retirement Financially

Let's get straight to it.

Leaving pro sports isn't just about leaving the field, the court, or the ice.

It's about leaving the financial rhythm you've known — and building a new one that can carry you for the next 40 or 50 years.

This chapter is about preparing for that shift.

Not in theory.

Not someday.

Now.

Because whether you're ready or not, the day is coming when the game clock hits zero — and the financial game clock starts ticking louder than ever.

And if you build the right transition plan now, you're not just surviving retirement.

You're living it on your terms.

Understanding the Shift: From Checks to Choices

When you're playing, you have a season.

You have paychecks hitting your account every two weeks (or every week, depending on your league).

You have endorsement income.

You have bonus structures.

There's movement. There's momentum.

You *know* when the money's coming.

But when you retire?

It flips.

Suddenly, you're not getting paid for being you anymore.

You're getting paid based on what you **planned**, what you **saved**, and what you **built** during your career.

Money doesn't move automatically anymore.

You have to move it.

And that requires a completely different mindset.

You're shifting from an **income mindset** to a **management mindset.**

This is where a lot of players — even the legends — stumble.

Not because they're stupid.

Because they didn't see the shift coming.

You're going to see it coming.

Step 1: Know Your Retirement Financial Starting Line

Before you can plan your post-career life, you have to know exactly where you're standing.

Here's what you need to map out:

- **Liquid Cash** (checking accounts, savings accounts, emergency funds)
- **Investment Accounts** (brokerage accounts, Roth IRAs, Traditional IRAs, SEP IRAs, 401(k)s)
- **Real Estate Assets** (homes, rental properties, mortgages)
- **Endorsement Contracts Still Paying Out** (structured settlements, equity stakes)
- **League Pensions and Benefits** (NFLPA, NBPA, MLBPA, WNBPA, NHLPA)
- **Deferred Compensation** (salary deferrals, bonuses still owed)

- **Business Ownership Stakes** (restaurants, companies, franchises)
- **Debt** (credit cards, mortgages, private loans, personal IOUs)
- **Monthly Expenses** (fixed and variable — your real budget)

Don't guess.

Don't ballpark it.

Know it.

You can't plan where you're going if you don't know where you're starting.

This is your financial field position.

Are you starting at your opponent's 20-yard line or on your own 5-yard line?

Big difference.

Step 2: Calculate Your Burn Rate

Your burn rate is the amount of money you'll spend each month — and each year — after you retire.

Not during your playing days.

Not when you're traveling 30 weeks a year with the team.

After.

When you're living regular life.

Calculate it honestly:

- Housing
- Cars
- Food
- Family support
- Kids' education
- Healthcare
- Vacations
- Taxes
- Lifestyle habits (good or bad)

- Business investments
- Charity and giving
- Random unexpected expenses

If you don't calculate your burn rate, you're playing financial roulette with your future.

You need to know:

- **Monthly survival number** (bare minimum expenses)
- **Monthly living number** (comfortable, enjoyable life)
- **Monthly dream number** (travel, splurges, big experiences)

Know all three.

Plan for the middle.

Step 3: Understand How Taxes Change After You Retire

Here's the curveball a lot of guys miss:

When you stop playing, your taxes don't magically get easier.

In fact, in many cases, they get trickier.

You'll move from W-2 employee income (team salary) to 1099 self-employment income (endorsements, appearances, business consulting, speaking gigs).

You'll still owe:

- Federal income taxes
- State income taxes (depending on where you live)
- Self-employment taxes (if you're consulting or running a business)

And if you're withdrawing from investment accounts, there are capital gains taxes, ordinary income taxes, and penalties if you pull money out of retirement accounts too early.

Bottom line:

You need a real tax strategy for post-career life — not just a tax preparer who plugs numbers into a software program.

You need someone who can *plan* your tax moves 5, 10, 15 years ahead.

This isn't just about saving a few bucks.

It's about keeping your freedom.

Step 4: Shift from Growth to Preservation

When you're young and earning millions, you can afford to swing for the fences with investments.

You can go after higher-risk, higher-return strategies.

But after retirement?

The game changes.

Now it's about:

- Protecting what you built
- Growing it slowly and steadily
- Making sure it lasts your whole life

You still want growth — but you can't afford catastrophic losses anymore.

It's like switching from running a no-huddle, go-deep offense to a ball-control, clock-management game.

Still aggressive when needed.

But smart.

Calculated.

You have to prioritize **preservation** over **gambling.**

Because now, every dollar you lose is a dollar you can't replace with another contract.

Step 5: Build a New "Income Stream" in Retirement

Here's the simple truth most players never hear until it's too late:

You have to **manufacture** your own income after you stop playing.

No team is sending you checks anymore.

You have to build a system where:

- Investment dividends pay you
- Rental properties pay you
- Business profits pay you
- Endorsements (if any remain) pay you
- Royalties and licensing fees pay you
- Pension distributions pay you
- Retirement account withdrawals pay you

You have to create **multiple small paychecks** to replace **one big paycheck.**

This is your new offense.

You're still scoring points — just in a different way.

Step 6: Protect Yourself from the Two Big Killers: Lifestyle Inflation and Family Pressure

Once you retire, something weird happens.

People around you act like you're richer than you've ever been — even though you're no longer earning like you used to.

They'll say:

- "You should buy a bigger house."
- "You should invest in this new business with me."
- "You should sponsor this event."
- "You should pay for the whole family trip."

And if you don't have a plan?

You'll say yes.

Not because you want to.

Because you don't know how to say no.

Lifestyle inflation and family pressure are silent killers of retired athletes' wealth.

Your defense?

A real, written, non-negotiable post-career budget and wealth preservation plan.

It's not about being stingy.

It's about being strategic.

You can still bless people.

You just have to bless yourself first.

Step 7: Structure Your Accounts for Different Phases of Retirement

Not all your money should be in one big pile.

That's like having one giant locker room for every team in the league. Total chaos.

You need separate "lockers" for different phases of your post-career life.

Here's a simple structure:

Short-Term Accounts (0–5 years after retirement)

- High-yield savings
- Short-term bonds
- Conservative brokerage accounts
- Cash reserves
- Any guaranteed income sources

Mid-Term Accounts (5–15 years after retirement)

- Moderate-growth investments
- Conservative stocks
- Real estate income
- Structured settlements
- Some pension income, if applicable

Long-Term Accounts (15+ years after retirement)

- Retirement accounts (IRA, Roth IRA, 401(k))
- Deferred compensation
- Growth stocks
- Long-term real estate holdings
- Business equity you're holding onto

You want the early money accessible and low risk.

You want the later money working harder, growing patiently for your 60s, 70s, and beyond.

It's a lot like managing your playing career.

You trained differently for a rookie mini-camp than you did for a playoff game.

Your money needs the same kind of customized game plan.

Step 8: Understand When to Start Taking Pension Payments

If you're lucky enough to be part of a league with a pension — NFL, NBA, MLB, WNBA, NHL — you need to understand your options.

You usually get to choose:

- Start payments earlier for smaller checks
- Wait longer for bigger checks

It's a lot like deciding when to leave college early for the draft.

If you come out early, you might make money faster but risk leaving some growth on the table.

If you wait, you might get a bigger payday — but you risk injury (or other financial needs) along the way.

Same idea here.

Factors to consider:

- Your current cash flow needs
- Your health and family medical history
- Your spouse's financial needs
- Other investment income
- Tax implications of early vs. delayed withdrawals

No blanket answer works for everyone.

You need a personalized strategy — like a custom playbook.

This is why having a trusted financial advisor *who understands athletes* (not just "rich people") is critical.

Step 9: Create a Smart Withdrawal Strategy

Here's the deal:

If you just pull money randomly from different accounts, you'll burn through it faster than you realize.

You need a **smart withdrawal strategy.**

The basics:

- Tap taxable accounts first (savings, brokerage)
- Tap tax-deferred accounts next (Traditional IRA, 401(k))
- Save Roth IRA accounts for last (they grow tax-free longer)

This sequence lets your tax-advantaged accounts grow longer while minimizing your taxes early on.

It's like playing a long season — you manage your starters differently in Game 1 than you do in the playoffs.

Same with your money.

Manage it for the long haul — not just the short sprints.

Step 10: Protect Your Mindset in Retirement

Nobody talks about this enough.

When you retire, you lose:

- Structure
- Competition
- Camaraderie
- Public validation
- Instant credibility

You go from "star athlete" to "regular person" overnight.

That emotional crash is real.

And if you're not prepared for it, you can start making desperate, stupid financial moves just to feel "important" again.

Buying stuff you don't need.

Saying yes to dumb investments.

Sponsoring random projects.

Overextending yourself for friends and family.

Protect your **mind** first.

- Find new goals.
- Build new communities.
- Stay physically active.
- Learn new skills.
- Focus on new financial challenges (like investing smarter or mentoring others).

A healthy mind supports healthy money decisions.

It always has.

It always will.

Real-World Examples: The Good, the Bad, and the Ugly

Let's talk about what happens when players get it right — and when they get it wrong.

The Good Example:

- NFL offensive lineman plays 7 years
- Saves 70% of his earnings every year
- Buys one modest home, no second house
- Diversifies investments (stocks, bonds, real estate)
- Starts financial education courses during career
- Transitions into private equity after football
- Still living comfortably 15 years after retirement

The Bad Example:

- NBA guard plays 5 years
- Lives paycheck to paycheck
- Buys three houses and four cars
- Invests heavily in bad businesses run by friends
- No pension strategy, burns through savings
- Forced to work retail at age 38

The Ugly Example:

- MLB pitcher plays 4 years
- Makes $12 million
- Lets agent control everything

- Never checks statements
- Ends up scammed for $6 million
- Bankruptcy at 35
- Mental health struggles follow

Moral of the story:

Talent gets you rich.

Planning keeps you rich.

Action Steps: Your Retirement Playbook

- Build your Financial Starting Line Sheet
- Calculate your Burn Rate
- Design your New Income Stream Strategy
- Lock in your Tax Plan
- Segment your accounts by timeline
- Decide when to tap pensions and retirement funds
- Build a Withdrawal Strategy
- Guard your Mindset
- Keep learning. Keep growing. Keep playing the financial game smart.

Final Words on Retiring Like a Champion

Look, stepping away from pro sports is emotional.

There's no sugarcoating it.

But your career ending on the field doesn't mean your winning ends in life.

This next chapter is about owning your future *even more fiercely* than you owned your playing days.

It's about putting the same discipline, the same work ethic, the same pride you had in your game — into your financial life.

Because that's where legends are really made.

Not just on ESPN highlights.

But 20, 30, 40 years later — living free, providing for your family, giving back to your community, and living with dignity.

That's real greatness.

And it's within your reach — starting today.

Your best plays are still ahead of you.

Stay smart.

Stay steady.

Stay hungry.

Chapter 46: Protecting Your Mental Health During and After Pro Sports

Introduction: Your Mind Is Your Most Valuable Asset

When you first start out in sports, it's all about the body.

Speed. Strength. Endurance. Power.

But the longer you stay in the game, the more you realize something deeper:

Your mind is your real franchise player.

Without mental toughness, the body crumbles.

Without emotional resilience, talent fades.

Without clear thinking, money disappears.

And when your playing days eventually end — whether by choice, by injury, or just by time — it's not your body that takes the hardest hit.

It's your mind.

That's why protecting your mental health isn't optional.

It's essential — before, during, and after your career.

Today, we're going to have the conversation too many athletes never get to have until it's too late.

Let's get into it.

The Silent Battles Athletes Fight (But Rarely Talk About)

You probably already know the public narrative:

- "They're rich. They're famous. They have it easy."
- "What could they possibly be stressed about?"
- "If I had that kind of money, I'd be happy forever."

But behind the scenes, here's the real story for a lot of pros:

- Crippling performance anxiety
- Loneliness on the road
- Family stress piling up back home
- Injuries taking a toll physically and mentally
- Financial pressure despite high salaries
- Fear of failure every time you suit up
- Fear of becoming irrelevant when the cheering stops
- Depression when facing retirement
- Identity crisis when you're no longer "the athlete"

The truth is, athletes are **trained to hide pain**, not express it.

You're trained to "walk it off," "stay tough," and "play through it."

And that survival strategy can work for a while — until it doesn't.

At some point, if you don't manage the stress, it will manage you.

And that has massive implications for your mental health... and your financial health too.

Why Financial Pressure Makes Mental Health Even Tougher

Money is a double-edged sword for athletes.

On one hand, it brings opportunities, security, freedom.

On the other hand, it brings responsibility, pressure, and fear.

The stakes feel higher when you realize:

- One bad contract can erase millions.
- One bad investment can devastate your family.
- One injury can end it all overnight.
- One year off the roster can erase years of work.
- One lawsuit can wipe you out.

You're not just playing a sport.

You're managing a business.

You're protecting a brand.

You're carrying the hopes and dreams of entire families, friends, and communities.

It's exhausting.

And when financial literacy is low — when you don't know what's happening with your own money — the anxiety multiplies.

You start feeling like you're one bad decision away from disaster.

That kind of mental weight will eventually break you if you don't have the right coping strategies.

So protecting your financial literacy *and* your mental health go hand in hand.

You can't build wealth without peace of mind.

You can't protect peace of mind without smart financial moves.

They work together — or they fall apart together.

Signs Your Mental Health Might Be Struggling (Even If You're Still Performing)

Mental health issues rarely start with an explosion.

Most of the time, it's a slow burn you don't notice right away.

Here are some early warning signs to watch for:

- Feeling numb instead of excited before games
- Constantly irritated by teammates, coaches, or media
- Losing sleep, even on off days
- Eating way more or way less than usual
- Obsessing over money, even if you're financially stable
- Pulling away from family and friends
- Feeling like you have no identity outside of your sport
- Dreading practices, games, or even public appearances
- Random outbursts of anger or sadness that don't make sense
- Using substances to "escape" more than usual (alcohol, painkillers, weed)

If you see any of these popping up, it's a sign:

Something inside you is waving a red flag.

Ignoring it won't make it go away.

It will just get louder, until it forces you to listen.

And trust me — it's better to handle it early than after it blows up your life.

The Financial Toll of Ignoring Mental Health

When athletes let mental health struggles fester without support, here's what often happens financially:

- Impulsive purchases trying to fill the emotional void
- Trusting the wrong people out of loneliness or fear

- Letting others manage your money without oversight
- Blowing through retirement savings prematurely
- Paying massive legal fees after emotional outbursts or DUIs
- Burning bridges with sponsors, teams, and media partners
- Losing focus on endorsements, branding, and business opportunities

Your financial life and mental health are tied together like your left and right legs.

If one goes down, the other stumbles too.

That's why this chapter matters so much.

Step-by-Step Game Plan: Protecting Your Mental Health

Step 1: Build a "Personal Team" Off the Field

You already know how important your team is on the court, field, or ice.

You need a team **off** the field too.

Your Personal Team might include:

- A therapist or mental coach who understands athletes
- A financial advisor who respects your emotional journey
- A spiritual advisor, pastor, or mentor if faith is important to you
- A small circle of trusted friends who love you, not your status
- A business advisor or lawyer who protects your future interests

You need people in your life who see the whole you — not just the highlights.

Step 2: Normalize Mental Health Conversations

Mental toughness doesn't mean suffering in silence.

Toughness means handling your business — and getting help when needed.

Talk openly about:

- Stress
- Fear
- Money anxiety
- Life after sports
- Family pressure

Normalize it in your locker room.

Normalize it in your friend group.

Normalize it in your family.

The more you talk, the more you heal.

The more you heal, the better you perform.

Step 3: Schedule Mental Health Check-Ins Like Physicals

You don't just go to the doctor when you're dying.

You do annual checkups to catch problems early.

Do the same thing for your mind.

- Find a therapist you vibe with
- Schedule quarterly or semi-annual sessions
- Treat it like a financial audit — preventative maintenance

Step 4: Create Your "Life After Sports" Vision Early

You need a life plan before your sport ends.

Don't wait until you're cut, injured, or retired to figure it out.

Ask yourself:

- What would excite me if I couldn't play anymore?
- How do I want to contribute to the world?
- What skills do I want to develop?
- How can I build wealth outside of sports?
- What legacy do I want to leave?

Having a bigger purpose will cushion the blow when your playing days end.

It gives you something to run toward — not just something you're running away from.

Step 5: Budget for Mental Health Services

Just like you budget for:

- Housing
- Food
- Training
- Travel

You should **budget for mental health** too.

- Therapy sessions
- Life coaching
- Mindfulness apps
- Mental wellness retreats

Investing in your mind is one of the best financial moves you'll ever make.

It keeps you in the game longer.

It protects your money better.

It makes every dollar you earn work harder.

Real-World Examples: Athletes Who Faced the Mental Health Challenge

Kevin Love (NBA):

Opened up about his panic attacks and therapy work.

Result: Extended career, new endorsements, respected mental health advocate.

DeMar DeRozan (NBA):

Shared his battles with depression.

Result: Broke stigma, inspired other players, created second career opportunities post-basketball.

Serena Williams (Tennis):

Spoke about managing pressure, expectations, and motherhood stress.

Result: Greater brand partnerships focused on wellness, motherhood, and empowerment.

Michael Phelps (Olympics):

Battled suicidal depression after winning it all.

Result: Started mental health foundation, built enduring legacy beyond swimming.

Chapter 47: Dealing with Injury and Early Retirement Financially

Introduction: The Game Can End Sooner Than You Expect

When you lace up those shoes, pull on that jersey, or step onto that court, field, ice, or track — you never think *today* could be your last day.

You prepare for gàmes.

You prepare for playoffs.

You prepare for championships.

But how many of us prepare for *the end*?

Especially an end we didn't choose?

One awkward landing.

One missed tackle.

One torn ligament.

One doctor's report.

One trade that never comes.

Suddenly, the career you worked your whole life to build can be over in a blink.

And if you're not ready financially, emotionally, and mentally, early retirement doesn't just hurt your pride — it can wreck your future.

That's why this chapter is so critical.

Today, we're going to get real about it — while you still have the power to prepare.

Because if you control the financial side, you stay in control of your life — even when the game says you're done.

Why Early Retirement Hits Athletes Harder Than Almost Any Other Profession

Most people spend 30 to 40 years in their chosen career before retirement.

Teachers.

Doctors.

Engineers.

Lawyers.

Accountants.

They start slow. They peak in their 50s or 60s. They have time to save, build, adjust.

Athletes don't get that luxury.

Your peak earning years are front-loaded.

You make the bulk of your lifetime income in your 20s and early 30s.

And then it's over.

If an injury speeds that up even more — you could be facing "retirement" at 26, 28, or 30 years old.

Meanwhile:

- Your friends are just finishing law school.
- Your siblings are just getting their first promotions.
- Your old college classmates are still renting apartments.

And you're already living in a million-dollar house... wondering what happens now.

It's backwards compared to the regular world.

And if you don't understand that — if you plan like a "regular person" instead of like an athlete — your money will disappear **way faster** than you ever imagined.

Common Financial Mistakes After Injury or Early Retirement

Here's what happens to too many athletes who get injured or retire early:

- **Denial Spending:**
- They keep living like they're still making game checks… even when the checks stop.
- **Delayed Adjustments:**
- They don't downsize expenses fast enough — homes, cars, vacations, gifting.
- **Risky Investments:**
- They chase "get rich quick" deals to replace lost income.
- **Isolation:**
- They pull away from advisors, teammates, mentors — and make money moves out of fear or shame.
- **Overtrust:**
- They hand their last pile of money to unqualified friends, family members, or shady "business managers" hoping to stretch it.

Every one of these mistakes is avoidable — if you plan **before** you need to.

That's what we're going to do right now.

Step-by-Step Game Plan: Financial Preparation for Injury or Early Retirement

Step 1: Face the Possibility Head-On

Nobody wants to think about injury or early exit.

But pretending it can't happen to you is like pretending you don't need insurance because you're "a careful driver."

It's not about expecting disaster.

It's about being **ready** for anything.

Start asking:

- If my income stopped tomorrow, how many months could I survive without touching investments?
- Have I maxed out my retirement accounts *now*, while I'm earning big checks?
- Do I know exactly what my burn rate is — monthly, annually?
- How fast could I downsize if needed?
- Do I have a clear post-sports plan (business, school, passion projects) that could kick in if needed?

Step 2: Build a "Career End" Emergency Fund

Most people aim for 3-6 months of living expenses in an emergency fund.

Athletes should aim higher.

Because your career ending isn't just a "temporary job loss."

It's a permanent identity shift.

Build at least 2 years' worth of living expenses in a secure, liquid emergency fund.

Yes, two full years.

Why so much?

Because when the game ends, you'll need:

- Time to grieve

- Time to reframe your identity
- Time to reskill or reposition
- Time to build a second career the right way

You don't want to be *desperate* during that transition.

You want to be *calm, patient,* and *strategic.*

That emergency fund buys you that peace.

Step 3: Insure Yourself Wisely

One torn ACL.

One broken neck.

One catastrophic injury.

If you don't have the right insurance, you could lose millions — even if the league offers some protections.

Types of insurance you should discuss with your advisor:

- Career-ending disability insurance
- Loss-of-value insurance (especially during contract years)
- High-deductible health insurance (for post-retirement care)

It's not glamorous.

It's not Instagram-worthy.

But it's the reason some athletes stay millionaires while others go broke after an injury.

Step 4: Create a "Downshift Budget" Ahead of Time

Before the injury happens... before the call comes...

Build a Plan B Budget.

This budget should reflect:

- No game checks
- Only investment and passive income
- Reduced living expenses
- Limited luxury spending
- Clear health care and insurance costs

Name it.

Save it.

Be ready to execute it if you ever need it.

You don't want to be figuring this out when emotions are running high.

You want to be flipping to your playbook... and running the play.

Step 5: Explore Second Career Income Streams Early

Start thinking about second-act income while you're still playing.

- Broadcasting
- Coaching
- Real estate
- Business ownership
- Financial advising (especially for other athletes)
- Brand partnerships
- Motivational speaking
- Consulting

You don't have to wait until you're officially retired to start learning new skills.

Think of it like cross-training:

Working different muscles while you're still at peak fitness.

The athletes who transition best financially aren't the ones who sit around waiting for inspiration.

They're the ones who build new playbooks while they're still in the game.

Real-Life Examples: Financial Survivors After Early Retirement

Andrew Luck (NFL):

Walked away from football early due to mental and physical toll.

Planned finances wisely. Still wealthy. Focused on family and education now.

Brandon Roy (NBA):

Career cut short by knee injuries.

Pivoted to coaching and mentoring, stayed connected to basketball, built second income stream.

Maya Moore (WNBA):

Paused her career to focus on social justice work.

Leveraged endorsements, education, and speaking opportunities to stay financially independent.

These athletes made tough choices — but smart financial moves before disaster hit.

You can too.

Mental Strategies to Handle Sudden Career Endings

Let's be real: it's not just about the money.

When an injury or early retirement ends your career, the emotional fallout is just as real — and just as dangerous — as the financial stress.

You aren't just losing a paycheck.

You're losing:

- A sense of purpose
- A daily schedule
- A locker room full of brothers and sisters
- Applause, respect, admiration
- The identity you've had since you were 5, 10, 15 years old

If you don't prepare mentally, all the money in the world won't save you from spiraling.

Here's how to get ahead of it:

1. Acknowledge It's a Loss — Not Just a Transition

Too often, athletes try to "tough guy" their way through retirement.

They pretend it's no big deal.

They pretend they're "too busy" to feel anything.

They deny, distract, and detach.

But denial doesn't protect you.

It delays your healing.

Early retirement is a form of grief.

It's okay to mourn.

It's okay to hurt.

It's okay to feel lost for a while.

Let yourself process it fully — so you can move forward clean, clear, and ready.

2. Find a New Locker Room

When your career ends, you lose your team — literally.

You lose the locker room energy.

The jokes, the brotherhood, the sisterhood.

The shared battles, the victories, even the defeats.

And isolation can be brutal if you're not ready.

Find or build a new team:

- Business masterminds
- Fitness groups
- Entrepreneurs networks
- Athlete alumni associations
- Men's groups, women's groups, faith-based groups

You need to keep iron sharpening iron.

You need people who challenge you, encourage you, and check you when you start slipping.

3. Reframe Your Identity

You are not just an athlete.

You never were.

You are:

- A leader
- A competitor
- A strategist
- A teammate
- A brand
- A builder
- A visionary

Athleticism was just the first platform you built on.

Now it's time to build your next platform — using the same DNA that made you elite on the field.

Financial Rebuilding Checklist for Post-Injury Life

If your career ends earlier than expected, here's your **post-injury money checklist**:

1. Reassess Net Worth Immediately

Inventory:

- Checking accounts
- Savings
- Investment portfolios
- Retirement accounts
- Endorsement or sponsorship deals still active
- Real estate
- Business equity
- Cars, collectibles, luxury goods

Get a clear, unemotional snapshot of your real financial standing.

2. Adjust Lifestyle

Within 60 days of early retirement:

- Cut housing costs by 20–30% if needed
- Eliminate multiple car payments
- Scale back on staff (assistants, chefs, stylists) if necessary
- Pause all major discretionary purchases
- Create a cash flow budget based only on passive income

Every dollar you save now buys you *time* and *freedom* later.

3. Meet With Your Financial Team

Convene your CPA, financial advisor, estate planning attorney, and insurance agent.

Topics to cover:

- Update insurance needs post-career
- Review tax implications of career-ending payouts
- Discuss safe withdrawal rates for retirement funds
- Rebalance investment risk based on new goals
- Adjust estate plans if dependents or beneficiaries have changed

4. Prioritize Health Coverage

Athletes transitioning out of leagues often lose team-sponsored health insurance.

Options to consider:

- COBRA coverage (temporary but expensive)
- Private insurance marketplace
- Special athlete-specific insurance plans

5. Create a "Second Career" Business Plan

Not just dreams — an actionable plan.

Elements to outline:

- Industry you want to enter
- Certifications or education needed
- Start-up costs
- Timeline for launch
- Network connections to leverage

Move thoughtfully — not impulsively.

Investment Allocation Shifts After Retirement

When you're playing, you can afford to take some investment risks.

You have huge game checks coming every week, every month, every season.

But once those checks stop?

The investment strategy must change.

Key shifts to consider:

1. Move from Aggressive Growth to Balanced or Conservative

You need to protect principal now — not just chase returns.

Shift some of your portfolio into:

- Bonds
- Dividend-paying stocks
- Index funds
- Real estate cash flow properties
- Annuities (only if structured properly)

2. Emphasize Liquidity

Illiquid investments (like start-up ventures, exotic real estate, or private equity funds) can trap your money for years.

After early retirement, you need **access** to your cash — not just paper wealth.

Aim to keep a portion of your assets easily available without heavy penalties or long lock-up periods.

3. Reassess Risk Tolerance Every 12 Months

Your emotional risk tolerance might change after the adrenaline fades.

Check in with yourself — and your advisor — yearly.

Update your investment allocations to match your new mindset.

Rebranding Yourself After Retirement

Think of your athletic career as your "first brand."

Now it's time to build your "second brand."

How you present yourself to the world post-career matters — financially, socially, emotionally.

Elements of a successful rebrand:

- Professional bio reflecting your transition story
- Clean, updated social media presence
- New headshots and brand visuals
- Updated resume or portfolio if pursuing a corporate or entrepreneurial path
- Thoughtful networking strategy (alumni events, business groups, speaking gigs)

Remember:

The skills that made you great in your sport — discipline, resilience, competitiveness — are exactly what make you valuable in your next chapter.

Own that.

Final Words of Encouragement

Listen — if you're reading this chapter because you're already facing injury or early retirement, know this:

You are not a failure.

Your value was never tied solely to your ability to score points, hit home runs, dunk basketballs, throw touchdowns, or win titles.

Those things were amazing.

They opened doors.

They built platforms.

They changed lives — including yours.

But your true power was never the jersey on your back.

Your true power is the person inside the jersey.

The discipline.

The perseverance.

The fight.

The focus.

The ability to adapt, train, overcome, and dominate — in *anything* you choose next.

Early retirement might change the game.

But it doesn't change the player.

Suit up for the next chapter.

Own your story.

Own your finances.

Own your future.

Because *your best days are still ahead of you* — and nobody can take that away.

Chapter 48: Building a Personal Brand Beyond Your Sport

When you lace up your shoes, strap on your pads, or pull on your jersey, you're representing more than a team.

You're representing a brand.

In your playing days, that brand is often tied tightly to your sport — your stats, your highlight reels, your championships.

But here's the truth that separates athletes who fade away from those who *build legacies*:

Your real brand — the one that lasts — is about who you are **off the field**.

Because one day the stadium lights will turn off.

The season will end.

The fans will move on to the next big name.

And what you've built beyond your sport is what will either carry you forward — or leave you scrambling for relevance.

This chapter is about making sure you build a brand that outlasts your playing days, and creates freedom, purpose, and opportunities for decades to come.

Let's go.

Step One: Understand What a Personal Brand Really Is

Your personal brand isn't your Instagram page.

It isn't your logo.

It isn't even your nickname.

Your personal brand is:

- What people say about you when you're not in the room
- The feeling people get when they hear your name
- The trust and credibility you have — or don't have
- The emotional connection people feel toward your story

Your personal brand is your reputation, your value, and your promise — all rolled into one.

And the earlier you start intentionally building it, the more options you'll have after your playing days are done.

Step Two: Separate Your Identity From Your Sport

When you've been "the basketball player," "the football star," "the baseball phenom," or "the fastest on the track" your whole life, it's easy to *become* the sport.

But you are not just your sport.

You're a whole person with talents, passions, skills, and stories that have nothing to do with a scoreboard.

Athletes who struggle post-career often feel lost because they never built anything outside their sport.

They thought "athlete" was their only identity.

Don't fall into that trap.

Start defining who you are outside of the uniform — *now.*

Ask yourself:

- What causes am I passionate about?

- What industries or topics excite me?
- What life experiences shaped me?
- What challenges have I overcome that others could learn from?

Your story off the field is just as powerful as anything you do on it.

Step Three: Clarify Your Brand Pillars

Every strong personal brand stands on clear pillars — 3 to 5 key ideas or values you represent.

For example:

- Leadership
- Resilience
- Entrepreneurship
- Faith
- Financial education
- Community service
- Mental health advocacy
- Athlete empowerment
- Social justice
- Creative expression

You don't have to be all things to all people.

You just have to be *very clear* about the few things you stand for — and then consistently live them out.

When someone hears your name, they should immediately associate you with those pillars.

Step Four: Be Strategic With Your Social Media

Social media can make or break your brand faster than almost anything else.

It's your digital storefront.

It's how most people will meet you long before they ever shake your hand.

Here's how to use it smartly:

- Stay consistent with your message
- Share content aligned with your brand pillars
- Highlight your off-the-field activities and interests
- Avoid reckless posts that could damage your reputation
- Respond thoughtfully — not emotionally — to criticism
- Use professional photos and clean bios

Remember: every post either builds trust or destroys it.

Every comment either adds value or subtracts it.

Your social media should tell the world: **I'm more than an athlete — and here's the proof.**

Step Five: Leverage Your Playing Platform While You Have It

The time to start building your brand is **now** — while you're still active, visible, and relevant.

Use your platform to:

- Speak at schools, camps, and charity events
- Start a blog, podcast, or YouTube channel about your interests
- Partner with brands that align with your values
- Mentor younger players coming up behind you
- Write articles or opinion pieces for local newspapers or sports media

The more seeds you plant during your career, the bigger your harvest will be after it's over.

Step Six: Control Your Narrative

If you don't tell your story, someone else will.

And trust me — they won't always tell it right.

You need to control your narrative by:

- Sharing your journey authentically
- Owning your wins and your losses
- Speaking openly about your transitions and lessons
- Framing your past challenges as preparation for future success

A strong personal brand doesn't come from pretending to be perfect.

It comes from being real — and showing others what's possible.

Step Seven: Build Real Relationships, Not Just Followers

There's a big difference between an audience and a network.

An audience claps for you.

A network *opens doors* for you.

You need both.

Use your playing career to build genuine relationships with:

- Business leaders
- Entrepreneurs
- Nonprofit executives
- Media professionals
- Educators
- Coaches
- Former athletes who've made successful transitions

Invest in these relationships:

- Have real conversations
- Send handwritten thank-you notes
- Follow up after events
- Offer value before asking for favors

Relationships — not followers — are what build long-term brand equity.

Step Eight: Create Multiple Streams of Impact (Not Just Income)

Yes, a strong brand can eventually help you make more money.

But the biggest brands are built on **impact first** — not just income.

Think about how you can:

- Inspire others through your story
- Create opportunities for your community
- Empower younger athletes
- Champion causes you believe in
- Leave a legacy bigger than trophies or stats

When you focus on impact, the income takes care of itself — endorsements, speaking gigs, book deals, business partnerships, consulting opportunities, and more.

Step Nine: Keep Evolving

You're going to grow and change after your playing career — and your brand should too.

Don't lock yourself into a version of yourself that no longer fits.

Stay flexible. Stay curious. Stay evolving.

The best brands — and the best people — keep learning, stretching, and leveling up.

Even after you retire, your brand journey is just beginning.

Final Play: Brand Like a Champion

Building a personal brand beyond your sport is about more than PR.

It's about building a life that's rich with purpose, passion, and possibility — long after the final whistle blows.

Here's the truth:

Your stats will fade.

Your trophies will gather dust.

Your jersey will hang in a closet.

But your impact — and the brand you build around it — will live on.

Start building it today.

Own your story.

Own your voice.

Own your future.

Because you are — and always have been — so much more than an athlete.

You're a leader.

You're a creator.

You're a builder.

Now it's time to show the world.

Part 6: Deep Dives By Sport

No two sports are the same — and neither are the financial realities that come with them.

In this section, we take a deep dive into the specific financial nuances, challenges, and opportunities that come with different professional sports.

Each league, each system, and each career path has its own rules, rhythms, and risks.

What works for an NFL player doesn't always work for an MLB veteran.

What's normal for a WNBA star might be completely different from a pro golfer or tennis player traveling the world.

You need financial literacy that's *tailored* to your sport — not just general advice that doesn't fit your reality.

This part of the book covers:

- How contracts are structured differently sport-to-sport
- How pensions, benefits, and healthcare plans vary
- How pay cycles, off-seasons, and career length impact financial planning
- Common traps athletes fall into within their specific leagues
- Smart strategies for maximizing earnings and minimizing risks, customized to your sport

Whether you're signing a 10-day contract in the NBA, a minor league deal in baseball, a rookie contract in the NFL, or traveling the world as a tennis or golf pro, this section will break it all down.

It's about knowing your field — on and off the court.

It's about understanding your sport's financial blueprint so you can game plan smarter, protect yourself longer, and build wealth that outlasts your playing days.

You've worked too hard to leave it to chance.

Let's dive in — sport by sport — and set you up for true, lasting financial success.

Chapter 49: Football (NFL, CFL, XFL, USFL) — Average Salaries, Career Span, Unique Financial Issues

When you put on the pads and strap on the helmet, you're stepping into one of the most physically demanding, financially unpredictable, and emotionally charged sports in the world. Football isn't just a game — it's a business, and it's a business that moves fast, hits hard, and doesn't wait for anyone to catch up. Whether you're signing with the NFL, the CFL, the XFL, the USFL, or another emerging league, your financial foundation starts the moment you ink your first deal.

For athletes in football, money doesn't just come differently — it *flows* differently. It's lumpy. It's seasonal. It's taxed aggressively. It's packed with hidden pitfalls and golden opportunities, depending on how you play your cards.

Let's sit down and break it all down — player to player, one real conversation at a time.

Understanding the Landscape: Football's Unique Financial Terrain

Unlike baseball or basketball, football contracts are rarely fully guaranteed. You might sign for "millions," but if you get injured in Week 2, you could see a fraction of it. The non-guaranteed nature of NFL, CFL, and even newer league contracts demands a different mindset.

In football, the *average career length is brutally short.*

- NFL average career: about **3.3 years**.
- CFL average career: about **3.2 years**.
- XFL and USFL? Many players get **one season** or even **just a training camp**.
- This is a sprint, not a marathon.

You can't afford to think about money the way your friends with 40-year corporate careers do. You need urgency. You need structure. You need protection.

Football is a "now" game. But your financial life needs to be a "later" game, too.

Average Salaries: What They Really Mean

When people hear about NFL contracts, they think everyone is a millionaire. Reality check: they're not.

- NFL rookies on minimum salaries in 2024 make around **$750,000** — before taxes, agent fees, union dues, and living costs.
- CFL players? The minimum salary is about **$70,000 CAD** — roughly **$50,000 USD** depending on exchange rates.
- XFL and USFL players? Many make **$50,000–$60,000** for an entire season.

Those numbers can sound big to someone not used to professional sports money. But here's what you have to remember:

Football money is temporary money.

You could be done next year. Next month. Next week.

You have to treat every check like it might be your last.

The Real Cost of Playing Football

Every hit you take carries a physical cost — and a financial one.

Medical expenses, rehabilitation, surgeries, long-term health issues like CTE — they don't just cost you physically. They can cripple your future earnings if you're not careful.

Insurance is your invisible teammate.

Disability insurance. Loss of value insurance. Gap coverage.

If you don't have the right protection, one injury could derail not just your career, but your entire financial future.

You're not just managing your earnings.

You're managing *risk*.

And in football, risk is *everywhere*.

Taxes Hit Harder Than Linebackers

In football, you often pay taxes in multiple states — every state you play an away game in, plus the state you live in.

It's called the "jock tax," and it's brutal.

- You might owe California taxes if you play the Chargers.
- New York taxes if you visit the Giants or Jets.
- Louisiana taxes if you take on the Saints.

Meanwhile, your home state might not care — they still want their cut too.

If you're not careful, you'll owe tens of thousands more than you expect at tax time.

You have to set aside taxes *early and aggressively*.

Think **35–40% of every paycheck** tucked away immediately, no exceptions.

If you don't, tax season could hit you harder than a blindside sack.

Budgeting for a Short Career: Your Real Window

If the average NFL career is 3.3 years, and you live 70–80 years, that means your "prime earning window" is **less than 5%** of your total life.

Think about that.

You're making most of your lifetime earnings in a tiny sliver of your life.

You have to stretch it over *decades* — not just seasons.

It's like getting handed all your grocery money for the next 60 years at once.

You have to ration it. Invest it. Protect it. Grow it.

That means:

- **Saving first, spending second.**
- **Living like your career could end tomorrow — because it might.**
- **Building passive income streams early.**
- **Treating every dollar like it's a starter seed for your post-football life.**

Unique Challenges in Each League

NFL

- **Non-guaranteed contracts**: You might be cut at any time.
- **Large signing bonuses**: Paid upfront but fully taxed.
- **Enormous pressure**: Expectations from family, friends, and the

public.

CFL

- **Lower salaries**: Most players need off-season jobs.
- **Currency exchange risks**: Paid in Canadian dollars, spending in U.S. dollars.
- **Shorter seasons**: 18 games, tighter pay windows.

XFL and USFL

- **Volatility**: Leagues still fighting for survival.
- **Lower base pay**: Many players make less than $5,000 per game.
- **Exposure over money**: Many use these leagues as stepping stones.

No matter the league, **you have to play chess, not checkers** with your money.

Pros and Cons of Football Financial Life

Pros:

- Potential for high earnings quickly.
- Platform for endorsement deals if you build your brand.
- Union benefits and pensions if you vest long enough.

Cons:

- Short careers.
- High physical risk.
- High taxation across multiple states.
- Non-guaranteed income and constant threat of being cut.

Action Steps Every Football Player Should Take Immediately

- **Hire a second opinion CPA** who specializes in multi-state tax returns.
- **Open a separate savings account** just for taxes.
- **Create an offseason budget** that assumes you earn no new money.
- **Buy disability insurance immediately.**
- **Plan your exit strategy now** — don't wait until you're released or retired.

You need a money game plan just like you need a game plan on the field.

Real-World Scenarios

"Imagine you're a rookie cornerback. You just got a $100,000 signing bonus. Your agent fee is 3%. Taxes will take around 40%. You buy a car, help your mom, and get an apartment near the team's facility. Two months later, you're waived. Suddenly, you have no income, but your bills keep rolling in."

It happens **every year** — and it doesn't just happen to the "bad" players. It happens to good ones, too.

You need a strategy to **last** — not just a strategy to *flash*.

Sports Analogies from All Sports

Saving during your career is like:

- **Basketball**: Playing defense first so you can run fast breaks.
- **Baseball**: Building your bullpen — because you're not going to pitch nine innings every game.
- **Tennis**: Having a second serve ready when your first serve fails.
- **Golf**: Taking the safe shot when you could try to drive the green —

playing the long game.

- **Soccer**: Defending your own goal before pushing forward.

In every sport, the pros who win **think long-term**.

Final Thoughts: Football Is Temporary — Wealth Can Be Forever

When the crowd noise fades, the highlight reels end, and the locker room empties out for the last time, your life will still be in front of you.

The money you protect, the habits you build, the investments you make, and the brand you create — *those are the things that will last.*

You're not just playing to win today.

You're playing to win the next 50 years.

And with the right financial playbook, you can.

1. Separate Subsections by League:

- NFL: Salary ranges, career risks, concussion/health considerations, early retirements.
- CFL: Salary differences, shorter seasons, need for dual careers.
- XFL/USFL: Pay structure, instability of leagues, realistic expectations.
- WNBA (already mentioned but can re-anchor for flow): salary caps, overseas play.

2. Football Player Retirement Readiness Checklist:

- Timeline when you should start prepping (Year 1 of career!)
- Health care planning post-career
- Budgeting post-checks
- Estate and trust setup
- Setting up streams of passive income

3. Rookie Mistakes Cautionary List:

- 20+ real financial mistakes football players make
- Real-world examples without naming names
- Immediate ways to avoid them

4. Sample Football Player Financial Plan Timeline:

- Year 1 Rookie Year: Budget, taxes, basic investments
- Years 2-4: Business building, buying property (cautiously)
- Years 5+: Preparing for a second career, branding, heavier investing
- Retirement Year: Transition plan, mental health support, tax planning

5. Deeper Real-World Scenarios (Relatable Stories Section):

- "You just got cut in preseason: now what?"
- "Your best friend from college pitches a shady business idea."
- "Your agent didn't handle your taxes right."
- "You are offered an overseas playing opportunity: pros and cons."
- "You have a career-ending injury: how your financial planning saves you."

Chapter 50: Basketball (NBA, WNBA, Overseas Leagues) — Managing Year-Round Income and Endorsements

The Game Doesn't End When the Buzzer Sounds

Let's get real for a second:

In basketball, your money moves need to be just as strategic as your footwork. Whether you're signing an NBA rookie deal, balancing a WNBA salary with an overseas contract, or making the most of an endorsement opportunity, the way you manage your cash today sets the tone for your freedom tomorrow.

Unlike the NFL, where players get paid in-season only, NBA and WNBA players often have the option to structure their paychecks year-round.

Sounds great, right?

It can be.

But it also means if you're not smart, you can still burn through it all — fast.

This chapter is your off-court playbook.

It's about how to manage year-round income, endorsements, taxes, and all the hidden traps that come with a basketball career — so you don't dribble away your financial future.

Understanding Your Basketball Income Streams

When you sign a contract, it's tempting to think you're set.
But basketball income isn't just *one* number. It's a mix of:

- Salary
- Signing bonuses
- Endorsements
- Appearances
- Performance incentives
- Playoff bonuses
- Merchandising royalties
- Overseas contracts (for WNBA players and some NBA free agents)
- Summer league or short-term contracts

Each stream comes with its own tax treatment, timeline, and rules.
If you treat all that money like it's just "one big pool," you're setting yourself up for a financial full-court press you won't be able to break.

NBA: Structure, Salaries, and the Illusion of Big Checks

Average Salary:
As of 2024, the average NBA salary hovers around $9.7 million.
But don't be fooled — the *median* salary (what the middle player earns) is much lower, around $4-5 million.
Salary Structure:
NBA players can elect to receive:

- **In-season payments:** Paid biweekly during the season (roughly October through April).
- **Year-round payments:** 24 paychecks spaced out across the full calendar year.

Choosing year-round payments can be a game-changer for budgeting, especially for younger players.

It turns the financial rollercoaster into more of a smooth ride — if you manage it right.

Endorsements:

Top NBA stars make *more* from endorsements than their on-court salary.

But for most players, endorsements are *seasonal* and *volatile* — meaning you can't count on them like a salary.

WNBA: Salaries, Overseas Play, and Managing the Grind

Average Salary:

In 2024, the average WNBA player salary is about $120,600.

Top players, like Breanna Stewart or A'ja Wilson, can push past $250,000 — but the majority earn less.

Year-Round Reality:

To supplement their income, many WNBA players head overseas in the off-season, playing in leagues in Russia, Turkey, Australia, or Spain.

- Overseas deals can pay anywhere from $100,000 to $1 million+, depending on the player and country.
- But there's risk: unstable contracts, cultural barriers, physical toll.

Managing two salaries from two countries (with two different tax systems) is complex.

You NEED a good financial team who understands international taxes and budgeting — not just U.S. basics.

Overseas Leagues: NBA G-League, EuroLeague, Australia's NBL, China's CBA

NBA G-League:

Salaries for 2024 range from $40,500 to $80,000+.

Two-way contract players (split time between G-League and NBA) can earn up to $500,000.

EuroLeague:

Top-tier players can make $500,000 to $5 million tax-free (many clubs pay taxes for the players).

Australia NBL:

Salaries are competitive ($100,000 to $500,000), and Australia offers strong player protections.

China CBA:

Contracts can be extremely lucrative ($1 million+), but are short-term and come with heavy lifestyle adjustments.

Pros and Cons of Managing Year-Round Basketball Income

Pros:

- Predictable cash flow.
- Easier to stick to a monthly budget.
- Better planning for investments, taxes, and business opportunities.

Cons:

- Taxes still come due at specific times (April, quarterly estimates).
- Temptation to overcommit financially.
- If an endorsement dries up, your budget could get tight fast.

Action Steps: How to Structure Your Cash Flow

1. Know Your Payment Schedule.

Request your salary structure from your team and agent. Choose whether you want year-round or in-season.

2. Build a "Fixed Budget" Lifestyle.

Set your *lifestyle* around a minimum cash flow — not the maximum.

Think of endorsements and bonuses as *extra*, not part of your everyday living money.

3. Automatic Saving.

Set up automatic transfers:

- 20% to taxes
- 20% to investments
- 10% to savings
- 50% for lifestyle expenses

4. Plan for the Endorsement Drought.

Your marketability peaks early in your career. Save bonus income aggressively.

5. Get Professional Tax Help.

Especially if you have overseas income, multiple states you play in, or different types of contracts.

Real-World Scenarios

Scenario 1: Rookie on a Non-Guaranteed Contract

You sign a two-year deal. Year one pays you $900,000, but year two isn't guaranteed.

If you spend like you have a two-year deal, you're gambling your future.

Budget based on what's guaranteed.

Scenario 2: WNBA Player Balancing Two Paychecks

You earn $120,000 in the WNBA and $400,000 overseas.

But you get paid in Euros, and taxes are tricky.

Hire an international tax specialist. Don't wing it.

Scenario 3: Mid-Career NBA Player with Endorsements

You're earning $5 million in salary and $2 million in endorsements.

Plan as if you're earning $5 million.

Save every penny of endorsement money toward your long-term investments.

Rookie Mistakes to Avoid

- Buying a $2 million house off your rookie deal.
- Banking on endorsement deals that disappear after a bad season.
- Not setting aside cash for taxes.
- Spending playoff bonuses like they're guaranteed every year.
- Assuming overseas contracts are "easy money" (they're not — cultural adjustment is real).

Building Year-Round Wealth: The Basketball Blueprint

Start with these key habits:

- Live off one income stream (salary).
- Invest other income streams (endorsements, bonuses).
- Protect your health (your body is your real "business").
- Build passive income now — before you "need" it later.

Final Timeout Talk

Basketball is beautiful — it's fast, it's global, it's lucrative.

But your playing days are short, no matter how long your highlight reels are.

Managing year-round income smartly isn't about playing defense.

It's about running your *off-court offense* — creating sustainable, durable, championship-level wealth that lasts long after your last buzzer beater.

Remember:

You're not just building a career.

You're building a life.

Basketball Career Financial Timeline: Rookie Year to Retirement

Rookie Year: Foundation Year

- **Set up your financial team.**
- Hire a CPA, financial advisor (fiduciary only), and a lawyer to review contracts.
- **Choose year-round pay if possible.**
- Smooth cash flow = less financial anxiety.
- **Create two budgets.**

1. *Guaranteed Contract Budget*
2. *Optimistic Scenario Budget* (only use if extra years/bonuses vest)

- **Start investing early.**
- Open a Roth IRA (or traditional IRA, depending on your income limits).
- **Rent, don't buy (yet).**
- You could get traded or cut. Flexibility matters.

Years 2–4: Establish and Grow

- **Maximize retirement accounts.**
- 401(k) contributions
- NBA/WNBA pension contributions

- SEP IRA if you have substantial endorsement income
- **Live below your means.**
- Drive a nice car, not a flashy liability.
- **Negotiate smart endorsement deals.**
- Take equity over quick cash (if the company is legit).
- **Set up a rainy-day fund.**
- 12 months of expenses saved.
- **Start investing in passive income streams.**
- (e.g., rental property, dividend stocks, low-fee index funds)

Years 5–8: Peak Earnings Years

- **Protect yourself.**
- Disability insurance. Asset protection trust. Estate planning.
- **Diversify investments.**
- You don't want all your wealth riding on the stock market.
- **Think about brand expansion.**
- Podcast? Clothing line? Speaking engagements?
- **Set "leave the game" financial benchmarks.**
- How much saved = freedom to walk away on your terms.

Years 9–Retirement: Transition Planning

- **Shift your mindset.**
- You're not just a player — you're a businessman, an investor, a brand.
- **Slow your burn rate.**
- Spend like you're semi-retired.
- **Finalize your second career plans.**
- Broadcasting? Coaching? Real estate? Business ownership?
- **Stay physically and mentally strong.**
- Health is wealth — literally.

Common Cautionary Tales: Where Players Went Wrong

Overspending Off Rookie Deals

- Buying five cars, three houses, and flying 20 friends to Vegas… after one contract signing.
- Rookie contracts (especially in the WNBA or G-League) can disappear *fast*.

Chasing Bad Endorsements

- Signing with shady supplement companies.
- Endorsing crypto projects without understanding the legal risks.

Ignoring Taxes

- Getting hit with massive state taxes when traded mid-season.
- Forgetting overseas tax obligations from off-season contracts.

"I'll Save Later" Syndrome

- Thinking you'll save "when you get your next big contract" — and then injuries, trades, or roster cuts happen.

Sample Basketball Player Cash Flow Plan

Monthly (Year-Round Income)

- 20% → Taxes
- 20% → Investments (brokerage account, real estate)
- 10% → Retirement savings (401(k), IRA)

- 10% → Big purchases fund (house down payment, etc.)
- 10% → Charitable giving or family support (set strict limits)
- 30% → Living expenses

Off-Season (Endorsements or Overseas Play)

- Save 90% of after-tax earnings.
- Only 10% toward lifestyle "splurges."

Bonus: Quick Rules of Thumb for Basketball Players

- **Live like a 10th man, invest like a starter.**
- **Think in 10-year chunks, not 10-month bursts.**
- **If the endorsement isn't aligned with your values, it's a no.**
- **Play overseas for cash, not clout.**
- **Make your money work harder than your body.**

Quick Sports Analogies

- **Basketball:** Think like a point guard. Set up your financial plays BEFORE the shot clock runs down.
- **Baseball:** It's not about one home run. It's about consistent base hits — savings, investments, smart spending.
- **Soccer:** Good positioning matters. A solid financial foundation keeps you ready no matter where life passes the ball.
- **Track:** Sprint today, but pace yourself for the marathon of life after sports.

Final Locker Room Talk for Basketball Players

Your playing career is just one season in the game of life.

The real "dynasty" you're building is your financial legacy — one smart decision, one good habit, one opportunity seized at a time.

Stay humble.

Stay focused.

And never forget:

You're not just making highlights for today.

You're creating freedom, stability, and generational wealth for tomorrow.

Deep Dive: NBA, WNBA, Overseas — The Financial Realities

NBA: Big Money, Big Responsibilities

Average NBA Salary:

Over $9 million (but that's skewed by the top 1%).

Real Story:

Many players — especially second-round picks and journeymen — sign minimum deals or two-way contracts around $500K to $2 million per year.

Unique NBA Financial Challenges:

- **State Income Taxes:**
- Play 41 home games + 41 road games = taxed in multiple states ("jock tax").
- **Guaranteed Money vs Non-Guaranteed Deals:**
- Fully guaranteed contracts are gold. Partial guarantees = career instability.
- **Lifestyle Inflation:**
- The NBA culture pushes luxury living. Private jets. Custom jewelry. Multi-million-dollar homes.
- **Short Career Risk:**
- Average NBA career = about 4.5 years.
- (If you're not LeBron, you don't have 20 years to "figure it out later.")

Smart NBA Moves:

- **Negotiate year-round payments.**
- Some players opt for 12-month direct deposits to smooth out cash flow.
- **Play the long game with endorsements.**
- Build equity partnerships (tech startups, clothing brands) instead of just cash deals.
- **Protect your off-court brand.**
- What you tweet, post, or say matters — future endorsements depend on it.

WNBA: Building Wealth on a Different Scale

Average WNBA Salary:

Around $130,000 — top players up to ~$250,000+.

Real Story:

Most WNBA players supplement income by playing overseas in the off-season.

Unique WNBA Financial Challenges:

- **Double seasons, double wear-and-tear.**
- Playing year-round strains the body — and shortens careers.
- **Lower U.S. endorsement exposure.**
- Compared to NBA players, brand deals are smaller and fewer.
- **Need for aggressive saving.**
- Smaller salaries mean there's less room for financial mistakes.
- **Retirement plans are vital.**
- Every dollar invested early counts triple in the long run.

Smart WNBA Moves:

- **Max your 401(k) immediately.**

- Take full advantage of league match programs.
- **Use overseas contracts wisely.**
- Save 90% of after-tax earnings from Europe or Asia. Build that wealth!
- **Brand yourself authentically.**
- Authentic, relatable players (think Sue Bird, A'ja Wilson) win long-term endorsements.

Overseas Basketball: Adventure and Challenges

Typical Overseas Pay:

Anywhere from $40,000 to $500,000+ depending on the league (EuroLeague = top tier).

Unique Overseas Financial Challenges:

- **Currency risks.**
- Payment in euros, yen, or local currencies = exchange rate volatility.
- **Delayed or missed payments.**
- Some overseas clubs don't always pay on time (or at all).
- **Tax Confusion.**
- U.S. citizens must report foreign income. Double taxation danger.
- **Isolation Risk.**
- No financial team on-site. Easy to overspend out of boredom or loneliness.

Smart Overseas Moves:

- **Negotiate contracts carefully.**
- Include payment timelines, housing, bonuses, and late-payment penalties.
- **Bank locally + in the U.S.**
- Set up international and U.S. accounts to avoid huge wire fees.
- **Invest remotely.**

- Work with a U.S.-based advisor you trust.

Off-Season Financial Checklist for Basketball Players

1. **Update all financial accounts.**

- Direct deposit
- Endorsement payments
- Brokerage accounts

1. **Review your spending habits.**

- Where did you waste money last season?
- What habits need fixing?

1. **Pre-pay major bills.**

- Rent/mortgage
- Insurance
- College funds for kids

1. **Max out savings opportunities.**

- 401(k)
- Roth IRA
- Brokerage account contributions

1. **Create a "bare minimum" budget.**

- If endorsements slow down, you still stay safe.

1. **Schedule medical check-ups.**

- Healthy player = longer career = longer income stream.

1. **Audit your financial team.**

- Is your CPA saving you taxes?
- Is your financial advisor delivering real value?

Rookie Mistakes Basketball Players Must Avoid

- **Spending based on your "potential" contract, not your current reality.**
- **Falling for fast-money endorsement traps (crypto coins, shady brands).**
- **Letting a "buddy" run your finances without licenses.**
- **Renting luxury properties instead of buying smartly (or vice versa).**
- **Blowing signing bonuses on jewelry, cars, or parties before your second contract.**

Sample Timeline: Building Wealth as a Basketball Player

Rookie Year:

- Budget like you're undrafted.
- Open retirement accounts.

Year 2–3:

- Invest steadily.
- Avoid lifestyle inflation.

Year 4–6:

- Diversify income (real estate, equity in brands).
- Plan for post-playing career.

Year 7–10:

- De-risk portfolio.
- Increase cash reserves.

Retirement Transition:

- Activate pensions.
- Start "life after basketball" businesses or media ventures.

Final Locker Room Talk

Basketball gave you a platform.

What you build off that platform — financially, professionally, personally — is completely up to you.

Stay humble.

Stay strategic.

Stay ready — on and off the court.

You've got the ball.

Now dribble it smart, pass wisely, and shoot your shot... toward lifelong financial freedom.

Navigating Overseas Basketball: Europe vs. Asia

Europe: Higher Prestige, Higher Pressure

- **Top Leagues:**
- EuroLeague (Spain, Turkey, Greece, Russia, Italy), ACB (Spain), France Pro A, Turkey Super League.
- **Typical Salary Range:**
- $100,000 to $2 million+ (depending on country, experience, and team).
- **Pros:**
- Strong competition (NBA scouts often watch EuroLeague).
- Big markets for endorsement deals (think Adidas, Puma, Nike Europe).
- Good infrastructure — apartments, drivers, medical care.
- **Cons:**
- Cultural adjustment.
- Language barriers.
- Tough travel schedules across Europe.
- Some countries (e.g., Turkey, Russia) have delayed payment risks.

- **Tax Notes:**
- Some countries take taxes at the source (e.g., Spain), others don't.
- Always ask for *net salary contracts* — where the club covers your taxes.

Asia: Big Checks, Shorter Seasons

- **Top Leagues:**
- Japan B.League, Korean Basketball League (KBL), Chinese Basketball Association (CBA).
- **Typical Salary Range:**
- $300,000 to $1 million+ (CBA superstars make even more).
- **Pros:**
- Shorter seasons — earn a full season's pay in 3-6 months.
- Paid housing, drivers, meals often included.
- Fan support is massive (especially in China).
- **Cons:**
- Huge cultural adjustments.
- Language barriers.
- Isolation issues for American players.
- Some CBA teams have unpredictable pay issues if not a top club.
- **Tax Notes:**
- U.S. citizens must report all foreign income.
- Certain countries offer lower tax rates but plan ahead for U.S. obligations.

What to Look For In An Overseas Basketball Agent

- **Experience in that market:**
- Not every agent knows Europe or Asia. Ask:
- *"How many players have you placed in ____ league?"*
- **Relationship with clubs:**
- A good agent has direct contacts — not working through shady

middlemen.

- **Contract expertise:**
- Net salary? Late-payment penalties? Housing covered? Paid insurance?
- **Visa and relocation help:**
- Make sure they assist with work visas, housing, and setting up bank accounts.
- **Emergency plan:**
- If you get cut early (it happens), do they have another gig lined up fast?

Sample Endorsement Negotiation Checklist for Basketball Players

When your agent brings you a deal — sneaker contract, clothing collab, energy drink — run through this:

1. **Exclusivity:**
2. Can you still sign with others? (Shoe contracts often require exclusivity.)
3. **Duration:**
4. 1 year? 3 years? 5 years? Shorter deals = more flexibility.
5. **Payment structure:**
6. Upfront? Monthly? Performance bonuses?
7. **Use of your likeness:**
8. Will they own photos, commercials, your name forever?
9. **Renewal rights:**
10. Can you renegotiate after a big season?
11. **Termination clauses:**
12. What happens if you get injured or traded?
13. **Equity vs. cash:**
14. Getting partial ownership in a startup could beat a simple $20K

cash payment.

How to Build Your Basketball Brand the Right Way

Focus Areas:

- **Authenticity:**
- Fans smell fake from a mile away.
- **Consistency:**
- Don't promote a health brand today and a junk food brand tomorrow.
- **Professionalism:**
- Every tweet, Instagram post, and interview matters.
- **Relationships:**
- Treat small brands well — they might blow up later (think about Steph Curry and Under Armour).
- **Long-Term Mindset:**
- Build a legacy brand, not just a "one-season wonder."

Rookie to Vet: Financial Moves Based on Your Basketball Career Stage

Rookie Contract Years (NBA/Overseas/Asia):

- Live cheaply.
- Stack savings.
- Avoid risky investments.
- Hire a CPA who knows athlete taxes.

Prime Contract Years (NBA Second Contract or Top Overseas):

- Diversify investments (real estate, index funds).

- Protect assets (insurance, LLCs).
- Cut unnecessary expenses.
- Maximize retirement accounts.

Veteran Years (End of Prime or Declining Years):

- Reduce risky assets.
- Increase cash reserves.
- Invest in businesses that don't depend on your name.
- Build streams of passive income.

Post-Career Transition:

- Turn endorsements into consulting gigs.
- Transition to coaching, broadcasting, entrepreneurship, or investing.

Year-Round Income Strategy for Basketball Players

Basketball doesn't operate on a 12-month paycheck for most players. You MUST manage cash flow smartly.

- **Off-Season Savings:**
- Save at least 6 months of living expenses before the season ends.
- **Automate Fixed Costs:**
- Rent, car payments, insurance should be on autopilot.
- **Season Bonus Planning:**
- Treat bonuses as "future money," not spending money.
- **Endorsement Management:**
- Save 50%+ of all endorsement money (after taxes).

Final Words: Think Like a CEO

Your basketball career is your startup.

Your personal brand is your product.

Your money is your business capital.

Treat every dollar like an investor would — not a lottery winner.

The best players aren't just physically talented.

They're financially prepared, mentally focused, and long-term driven.

You are the CEO of YOU.

Own your game.

Own your money.

Own your future.

Chapter 51: Baseball (MLB, MiLB) — Long Minor League Roads, Big-League Money Management

There's something different about baseball.

If you're reading this chapter, you already know.

Baseball isn't like football or basketball where a player often jumps straight into the big leagues with big paychecks on Day 1.

In baseball, the journey is long.

It's bus rides, cheap hotels, late-night fast food, playing in front of a few hundred fans at a dusty ballpark.

It's earning $1,200 a month while chasing a $10 million dream.

And that's why understanding money — really understanding it — matters even more for baseball players.

Because in baseball, the grind is financial before it's ever glamorous.

The Financial Reality of Minor League Baseball (MiLB)

The Harsh Paycheck Truth

Let's keep it real:

For most minor leaguers, the money is bad. Historically bad.

Before recent improvements, minor league players often made between $5,000 and $15,000 **for an entire season** — not per month, per year.

Many worked second jobs in the offseason to survive.

Even now, with improvements:

- Rookie ball/short-season players: ~$400–$500/week
- Single-A: ~$500–$700/week
- Double-A: ~$600–$850/week
- Triple-A: ~$700–$1,000/week

That's only during the season.

Offseason? No pay unless you're on a 40-man roster.

And no, signing a big bonus doesn't guarantee anything long-term.

Plenty of guys blow through their signing bonus — taxes, agent fees, family support — and find themselves broke by Year 2.

Surviving the Minors: Smart Money Moves

If you're in the minors:

- **Save half** of every paycheck if you can.
- **Split rent** with multiple roommates.
- **Meal prep** instead of eating out.
- **Drive a reliable used car**, not a flashy one.
- **Skip luxury purchases** — you haven't "made it" yet.
- **Get offseason work** that doesn't risk injury (coaching, camps, sales).

Financial survival in MiLB is like a long road trip:

It's less about speed, more about endurance.

Signing Bonuses: Blessing or Curse?

Signing bonuses sound amazing on ESPN.

"First-round pick signs for $5.5 million!"

What they don't tell you:

- **Agent fees**: ~3–5%
- **Taxes**: 37% federal, plus state taxes depending where you sign
- **Living expenses**: housing, insurance, offseason training

If you signed for a $1 million bonus, you might keep $500,000 after taxes and fees.

Maybe less.

That's still a lot of money — but not "I'm set for life" money.

Especially if you live like a rock star instead of a ballplayer on the rise.

Transitioning to the Majors: Money Changes, Habits Shouldn't

When you finally get that call-up to "The Show," everything changes.

- MLB minimum salary: $740,000+ (2024 numbers)
- Meal stipends, better hotels, chartered flights, union benefits

But here's the danger:

Your habits from the minors must stay disciplined.

If you suddenly start living like a millionaire, thinking it'll last forever, you're setting yourself up for trouble.

Remember: the average MLB career is **only about 3.3 years**.

You have a narrow window to earn, invest, and set yourself up for life.

Real Talk: Money Mistakes Baseball Players Make

Rookie Mistakes

- **Blowing signing bonuses** on cars, jewelry, trips
- **Underestimating taxes** — paying taxes late = penalties and interest
- **Forgetting offseason expenses** when the checks stop
- **Loaning money to family and friends** with no repayment plan
- **Overinvesting** in risky businesses pitched by "buddies"

Veteran Mistakes

- **Lifestyle creep** — when your spending grows faster than your earnings
- **No offseason income strategy** for after retirement
- **Late career financial planning** — you should be planning before you hit 30

The Importance of a Season-Based Cash Flow Plan

Baseball money comes fast and seasonally.

- **During the season**: Paychecks every two weeks.
- **Offseason**: No team paychecks unless arbitration-eligible or on a guaranteed MLB deal.

You must **stretch your season earnings** across 12 months.

Think of it like pitching:

You can't throw 100 mph every pitch for nine innings — you'll gas out.

Same with spending:

If you spend like it's the World Series every month, you'll be broke by December.

Long-Term Wealth Strategy for Baseball Players

1. **Emergency Fund**
2. Save 6–12 months of living expenses. Always.
3. **Debt Management**
4. Avoid stupid debt.
5. No $80,000 car loans when you make $30,000/year.
6. **Smart Investing**

- IRAs (Roth if early-career)
- Brokerage accounts
- Real estate when you're ready

1. **Retirement Planning**
2. Max out MLB pension contributions when eligible.
3. Save additional in private accounts too.
4. **Insurance Protection**

- Disability insurance
- Health insurance during and after career
- Life insurance if you have dependents

Special Section: Minor Leaguer Budget Sample

Let's say you're playing Single-A ball:

- Salary: ~$600/week x 5 months = $12,000 gross
- After taxes: ~$9,000

Expenses:

- Rent split 3 ways: ~$300/month = $1,500 total
- Food: $200/month = $1,000 total

- Transportation (cheap used car): $2,000–$3,000 all-in

Leftover for savings? Maybe $3,000–$4,000 at best.

Lesson:

Every dollar must be managed carefully.

Your margin for error is razor-thin.

Special Section: MLB Player Financial Timeline

Rookie Year (Debut)

- Save 50%+ of income
- Max out 401(k) plan and MLB pension contributions
- Hire a CPA, not just an agent

Years 2–4 (Prime Earning)

- Diversify: 401(k), Roth IRA, brokerage account, real estate
- Hire a fee-only financial advisor
- Set up a personal LLC for endorsements

Years 5+ (Late Career)

- Lower risk investments
- Pay off all debt
- Build passive income streams
- Transition to post-baseball plans early

Final Word for Baseball Players

The road is long.

The paychecks are uneven.

The dream can be snatched away by injury, trades, or bad luck.

Your best defense isn't just your glove or your bat — it's your financial brain.

Play smart.

Save smarter.

Invest smartest.

Make sure you don't just play for a few years — but live well for decades after.

Red Flags to Watch for When You Finally Get Called Up

Getting called up to The Show is everything you've worked for — but it also opens up new risks, not just on the field, but financially too.

Here are the financial *red flags* you must recognize immediately.

1. Sudden Lifestyle Inflation

Just because you're finally earning $740,000 (or more) doesn't mean you should spend like it.

Watch out for:

- Upgrading your apartment before you're ready
- Buying luxury cars (plural) when you barely own one outright
- Shopping sprees for clothes, jewelry, and watches
- Booking luxury vacations every offseason

The first year you're in the majors is the worst time to splurge.

You're not guaranteed another contract yet.

Stay humble, stay disciplined.

2. Family and Friends "Emergency" Requests

There will be sudden, urgent needs:

- "Mom needs a new house."
- "Cousin needs to start a business."
- "Old high school buddy just needs a small loan."

You have to say no (or delay decisions until you have a full financial team review it).

Emotional decisions = financial disasters.

3. Sketchy Financial Advisors and Business Pitches

Now that you have money, people with "great" ideas will find you.

- Real estate schemes
- Restaurant investments
- Cryptocurrency deals you don't understand
- NFT art your trainer's barber's cousin is promoting

If you don't understand it **clearly enough to explain it to a 10-year-old**, don't invest in it.

Building a Financial Offseason Plan (Whether You're in MiLB or MLB)

Baseball seasons are short compared to real life.

Here's how to build an offseason plan that keeps you sharp financially.

October

- Review your season earnings and total net income.
- Meet with your CPA and financial advisor to plan year-end tax strategies.

November

- Check if you need to make estimated tax payments.
- Rebalance investment accounts if needed (sell some winners, harvest some losses).

December

- Finalize any charitable contributions you want for tax deductions.
- Set cash aside to cover January–March expenses without new paychecks.

January–February

- Analyze offseason expenses.
- If needed, pick up safe offseason work (clinics, camps, TV gigs).
- Focus on training without draining your bank account.

Offseason is when financial discipline separates long careers from short ones.

Understanding MLB and MiLB Pension Systems

Minor League Players

Minor league players historically had little to no pension protection — but **that's changing**.

New agreements are adding health benefits and small pensions based on years of minor league service.

Still, nothing compares to MLB benefits.

Major League Players

Once you're on an MLB roster (even briefly), you start earning pension credits.

Some highlights:

- **43 days** of service = eligibility for some benefits.
- **10 years** of service = maximum pension payout.

The pension can be a **lifesaver** post-retirement.

Don't ignore it.

Protect your service days like gold.

Real-World Stories: Financial Home Runs and Strikeouts

Home Run Story

A minor leaguer drafted in the 12th round got a $150,000 signing bonus.
He immediately:

- Saved $75,000 in a high-yield savings account.
- Bought a used Honda Civic for $8,000 cash.
- Got a side gig coaching kids in the offseason.
- When he made it to MLB three years later, he had $50,000 still saved, no debt, and rolled it into investments.

Now he's 28, owns two rental properties, and isn't sweating retirement.

Strikeout Story

Another top-5 draft pick signed for $3 million.
He immediately:

- Bought a $200,000 car.
- Bought a $1.1 million house.
- Gave $500,000 away to family and friends.
- Had $200,000 left… which he invested in a nightclub venture that flopped.

When injuries ended his career in Year 4, he had **almost nothing left.**
Big contract doesn't mean big safety unless you protect it.

Your Baseball Career Timeline (Financial Edition)

Rookie Minor Leaguer

- Save every extra dollar.
- Hustle offseason side gigs that don't risk injury.
- Build your emergency fund.

Double-A / Triple-A Prospect

- Live cheaply still.
- Start basic investing (Roth IRA, simple brokerage accounts).
- Avoid flashy lifestyle upgrades.

40-Man Roster MLB Player

- Max out retirement accounts.
- Build passive income (real estate, index funds).
- Hire a **true** fiduciary financial advisor.

MLB Starter

- Protect your contract.
- Limit risky private investments.
- Diversify: business, real estate, stocks, bonds.

Veteran MLB Player

- Plan for career sunset (age 32–36 for most).
- Lock in lifetime income streams.
- Build your post-baseball second career gradually.

A Real Talk Moment: Baseball Is Brutal

- **Baseball is failure** 7 out of 10 times — and that's considered "good."
- **Financial planning** needs to be 10 out of 10 — because one mistake can ruin the dream.

You can't control:

- Injuries
- Trades
- Politics
- Slumps

But you can absolutely control:

- How you save
- How you invest
- How you protect yourself and your future family

That's true greatness — even beyond the diamond.

Closing: Play the Long Game, Not the Short Inning

The guys who survive the Minor League grind financially?
They don't just survive — they **thrive**.
They don't live for the highlight reel today.
They live for the freedom tomorrow.

- Be the guy who retires with choices.
- Be the guy who uses baseball to build a life — not just a few highlight videos.
- Be the guy whose money still wins even after the final out.

You worked too hard to blow it now.

Stay smart. Stay humble. Stay hungry.

Your future self will thank you for it.

Chapter 52: Soccer (MLS, NWSL, International) — Managing Contracts Abroad, Currency Exchange Risks

Soccer players live in a unique financial world compared to almost any other athlete.

Whether you're drafted into MLS or NWSL, sign your first international contract with a club in Europe, or bounce around on short-term loans and transfer deals, one truth remains:

You must manage your money smarter, because your career will almost certainly be less predictable than players in other sports.

Let's get into it — the real talk you need about contracts, taxes, currency exchange, and long-term financial moves as a soccer pro.

The Financial Landscape of Pro Soccer

Soccer is a global game, and that means the financial rules change depending on where you are.

MLS and NWSL (United States-Based Soccer)

- **MLS average salary (2023)**: Around $500,000
- Note: Huge disparity between star players (millions) and average players.
- **NWSL average salary (2023)**: Around $54,000, with top players

earning six figures.

- **Key Issue**: Cost of living often varies wildly between cities (New York vs. Kansas City vs. Houston).

International Soccer

- **Top European Leagues (Premier League, La Liga, Serie A)**: Millions per year.
- **Smaller Leagues (Norway, Denmark, Eastern Europe)**: $40,000–$150,000 per season.
- **Key Issue**: Currency risk, unstable contracts, and being paid in a foreign currency.

Why Soccer Contracts Are Different

Soccer players deal with a lot more instability than athletes in other major sports.

You might have:

- One-year deals
- Six-month loans
- Trials and training stints before signing
- No guarantee of being re-signed even after a good season

You must **treat every dollar like it could be your last paycheck** — because sometimes it will be.

How Currency Exchange Can Make (or Break) Your Bank Account

Getting paid in euros, pounds, or yen sounds glamorous — until you realize that a 10% swing in the exchange rate can cost you tens of thousands of dollars.

Real-World Example

Let's say you're playing in Sweden.

- Your contract is worth 600,000 SEK (Swedish Krona).
- When you sign, 1 USD = 10 SEK.
- So you think you're earning around $60,000 USD.

But then the currency shifts:

- 1 USD = 11 SEK.

Now your 600,000 SEK is worth about $54,545 USD.

That's a loss of over $5,000 without you doing anything wrong.

Multiply that across a few years — or when transferring a big signing bonus — and it gets scary fast.

Action Steps: Managing Currency Exchange Risks

1. Negotiate Payment in U.S. Dollars (if Possible)

Some foreign clubs will agree to pay you in USD, especially if you're American.

It protects you from currency swings.

2. Use Professional Currency Brokers

When transferring money from your foreign bank to your U.S. account:

- Use currency brokers like Wise, OFX, or a private bank with low fees.
- Never accept terrible exchange rates from random wire services.

Saving 1–2% on every transfer adds up massively over time.

3. Time Transfers Strategically

Work with your financial advisor to time big conversions when rates are favorable.

A swing of a few cents can be worth thousands.

Taxes: The Silent Killer of Soccer Wealth

Playing abroad doesn't exempt you from U.S. taxes.

As a U.S. citizen, you owe:

- Federal income taxes on your worldwide income.
- Potential state income taxes (depending on your residency).

You may qualify for:

- The **Foreign Earned Income Exclusion** (around $120,000+ excluded).
- **Foreign tax credits** if you pay taxes in another country.

But it's complicated — you need a CPA who understands **expat athletes.**

Do not use TurboTax.

Do not DIY your taxes when playing abroad.

Get a pro.

Structuring Your Soccer Income

1. Pay Yourself a Salary

Even if you're living abroad, create a U.S. LLC or personal corporation (if appropriate) and pay yourself a modest salary.

This structure can:

- Reduce self-employment taxes
- Protect assets
- Separate business from personal finances

Always talk to a CPA before setting this up.

2. Build Your Emergency Fund Bigger

Soccer careers are fragile.

If you're normally told to have 6 months of expenses saved, as a soccer player **you should aim for 12 to 18 months.**

Why?

- Sudden injury = out of contract.
- Team financial issues = delayed paychecks.
- Political instability = entire leagues collapse (it happens).

Endorsements: Manage Them Separately

If you land endorsements — shoe deals, energy drinks, local ads — **keep those earnings separate.**

- Set up a second bank account.

- Save at least 30% of endorsement income for taxes.
- Invest endorsement income separately from your salary.

Endorsements can vanish quicker than your contract, so don't count on them lasting forever.

Real-World Scenarios: Money Wins and Money Fumbles

Money Win

A U.S. defender signs a contract in Germany for $300,000.
He:

- Hires a U.S.-based financial advisor specializing in athletes abroad.
- Converts monthly earnings carefully.
- Maxes out Roth IRA contributions each year.
- Lives on 50% of net income.

After three years, he's got $400,000 saved — despite playing on lower-tier European teams.

Money Fumble

An MLS player transfers to a South American club.
He:

- Takes all earnings in local currency without understanding conversion fees.
- Pays 30% taxes in the foreign country but forgets U.S. obligations.
- Buys a luxury car in cash.
- Lives large because "it's cheaper down here."

Result:

Two years later, he owes $50,000+ in back taxes to the IRS and has to sell assets to cover it.

Rookie Mistakes to Avoid (Especially Abroad)

- Ignoring exchange rates.
- Assuming your team will always pay you on time (some won't).
- Believing a short-term contract guarantees long-term security.
- Forgetting about U.S. taxes.
- Failing to keep U.S. credit history active.

Your Soccer Career Timeline (Financial Version)

Early Years (Academy, College, First Contracts)

- Build emergency savings.
- Stay extremely frugal.
- Start basic investing (Roth IRA, savings account).

Prime Years (MLS/NWSL Starter, European Clubs)

- Maximize earnings.
- Lock in low taxes legally.
- Protect money from bad investments.

Late Career (Overseas Short-Term Contracts, Final MLS/NWSL Deals)

- Shift from aggressive growth to income preservation.
- Start planning your second career.
- Minimize debt at all costs.

Mental Health, Isolation, and Finances

Living abroad can be lonely.

Many players overspend out of:

- Boredom
- Loneliness
- Trying to "feel at home"

Recognize emotional spending for what it is.

Build routines.

Find community.

Stay focused.

Your financial health is tied closely to your emotional health.

Final Whistle: Your Gameplan for Soccer Success

Soccer can offer an incredible life.

You can:

- See the world.
- Earn great money.
- Build a brand internationally.

But only if you approach it with the same discipline you bring to the field.

- Respect your money like you respect the game.
- Protect your money like you protect your body.
- Play for the long haul — financially and personally.

If you do that, you won't just be a good player.

You'll be a legend — on and off the pitch.

The world is wide open to you.

Be smart.

Be ready.

Be relentless.

Chapter 53: Hockey (NHL) — Pensions, Seasonal Pay, Insurance Strategies

Hockey is a different beast.

From the moment you lace up your skates in juniors or get drafted into the NHL, the money, the risk, and the career path you face are different from almost any other pro athlete.

You have a shorter window than you think.

You have some of the highest physical risk outside of football.

And you have huge opportunities — if you manage your money with the same precision you bring to your shifts.

Let's dig into it.

Understanding the Financial DNA of an NHL Career

Most rookies enter the league thinking they'll have time.

Time to figure it out.

Time to "make the real money later."

Reality check: the average NHL career lasts **about 5 years**.

For many players, it's even shorter.

And while NHL salaries have risen over the years:

- The **league minimum** for the 2023–24 season is **$775,000**.
- The **average NHL salary** is roughly **$3.5 million**.

- The **median salary** is much lower — around **$2 million**.

Half the league isn't making superstar money.

And even the players making millions can lose it faster than they realize if they don't build a solid plan.

Hockey Careers Are Heavy on Seasonal Pay

Unlike corporate jobs where you get 24 or 26 paychecks a year, in the NHL:

- You're typically paid **bi-weekly during the season only**.
- No paychecks during the offseason unless specified otherwise.
- Bonuses (signing, performance, roster) are lumped into specific dates.

Which means:

You're making a full year's living in 6–7 months.

And if you don't pace yourself, you can hit the summer broke — even if you had a strong season.

Action Steps: Managing Your Seasonal Pay Flow

1. Break Your Pay into a 12-Month Budget

Divide your total after-tax income across 12 months, not just the season.

Example:

- You earn $1,000,000 gross = ~$550,000 after taxes and agent fees.
- $550,000 ÷ 12 = ~$45,833 per month you can "spend" or allocate.

Even when the paychecks stop in June, you still have monthly structure.

2. Set Up Automatic Transfers

When you get paid during the season:

- Automatically move money into an offseason savings account.
- Pay yourself a monthly "salary" from that account year-round.

Think of it like conditioning your financial muscles.

It's discipline.

It's survival.

3. Build a True Emergency Fund

Hockey can turn fast:

- Injuries.
- Trades.
- Buyouts.

Save **at least 12–18 months' worth** of essential expenses early in your career.

Protect yourself like you protect your net.

Pensions: Your Quiet Lifeline

The NHL pension plan is **one of the strongest in pro sports** – but you have to understand it.

Basics of the NHL Pension

- You need **160 credited games** to qualify for the pension.
- Your pension grows with each additional credited season.
- Full benefits are based on a player with 10 credited seasons.
- The pension is calculated based on a formula tied to salary and years of service.

Important: Even if you only play a few years, you're still eligible for reduced benefits starting around age 62–65.

Pro Tip: Never lose track of your credited games.

One season at 80 games = 80 credited games.

Why You Must Know Your Pension Details Now

Too many players ignore their pension until their 40s or 50s — when it's harder to fix mistakes or optimize payouts.

- Know your vested status.
- Know your estimated future benefits.
- Coordinate your private investments with your pension for full retirement coverage.

Remember: Your pension is a **floor**, not a **ceiling**.

You still need to save aggressively outside of it.

Insurance Strategies for Hockey Players

Hockey players have some of the highest injury risks in all of pro sports.

You need more than just standard health insurance.

Key Types of Insurance You Need

1. Career-Ending Injury Insurance

Protects your future earnings if an injury forces early retirement.

2. Disability Insurance

Provides income if you are temporarily unable to play.

3. Loss-of-Value Insurance

If your market value drops due to injury before your next contract, this coverage can replace part of the lost income.

4. Life Insurance

Critical once you have dependents or significant assets.

Action Steps: Insuring Your Future

1. **Buy Coverage Early**
Premiums are lower the younger and healthier you are.
2. **Review Policies Every Contract Year**
Make sure your coverage aligns with your current earning potential.
3. **Work With Advisors Who Understand Athletes**
Not every insurance agent understands the risk profile of a hockey career.
You want specialists.

Real-World Examples: Money Wins and Money Fumbles

Money Win

An NHL defenseman signs a modest rookie deal.
Instead of buying luxury items:

- He lives on 30% of his after-tax income.
- Saves 20% into retirement accounts.
- Invests 20% into diversified taxable accounts.
- Keeps 30% in cash for offseason living.

By the end of his first contract (3 years), he's sitting on $600,000+ in net worth — before he signs his next deal.

Money Fumble

A high-drafted forward signs a $4 million contract.

- Buys two luxury cars.
- Buys a $2 million home (with no long-term plan).

- Supports 6 friends and family members.

Gets injured in Year 2.

Never plays another NHL game.

Has no emergency fund, no savings, a giant mortgage, and tons of regrets.

Rookie Mistakes to Avoid in Hockey

- Spending every in-season paycheck like the next one is guaranteed.
- Forgetting that you have no offseason paycheck.
- Relying only on your pension for retirement.
- Buying a massive home before securing a long-term contract.
- Ignoring loss-of-value insurance before signing big contracts.

Your Hockey Career Timeline (Financial Version)

Junior/College Years

- Live as cheaply as possible.
- Build early financial literacy.
- Avoid taking on bad debts.

Entry-Level NHL Years (Years 1–3)

- Save at least 50% of after-tax income.
- Build an emergency fund immediately.
- Start long-term investing.

Prime Contract Years (Years 4–10)

- Max out investments (Roth IRA, SEP IRA, 401(k) equivalents).
- Protect earnings with insurance.

- Plan for career transitions post-playing.

Late Career (Years 10–Retirement)

- Shift investment strategy toward income preservation.
- Solidify second-career plans.
- Maintain health, both physical and mental, for longevity.

The Quiet Trap: Lavish Lifestyle Pressure in Hockey

Hockey culture can be:

- Low-key off the ice.
- Lavish when it comes to houses, cars, and vacations.

Remember:

Many players live paycheck-to-paycheck, even in the NHL.

Avoid the flexes.

Avoid the peer pressure.

You're building generational wealth — not a highlight reel of luxury purchases.

Final Whistle: Your Hockey Financial Gameplan

You've spent your life training to master skating, stickhandling, shooting, and reading the game.

Now it's time to master money the same way:

- With preparation.
- With patience.
- With vision.

You don't just want a good hockey career.

You want a great life.

You want to make sure that when the final horn sounds on your playing days, you're still skating — financially strong, confident, and free.

Own it.

Control it.

Build it.

Your future is yours to win.

Chapter 54: Golf, Tennis, Track — Independent Contractors, Prize Money, and Taxes

If you're a golfer, tennis player, or track athlete, your money world works differently from most team-sport athletes.

You're not signing a salary-based contract with guaranteed checks.

You're not part of a season-long team payroll where someone else handles taxes for you.

You're an independent contractor.

That changes everything.

Let's walk through it together, because understanding this difference is what separates the athletes who *build real wealth* from the ones who *struggle quietly even while winning medals.*

Independent Contractor = You Are the Business

When you're an independent contractor:

- You don't get a traditional paycheck.
- No taxes are withheld automatically.
- You're responsible for paying your own taxes — federal, state, local, and even foreign.
- You have to manage travel, hotels, trainers, entry fees, and equipment

costs — often upfront.
- You're not just an athlete anymore. You are a *business owner*.

That's a mental shift you have to make early and often.

You're not just "playing" professionally.

You're *operating* professionally.

Pros and Cons of Being an Independent Contractor Athlete

Pros

- **Unlimited Earning Potential**: No salary cap. Win big, earn big.
- **Flexible Schedules**: Choose your tournaments, meets, or events.
- **Brand Building**: You're free to build your own brand without team restrictions.
- **Tax Deductions**: You can deduct a lot of legitimate business expenses (flights, hotels, coaching fees, equipment, agents).

Cons

- **No Guaranteed Income**: If you don't place, you don't get paid.
- **Self-Employment Taxes**: You pay both the employer and employee side of Social Security/Medicare taxes.
- **Risk of Overspending**: Without steady paychecks, it's easy to blow through money.
- **Accounting Complexity**: You need serious tax and bookkeeping help to stay compliant.

Managing Prize Money: Plan Like a Pro

Winning a $50,000 golf purse or a $75,000 second-round tennis payout is amazing — but don't mentally treat it like free money.

It's business revenue, not personal income.

Here's how you should treat prize money:

1. **Set Aside Taxes Immediately**

- As a rule of thumb: **Set aside at least 40%**.
- Higher if you're in a high-tax state or playing internationally.

1. **Reimburse Your Business First**

- Cover tournament entry fees, travel, coaching expenses first.
- What's left is your profit.

1. **Save a Large Percentage**

- Save at least **30-50%** of your *after-expenses, after-tax* winnings.
- Invest in retirement accounts if possible.

1. **Pay Yourself a Salary**

- Instead of living off volatile earnings, pay yourself a steady "salary" from your business account.
- Helps you plan, budget, and invest wisely.

Real Talk About Self-Employment Taxes

In the U.S., if you're self-employed:

- You pay **15.3%** for Social Security and Medicare on top of your income tax.

- There are no employer matches — you're the employer.

This sneaks up on athletes who aren't prepared.

If you're making $250,000 in prize money, you're not clearing $250,000.

You could owe:

- ~15.3% self-employment tax
- ~24-37% federal income tax
- State income taxes depending on where you live or compete
- Foreign taxes depending on where you compete internationally

How Taxes Hit Athletes Differently by Sport

Golf

- Prize money is taxed in the country/state where earned.
- Sponsorship income adds another layer.
- Deductible expenses are a must to minimize tax burden.

Tennis

- Same challenges as golf.
- Grand Slam winnings taxed at source countries first.
- Travel logistics are brutal financially if unmanaged.

Track and Field

- Appearance fees, sponsorships, and bonus structures vary widely.
- Fewer "tour" opportunities than golf/tennis.
- Expenses (coaching, training, medical) often higher proportionally to earnings.

Example: Tennis Prize Money Breakdown

Let's say you make it to the quarterfinals at the Australian Open:

- Prize Money: $500,000 AUD (~$330,000 USD)
- Australian taxes: ~32.5% withholding
- U.S. taxes: Credit given, but you may owe additional
- Agent commission: 10% (~$50,000 AUD)
- Coaching/travel costs: ~$30,000 AUD

After all taxes and expenses, you might net closer to **$180,000–$200,000 USD** — not the $330,000 headline number.

Key Action Steps for Golfers, Tennis Players, and Track Athletes

1. Hire a Good CPA — Early

- Find someone who understands athletes and international tax issues.

2. Create an LLC or S-Corp

- Formalizes your business.
- Potentially lowers self-employment taxes.
- Helps protect your personal assets.

3. Open Retirement Accounts

- SEP IRA, Solo 401(k), or Roth IRA.
- Start investing your money early.

4. Budget Seasonally

- Plan for income bursts, not steady paychecks.
- Budget across 12 months, not based on your last tournament win.

5. Insure Yourself

- Disability insurance is critical when your body = your business.
- Consider loss-of-earnings riders for high-earning players.

Rookie Mistakes to Avoid

- Spending prize money immediately.
- Forgetting to account for taxes.
- Not deducting legitimate business expenses.
- Waiting too long to set up a business structure.
- Ignoring international tax rules when competing abroad.
- Paying friends/family to "help" without proper contracts and paperwork.

Real World Story: Track Athlete Financial Win

A U.S. sprinter:

- Forms an LLC early in her career.
- Hires a CPA with Olympic client experience.
- Lives frugally even after winning World Championship medals.
- Invests 50% of her after-tax income every year.

By the time she retires at 32, she owns her house outright, has $2 million in investments, and is launching a speaking/coaching business.

Building Wealth While Traveling the World

Competing internationally is one of the greatest opportunities — and one of the sneakiest threats.

Currency risk is real:

- If you earn prize money in Euros but the USD strengthens by 10% before you convert it, you lose purchasing power.

Work with a financial advisor who understands:

- Currency risk management
- Bank account structures for athletes
- Managing international taxes

Personal Brand = Business Asset

In golf, tennis, and track, your brand can:

- Bring in endorsements.
- Open up broadcasting, coaching, or entrepreneurial opportunities after competition ends.

Invest in your brand just like you invest in your game:

- Clean, professional social media.
- Personal website and email list.
- Smart, authentic public appearances.

Build something that endures after your last competitive match, round, or race.

Sports Analogies: Golf, Tennis, Track

Golf: Financial management is like course management. You don't bomb it on every shot. You strategize every hole based on wind, hazards, and your strengths.

Tennis: It's not just about big serves — it's about consistent returns. In money, consistency beats flash.

Track: It's not about the first 10 meters of the race — it's about maintaining form all the way through the finish line.

Same with money:

Sustainability matters more than speed.

Encouragement: Your Business, Your Legacy

You're not just playing a sport.

You're building a business.

You're building a future.

You're creating a financial legacy that can outlast your last medal, your last match, your last tournament.

Handle your money like you handle your sport:

- Focused.
- Strategic.
- Relentless.
- Long-term.

You have the power.

You have the opportunity.

You just need the plan.

Chapter 55: MMA, Boxing, Wrestling — Managing Uneven Fight Incomes and Sponsorships

If you're stepping into a cage, a ring, or an arena, your money world looks a whole lot different than someone signing a multi-year team contract.

In combat sports like MMA, boxing, and professional wrestling:

- Your income can come in *massive bursts* — but only a few times a year.
- Your expenses are constant — camp costs, trainers, gym fees, travel, gear.
- Your health window is tight — injury can end a career overnight.
- Sponsorships and endorsements are volatile — rising with your fame, disappearing with a single loss.

You're not just a fighter.

You're a CEO managing a high-risk, high-reward business.

The sooner you think like a business owner — not just a competitor — the faster you build long-term financial security.

Let's talk about how to do it smartly.

Fight Income: Feast and Famine Cycles

In combat sports, money often comes in chunks:

- Fight purses
- Win bonuses
- Performance bonuses
- Sponsorship deals (some guaranteed, some not)
- Pay-per-view points (for big names)
- Merchandise sales
- Appearance fees

But even if you bank $100,000 from a fight — or $2 million from a title match — you might not fight again for 6-12 months.

You must budget like a marathon runner, not a sprinter.

The worst financial mistake a fighter can make is to live like the last purse is guaranteed to happen again next month.

Pros and Cons of Fight-Based Income

Pros

- **Big Upside**: One win can change your financial life overnight.
- **Brand Growth**: Fame builds faster in fight sports when you succeed.
- **Negotiation Power**: Winning gives you leverage to demand better deals.

Cons

- **Unpredictable Paydays**: Injuries, cancellations, bad matchups can stall your income.
- **High Expenses**: A fight camp can cost $10,000-$100,000+.
- **Short Career Span**: Most fighters peak financially for 3-7 years.

- **Pressure to "Win or Starve"**: Leads to poor financial decisions under stress.

Sponsorships: Temporary Boosts, Not Permanent Foundations

Sponsorship money is great.

But it's seasonal.

It depends heavily on:

- Winning
- Staying visible
- Staying marketable
- Staying healthy

Never base your long-term financial life on temporary sponsorships.

Treat sponsorship money like bonus money.

Not base salary.

Bank it.

Invest it.

Don't spend it like it will always be there.

Real Talk: Fight Purses Are NOT Pure Profit

Let's break down a typical fighter's purse:

- $100,000 purse (show + win bonus)
- -10% to manager ($10,000)
- -10% to trainer/coaches/camp fees ($10,000)
- -15-40% taxes depending on location ($15,000-$40,000+)
- -Travel, nutritionist, training, gym fees ($5,000-$15,000)

Real Net Pay:

Closer to **$30,000-$50,000** — not $100,000.

And if you lose?

No win bonus.

Smaller sponsorship visibility.

Longer gap before your next fight.

How to Budget Fight Income

Step 1: Create a "Yearly Needs Budget"

Figure out:

- Rent/mortgage
- Utilities
- Car payments
- Food, gas, insurance
- Family support, if any

Multiply monthly essentials x 12.

That's the bare minimum you need.

Step 2: Divide Big Purses Across the Year

Don't treat a $150,000 win like $150,000.

Treat it like $12,500/month for the next 12 months.

Step 3: Save Automatically

Out of every fight purse:

- Set aside 40% immediately for taxes.
- Save another 30% for long-term investing.

Live on the rest — smartly.

Taxes for Fighters: Brutal but Manageable

You owe:

- Federal income taxes
- State income taxes (where you live AND where you fight)
- Self-employment taxes

And in some cases, international taxes if fighting abroad.

Hire a fighter-savvy CPA early.

Set up quarterly estimated tax payments.

Otherwise, that $300,000 title fight can turn into a $100,000 tax nightmare next year.

Setting Up Your Business: LLCs, Trusts, and Beyond

Smart fighters:

- Set up LLCs early (for sponsorship and fight income)
- Pay themselves a steady "salary" through their LLC
- Separate personal and business expenses

Super-smart fighters:

- Set up retirement accounts early (SEP IRA, Solo 401(k))
- Build trusts to protect assets from lawsuits
- Diversify income streams beyond the cage or ring

It's not flashy.

It's not "Instagram-cool."

But it's how real wealth is built behind the scenes.

Rookie Mistakes Fighters Make (And How to Dodge Them)

- **Blowing fight purses on cars, chains, watches.**
- **Trusting the wrong people to "invest" their money.**
- **Ignoring taxes until the IRS comes knocking.**
- **Living paycheck-to-paycheck between fights.**
- **Believing one big fight = forever rich.**

Instead:

- Save aggressively.
- Invest early.
- Build multiple income streams.
- Stay humble, stay hungry, stay prepared.

Case Study: Boxer Financial Win Story

A rising star in boxing:

- Wins a $200,000 fight purse.
- Banks 50% immediately into an investment account.
- Lives off a $60,000 yearly budget.
- Invests bonus sponsorship deals.
- Hires a solid tax professional.
- Prepares for life after fighting with business education.

Result?

Even after two major injuries and a 2-year break from boxing, he's financially stable, owns two rental properties, and has zero debt.

Building Wealth in Combat Sports: Your Real Game Plan

1. **Treat Fighting Like a Business**

Every fight = business revenue.
Every camp = business expense.

1. **Protect Your Money**

Save early, save often.
Set up strong bank and investment structures.

1. **Control Your Brand**

Your public image affects your sponsorship value.
Stay professional online and off.

1. **Invest in Education**

Take courses.
Learn investing basics.
Prepare for life after the spotlight.

1. **Prepare for Injury and Aging**

Your body won't stay 100% forever.
Your finances have to last longer than your fight career.

Combat Sport Analogies: Fighting and Finances

Boxing: It's not the knockout punch — it's winning on points.

Manage your money one smart decision at a time.

MMA: It's not just striking — it's jiu-jitsu, wrestling, cardio, strategy.

Managing wealth requires *multiple* disciplines too.

Pro Wrestling: The show is entertainment — but contracts, royalties, and rights are business.

Always negotiate with the big picture in mind.

A Final Word: Fighting for Your Future

You fought to get here.

You fought through amateur ranks, injuries, sacrifices, and doubters.

Now, you have to fight one more battle — the battle to protect and grow your financial future.

You have every tool you need:

- Your work ethic.
- Your resilience.
- Your ability to adapt.

Money management is just another opponent.

You can beat it.

You will beat it.

And when the last bell rings, you'll walk away not just with memories — but with real wealth, real peace, and real power for life beyond the cage, the ring, or the mat.

Chapter 56: Women's Pro Sports (WNBA, Soccer, Tennis, MMA) — Lower Average Salaries, Smarter Planning Needed

When you look at women's professional sports, one thing becomes clear fast:

The financial game is different.

Not because the talent is lower.

Not because the grind is easier.

Not because the sacrifices are smaller.

The reality is, **the money isn't the same yet** — but the financial stakes absolutely are.

For women in the WNBA, NWSL, tennis tours, MMA promotions, and beyond, *managing your money smartly isn't just a good idea — it's survival.*

And when you do it right?

You're not just protecting yourself.

You're setting a standard for the next generation.

Let's talk about how.

The Financial Reality in Women's Sports

In almost every major women's league:

- Salaries are lower.
- Sponsorships are harder to secure (unless you're at the very top).
- Off-season income often matters more than in-season pay.
- Career spans are just as fragile — or even more so — due to injuries, market instability, and team closures.

This is not negativity.

This is clarity.

And clarity gives you power.

When you know the landscape, you can play the game better than anyone expects.

Breaking It Down: Sport by Sport

WNBA

- Average base salary: ~$120,600 in 2024
- Supermax salary: ~$241,984
- Offseason play: Many WNBA players go overseas (Russia, Turkey, Spain, etc.) to supplement income.
- Endorsements: Top players like Breanna Stewart and A'ja Wilson have sneaker deals, but most do not.

NWSL (Women's Soccer)

- Average salary: ~$60,000 to $80,000
- Top players (USWNT members): Higher thanks to bonuses and sponsorships.
- Offseason: Many players seek off-field endorsements, coaching

clinics, or training gigs.

Tennis

- Huge disparity:
- Top players (Serena Williams, Naomi Osaka): Tens of millions in prize money + endorsements.
- Mid-level: Break even after travel, coaching, equipment.
- Low-level pros: Losing money unless consistently winning ITF events.

Women's MMA

- UFC, Bellator, PFL women's divisions growing fast.
- Fight purses: $10,000 to $500,000 depending on name recognition.
- Sponsorships: Improving, but still way behind men.

The Pros and Cons of Lower Pay

Pros

- Greater incentive to diversify income early.
- Financial habits are built with discipline from day one.
- Closer-knit communities that often help each other out.

Cons

- More financial pressure off the field/court/ring.
- Harder to invest early if living paycheck to paycheck.
- Increased career burnout if finances aren't stabilized.

Action Steps for Smarter Planning

1. Save Aggressively During Playing Years

- Aim to save 40-50% of net income if possible.
- Create an emergency fund that covers at least 12 months of living expenses.
- Save every bonus, sponsorship, and off-season check — not just your regular salary.

2. Master Offseason Income

- Coaching
- Speaking engagements
- Clinics and camps
- Content creation (YouTube, podcasts, Patreon)
- Consulting roles in brands or sports organizations

Your second income stream isn't optional. It's essential.

3. Invest Early — Even If Small

- Open a Roth IRA or Solo 401(k) as soon as possible.
- Set up automatic contributions, even if it's $100 a month.
- Learn basic index fund investing.

You may not have millions today — but compounding is real.
The earlier you start, the more options you'll have later.

4. Understand Healthcare and Insurance

- Disability insurance is critical for athletes, but even more for women who often have fewer guaranteed contracts.
- Know your options for health insurance if injured or released.
- Explore supplemental insurance options (accident, cancer, hospital indemnity).

5. Negotiate Everything

- WNBA? NWSL? UFC? Fight for appearance fees, bonuses, jersey sales cuts — whatever you can.
- Tennis? Negotiate exhibition fees and sponsor activation fees.
- MMA? Negotiate win bonuses, not just show money.

Every contract is negotiable.

Get professional help (agent or attorney) — and *always* read the fine print yourself too.

Real-World Story: Financial Win in Women's Sports

A WNBA player:

- Makes $80,000 salary.
- Plays overseas for another $150,000 during offseason.
- Banks 60% of both incomes into an investment account.
- Lives off a $40,000 yearly budget.
- Starts a basketball training academy in the off-season.
- Retires at 34 with $600,000+ saved, owns a home, no debt.

You don't have to be a household name to win financially.

You just have to play the money game smarter than the system expects.

Rookie Mistakes in Women's Sports

- Living like a top-5 player on a mid-tier salary.
- Assuming endorsements will come automatically (they won't).
- Not prioritizing savings because "I'm young."
- Ignoring the power of offseason income.
- Staying financially tied to poor management or bad advice.

How to Build a Lifetime Financial Advantage

Start Early

- Save before you think you "deserve" to.
- Invest before you think it's a "big" amount.
- Educate yourself before you think you "need" to.

Think Business

- You are the CEO of your career.
- Every deal, every endorsement, every dollar matters.

Plan for Post-Career While Playing

- Don't wait until the final whistle to start preparing.
- Build your second career while still competing.

Guard Your Brand

- Reputation builds wealth.
- Scandals, bad deals, reckless spending all kill future opportunities.

Real-World Scenarios for Women's Athletes

Scenario 1: WNBA Player

You sign a 3-year $250,000 total contract.
Your agent takes 4%.
Taxes take 35%.
You net ~$135,000 over 3 years.
That's about $45,000 per year.
You must:

- Budget smartly.
- Consider offseason overseas play.
- Build a second income stream.
- Save a portion of each paycheck automatically.

Scenario 2: Pro Tennis Player

You're ranked #120 in the world.
Prize money: $150,000 before taxes.
Travel expenses: $80,000.
Coaching fees: $30,000.
Leftover: ~$40,000 net.
You must:

- Budget like a working professional, not a millionaire.
- Pick tournaments carefully.
- Find sponsors to offset costs.
- Save aggressively during hot streaks.

Women's Sports Analogy: Money Management is Like Training

In every sport:

- You don't win by training once and quitting.
- You don't build muscle by lifting once.
- You don't master technique overnight.

Money is the same.

- Daily reps.
- Small wins.
- Consistency beats flash.

A Final Word: You Are the Blueprint

The future of women's sports is growing fast.

But the system won't automatically take care of you.

You have to fight for:

- Your money.
- Your brand.
- Your second act.

Every smart financial move you make isn't just about you.

It's about every player who comes after you — inspired by your blueprint.

You are not just a player.

You are a pioneer.

Own it.

And build a legacy that's bigger than any scoreboard.

Chapter 57: Other Emerging Pro Sports: Lacrosse, Rugby, Pickleball, eSports — Financial Realities

The world of professional sports is bigger than just the NFL, NBA, MLB, NHL, and WNBA.

There are athletes grinding, thriving, and building brands in sports like lacrosse, rugby, pickleball, and eSports.

These sports may not have billion-dollar TV deals — yet — but they are growing fast. And the money, while different, still demands serious financial literacy.

Here's the truth:

Emerging sports require emerging financial strategies.

You're not playing with 10-year, $100 million contracts.

You're not banking on guaranteed pensions at 45.

You're building a career in real-time — while also building the sport.

That's powerful.

But it means your financial game plan has to be sharper, smarter, and even more disciplined than athletes in bigger leagues.

Let's walk through how to win financially in these rising fields.

The Financial Landscape of Emerging Sports

Across these sports — lacrosse, rugby, pickleball, eSports — the financial themes are remarkably similar:

- Lower base salaries or prize money
- Greater dependence on endorsements, sponsorships, and content creation
- Higher personal costs (travel, equipment, coaching)
- Shorter contracts, sometimes event-by-event
- Less institutional financial support (pensions, healthcare, retirement plans)
- Huge opportunity for early brand building

If you think of pro sports like a pyramid:

- The NFL and NBA are at the very top (money-wise).
- Sports like lacrosse, rugby, pickleball, and even some levels of eSports are still climbing up the mountain — fast.

You are an entrepreneur as much as an athlete.

Breaking It Down: Sport by Sport

Professional Lacrosse

- **Leagues**: PLL (Premier Lacrosse League), NLL (National Lacrosse League)
- **Average salaries**: ~$35,000–$50,000 in PLL (higher with sponsorships)
- **Structure**: Seasonal tournaments and games
- **Offseason**: Players often coach, run camps, or work other jobs.

Professional Rugby

- **Leagues**: MLR (Major League Rugby in the U.S.), international clubs (Europe, Japan)
- **Average salaries**: ~$30,000–$70,000 in U.S. MLR; up to $200,000+ abroad
- **Structure**: Full seasons, domestic and international play
- **Offseason**: Similar to football, some downtime, but opportunities for coaching and clinics.

Professional Pickleball

- **Leagues**: PPA Tour, APP Tour
- **Average earnings**: ~$15,000–$100,000+ annually from tournaments, sponsorships, and clinics
- **Structure**: Year-round tournaments
- **Offseason**: Nonexistent — you build your own schedule.

Professional eSports

- **Leagues**: Vary by game — League of Legends, Overwatch, Fortnite, etc.
- **Average earnings**: $40,000–$60,000 for salaried pros; up to millions in prize money for top-tier players.
- **Structure**: Seasonal leagues, major international tournaments
- **Offseason**: Limited; content creation (streaming, YouTube, brand deals) fills the gaps.

The Pros and Cons of Emerging Sports

Pros

- Early movers in the sport can become faces of their league.
- Brand partnerships are eager to find authentic athletes.
- Flexibility in building multiple income streams.
- Closer connection to fanbases.

Cons

- Lower guaranteed income.
- Higher risk of injuries with less financial protection.
- League instability (team closures, league shutdowns are possible).
- Must manage and create your own benefits (health insurance, retirement plans, etc.).

Action Steps to Dominate Financially

1. Treat Yourself as a Business — Right Now

Set up:

- LLC or S-Corp to manage income, expenses, and sponsorship deals.
- Business bank account separate from your personal account.
- Basic bookkeeping software (QuickBooks, Wave, etc.).

2. Prioritize Building a Brand Alongside Building Stats

- Build an online presence (social media, YouTube, TikTok, LinkedIn).
- Create a simple, clean personal website.
- Offer clinics, lessons, or consulting in your sport.
- Network like crazy at tournaments, events, conferences.

Your personal brand can eventually earn more than prize money.

3. Save Like You're a Seasoned Vet, Even If You're a Rookie

- 50%+ of net income should go to savings/investing if possible.
- Create a cash reserve to survive dry periods (like no tournaments or events).
- Invest small amounts early in index funds, IRAs, or simple portfolios.

4. Plan for Health Care and Insurance Separately

- Buy private health insurance if your league doesn't offer it.
- Consider disability insurance — even if it feels expensive.
- Build an emergency medical fund for unexpected injuries.

5. Diversify Income Streams Early

- Coaching clinics
- Online courses or e-books
- Branded merchandise
- Sponsorships
- Content creation
- Speaking engagements

Don't rely on prize money alone.

Real-World Stories: Emerging Sport Wins

Lacrosse Star

- Salary: $40,000
- Clinics: $60,000 annually
- Sponsorships: $20,000 (gear and training endorsements)
- Online Academy: $15,000 in first year

Total Annual Earnings: $135,000+

Pickleball Champion

- Tournament Winnings: $70,000
- Sponsorship Deals: $25,000
- Clinic Hosting: $10,000
- YouTube Channel Revenue: $5,000

Total Annual Earnings: $110,000

Rookie Mistakes in Emerging Pro Sports

- Living like a superstar after one good season.
- Not paying quarterly taxes on independent contractor income.
- Not understanding basic contracts (appearance fees, exclusivity clauses).
- Not investing in basic insurance and financial planning.
- Not building a professional image and presence.

Analogies: Money is Training

- You don't win your sport by practicing once.
- You don't build a strong body without reps.
- You don't build a lasting financial life without discipline.

Winning financially is daily habits, just like winning games or matches.

Real-World Scenarios

Scenario: eSports Player

You win $120,000 in prize money one year.
After taxes (~35%) and team cuts (~10%), you're left with ~$66,000.
You need to:

- Set aside at least 30% of net income for taxes.
- Save aggressively for future downtime.
- Diversify into content creation or coaching before income slows.

Scenario: Rugby Player

You sign a $50,000 MLR contract.
You get injured midseason — non-guaranteed contract.
You need to:

- Have emergency savings.
- Have disability insurance.
- Have an offseason backup plan (coaching, clinics, camps).

The Future of Emerging Sports

Sports like lacrosse, rugby, pickleball, and eSports are exploding.
If you get your money right now:

- You'll ride the wave.
- You'll build wealth while the sport builds fandom.
- You'll become the blueprint for future players.

Closing Encouragement: You Are Building It While Playing It

You aren't just athletes in emerging sports.

You are the pioneers.

You are the architects.

And when you manage your money smartly, you create freedom that lasts far beyond your playing years.

Build wealth now, while the stadiums are still filling up.

Because someday, people will say they remember when you changed the game — on the field, and in your financial life.

Own it.

Chapter 58: Financial Literacy for International Pro Athletes — Different Laws, Different Taxes

Let's keep it real from the start.

When you take your game global — whether you're a soccer player in Europe, a basketball player in Australia, a tennis pro traveling the world, or an eSports star bouncing between continents — you are not just crossing borders.

You are crossing **legal systems**, **tax codes**, **currency policies**, and **financial expectations** that can either set you up beautifully or tear you apart financially if you're not careful.

The money might hit your bank account the same way — numbers on a screen.

But **what those numbers mean**, **how they're taxed**, and **how they work for you** is completely different.

This chapter is your game plan for surviving and thriving financially when your career goes international.

No fluff. No sugarcoating.

Let's build it.

Playing Abroad: Why the Financial Game Changes Immediately

When you sign that contract overseas, you're no longer just a U.S. taxpayer or hometown hero.

You are now:

- A foreign worker in another country
- A subject to their tax laws
- Possibly still a U.S. taxpayer (if you're American)
- A currency exchanger
- A businessperson under multiple jurisdictions

Each one of those realities has real, tangible financial consequences.

What Changes When You Play Internationally?

1. **Taxes**:
2. You could owe taxes both in the country you're playing in *and* back home (U.S. or otherwise).
3. **Currency Risks**:
4. The value of your earnings can change with the strength or weakness of the U.S. dollar, Euro, Yen, Pound, Peso, etc.
5. **Contract Structures**:
6. Contracts might be *net* of taxes (team pays your taxes for you) or *gross* (you're responsible).
7. **Insurance**:
8. Health, disability, and life insurance might need private policies abroad — or your home policy might not cover you.
9. **Legal Protections**:
10. Employment rights, dispute resolution, union protections, and even basic contract enforcement vary by country.

11. **Banking**:
12. You may need foreign bank accounts — and know how to move money legally across borders.
13. **Retirement Planning**:
14. You may not qualify for retirement benefits in a foreign country. You have to build your own.

Taxes for International Athletes: The Quick Realities

If you're a U.S. citizen or green card holder, the IRS taxes you on your **worldwide income** — even if you live abroad.

There are some protections:

- **Foreign Earned Income Exclusion (FEIE)** — allows you to exclude ~$120,000+ of foreign income (updated annually) if you meet certain residency tests.
- **Foreign Tax Credit (FTC)** — allows you to offset U.S. tax with taxes paid to foreign governments.
- **Tax Treaties** — special deals between countries to prevent double taxation.

BUT:

The rules are strict.

The paperwork is brutal (especially FBARs and FATCA reporting if you have foreign bank accounts).

And penalties for messing it up are savage.

This is not "do it yourself" territory.

You need a CPA who understands international tax law for athletes.

Currency Exchange Risks

When you earn in foreign currencies, your real earnings depend on:

- Exchange rates
- Transaction fees
- Timing of transfers

Scenario Example:

- You earn €500,000 in Spain.
- The Euro drops 10% against the Dollar by the time you move your money home.
- You just lost ~$50,000.

Solution:

Work with a bank or financial advisor familiar with **currency hedging** or **smart timing strategies** for large transfers.

How Contracts Vary Across Borders

In the U.S., sports contracts are heavily regulated and standardized.

Internationally?

Not so much.

Key differences:

- Contracts might be net of taxes (team covers your income tax).
- Some countries allow teams to terminate contracts easily.
- In others, player rights are better protected.
- Payment schedules (monthly, quarterly, lump-sum) vary.
- Bonus structures might be extremely vague.

Action Step:

Hire a bilingual or international sports agent or attorney familiar with that specific country's league and laws.

Do NOT assume your U.S. agent can just "figure it out."

Insurance Realities Abroad

Don't assume you're covered.

- Domestic health insurance often won't cover you overseas.
- Teams might offer basic coverage — but not always great.
- Disability policies might not kick in if you get hurt overseas.

Solutions:

- Buy an **international health policy**.
- Buy **private disability insurance** (protects your income if you're hurt).
- Buy **emergency evacuation insurance** if playing in risky regions.

Managing Your Money Across Borders

Set Up Smart Banking

- Open a **local bank account** for basic living expenses.
- Maintain a **U.S. account** for long-term savings and investment.
- Use **low-fee international transfer services** like Wise or Revolut.
- Avoid high currency conversion fees.

Handle Your Credit Wisely

- Keep using a U.S. credit card (with no foreign transaction fees) to build credit history.
- Pay bills automatically to maintain U.S. credit scores.

- Don't close U.S. bank accounts even if you live abroad.

Build Emergency Reserves in Both Currencies

- You'll want 3–6 months' living expenses in the **currency you're paid in**.
- Plus, a U.S. reserve fund if your international gig ends unexpectedly.

Real-World Story: Basketball Player in Italy

Marcus signs a €250,000/year deal in Italy.

He thinks it's all his.

But:

- Team only covers local taxes.
- U.S. IRS still wants their share.
- He pays an extra $40,000 in U.S. taxes.
- The Euro weakens, costing him another $15,000.
- Agent fees weren't properly negotiated internationally (higher).

In the end?

He pockets closer to $110,000 than the $250,000 he dreamed about.

Rookie Mistakes International Athletes Make

- Assuming their team pays all taxes.
- Moving all their money without currency planning.
- Not reading the fine print on contracts.
- Not planning for an unexpected early exit.
- Ignoring health and disability insurance needs.
- Letting U.S. credit scores lapse.

Action Steps for International Athletes

1. **Hire a qualified CPA specializing in international tax law.**
2. **Hire an attorney fluent in international sports contracts.**
3. **Buy your own international health and disability insurance.**
4. **Plan your banking setup before you leave.**
5. **Understand the currency you'll be paid in — and how you'll move it.**
6. **Ask for clarity: Net of tax or Gross of tax?**
7. **Read your entire contract carefully — in English if needed.**
8. **Set up a U.S. retirement plan even if working abroad (Roth IRA, SEP IRA, Solo 401(k)).**
9. **Treat your playing income as business income — plan and save aggressively.**

Sports Analogies: International Play is Like an Away Game Every Day

You know how when you're on the road, the refs call the game differently?

The fans are louder?

The environment is unfamiliar?

Playing internationally is the same — financially.

You can win away games.

You just need to **study the court**, **understand the conditions**, and **prepare like a champion**.

Final Encouragement: You Are Building a Global Legacy

Playing internationally is an incredible adventure.

It tests your skills.

It grows your brand globally.

And if you manage your money wisely, it can set you up for life — even if your playing days end thousands of miles from home.

The ball is in your hands.

Play it smart.

Quick Checklist: 20 Things to Know Before Signing an International Contract

1. **Net vs. Gross** — Is your salary net of taxes (team pays) or gross (you pay)?
2. **Tax Rate** — What is the local income tax rate in that country?
3. **U.S. Tax Impact** — Will you still owe U.S. taxes? (Most Americans do.)
4. **Tax Treaties** — Does the U.S. have a treaty with that country?
5. **Currency** — What currency are you being paid in?
6. **Exchange Rate Volatility** — How stable is that currency historically?
7. **Payment Timing** — Monthly, quarterly, lump sum? What happens if late?
8. **Bank Accounts** — Can you easily open a local account?
9. **Wire Fees** — How much will it cost to move money home?
10. **Contract Termination** — Under what conditions can the team terminate your deal?
11. **Health Insurance** — Does the team provide it? Is it good enough?
12. **Disability Insurance** — Do you have your own coverage?

13. **Visas and Work Permits** — Who handles it and how long is it valid?
14. **Retirement Plans** — Will you have any pension contributions?
15. **Living Expenses** — Who pays for housing, transportation, visas, relocation?
16. **Language Barriers** — Is there a translation of your contract?
17. **Agent Fees** — Are international fees different from domestic ones?
18. **Bonus Payments** — Are bonuses guaranteed or performance-based?
19. **Legal Recourse** — How easy is it to sue or enforce rights if needed?
20. **Exit Strategy** — If you leave midseason, what happens financially?

Sample Financial Timeline for an Overseas Pro Athlete

Pre-Signing

- Interview an international agent and attorney.
- Hire a CPA familiar with foreign-earned income.
- Research the country's tax system and currency.
- Understand local banking, visas, and insurance needs.

First 30 Days After Signing

- Open a local bank account.
- Set up automatic savings into U.S. retirement accounts.
- Buy international health and disability insurance.
- Arrange currency transfer strategies.

During Season

- Keep copies of every pay stub and contract addendum.
- Track all wire transfers and currency exchanges.
- Pay estimated U.S. taxes if necessary.
- Maintain U.S. credit score activity.

Offseason or Exit

- Move money back strategically (timing matters with exchange rates).
- File foreign bank account reports (FBAR/FATCA) if required.
- Meet with CPA for end-of-year international tax planning.
- Update estate plans and insurance based on new assets.

Common International Tax Traps for Athletes

Trap 1: Thinking Foreign Income is "Tax-Free"

Reality: The IRS taxes American citizens on worldwide income.

Trap 2: Missing the FEIE Residency Test

You must meet **physical presence** or **bona fide residence** tests to exclude income.

Missing even one day can cost you tens of thousands in taxes.

Trap 3: Forgetting to File FBAR or FATCA

If you have over $10,000 combined in foreign accounts, you must file the FBAR.

Failure = Huge penalties.

Trap 4: Mismanaging Currency Conversions on Tax Returns

You must report foreign income in U.S. dollars using IRS-approved exchange rates — not just your "bank app" rates.

Trap 5: Trusting the Team's Accountant

They work for the team — not you. Hire your own financial team.

Deep Dive: Unique Risks by Sport

Basketball Players (EuroLeague, Australia's NBL)

- Net contracts are common, but verify the guarantee level.
- Some clubs have spotty payment reputations.
- Understand early termination clauses.

Soccer Players (Europe, Asia, South America)

- "Image rights" agreements (endorsements vs. salaries) can cause tax confusion.
- Some countries require players to use specific agents or lawyers.

eSports Players (Asia, Europe)

- Prize money taxes vary wildly by country.
- Visa issues are common — overstaying can ruin future work opportunities.

Final Encouragement: Global Play, Global Planning

You were brave enough to take your game around the world.

Now you have to be just as brave — and smart — about your finances.

Being an international pro athlete means you are part athlete, part CEO, part diplomat, and part money manager.

Own that role.

Protect what you're building.

You've worked too hard — from childhood practices to college tryouts to signing that pro contract — to let financial ignorance steal your opportunity now.

Play global.

Think global.

Plan global.

Because true financial freedom knows no borders.

Top 10 Countries Where Pro Athletes Keep More of Their Money

Not all countries tax athletes the same.

Some are much better for your wallet than others.

Here's where playing can really help you **keep** what you earn:

1. **Monaco** —
2. No personal income tax.
3. If you're in tennis, motorsports, or high-end soccer, it's a financial dream.
4. **United Arab Emirates (Dubai, Abu Dhabi)** —
5. No personal income tax.
6. Growing scene for golf, soccer, and combat sports.
7. **Saudi Arabia** —

8. No personal income tax.
9. Massive contracts in soccer, golf, and boxing.
10. **Singapore** –
11. Low tax rates (~22% max).
12. Fast growing for Formula 1, MMA, and eSports.
13. **Switzerland** –
14. Negotiable flat-rate tax deals for foreign high-net-worth individuals.
15. Common for tennis stars, cyclists, skiers.
16. **Bermuda** –
17. No income tax, but cost of living is extremely high.
18. **Ireland** –
19. Athletes can claim tax relief on career earnings under the "artist exemption" if structured properly.
20. **Qatar** –
21. No personal income tax.
22. Growing sports hub: World Cup host, tennis, golf.
23. **Florida, USA (playing for a Florida-based team)** –
24. No state income tax + U.S. federal tax only.
25. Great for NBA, NFL, MLB, MLS players.
26. **Texas, USA (Dallas, Houston, Austin)** –
27. No state income tax.
28. Same federal obligations but huge salary savings compared to high-tax states like California or New York.

Important Reminder:

Living in a no-tax country doesn't automatically erase your U.S. federal obligations as a U.S. citizen!

7 Worst Financial Mistakes International Athletes Make (Real-World Stories)

Mistake 1: "I Thought They Were Paying the Taxes"

Player signed a *net contract* but didn't realize the team was slow paying tax authorities.

Result: Huge unexpected tax bill back home.

Mistake 2: "I Left Mid-Season Without Checking the Fine Print"

Athlete terminated the contract early.

Owed the team a portion of signing bonus and relocation fees back.

Mistake 3: "I Got Paid in Cash Under the Table"

Looked good short-term.

But no paper trail = no proof of earnings = no retirement contributions and no visa renewal.

Mistake 4: "I Didn't File My U.S. Taxes"

Assumed foreign earnings didn't matter.

IRS penalties stacked up.

Had to pay double years later.

Mistake 5: "I Didn't Hedge the Currency"

Earned $500,000 in another currency.

When it was time to transfer back home, the exchange rate dropped — lost 15% value instantly.

Mistake 6: "I Forgot About FBAR and FATCA"

Had over $10,000 in a foreign bank account.

Didn't file the right forms.

Massive penalties, even though it was just savings.

Mistake 7: "I Didn't Plan for Moving Home"

Sold a home overseas at a huge gain.

Forgot that foreign capital gains must be reported in the U.S.

Key Questions to Ask Before Accepting an International Contract

Before you sign anything, ask these questions:

1. Is the salary net or gross?
2. What is the income tax rate in the country?
3. Does the team guarantee full salary no matter what?
4. What happens if I get injured?
5. Who pays for housing and living expenses?
6. Who handles visas and work permits?
7. Am I allowed to leave early if things don't work out?
8. How is bonus money structured — and taxed?
9. Will I need to set up a local business entity (for endorsements)?
10. Who handles my U.S. taxes while I'm abroad?
11. Will I still be covered by my U.S. health insurance?
12. Are there currency transfer restrictions in the country?
13. How reliable is the country's legal system for contracts?
14. Will the team cover relocation costs back home if necessary?
15. What benefits (pension, health) does the team provide, if any?
16. What is the exit tax policy (if you leave mid-contract)?
17. Can I bring family members — and are they covered legally?
18. How often will I be paid — monthly, quarterly, lump sum?
19. Does the team have a reputation for paying players on time?
20. Who do I call if there's a dispute — agent, lawyer, league?

Quick International Athlete Money Rules (Memorize These)

- **File U.S. taxes no matter what.**
- **Report all foreign accounts over $10,000.**
- **Have a U.S. CPA familiar with international income.**
- **Use a multi-currency bank account if possible.**
- **Don't trust the team's accountant without independent verification.**
- **Plan for currency fluctuations.**
- **Don't get paid cash under the table without contracts.**
- **Confirm insurance is valid internationally.**
- **Save aggressively — many overseas careers are short.**
- **Plan an exit strategy before you need one.**

Final Words of Wisdom: You're Not Just an Athlete — You're a Global Entrepreneur Now

Playing pro sports internationally isn't just about athletic talent.

It's about navigating new systems, taxes, banking, insurance, immigration laws, real estate, and personal brand protection.

You are your own walking business now.

And if you treat your career like a business, you'll be able to:

- **Extend your playing years**
- **Grow real wealth**
- **Transition smoothly post-career**
- **Take care of your family for generations**

You didn't grind this hard to build a life overseas just to give it away to bad contracts, bad taxes, or bad planning.

So stay smart.

Stay ready.
Stay global — in mind and money.
Your game opened doors.
Now your financial literacy will keep them open.

Chapter 59: Lessons from Legends — Smart Moves (and Big Mistakes) by Famous Athletes

When you make it to the pros, there's no shortage of people who want to give you advice.

But sometimes, the best lessons aren't from speeches — they're from **watching what others actually did** with their money, their brand, and their opportunity.

You don't have to learn everything the hard way.

You can learn by studying the blueprint laid out by athletes who came before you — the smart plays and the fumbles.

Let's walk through it, real talk style.

Smart Money Moves by Famous Athletes

Magic Johnson — *Owning the Game Outside the Game*

When Magic retired, he didn't just sit on his playing checks.

He **built an empire** — movie theaters, Starbucks franchises, sports teams.

Magic turned fame into ownership.

He understood early: **you are the business, not just the athlete**.

Lesson: Build businesses that will outlast your playing days.

Use your platform to create cash flow streams that work for you.

Venus and Serena Williams — *Ownership Over Endorsements*

The Williams sisters didn't just take checks to promote brands.

They **negotiated ownership stakes** in companies they believed in.

When Serena invested in startups, she built her venture capital firm.

Venus negotiated equity deals in wellness brands and interior design companies.

Lesson: Instead of just endorsing brands, **own part of them**.

Be part of the upside.

LeBron James — *Building a Brand Bigger Than Basketball*

LeBron wasn't just about points and rings.

He built SpringHill Entertainment, invested in Blaze Pizza, bought into Liverpool FC.

He partnered with Nike for a **lifetime deal**, one of the most lucrative in sports history.

Lesson: Your brand power is **multipliable**.

Every year you stay consistent and smart, your off-court opportunities grow.

Shaquille O'Neal — *Investing Where He Eats*

Shaq became a franchise mogul — owning Auntie Anne's, Five Guys, car washes, fitness centers.

His rule was simple: **If he liked the business, he bought into it**.

Lesson: You don't have to invent the next big thing.

Sometimes the smartest move is investing in what you already use, love, and believe in.

Big Financial Mistakes Famous Athletes Made (and What We Can Learn)

Mike Tyson — *Spending Faster Than You Earn*

Mike Tyson earned over $400 million in his career.

He spent it faster than it came in — on houses, cars, jewelry, tigers, entourages.

By his early 30s, he declared bankruptcy.

Lesson: It doesn't matter how much you make if you don't **manage**

the inflows and outflows.

A $20 million contract with $25 million in spending still equals broke.

Antoine Walker — *Too Many Yes's, Not Enough No's*

Walker made over $110 million during his NBA career.

He lost it through bad investments, real estate collapses, and constantly bailing out friends and family.

Lesson: Your heart is big — but your wallet has to have **boundaries**.

It's okay to say **no**, even to people you love.

Evander Holyfield — *Living Too Big, Too Long*

Holyfield earned more than $250 million boxing.

At one point, he owned a 109-room mansion.

Between maintenance, taxes, child support for 11 kids, and bad business moves, the money bled out.

Lesson: Lifestyle inflation can **crush even the richest athletes**.

Live well, but live smart.

Big doesn't always mean better.

Latrell Sprewell — *Pride Over Planning*

Offered a $21 million contract extension, Sprewell famously said, "I got my family to feed."

He declined — and never signed another big deal again.

Lesson: Pride doesn't pay the bills.

Negotiation is smart.

Overplaying your hand out of ego is not.

Actionable Lessons for You — Right Now

Lesson 1: Invest Early and Often

The best investment is **time in the market**, not timing the market.

Start your retirement accounts the minute you sign your first pro contract.

Lesson 2: Own Equity, Not Just Endorsements

If you have a choice between a check and a small ownership slice — think bigger picture.

Equity can outpace cash.

Lesson 3: Protect Your Downside

Every athlete is one injury, one bad season, or one lockout away from reality hitting hard.

Build emergency funds and disability insurance while things are good.

Lesson 4: Build Brand Consistency

Your brand isn't just your performance stats.

It's how you treat people.

It's how you handle business.

It's the story people tell about you when you're not in the room.

Lesson 5: Choose Your Team Carefully

Surround yourself with professionals who **work for you**, not just hang around you.

Financial advisors, attorneys, accountants, and agents should be vetted like you're hiring for a championship roster.

Real Talk: How to Think Like a Legend Starting Now

When you see the greats who made it both during and after their playing careers, one thing becomes clear:

They treated their money with the same intensity they treated their game.

They studied it.

They respected it.

They protected it.

They didn't expect someone else to do it for them.

They built the muscle — even if they started out not knowing much.

You don't have to become a Wall Street expert overnight.

You just have to:

- Stay humble enough to keep learning.
- Stay wise enough to ask questions.

- Stay strong enough to say no when it matters.

Final Drill: If You Want to Win Long-Term

Practice Money Moves Like You Practice Your Sport

- Review your budget monthly like watching film.
- Check your investment accounts quarterly like game stats.
- Set annual goals like training camp plans.

Small habits win championships — financially and athletically.

You already beat the odds by getting here.

Now beat the odds again by staying financially free after the spotlight dims.

Because remember:

The ball stops bouncing.

The cleats get hung up.

The gloves come off.

But **your financial legacy** — that lasts forever.

Bonus Section: Winning Money Moves and Avoidable Mistakes

Top 10 Smartest Financial Moves Ever Made by Athletes

1. **LeBron James investing in Blaze Pizza** before it exploded in popularity, turning a few hundred thousand dollars into tens of millions.
2. **Venus Williams studying business during her tennis career**, earning her degree and launching successful ventures in fashion and interior design.
3. **Shaquille O'Neal investing in Five Guys, Papa John's, car**

washes, and fitness centers — diversifying early.

4. **Kobe Bryant launching Bryant Stibel Venture Capital** before retirement, investing in technology, media, and data companies.
5. **Kevin Durant launching Thirty Five Ventures** — producing media, backing startups, and building ownership.
6. **Maria Sharapova creating Sugarpova candy company** while still dominating on the court.
7. **Roger Federer negotiating a $300 million deal with Uniqlo** after his Nike contract ended — leveraging timing and brand loyalty.
8. **Serena Williams creating Serena Ventures**, focusing on diversity-led startups while still competing professionally.
9. **George Foreman licensing his name to the George Foreman Grill**, earning more from grills than he did boxing.
10. **Magic Johnson's early investment into Starbucks and urban development projects**, creating generational wealth and community impact.

Takeaway:

The smart players didn't just think about their sport.

They thought about **ownership, entrepreneurship, and building value** beyond game checks.

Top 10 Biggest Money Mistakes Athletes Should Avoid

1. **Living paycheck to paycheck**, even on a $5M salary.
2. **Trusting the wrong people** — family, friends, agents — without checks and balances.
3. **Buying too many liabilities** (cars, houses, jewelry) that lose value instead of buying assets that grow.
4. **Making emotional investments** — giving money to everyone who asks without vetting.
5. **Ignoring taxes** — then getting crushed by IRS bills later.

6. **Overextending credit** — believing "future money" will cover current spending.
7. **Falling for get-rich-quick schemes** pitched by people with no real track record.
8. **Failing to insure yourself properly** — disability insurance, liability coverage, career-ending injury protections.
9. **Not planning for the "afterlife" of sports** — assuming endorsements or income will just "show up."
10. **Letting pride block advice** — refusing to hire or listen to professionals who can help you see what you don't know yet.

Takeaway:

Most bankrupt athletes didn't fail because they were "bad with money." They failed because they **didn't respect the basics**.

Sample Financial Game Plan: Rookie Signing a $1M Contract

Let's pretend you're a rookie who just signed a $1 million deal.

Here's a simple real-world plan to set you up for long-term success:

Step 1: Cut it in Half for Mental Accounting

- Assume you have **$500,000** after taxes, agent fees, union dues, etc.

Step 2: Create Buckets

- **Emergency Fund (10%)** → $50,000 in high-yield savings.
- **Living Expenses (20%)** → $100,000 for rent, groceries, car (reasonable budget, not flashy).
- **Investments (50%)** → $250,000 into a conservative-diversified portfolio (mix of index funds, blue-chip stocks, bonds).
- **Opportunity Fund (10%)** → $50,000 cash reserve for smart investments or business opportunities.

- **Fun Fund (10%)** → $50,000 for vacations, family gifts, or personal splurges — guilt-free.

Step 3: Hire a Financial Team

- Find a **fee-only financial planner** — not someone trying to sell you stuff.
- Find a **tax advisor** who understands athletes.
- Find an **attorney** to review deals, contracts, and investments.

Step 4: Plan Your "Next Contract" Before It Comes

- Assume no more money is coming until it's signed — stay financially conservative.

Step 5: Set 1-Year, 5-Year, and 10-Year Goals

- 1 Year: Build credit score, max out retirement contributions.
- 5 Years: Own a paid-off home if it makes sense.
- 10 Years: Have multiple income streams outside of sports.

Step 6: Keep Learning

- Read one book a year on investing, entrepreneurship, or financial planning.
- Meet with your financial team quarterly — even if nothing major changes.

Closing Real Talk

You're not here by accident.

You worked, you sacrificed, you bled, you hustled to become a professional athlete.

Now, you have a choice:

Be remembered as someone who dominated during the game and after it.

Be the blueprint, not the cautionary tale.

Learn from the legends.

Learn from the losses.

Learn from the wins.

Because the goal isn't just to get the bag.

It's to **keep the bag, grow the bag, and change lives because of the bag.**

You got this.

Part 7: Mastering Your Financial Legacy

At this stage, it's no longer just about managing game checks, negotiating contracts, or budgeting for offseason spending. It's about thinking **bigger**, **longer**, and **deeper**.

Part 7 is where we focus on building something that **outlives your playing days** — and even your lifetime.

You'll learn what it means to:

- Transition from just making money to **growing wealth** across generations.
- Protect yourself, your family, and your brand from the financial dangers that can unravel everything you worked so hard to build.
- Turn short-term fame into long-term financial freedom.
- Set up systems that allow your name, values, and impact to live on — whether you played two seasons or twenty.

This part covers essential topics like:

- Estate planning basics every athlete must know — wills, trusts, powers of attorney.
- Creating charitable foundations the right way (not just for the headlines).
- Teaching your kids and family about money so you aren't the last

financially savvy person in the bloodline.

- Avoiding legacy-killers like mismanagement, taxes, and lawsuits.
- Designing a *real plan* for giving back to your community without going broke.
- Understanding how financial literacy itself becomes one of the greatest gifts you can pass on.

Because the truth is this:

The real measure of your success isn't just the size of your last paycheck — it's what you leave behind when the lights go off and the crowd stops cheering.

Mastering your financial legacy means **thinking like a CEO**, even if you started as a rookie with nothing but raw talent and a dream.

In Part 7, you'll be equipped with the tools, mindsets, and strategies to **become the legend your family, your community, and your future generations will always be proud of**.

It's about **building something that lasts**.

And it starts right here.

Chapter 60: Giving Back the Smart Way — Foundations, Charities, and Donor-Advised Funds

When you first make it as a professional athlete, there's a moment — sometimes big, sometimes small — when you realize you now have the ability to help others in ways you once could only dream of.

Maybe it's buying your parents a house.

Maybe it's funding a local youth league where you grew up.

Maybe it's donating to causes you believe in or creating a scholarship in your family's name.

Maybe it's all of that, and more.

Giving back is one of the most powerful and fulfilling parts of success.

But here's the reality that too few people will tell you: **there's a smart way to do it — and there's a way that can quietly sabotage everything you've built.**

In this chapter, we're going to break it down — slowly, clearly, practically — so you can give generously without wrecking your finances, your peace of mind, or your long-term security.

We're going to cover:

- The emotional side of giving — why it feels good, but why you still need boundaries
- The pros and cons of foundations, private charities, and donor-

advised funds
- How to choose the right structure for your goals
- How to spot the "give to feel important" trap (and avoid it)
- Action steps to set up your giving plan now, not later
- Real-world examples of athletes who did it right — and those who learned the hard way
- How to build a giving legacy that actually lasts

Let's start where it always starts: with your heart — and then bring your head along too.

Giving From the Heart, But Guarding With Your Head

It's natural to want to give when you finally make it.

You remember the teachers who believed in you, the coaches who trained you for free, the friends who stuck by you when nobody knew your name.

You want to lift others up the way you were lifted.

That's good. That's beautiful.

But giving without a plan is like trying to play a game with no clock, no score, and no boundaries.

It can lead to burnout, regret, and — ironically — less help for the people you care about.

You have to protect the mission by protecting the money.

That's not selfish. That's stewardship.

You can't pour from an empty cup.

And your financial health is the cup.

Pros and Cons of Different Giving Structures

Let's talk about three of the most common ways athletes give back — and the real trade-offs involved.

1. Private Foundations

A private foundation is a legal entity you create and control.

Think of it like your own mini-charity, built with your own money.

Pros:

- Total control over where the money goes
- Can build your name into something bigger than your career
- Potential tax benefits (carefully managed)

Cons:

- Expensive to set up and maintain (lawyers, accountants, annual filings)
- Requires ongoing administration
- Can attract attention — good and bad — from people wanting handouts

Real Talk Tip:

Many athletes set up foundations because they think it's what "successful people do," but they underestimate the time, energy, and money it takes to run one properly.

If you don't want another full-time job after sports, think carefully.

2. Donor-Advised Funds (DAFs)

A DAF is like a charitable investment account.

You put money into it, get an immediate tax deduction, then recommend where the grants go over time.

Pros:

- Very low cost to set up

- Simpler than a private foundation
- Gives you flexibility — you can give today, next year, or ten years from now
- Keeps you relatively anonymous if you want

Cons:

- Less direct control compared to your own foundation
- Funds must go to registered nonprofits — you can't just give to individuals or businesses
- Some fees involved depending on where you set it up

Real Talk Tip:

DAFs are a phenomenal tool if you want to **separate the decision to donate money** from the **pressure to immediately decide where it should go**.

3. Direct Gifts and Sponsorships

Sometimes you just want to cut a check.

Sponsor a kid's AAU team. Pay tuition for a cousin. Help someone out directly.

Pros:

- Immediate impact
- Very personal and meaningful

Cons:

- No tax benefits (unless structured properly)
- Can create expectations, resentment, or dependency
- No legal protection if something goes wrong

Real Talk Tip:

Direct giving feels the best in the moment — but it's the riskiest financially and emotionally if it isn't managed carefully.

Common Giving Mistakes Athletes Make

Before we get into action steps, let's call out a few traps you need to see coming.

- **Giving too early:** Before you know your real financial picture.
- **Giving too much:** Leaving yourself financially vulnerable.
- **Giving to the wrong people:** Out of guilt, loyalty, or fear of being called "selfish."
- **Giving without structure:** No plan, no tracking, no accountability.
- **Giving for image:** Trying to look successful instead of actually building success.

You are not selfish for saying "Not yet" or "Not this way."

You're being smart.

How to Set Up a Smart Giving Strategy

Here's your game plan — step-by-step.

Step 1: Build your own financial foundation first.

No giving plan until you have:

- Emergency fund
- Retirement plan
- Debt management plan
- Estate plan basics in place

Step 2: Define your giving goals.

Ask yourself:

- Who or what do I want to impact?
- Am I thinking about this for my lifetime — or beyond?

Step 3: Choose the right structure.

- Private foundation if you want maximum control and legacy-building
- Donor-advised fund if you want low-maintenance flexibility
- Direct gifts if it's small, personal, and carefully considered

Step 4: Assemble your giving team.

You need:

- A financial advisor who understands philanthropy
- A tax professional to structure donations wisely
- An attorney if you're setting up a foundation

Step 5: Set giving boundaries.

Decide:

- What causes you'll support (stay focused)
- How much you'll give annually (set a percentage of income, not just "whatever feels good")

Step 6: Communicate clearly.

If you start giving — especially to family and friends — be honest about your limits.

Clear is kind. Confusing is cruel.

Step 7: Review and adjust annually.

Life changes. Finances change. Review your giving plan every year.

Real-World Examples: The Good, The Bad, and The Lessons

Good Example:

Dikembe Mutombo used a combination of a foundation and strategic partnerships to build hospitals and fund education programs in Africa — without going broke or burning out.

Bad Example:

Multiple athletes have set up foundations that folded within a few years because they were poorly managed, drained by overhead costs, or used for "image" instead of real impact.

Lesson:

Sustainable giving requires the same discipline, planning, and team-building as a winning sports career.

Final Words of Encouragement

Giving back is part of why you're here.

It's part of why you fought so hard to get to this level.

It's part of what will make your life bigger than your stat sheet or your bank account.

But you can't give what you don't have.

You can't serve others well if you don't protect yourself first.

Giving the smart way means:

- **Thinking like a CEO** about your philanthropy
- **Building systems** that outlast your playing days
- **Being intentional** about where your money, time, and energy go

When you do that, you don't just "give back."

You build something **forward**.

You turn success into significance.

And that, my friend, is the real championship ring.

Chapter 61: Teaching Financial Literacy to the Next Generation of Athletes

You made it.

You've walked the path that so many dream of but so few truly understand.

You've dealt with the fame, the freedom, the pressure, the mistakes, the lessons.

You know what it's like to be young and have the world open up—and how quickly it can close if you aren't smart with your money.

Now comes one of the greatest responsibilities and honors you'll ever have: **teaching the next generation**.

Not just about the sport.

Not just about the grind.

But about **life off the field, court, rink, octagon, or track.**

About **money. Freedom. Choices. Legacy.**

Because here's the truth:

If we don't teach them, the world will.

And the world doesn't always have their best interests at heart.

In this chapter, we're going to break down how to pass the torch wisely.

How to become not just an example — but a mentor, a guide, a builder of futures.

We'll cover:

- Why teaching financial literacy is just as important as teaching skills
- How to meet young athletes where they are
- How to make financial lessons stick
- The biggest financial traps for young athletes
- Action steps you can start taking right now
- A sample "Financial Literacy Game Plan" for the next generation
- Encouragement for your role as a leader beyond your playing days

Why Financial Literacy Matters More Than Ever

Every generation faces challenges.

But this one?

They're facing NIL deals at 16.

Sponsorships in high school.

Social media wealth traps.

Pressure from family, coaches, agents, and strangers before they've even learned to file taxes.

And most of them are walking into it without armor.

Without shields.

Without the tools they need to defend their future.

Teaching financial literacy isn't a luxury anymore.

It's a necessity.

It's protection.

It's empowerment.

It's survival.

And if you have even one athlete look at you and say,

"Man, because of you, I didn't blow it,"

you will have done something bigger than championships.

You will have changed a life.

How to Meet Young Athletes Where They Are

Here's the first lesson: **You can't lecture your way into their hearts.**

Young athletes today are:

- Distracted
- Overstimulated
- Worried about their image
- Pulled in a million directions

You have to approach them like a coach during tryouts:

Tough, but loving.

Patient, but demanding.

Direct, but understanding.

Rules for reaching them:

- **Keep it real.** No big words. No lectures. Straight talk only.
- **Use stories.** Real examples hit harder than abstract ideas.
- **Start with their dreams.** Tie money lessons to the life they say they want.
- **Respect their hustle.** Even if they're making mistakes, honor the fact that they're trying.

You're not there to preach.

You're there to guide.

You're there to arm them with weapons the world won't hand them.

How to Make Financial Lessons Stick

You want them to remember this stuff when the checks start hitting their accounts.

Here's the strategy:

1. Teach in reps, not lectures.

Just like they didn't master their sport in one practice, they won't master money in one conversation.

Teach small bites.

Over and over.

2. Tie money lessons to survival and success.

Example:

"If you blow your signing bonus, you could be broke before your second contract. If you invest it smartly, you might never HAVE to work again after your career."

3. Show, don't just tell.

Set up mock budgets.

Run practice NIL deals.

Show real-world examples of smart and dumb money moves by famous athletes.

4. Keep it personal.

Ask them:

- "What do you want your life to look like at 30?"
- "If you had $1 million today, what would you do first?"
- "What's the dumbest thing you've ever seen someone do with money?"

Get them talking.

Then guide them.

The Biggest Financial Traps for Young Athletes

If you can help them see these traps early, you can save them heartache later.

Trap #1: Spending for the 'Gram, Not for the Game.

Buying cars, jewelry, trips — not because they want to, but because they feel pressured to flex.

Trap #2: Not Paying Taxes.

Thinking money in = money to spend.

Forgetting about taxes, fines, back payments — and ending up bankrupt.

Trap #3: Trusting the Wrong People.

Family, friends, agents, "businessmen" who don't have their best interests at heart.

Trap #4: Thinking Short-Term, Not Long-Term.

Not realizing that an athletic career might be 5-10 years, but life is 70+.

Trap #5: No Emergency Plan.

Injuries. Trades. Endorsements drying up.

If they don't plan for sudden changes, they get crushed by them.

You can teach them to recognize the traps.

You can teach them to walk around them — not into them.

Action Steps You Can Start Taking Right Now

If you're serious about planting seeds for the next generation, here's your move list.

Step 1: Mentor one younger athlete.

Pick someone younger than you.

Have one real conversation a month about money.

Step 2: Normalize talking about money.

Remove the shame.

Make it as normal as talking about training or nutrition.

Step 3: Share your mistakes, not just your wins.

They'll learn more from your stumbles than your highlight reel.

Step 4: Push for financial literacy programs in your sport.

At camps.

At academies.

At schools.

Be the one who speaks up.

Step 5: Build or fund resources if you can.

Whether it's a scholarship, a seminar, or a book club — leave tools behind that others can use.

A Sample "Financial Literacy Game Plan" for Young Athletes

If you want to coach someone young, you can use this simple 12-month plan.

Month 1: Budgeting Basics — "Know your numbers."

Month 2: Saving — "Emergency fund = survival."

Month 3: Taxes — "Nothing's yours until Uncle Sam gets his."

Month 4: Credit and Debt — "Borrow smart or don't borrow at all."

Month 5: Investing Basics — "Make your money make babies."

Month 6: Contracts 101 — "Always read everything. Twice."

Month 7: Insurance 101 — "Protect what you can't afford to lose."

Month 8: Entrepreneurship Basics — "Not every idea is a good one."

Month 9: Scams and Predators — "If it sounds too good to be true, it is."

Month 10: Giving and Charity — "Generosity needs boundaries."

Month 11: Building a Personal Brand — "Your name is your future."

Month 12: Wealth Mindset — "Long game always wins."

You don't have to teach it perfectly.

You just have to teach it consistently.

Final Words of Encouragement

You're not just a player.

You're a leader.

You're a lighthouse.

Someone out there — maybe a kid who's never had anyone believe in them — is waiting for your words.

For your example.

For your blueprint.

Teaching financial literacy isn't about lecturing.

It's about unlocking freedom.

It's about showing them that money is a tool — not a trap.

And when you teach one athlete how to handle their money, you don't just change a career.

You change a family.

You change a community.

You change a legacy.

You don't need a podium.

You don't need a foundation.

You just need to care enough to start.

Be the coach you wish you had.

Be the mentor you wish you met.

Pass the torch — and watch the next generation light up the world.

Chapter 62: Why Financial Literacy Is an Ongoing Journey, Not a One-Time Lesson

By now, you know this truth deep in your bones:

Success in money — like success in sports — is never "once and done."

It's built rep by rep.

Day by day.

Season by season.

You can't show up to one practice and expect to win a championship.

You can't lift weights one time and expect to dominate on game day.

And you can't read one book, sit in one seminar, or sign one big deal — and expect to master your money for life.

Financial literacy is not a finish line.

It's a lifelong process.

It evolves as your life evolves.

It gets deeper as your challenges get bigger.

Today, we're going to dig into why treating financial literacy like an ongoing journey — not a one-time class — is one of the most powerful money moves you can make as a professional athlete, and for the rest of your life after the game.

The Myth of "Once and Done"

One of the biggest mistakes athletes (and honestly, a lot of people) make about money is thinking:

"Once I learn the basics, I'm good."

"Once I sign this first deal, I'm set."

"Once I make $5 million, I won't need to worry."

That mindset is a setup for disaster.

Because here's what's real:

- Contracts change.
- Tax laws change.
- Endorsements end.
- New financial tools come out.
- Economies rise and fall.
- Family situations evolve.
- Your goals evolve.

Money management is a living, breathing skill.

It needs maintenance.

It needs upgrades.

It needs attention.

Think about your sport.

Imagine if you said, *"I learned how to dribble once in middle school. I'm good."*

You'd get embarrassed on the court.

You'd get left behind.

Money works the same way.

Financial Literacy Across the Stages of Life

Let's get even more real.

Your money skills need to level up at every stage of your journey.

Rookie Stage:

You're learning how to handle a real paycheck.

You're setting up accounts, budgeting, paying taxes for the first time.

You need simple, sturdy basics.

Vet Stage:

You're juggling investments, endorsements, real estate deals.

You need a trusted team, regular audits, and bigger strategies.

Exit Stage:

You're planning retirement accounts, pensions, passive income streams.

You're thinking about kids, estate planning, and wealth preservation.

Legacy Stage:

You're funding scholarships, endowing charities, mentoring the next wave.

You're making sure your name means something for generations to come.

At every stage, **new financial skills are required.**

At every stage, **new traps are waiting.**

At every stage, **the game changes.**

And just like on the field, the athletes who stay sharp are the ones who last.

Why Your Relationship With Money Will Keep Evolving

Your relationship with money isn't static.

When you were broke in college, $1,000 felt like a fortune.

When you first signed, $100,000 might've felt like breathing room.

When you got that big contract, $5 million might've felt like *forever money*.

But then you realize:

- $5 million after taxes is closer to $2.5 million.
- Agent fees, family support, lifestyle costs eat into it.
- A $10,000 monthly lifestyle costs $120,000 a year...before taxes.
- Injuries happen.
- Careers get cut short.

What once felt infinite starts to look finite.

And **that's normal.**

It doesn't mean you failed.

It means you have to **keep learning.**

Keep growing.

Just like a quarterback has to study film every week.

Just like a point guard has to stay conditioned all year.

Just like a striker has to sharpen their footwork.

You have to stay ready with your money — or you will get caught slipping.

Financial Literacy Is a Defensive Skill — and an Offensive Skill

Defense wins championships.

But you can't win without scoring either.

Financial literacy is both.

On defense:

- Protecting your income from bad deals.
- Protecting your investments from bad risks.
- Protecting your name from bad branding moves.
- Protecting your wealth from lawsuits, taxes, scams.

On offense:

- Growing your investments steadily.
- Expanding your income streams.
- Leveraging smart tax moves to maximize your money.
- Building businesses, brands, and assets that last.

It's not enough to protect what you have.

You have to grow it.

And it's not enough to chase growth without protection.

You need both.

Every season.

Every stage.

Every year.

Financial Literacy Is Mental Conditioning

We talk about physical conditioning all the time.

Lifting. Sprinting. Recovery.

But financial literacy is a form of **mental conditioning.**

It's building the muscle of:

- Patience (when everyone else is spending crazy)
- Discipline (when the flashy purchase calls your name)
- Curiosity (to keep learning new money strategies)
- Courage (to fire bad advisors and protect your future)
- Awareness (to know when to pivot your plan)

It's setting the right habits:

- Checking your accounts monthly.
- Meeting with your CPA quarterly.
- Updating your estate plan every few years.
- Reviewing your investments regularly.

It's not a crash diet.

It's a permanent lifestyle.

Why the Best Athletes Stay Humble — With Their Bodies and Their Bank Accounts

The greatest athletes in history all have something in common.

It's not just talent.

It's not just hard work.

It's **humility.**

They know:

- They can always get better.
- There's always someone hungrier coming up behind them.
- One injury, one mistake, one bad moment can change everything.

Financial literacy demands the same humility.

The second you think, *"I know it all,"*

you're vulnerable.

Stay coachable.

Stay curious.

Stay hungry.

Whether you're a rookie or a 10-year vet, the same rule applies:

You have to keep learning.

Practical Steps to Keep Growing Financially

Here's how to treat financial literacy like a lifelong journey — not a one-and-done class.

1. Build your "Money Team."

- CPA
- Financial Advisor

- Estate Attorney
- Business Attorney
- Mentor

2. Schedule a "Financial Training Camp" annually.

Once a year, take 2-3 days to review:

- Net worth
- Cash flow
- Investments
- Taxes
- Estate plans
- Insurance

3. Stay curious.

Read one financial book a year.

Listen to financial podcasts.

Take a course if you need to.

4. Audit your team.

Just like you'd replace a coach who isn't helping you win, replace advisors who aren't protecting your future.

5. Protect your energy.

Not every "opportunity" deserves your time.

Not every pitch deserves a meeting.

Not every friend deserves an investment.

6. Teach someone else.

Nothing locks in your own learning like passing it on.

Real Talk: The Financial Literacy Journey Won't Always Feel Fun

Some seasons, it will feel easy.

Money will be flowing.

Investments will be growing.

Opportunities will be everywhere.

Other seasons, it will feel slow.

Markets will be down.

Endorsements will dry up.

Expenses will rise.

And in those tough seasons, your **habits** will protect you.

Your **mindset** will carry you.

Your **discipline** will separate you.

This is why we stay ready.

This is why we keep growing.

Not for the easy times — for the hard times.

Final Words: Your Legacy Is Bigger Than Your Career

At the end of the day, it's not just about you.

It's about:

- The kids who will see your example.
- The family members who will benefit from your wisdom.
- The communities you can uplift.
- The businesses you can build.
- The generations you can bless.

When you master financial literacy as a lifelong journey,

you don't just change your bank account.

You change your bloodline.

You become the one who breaks the cycle.

The one who builds.

The one who leaves a mark bigger than stats or highlights.

So keep learning.

Keep growing.

Keep sharpening your financial mind like your athletic body.

Your career might be 5, 10, maybe 15 years.

But your financial life?

Your legacy?

That can last forever.

Stay humble.

Stay ready.

Stay legendary.

Chapter 63: What You Can Learn from Other Industries (Business, Entertainment, Entrepreneurship)

When you step into the world of professional sports, you're not just an athlete anymore. Whether you realize it or not, you're now the CEO of your own brand, the face of your own franchise, the captain of your own ship. And like it or not, how you handle the business side of your career will determine whether you build lasting wealth or find yourself scrambling once the stadium lights go dark.

Athletes are unique. The money can come fast and heavy. The fame can be intoxicating. The pressures can be brutal. But here's the truth: you're not the first person to face these challenges. You can learn a lot—and I mean a LOT—from people in other industries who've had to navigate the same storms.

Business moguls, entertainers, entrepreneurs — they've all faced the flood of fame, fortune, temptation, and risk. And many of them have built empires that lasted far beyond their "playing days" in their own industries.

Let's sit down and break this down together.

Lessons from the Business World

Play the Long Game

Business leaders understand something critical: success isn't about one big play. It's about stringing together smart decisions over and over and over again.

You can't blow it all on one investment. You can't panic after a bad quarter. You stay steady. You adjust. You keep showing up.

Sports Analogy: Think about a football season. You might lose Week 1. Maybe you lose Week 2. But if you stay focused, improve, and win out the rest of the season, you can still make the playoffs. Business is the same. You don't "win" wealth with one paycheck. You win by consistently making smart moves.

Action Steps:

- Build a "seasonal" financial plan: know your "off-season" and "playoff push" financially.
- Set financial goals that stretch 1, 5, and 10 years out.
- Learn to be patient. Wealth isn't built in a single contract year.

Diversify Like a Boss

In business, smart CEOs never bet the farm on one thing. Even if they have a killer product, they keep developing new ones. They expand into different markets. They don't get too comfortable.

Sports Analogy: A basketball player who can only shoot is easier to guard. But if you can shoot, drive, pass, and defend, you stay valuable. You stay on the court.

Action Steps:

- Don't rely on just your game checks. Set up other streams of income.
- Learn about investments, but don't chase every "hot" deal.
- Stay flexible: your financial game plan should evolve as you do.

Know When to Hire a Team — and When to Be the Coach

The best CEOs build incredible teams. But they don't just hand over the keys and walk away. They stay involved. They ask questions. They make sure everyone is doing their job right.

Sports Analogy: You might trust your trainer, but you're still the one lifting the weights. You still have to show up. You still have to want it.

Action Steps:

- Build a trusted circle of professionals: CPA, financial advisor, lawyer, business manager.
- Stay engaged. Get reports. Ask questions.
- Remember: they work for you.

Prepare for Rebuilding Years

Sometimes, businesses hit rough patches. Good CEOs don't panic. They cut costs. They refocus. They rebuild.

Sports Analogy: Even dynasties like the Patriots or the Warriors have rebuilding years. It's part of the game.

Action Steps:

- Build a strong emergency fund: 12 months of living expenses.
- Keep your lifestyle below your income level.
- Expect the unexpected—and prepare for it.

Lessons from the Entertainment Industry

Your Brand Is Bigger Than Your Stats

Entertainers understand that it's not just about talent. It's about image, perception, and relationships.

Sports Analogy: You could be the leading scorer, but if you're toxic in the locker room, endorsements dry up. Fans turn. Teams hesitate.

Action Steps:

- Be mindful of your social media.
- Protect your reputation like it's gold—because it is.
- Choose your inner circle wisely.

Create Intellectual Property

Musicians, actors, writers—they all try to own their stuff. If you own your music, you get royalties forever. If you own your script, you can sell it 10 different ways.

Sports Analogy: If you invest in yourself — your brand, your business, your name — you keep earning long after your last game.

Action Steps:

- Trademark your name or logo if you're building a brand.
- Consider building businesses around your passions (fitness, fashion, media).
- Retain ownership whenever possible.

Don't Just Be Famous—Be Strategic

Fame is a tool. Not a finish line. Smart entertainers leverage fame to launch businesses, create partnerships, and build generational wealth.

Sports Analogy: Winning the MVP is awesome. But what you *do* with the MVP spotlight can change your whole future.

Action Steps:

- Think about your long game whenever you're in the public eye.
- Use big moments to connect with smart partners.
- Always ask: "How can this opportunity work for me beyond today?"

Lessons from Entrepreneurs

Take Calculated Risks — Not Wild Gambles

Entrepreneurs understand that you have to risk some things to grow. But they also know how to calculate those risks.

Sports Analogy: A quarterback who throws deep on 4th and 2 at midfield needs to know when to risk it—and when to play field position.

Action Steps:

- Only invest what you can afford to lose.
- Always do your homework before investing.
- Trust, but verify.

Stay Hungry, Stay Humble

The best entrepreneurs never get satisfied. They keep learning. Keep adapting. Stay humble enough to know they don't know everything.

Sports Analogy: A rookie who acts like a vet gets cut fast. A vet who keeps learning stays in the league longer.

Action Steps:

- Keep reading books, listening to podcasts, attending seminars.
- Surround yourself with people who are smarter than you.
- Always be a student of the game—and of money.

Build Systems, Not Just Hustle

Entrepreneurs who last build systems that make money while they sleep. They don't just grind until they burn out.

Sports Analogy: You can't play 48 minutes a night forever. You need a team. You need rest. You need a game plan.

Action Steps:

- Set up automatic investments and savings.
- Build businesses that don't need you present every second.
- Think bigger than just "working hard."

Real-World Scenario

Imagine you're three years into your pro career. You've earned a few million dollars. You're comfortable.

Then your college buddy hits you up: "Yo, let's open a restaurant. It'll be huge!"

Sounds fun, right?

Slow down.

Think like a CEO. Think like an entrepreneur. Think like an entertainer who knows that owning the restaurant's real estate is smarter than just putting your name on the menu.

Ask questions:

- What's the business plan?
- Who's running it?
- How much do I have to put in?
- How soon do I get paid back?
- What happens if it fails?

You're not saying no to your buddy. You're saying yes to protecting your future.

Be smart. Be steady. Be strategic.

Pros and Cons of Learning from Other Industries

Pros:

- You expand your financial IQ.
- You avoid mistakes others have made.
- You can build multiple streams of income.
- You protect your wealth and brand better.

Cons:

- It can feel overwhelming at first.
- Not every "lesson" applies directly to sports.
- You have to be disciplined to sort good advice from bad.

Final Action Steps

1. Pick 3 books by business leaders, entertainers, or entrepreneurs and read them this year.
2. Start following 3 business podcasts.
3. Create a "Wealth Playbook" — a simple document outlining your financial goals, action steps, and lessons learned.
4. Set up quarterly "Financial Film Sessions" where you review your money moves, just like you would game tape.
5. Connect with mentors in business and entrepreneurship outside of sports.

Closing Encouragement

You are not just an athlete.

You are a business.

You are a brand.

You are a builder.

Your career might be measured in seasons. But your wealth? Your legacy? That can be measured in generations.

Stay humble.

Stay hungry.

Keep learning.

Keep building.

And remember: every smart play you make today sets you up for more freedom, more impact, and more peace tomorrow.

This is your time.

Own it.

Own your career.

Own your future.

Own your financial life.

And if you ever feel overwhelmed, just remember:

Every CEO, every mogul, every legend—they all started right where you are.

One decision at a time.

One lesson at a time.

One smart play at a time.

You're ready.

Let's get it.

Chapter 64: Creating Generational Wealth the Right Way

Picture this.

You're not just playing for you. You're playing for your last name. You're playing for your future kids, grandkids, and great-grandkids. You're playing for a legacy that stretches long after the cleats are hung up, the lights dim, and the roar of the crowd fades into memory.

That's what this chapter is about: creating *real* generational wealth.

Not just "rich for now" money.

We're talking about "rich forever" moves.

Moves that echo through time.

Moves that mean your family's story changes—forever.

And here's the truth:

Creating generational wealth is not about hitting the lottery or signing one big contract.

It's about smart, steady, disciplined decisions—stacked day after day, year after year.

You don't have to be perfect.

You just have to be *intentional.*

Let's dive into how to do this—the right way.

Understanding Generational Wealth

Generational wealth means assets—money, real estate, investments, businesses, trusts—that can be passed down to your family.

It's not just about having cash.

It's about building assets that can outlive you.

Sports Analogy: Think about winning a championship. It's not about winning one regular season game. It's about building a whole system—offense, defense, special teams—that works under pressure, season after season.

Same with wealth.

It's about building a full system.

Why Most Athletes Struggle to Build It

Sudden Wealth Syndrome: You go from zero to millions overnight, without financial infrastructure.

Short Career Span: Most athletes' earning windows are brutally short compared to other industries.

Lifestyle Inflation: You live bigger because you earn bigger—but it's easy to lose control.

Bad Investments: Everyone has "the next big thing."

Lack of Planning: No estate plan. No trusts. No protection.

But none of these challenges are fatal.

You can beat every single one.

How?

Through strategy.

Through education.

Through choosing to build—on purpose.

The Blueprint for Generational Wealth

Step 1: Stabilize Your Finances First

Before you can think about building for the next generation, you have to secure your own foundation.

- Pay off bad debt.
- Build an emergency fund (12 months of expenses minimum).
- Create a season-based cash flow plan (when money comes in heavy, when it's light).
- Protect yourself with proper insurance (health, disability, life, umbrella).

Sports Analogy: Before a basketball team even thinks about running fast breaks, they lock down on defense first.

Lock down your defense—your foundation—first.

Step 2: Build a Simple, Sustainable Investment Plan

Forget chasing "hot" stocks.

Forget "crypto get rich quick" schemes.

Generational wealth is built on boring, consistent, powerful moves:

- Maximize retirement accounts (IRAs, 401(k)s, SEP-IRAs).
- Invest in index funds and ETFs—diversified, low-cost, and proven.
- Consider real estate investments.
- Automate your investments: set it and forget it.

Plain Language: You're not trying to "beat the market" every year. You're trying to *own* pieces of great companies—forever.

Step 3: Own Assets, Not Just Stuff

Assets make you money. Stuff costs you money.

A Ferrari is stuff.

An apartment building is an asset.

A $30,000 watch is stuff.

A portfolio of dividend-paying stocks is an asset.

Own assets.

Action Step: Before every big purchase, ask: "Will this grow in value or lose value?"

Step 4: Protect It All

Generational wealth can disappear in one lawsuit, one bad business deal, or one bad divorce.

Protect it.

- Get the right insurances.
- Work with lawyers to set up trusts, wills, and estate plans.
- Separate personal and business assets.
- Think about asset protection strategies (like LLCs, trusts, etc.).

Sports Analogy: Even the best offense needs a defense. You need guards to protect the quarterback.

Your wealth needs guards too.

Step 5: Educate Your Family

It's not enough to leave money.

You have to leave *money skills.*

Teach your kids. Teach your spouse. Teach your family.

Otherwise, the money evaporates.

Real-World Example: Studies show that 70% of wealth is lost by the second generation. And 90% is gone by the third.

Break that cycle.

Start the conversations early.

Step 6: Plan for Transition

You won't play forever. You won't live forever.

Set up a clear transition plan.

- Who gets what.
- When they get it.
- Under what conditions (trusts can control this).

This isn't about control. It's about stewardship.

Plain Language: You worked too hard to leave your wealth to chance.

Pros and Cons of Building Generational Wealth

Pros:

- Your hard work multiplies across generations.
- You create opportunities for your family.
- You break cycles of poverty.
- You gain peace of mind.

Cons:

- Requires patience and long-term thinking.
- Requires planning, discipline, and sometimes uncomfortable conversations.
- Not everyone around you will understand it.

But the cons are nothing compared to the *power* you gain.

Real Scenarios

Scenario 1: The Trap You earn $10 million. You spend $8 million on cars, houses, jewelry. You invest $2 million in "can't miss" ideas that flop. Five years post-career: broke.

Scenario 2: The Playmaker You earn $10 million. You live on $2 million. You invest $6 million. You build businesses and buy assets. Five years post-career: $15 million and growing.

Choose wisely.

Action Steps Starting Today

1. Meet with a fiduciary financial advisor.
2. Set a budget that protects your future.
3. Max out retirement accounts this year.
4. Buy one income-generating asset.
5. Create or update your will and estate plan.
6. Have a "money talk" with your family.
7. Keep learning: read one financial book every quarter.

Breakdowns of Important Ideas

Trusts vs. Wills:

- A will goes through probate (a long, public court process).
- A trust can transfer assets privately and faster.
- Trusts allow you to set conditions (e.g., "Junior gets $50k/year starting at 25 if he's working or in school").

Asset Protection:

- Separate personal and business liabilities.
- Use LLCs for businesses or rental properties.
- Have high insurance limits (especially umbrella policies).

Diversification:

- Don't put all your money in one investment.
- Spread it across stocks, real estate, bonds, businesses.
- Different assets react differently to market changes.

Lifestyle Creep:

- As you make more, it's tempting to spend more.
- Keep lifestyle upgrades modest.
- Save and invest raises and bonuses.

More Sports Analogies

Boxing: Protect your chin. One good punch can end the fight—just like one bad investment can wreck your finances.

Golf: Play the course, not just one shot. Plan your moves like a 72-hole tournament, not a one-swing miracle.

Soccer: Maintain shape. Don't overcommit on offense and leave yourself exposed.

Baseball: It's a marathon, not a sprint. Batting .300 over a career makes you a Hall of Famer—small wins add up.

Track and Field: Run your race. Focus on your lane, your plan, your pace.

Closing Encouragement

You've already done the hardest part.

You beat the odds.

You made it.

Now the real game begins.

Building generational wealth isn't about making one right move.

It's about making dozens of steady, strong moves—over time.

It's about:

- Protecting what you've built.
- Growing what you've earned.
- Teaching the next generation.
- Building systems that work while you sleep.

Your career will end.

Your earnings will slow.

But your impact?

That can last forever.

Imagine your grandkids, sitting around a dinner table decades from now, telling stories about how *you* changed everything.

Imagine the pride.

Imagine the security.

Imagine the freedom you create—not just for you, but for everyone who comes after you.

You have that power.

You have that opportunity.

And it starts today.

Own it.

Own your career.

Own your future.

Own your financial life.

Build the dynasty.

Be the legend—not just on the field, but off it too.

The next chapter of your story—the most important one—is waiting.

Let's write it.

Chapter 65: Final Playbook: 20 Non-Negotiables for Every Pro Athlete's Financial Game Plan

When the final whistle blows on your career, and the crowd goes home, what's left?

Your legacy.

Your wealth.

Your impact.

This chapter is about locking in your *non-negotiables* — the final, undeniable, ironclad plays you must run to protect everything you've worked for.

This is your final playbook.

No excuses.

No shortcuts.

Just 20 non-negotiables that every pro athlete must live by if they want to stay winning long after the game is over.

Let's get it.

1. Pay Yourself First

Before you spend a dime on anything else, invest in your future.

Action Step: Set up automatic transfers to savings and investment accounts the day your paycheck hits.

Sports Analogy: Defense wins championships. Paying yourself first is your financial defense.

2. Spend Like You're Undrafted

Live like you're still fighting for a spot.

Action Step: Create a budget based on 50% or less of your take-home pay.

Sports Analogy: Tom Brady always trained like he was the backup QB.

3. Build a One-Year Emergency Fund

Cover your personal expenses for 12 months — minimum.

Action Step: Park it in a high-yield savings account.

Sports Analogy: Soccer teams always have backup keepers ready. You need your backup too.

4. Max Out Retirement Accounts

Stack money while you're earning heavy.

Action Step: Max out IRAs, 401(k)s, or SEP-IRAs annually.

Sports Analogy: Baseball players build their stats over a season. You build retirement wealth over a career.

5. Diversify, Don't Gamble

Spread your investments across assets, not get-rich-quick schemes.

Action Step: Own stocks, real estate, and business interests—carefully.

Sports Analogy: A good golfer has a full bag of clubs, not just a driver.

6. Buy Assets, Not Just Stuff

Assets grow your wealth. Stuff drains it.

Action Step: Invest 2x more in assets than you spend on material things.

Sports Analogy: You can't win with highlight dunks alone. Fundamentals matter.

7. Protect Yourself with Insurance

One injury or lawsuit can destroy it all.

Action Step: Get top-tier disability, health, life, and umbrella insurance.

Sports Analogy: A hockey goalie wears pads for a reason.

8. Set Up a Trust and Will

Control your wealth beyond your lifetime.

Action Step: Hire an estate attorney to set up proper documents.

Sports Analogy: A good football coach scripts the first 15 plays. You script your legacy.

9. Hire a Fiduciary Financial Advisor

Only work with people legally obligated to act in your best interest.

Action Step: Interview at least three advisors before choosing.

Sports Analogy: You wouldn't let a coach who's paid by the other team call your plays.

10. Build a Board, Not a Bunch of Yes-Men

Surround yourself with experts who challenge and protect you.

Action Step: Assemble a CPA, attorney, advisor, and mentor.

Sports Analogy: Great teams have strong captains *and* strong coaches.

11. Plan for Taxes

Never let taxes blindside you.

Action Step: Save 35% of every check until you settle your tax bill.

Sports Analogy: In tennis, you have to anticipate the ball—not just react.

12. Own Your Endorsements

Control your brand, your name, your image.

Action Step: Trademark your name, slogan, or logo.

Sports Analogy: Serena Williams built her own brand, not just Nike's.

13. Create a Season-Based Cash Flow Plan

Income changes through the year—plan for it.

Action Step: Map out monthly cash flow in-season and off-season.

Sports Analogy: Baseball teams plan rotations across 162 games, not just Opening Day.

14. Keep Business and Personal Separate

Separate accounts. Separate decisions.

Action Step: Use business entities (LLCs) for side businesses.

Sports Analogy: No mixing locker rooms. Business stays business.

15. Learn to Say No

You can't fund everyone's dream.

Action Step: Practice gracious, firm "No" responses.

Sports Analogy: Great defense says "no" all night long.

16. Never Co-Sign Loans

If the bank won't trust them, why should you?

Action Step: Never co-sign—period.

Sports Analogy: You can't block shots for your teammate *and* your opponent.

17. Vet Every Investment

Trust but verify.

Action Step: Require written business plans, audited financials, and outside legal review.

Sports Analogy: A baseball scout checks every stat, not just the home runs.

18. Build Wealth While You're Still Playing

Don't wait until retirement.

Action Step: Invest consistently from your first pro paycheck.

Sports Analogy: Track stars don't wait until the final lap to start running.

19. Keep Educating Yourself

Stay a student of the financial game.

Action Step: Read one finance, business, or investing book every quarter.

Sports Analogy: The best coaches watch game tape every week.

20. Plan Your Transition Now

Career ends are sudden.

Action Step: Start exploring post-playing passions today.

Sports Analogy: A good boxer doesn't wait for the bell to start breathing right.

Closing Encouragement

Here's the deal:

Nobody wins a championship by accident.

Nobody builds generational wealth by accident.

It's intentional.

It's deliberate.

It's a daily choice to make smart moves even when no one's watching.

You're not just an athlete.

You are a leader.

You are a builder.

You are a champion for your future family—and for yourself.

The 20 non-negotiables in this chapter are your playbook.

Master them.

Live them.

Revisit them often.

This isn't just about having money.

It's about:

- Having peace.
- Having freedom.
- Having options.
- Having impact.

Your financial life is your ultimate championship season.

And the ring you win—is generational.

You're not alone.

You have the tools.

You have the talent.

You have the heart.

Now go build the dynasty.

Own your career.

Own your future.

Own your financial life.

The final buzzer hasn't sounded yet.

Your greatest victories are still ahead.

Let's go.

Closing Chapter: You Are the CEO of Your Life and Finances

If you've made it here, let's take a real moment together.

You're not the same person who cracked open the first chapter.

You've grown.

You've leveled up.

You've started seeing the game—and your life—differently.

This isn't just about understanding contracts, taxes, investments, and budgeting.

This is about something much bigger.

You are the CEO of your life.

You are the general manager of your future.

You are the head coach of your wealth journey.

No agent, no financial advisor, no business manager can care about your career and your money like you can.

You are the one in control.

You are the one who sets the vision.

You are the one who builds the team.

You are the one who makes the calls when it counts.

And here's the thing every true CEO knows: **leadership never stops.**

You don't "graduate" from responsibility.

You don't "finish" mastering your financial life.

You grow.

You learn.

You stay sharp.

Every season.

Every chapter.

Every stage of life.

Your financial literacy journey is a lifetime journey.

Just like your training never stops if you want to stay at the top of your game, your education about money, business, and life should never stop either.

Let's talk about how to keep that momentum alive.

Keep Investing in Your Knowledge

You already know how powerful investing money can be.

But investing in yourself?

That's the highest return you'll ever get.

Smart athletes keep training.

Smart CEOs keep learning.

Smart investors keep studying.

You've already built a solid foundation.

Now build on it.

Here's how:

- Set a goal to read at least four financial, business, or personal development books a year.
- Attend one financial education workshop, webinar, or seminar every year.
- Find a mentor—someone who's done it right.
- Schedule annual "financial checkups" with your advisor and CPA—just like you would with a team trainer.
- Subscribe to trustworthy financial newsletters or podcasts.
- Keep asking questions—no matter how much success you achieve.
- Keep upgrading your team—as you grow, your needs will grow too.

Sports Analogy: Great athletes never stop practicing the basics. Steph Curry still practices free throws. Serena Williams still drills her backhand. You keep mastering your financial fundamentals.

There's no offseason for wisdom.

There's no substitute for knowledge.

Stay sharp.

Stay hungry.

Stay curious.

Your future deserves it.

Resources to Keep You Winning

You're not on this journey alone.

I've built platforms, tools, books, and speaking engagements all designed to help you stay winning—financially and personally.

Here's where you can stay plugged in:

- FinancialLiteracyForNIL.com
- FinancialLiteracyForStudentAthletes.com
- FinancialLiteracyForProAthletes.com
- FinancialLiteracyForCollegeCoaches.com

Each platform is built with one goal: **to help you win.**

Not just in the game.

In life.

For you.

For your family.

For your future.

My Books

You can continue your journey with:

- Financial Literacy For NIL
- Financial Literacy For NIL for Parents of Student Athletes
- Financial Literacy For NIL for International Student Athletes
- Financial Literacy For NIL for High School Student Athletes
- Financial Literacy For Student Athletes
- Financial Literacy For Parents of Student Athletes

- Financial Literacy For Pro Athletes (this one!)

Each book builds on the last.

Each one is a new set of tools for the different stages of your journey.

Stack them.

Study them.

Apply them.

Speaking Engagements

Want me to come speak to your team, your organization, or your event?

I travel to meet athletes, coaches, families, and executives across the country.

We talk real.

We build real game plans.

We make financial literacy personal, powerful, and practical.

You can reach out through any of the platforms listed above to book a session.

This isn't just about giving speeches.

It's about changing lives.

Including yours.

Stay Connected

The financial world moves fast.

Opportunities change.

Laws change.

Markets change.

You want to stay sharp, stay updated, and stay connected with a community that's committed to growing with you.

Bookmark these:

- FinancialLiteracyForNIL.com
- FinancialLiteracyForStudentAthletes.com
- FinancialLiteracyForProAthletes.com
- FinancialLiteracyForNILForParentsOfStudentAthletes.com

- FinancialLiteracyForNILForHighSchoolStudentAthletes.com
- FinancialLiteracyForNILForInternationalStudentAthletes.com
- FinancialLiteracyForCollegeCoaches.com
- FinancialLiteracyForParentsOfProAthletes.com

Sign up for updates.

Check back for new resources.

Stay in the game.

Final Real Talk

You've been given a rare gift.

Talent.

Opportunity.

Resources.

Access.

What you do with it will define your life—and your legacy.

You can waste it.

Or you can grow it.

You can blow it.

Or you can build it.

You can chase short-term clout.

Or you can create generational impact.

You are the CEO.

You are the brand.

You are the business.

You are the dynasty.

Own it.

Protect it.

Grow it.

Every day, you get to write your story.

You get to choose how it goes.

You get to decide whether you're just another highlight clip—or whether you're the blueprint.

Whether you're just another stat line—or whether you're the standard.

You have everything you need.
Now go build it.
Brick by brick.
Decision by decision.
Play by play.
One smart move at a time.
One lesson applied at a time.
One win stacked on top of another.
Your future is wide open.
Your destiny is waiting.
And your best days?
They're still ahead.
Let's go.
Own your career.
Own your future.
Own your financial life.
Play smart.
Play long.
Win forever.
I believe in you.
Now it's your turn to believe in you, too.
Let's build the legacy.
Together.

About the Author

Pat Brown, MBA, is a former Division I football player turned financial educator, advisor, and fierce advocate for athletes navigating the complex world of money, wealth, and opportunity. After competing at the University of Kansas—where he served as a team captain and led at the highest level of collegiate athletics—Pat briefly played in the CFL before shifting his focus to business and financial education.

Motivated by the financial struggles he witnessed among teammates, peers, and even within his own family, Pat earned his MBA and committed his life to helping others make smarter, stronger financial decisions. Over the past two decades, he has worked as a wealth advisor, insurance specialist, and financial literacy speaker—teaching athletes, parents, and professionals about budgeting, credit, investing, taxes, entrepreneurship, and building generational wealth.

Pat is the founder of FinancialLiteracyForNIL.com, a platform designed to empower student-athletes with the tools, curriculum, and real-world knowledge needed to manage NIL income wisely. He also leads initiatives through FinancialLiteracyForStudentAthletes.com, FinancialLiteracyForProAthletes.com, and several other educational platforms, working with universities, high schools, athletic departments, and community organizations across the country.

Pat's mission is bigger than money—it's about helping athletes see themselves not just as competitors, but as CEOs of their own brand and future. A husband, father, and lifelong learner, Pat believes the game may end—but the habits, lessons, and impact you build through financial literacy last forever.

To connect with Pat for speaking engagements, workshops, or more information, you can reach him at:

- Email: **info@financialliteracyforproathletes.com**
- Phone: **785-979-9796**

Terms and Definitions

Financial Terms

1. **Asset** – Anything you own that has value, like cash, stocks, or real estate.
2. **Liability** – Money you owe, such as loans or credit card debt.
3. **Net Worth** – Total assets minus total liabilities.
4. **Liquidity** – How quickly you can turn an asset into cash.
5. **Investment** – Using money to buy assets that have the potential to grow in value.
6. **Diversification** – Spreading money across different investments to reduce risk.
7. **Portfolio** – A collection of financial investments.
8. **Interest Rate** – The cost of borrowing money or the reward for saving money, shown as a percentage.
9. **Principal** – The original amount of money invested or loaned.
10. **Compound Interest** – Earning interest on both the principal and the accumulated interest.
11. **Inflation** – The rise in prices over time, reducing purchasing power.
12. **Emergency Fund** – Savings set aside for unexpected expenses.
13. **Savings Account** – A bank account that earns interest on your deposits.
14. **Brokerage Account** – An investment account used to buy and sell securities.
15. **Index Fund** – A type of mutual fund that mirrors a stock market

index.

16. **ETF (Exchange-Traded Fund)** – A collection of investments traded like a stock.
17. **Bond** – A loan you give to a company or government that pays you back with interest.
18. **Stock** – A share of ownership in a company.
19. **Dividend** – A payment to shareholders from a company's profits.
20. **401(k) Plan** – A retirement savings plan offered by employers.
21. **IRA (Individual Retirement Account)** – A personal retirement savings account.
22. **Roth IRA** – An IRA where contributions are made after taxes but withdrawals are tax-free.
23. **Pension** – A retirement plan where an employer guarantees a specific payout.
24. **Annuity** – An insurance product that provides income for life.
25. **Real Estate Investment** – Buying property to earn income or profit.
26. **Capital Gains** – Profit from selling an asset for more than you paid.
27. **Asset Allocation** – How you divide your investments among different asset types.
28. **Risk Tolerance** – How much risk you're willing to accept in your investments.
29. **Credit Score** – A number that shows how well you manage debt.
30. **Debt-to-Income Ratio** – The percentage of your income that goes toward paying debts.
31. **Budget** – A plan for how to spend and save money.
32. **Cash Flow** – Money coming in and going out of your accounts.
33. **Estate Planning** – Preparing to pass on wealth to heirs after death.
34. **Beneficiary** – A person who receives money or assets from a will, trust, or insurance policy.
35. **Power of Attorney** – A legal document allowing someone else to make financial decisions for you.

36. **Insurance Premium** – The amount you pay for an insurance policy.
37. **Deductible** – The amount you pay out-of-pocket before insurance kicks in.
38. **Umbrella Insurance** – Extra liability insurance to cover major claims.
39. **Term Life Insurance** – Life insurance that covers you for a specific period.
40. **Whole Life Insurance** – Life insurance that covers you for life and builds cash value.
41. **Entrepreneurship** – Starting and running your own business.
42. **Business Credit** – Credit obtained in the name of a business.
43. **S Corporation** – A type of corporation with pass-through taxation.
44. **LLC (Limited Liability Company)** – A business structure that protects personal assets.
45. **Asset Protection** – Strategies to shield wealth from lawsuits or creditors.

Tax Terms

1. **Income Tax** – Tax paid on money earned from work or investments.
2. **Capital Gains Tax** – Tax on the profit from selling an asset.
3. **Estate Tax** – Tax on the transfer of wealth after death.
4. **Gift Tax** – Tax on money or property given to another person.
5. **Tax Deduction** – An expense that lowers your taxable income.
6. **Tax Credit** – Reduces the amount of tax you owe dollar-for-dollar.
7. **Standard Deduction** – A fixed amount that reduces taxable income.
8. **Itemized Deductions** – Specific expenses you list to reduce taxable income.
9. **Adjusted Gross Income (AGI)** – Income after adjustments but before deductions.

10. **Taxable Income** – Income on which taxes are calculated after deductions and exemptions.
11. **Filing Status** – Determines your tax rate (e.g., Single, Married Filing Jointly).
12. **Withholding** – Income tax taken out of paychecks by employers.
13. **Estimated Taxes** – Quarterly payments for income not subject to withholding.
14. **Self-Employment Tax** – Tax covering Social Security and Medicare for self-employed individuals.
15. **Payroll Tax** – Tax employers withhold for Social Security and Medicare.
16. **Alternative Minimum Tax (AMT)** – A separate tax calculation for high-income earners.
17. **Tax Bracket** – The income range that determines the tax rate you pay.
18. **1099 Form** – Tax form for independent contractors or other non-employment income.
19. **W-2 Form** – Tax form showing wages earned and taxes paid through an employer.
20. **Schedule C** – Tax form for reporting self-employed income and expenses.
21. **Depreciation** – Deducting the cost of an asset over its useful life.
22. **Tax-Deferred** – Paying taxes later instead of now (e.g., traditional IRA).
23. **Tax-Exempt** – Income not subject to taxes (e.g., municipal bond interest).
24. **Carryforward** – Applying unused tax benefits to future tax years.
25. **Amended Return** – A corrected tax return filed after discovering an error.
26. **Audit** – IRS examination of your financial information and tax returns.
27. **Penalty** – A fee for late filing, late payment, or underpayment of taxes.

28. **Extension** – Extra time to file a tax return (but not to pay taxes).
29. **Tax Shelter** – Legal strategies used to reduce taxable income.
30. **Charitable Contribution Deduction** – Tax deduction for donations to qualified organizations.

Attorney/Legal Terms

1. **Contract** – A legally binding agreement between two or more parties.
2. **Breach of Contract** – Failure to fulfill the terms of a contract.
3. **Indemnification** – Protection against financial loss or liability.
4. **Liability** – Legal responsibility for damages or losses.
5. **Negligence** – Failure to exercise reasonable care, causing harm.
6. **Due Diligence** – Research and analysis before entering a contract or investment.
7. **Confidentiality Agreement** – A contract to keep shared information private.
8. **Non-Compete Clause** – A contract preventing someone from working with competitors.
9. **Non-Disclosure Agreement (NDA)** – Agreement not to share specific information.
10. **Jurisdiction** – The authority of a court to hear a case.
11. **Arbitration** – Settling disputes outside of court with a neutral third party.
12. **Mediation** – A negotiation facilitated by a neutral person to resolve a dispute.
13. **Settlement** – An agreement reached by both parties to resolve a lawsuit.
14. **Plaintiff** – The person who brings a lawsuit.
15. **Defendant** – The person being sued or charged.
16. **Litigation** – The process of taking legal action through court.
17. **Power of Attorney (POA)** – Granting someone authority to act on your behalf.

18. **Trust** – A legal entity to hold and manage assets for beneficiaries.
19. **Executor** – The person appointed to carry out the terms of a will.
20. **Guardian** – Someone legally responsible for a minor or incapacitated adult.
21. **Probate** – The legal process of validating a will and distributing assets.
22. **Heir** – A person legally entitled to inherit property after someone\u2019s death.
23. **Incorporation** – Forming a legal corporation for a business.
24. **Fiduciary Duty** – A legal obligation to act in another person's best interest.
25. **Conflict of Interest** – A situation where personal interests could interfere with professional duties.

Important Disclaimer

This book, *Financial Literacy For Pro Athletes,* is written with the intent to educate, empower, and encourage professional athletes—and those who support them—to take control of their financial lives. The information shared throughout these pages is based on the author's personal experiences, professional insights, and over two decades of work in financial services, athlete education, and personal development.

However, it is critically important to understand the following:

Educational Purpose Only

All content in this book is presented strictly for general educational and informational purposes. The goal is to provide athletes with foundational financial concepts, frameworks for responsible decision-making, and awareness of common challenges and opportunities faced by those earning significant income through professional sports.

The strategies, ideas, and insights shared are intended to help you begin thinking critically about your financial future. This book is not personalized financial advice and should not be treated as a custom roadmap for your unique situation.

Every athlete's financial circumstances, legal obligations, and personal goals are different. What works for one player may not be appropriate—or even advisable—for another. Before making any decisions involving contracts, endorsements, investments, taxes, or legal matters, you should consult the appropriate licensed professional.

No Legal Advice

Although professional sports contracts, endorsements, and intellectual property issues have legal implications, this book does not provide legal advice. It is not a substitute for working with an attorney.

If you are signing contracts, reviewing endorsement agreements, forming a business entity, or managing your personal brand, you must seek advice from a qualified attorney who specializes in sports law, entertainment law, or contract law.

Rules governing endorsements, intellectual property, business operations, and liability vary by state, country, league, and team, and they continue to evolve. It is your responsibility to ensure that you are in compliance with all relevant laws and regulations.

No Financial or Investment Advice

While this book discusses important financial topics such as budgeting, saving, investing, tax planning, insurance, and wealth-building strategies, it does so from an educational standpoint only. It is not intended to offer personalized financial advice or investment recommendations.

You should not make any financial moves based solely on the content of this book. Always consult with a Certified Financial Planner, licensed financial advisor, or other qualified professionals before making decisions about investments, retirement planning, insurance coverage, cash flow strategies, or financial management.

The author does not represent or warrant that any strategies discussed will guarantee a specific outcome or result in financial success.

No Accounting or Tax Advice

This book is not authored by a CPA, tax attorney, or enrolled agent. Any references to tax strategies, deductions, business expenses, or IRS filings are based on a general understanding and publicly available information.

Tax laws, filing requirements, and deductions vary based on your income, residency, career structure (e.g., endorsement income, bonus income, salaries, performance incentives), and the state or country where you live or earn income. Athletes often face complex multi-state and international tax issues.

If you are earning professional income, you are strongly encouraged to seek advice from a licensed tax professional or accountant familiar with the unique financial and tax needs of pro athletes. Only a licensed expert can help you properly structure your income, calculate quarterly estimated taxes, and avoid unnecessary penalties or audit risks.

No Guarantees or Promises

Reading this book does not guarantee financial gain, career longevity, endorsement success, or long-term wealth. Financial success depends on many factors including your personal discipline, decisions, team of advisors, market conditions, and sometimes circumstances beyond your control.

This book provides motivation, education, and a starting point not guarantees. Any examples, case studies, or hypothetical scenarios included are for illustrative purposes only and do not represent promised outcomes.

Limitation of Liability

By reading this book, you acknowledge that the author, Pat Brown, MBA, and all affiliated brands or websites including FinancialLiteracyForProAthletes.com, FinancialLiteracyForNIL.com, FinancialLiteracyForStudentAthletes.com, FinancialLiteracyForCollegeCoaches.com, FinancialLiteracyForParentsOfProAthletes.com, and others are not responsible for any decisions you make or outcomes you experience based on the content provided.

Neither the author nor any affiliated organization will be liable for any loss or damage including financial loss, tax penalties, legal consequences, or business setbacks that may arise directly or indirectly from your use of the information contained herein.

Encouragement to Seek Professional Support

It is the author's strong belief that every athlete deserves access to a qualified, trustworthy team of professionals including financial advisors, accountants, attorneys, insurance specialists, and business managers who understand the unique opportunities and challenges professional athletes face.

This book is meant to complement, not replace, the role of your professional team.

If you do not currently have a qualified financial advisor, CPA, or attorney specializing in sports or athlete income management, you are encouraged to start building your team as soon as possible. Making smart financial decisions early can have a profound impact on your wealth, freedom, and long-term legacy.

Remember: You are the CEO of your career. Owning your financial life is a championship move one that will serve you long after your playing days are over.

Stay sharp. Stay smart. Stay protected.

Key Financial and Tax Dates for Pro Athletes (NFL, NBA, WNBA, Soccer, MLB, Hockey, and More)

As a professional athlete, your financial game plan must be just as sharp as your performance on the field, court, pitch, or ice.

Here's a month-by-month breakdown of the key financial and tax dates every pro athlete needs to know—whether you're in the NFL, NBA, WNBA, MLB, NHL, MLS, or any other league.

Use this as your playbook to stay ahead, avoid penalties, maximize deductions, and protect your future.

January

Jan 1 – New Tax Year Begins

- Start tracking all income, endorsement deals, bonuses, appearance fees, and business expenses.
- Set up or refresh your bookkeeping system (Google Sheets, QuickBooks, Keeper Tax, etc.).
- Open or maintain a separate business bank account.
- Rule of Thumb: Save 25%-30% of every dollar you earn for taxes.

Jan 15 – 4th Quarter Estimated Tax Payment Due

- If you owed $1,000 or more last year and didn't have enough withheld, you must make this payment.
- Form to Know: IRS Form 1040-ES.

Jan 31 – Deadline for Receiving Tax Forms

- Watch for:
- Form 1099-NEC (for endorsement income, appearances, etc.)
- Form 1099-K (for platform payments like Venmo, PayPal, etc.)
- W-2 (if you had salary income from any employment)

Tip: Create a "2024 Taxes" digital folder now to store everything.

February

- Start organizing your tax documents: contracts, receipts (travel, training, marketing), mileage logs.
- Prepare to complete:
- Schedule C (for self-employed income)
- Schedule SE (for self-employment taxes)

March

March 15 – Tax Filing Deadline for LLCs and S-Corps

- If you operate your brand or endorsement deals through an LLC taxed as an S-Corp, file your business return.
- Form to Know: Form 1120-S.

April

April 15 – Major Federal Tax Deadline

- File your individual tax return (Form 1040).
- Make 1st Quarter Estimated Tax Payment for the new year.
- Last day to contribute to an IRA or HSA for the previous year.
- Extension Form: IRS Form 4868 (if you need extra time).

Tip: File even if you can't pay. Penalties are much higher for failing to file than for failing to pay.

June

June 15 – 2nd Quarter Estimated Tax Payment Due

- Keep up with quarterly tax payments to avoid IRS penalties.

Mid-Year Review:

- Recalculate your tax estimates if your income (or endorsements) has jumped.
- Adjust your savings percentage if necessary.

July

July 1 – Mid-Year Financial Review

- Reassess contracts, financial goals, tax withholding, and budget.
- Evaluate forming or upgrading your business entity (if consistent off-field income continues).

September

September 15 – 3rd Quarter Estimated Tax Payment Due

- Organize receipts, contracts, and endorsements ahead of the final tax push.

Tax Prep Tip:

- Start prepping early before playoffs, bowl games, or travel season gets heavy.

October

October 1 – FAFSA Opens (For Younger Athletes)

- Important for pro athletes pursuing degrees or supporting family members in college.

- NIL income (for younger players) may affect financial aid eligibility.

October 15 – Extended Tax Return Deadline

- Final day to file if you requested an extension.

November

Year-End Planning Begins

- Meet with your financial team (advisor, CPA, agent).
- Maximize deductions (buy gear, update websites, renew media kits).
- Review investments and consider charitable contributions for tax planning.

Rule of Thumb:

- Document every expense linked to your career.
- Keep track of professional training, coaching, marketing, travel, and equipment.

December

December 31 – Final Day for Major Tax Moves

- Last day to:
- Purchase business-related items (for deductions).
- Book last-minute endorsement income.
- Contribute to some retirement accounts (Solo 401(k), SEP IRA).
- Calculate whether you met the IRS Safe Harbor Rule:
- Pay at least 100% of last year's tax liability (or 110% if you earned over $150,000).

Bonus: Best Financial Practices for Pro Athletes

- **Save 25%-30% of Every Payment** for taxes immediately.
- **Separate Business and Personal Finances** — different accounts, different credit cards.
- **Track All Expenses** — every plane ticket, hotel, meal, and gear purchase.
- **Hire a Professional** — work with a CPA, financial advisor, and attorney who understand athlete finances.
- **Know Your State and City Taxes** — different states (and cities) have different rules.
- **Use Free Tools** — Google Sheets, QuickBooks Self-Employed, Keeper Tax, MileIQ for mileage tracking.

Final Encouragement

Managing your financial calendar is just like managing your training schedule.

The more intentional you are, the stronger your foundation becomes.

Small, smart moves every month stack up into lifelong wealth, freedom, and impact.

You're not just playing for today.

You're building for tomorrow—and for every season after that.

Own your calendar.

Own your money.

Own your legacy.

Stay ready.

Stay sharp.

Win forever.

Pension Playbook: Maximize Your Lifetime Benefits

1. First Year in the League

- Schedule a meeting with your union representative (NFLPA, NBPA, MLBPA, WNBPA, etc.)
- Get a copy of your Pension Summary Plan Description
- Ask specifically how many seasons, games, or days you need to be vested
- Enroll in your 401(k) or defined contribution retirement plan immediately
- Contribute enough to capture any available matching contributions

2. Each Playing Season

- Confirm your credited seasons or vesting progress at midseason and again at the end of the season
- Max out your retirement plan contributions if possible
- Meet with an independent financial advisor to review cash flow, investments, and tax strategies
- Make sure your beneficiary designations are current

3. If You Get Injured or Traded

- Confirm how the injury or trade impacts your vesting, credited seasons, or eligibility for benefits
- Review your disability insurance policies and protections
- Strengthen your emergency fund in case of shortened earnings or unexpected medical costs
- Stay proactive about career development and education in case of early retirement

4. After Three to Five Years in the League

- Double-check that you are officially vested in your pension and long-term benefits
- Create a personal "exit strategy" plan even if you are still playing well
- Estimate what your retirement pension will be
- Forecast how your cost of living may change after retirement
- Identify opportunities to continue growing your income and wealth after your playing career
- Begin networking for life after sports — mentorships, certifications, entrepreneurship, or broadcasting opportunities

5. Final Playing Season

- Notify your league or players association if you are eligible to trigger pension benefits
- Finalize health insurance coverage options for after your career ends (league retiree plans, COBRA, private coverage)
- Conduct a full financial audit: investments, savings, insurance, debts, and cash flow
- Prepare mentally and emotionally for the transition to life after professional sports

6. After Retirement

- Submit paperwork to begin pension payments once you meet the eligibility age or service requirements
- Stay informed about CBA renegotiations because future improvements could apply retroactively to retirees
- Protect your retirement nest egg through smart investing and disciplined budgeting
- Continue to expand your network; the relationships built during your career can fuel your second career
- Periodically review your financial plan and retirement distributions

Pro Tips for Every Stage

- Always document every official letter, contract, confirmation of benefits, and pension statement you receive.
- Understand that pensions often increase the longer you wait to take them. Sometimes delaying by a few years can significantly increase your monthly check.
- Never assume you will keep earning new big money after retirement. Save aggressively while you are earning the most.
- Make long-term decisions when you are clearheaded, not when you are emotionally exhausted from leaving the game.
- Always seek a second opinion before making major financial moves after your playing career ends.

The Championship Mindset

In sports, knowing the play clock is critical. You have to know how much time is left and what the situation demands.

Your pension and benefits are your play clock for life after the game.

You must protect them the way you protect a championship lead in the fourth quarter.

Many athletes lose their pensions through bad decisions, bad advice, or lack of planning.

But you are different. You have worked too hard to fumble your future now.

Being financially disciplined after your career is not weakness.

It is strength. It is wisdom.

It is how you extend your greatness beyond the game itself.

Your mission now is to set yourself up to be as legendary with your money as you were with your athletic performance.

You owe that to yourself, your family, and your future.

The scoreboard is still running.

The game is not over.

Win this next half of your life.

Bonus Section: Pension Strategies for Players Who Went International

Playing overseas — whether in the EuroLeague, Japanese baseball, Australia's NBL, or other international leagues — changes your pension and retirement landscape. Here's how to think about it:

Understand What You Are (And Aren't) Eligible For

- If you were vested in an American league (NFL, NBA, WNBA, MLB) before going overseas, your domestic pension is still yours.
- Time spent overseas typically does not count toward additional vesting or increasing domestic pension benefits.
- Most international leagues do not offer robust pensions comparable to U.S. players associations.

Best Practices

- Maximize private savings: Open or contribute heavily to a Roth IRA, Traditional IRA, SEP IRA, or Solo 401(k) while playing abroad.
- Keep track of all documentation: Overseas leagues may have supplemental retirement accounts, but they are often complicated to access or transfer.
- Protect your health: Medical coverage overseas may differ dramatically. Secure private long-term insurance if needed.
- Set aside a "reverse emergency fund": A cash reserve specifically for your return to the U.S., in case of relocation, education costs, or retraining for a second career.

Strategic Moves

- Hire a tax professional who understands international income treaties and reporting rules (like FBAR for foreign accounts).
- If you earn significant overseas income, consider setting up a U.S.-based entity (like an LLC) for certain endorsement or business income.
- Avoid lifestyle creep while overseas; save in U.S. dollars as often as possible.

Key Mindset

Your U.S. pension is your foundation. Your overseas earnings are your bonus. Treat them as separate teams you must manage carefully.

Bonus Section: Second Career Checklist Tied to Pension Start Date

Most athletes retire from sports long before they retire from working. Here's how to structure your transition:

While Still Playing

- Start networking heavily in areas of interest: business, media, coaching, entrepreneurship.
- Take offseason internships, online courses, certifications.
- Build a LinkedIn profile and professional social media presence separate from your athlete brand.
- Begin exploring industries and roles you could see yourself thriving in post-sports.

1–2 Years Before Retirement

- Meet with a career coach or mentor to sharpen your transition plan.
- Update your resume and gather letters of recommendation.
- Set a "post-career budget" that reflects your new cost of living without player income.
- Attend networking events beyond the sports world: finance, healthcare, tech, real estate, etc.

At Retirement

- Decide if you will begin collecting your league pension immediately or delay for a higher payout.
- If delaying, plan how you will replace income for the delay period (consulting, part-time work, new full-time career).
- Clarify your health insurance coverage (league retiree plan, private

marketplace, etc.)

- Secure an independent financial advisor to project income, expenses, and investment returns based on your new life chapter.

After Retirement

- Reassess your living situation: should you stay in your current home, relocate for career opportunities, or downsize?
- Maintain or accelerate savings and investing even if income drops.
- Keep your personal brand active: speaking engagements, podcasts, writing, nonprofit work, coaching.
- Check in with your pension administrator annually to ensure no paperwork issues or miscommunications.

The Goal

Don't think of retirement from sports as the end. Think of it as **halftime.** You are simply preparing for the second half of your life and career.

Bonus Section: Common League Benefit Upgrades to Watch for in CBA Renewals

Every time your league renegotiates its collective bargaining agreement (CBA), **pay attention.**

CBA renewals often change pensions, health benefits, disability insurance, and post-career programs.

Key Changes That Sometimes Occur

- **Increased Pension Multipliers:** The dollar amount credited per year of service may rise, boosting future monthly payouts.
- **Earlier Vesting:** Vesting requirements could be lowered from, say, five years to three years, allowing more players to qualify.

- **Retiree Health Plans Expanded:** Additional health coverage may be added for retirees (sometimes including dental, vision, and mental health services).
- **Lump-Sum Buyouts:** Some leagues offer older retirees the option to take a lump-sum payment instead of monthly pension checks.
- **Benefit Portability:** New rules might allow easier rollovers of 401(k) plans or benefits between teams and leagues.
- **Expanded Career Transition Programs:** New education grants, career training stipends, or networking programs may be created.
- **Increased 401(k) Match or Contribution Limits:** New CBAs can improve employer (league/team) matching on player retirement contributions.

How to Stay Informed

- Stay connected with your players' association even after retiring.
- Subscribe to union newsletters and benefit plan updates.
- Attend retiree informational sessions or webinars.
- Ask your financial advisor to watch for relevant updates if you don't want to stay plugged in yourself.

Why It Matters

Even small CBA tweaks can increase your lifetime benefits by tens or hundreds of thousands of dollars.

You fought hard for those benefits — maximize them.

Closing Mindset

Managing pensions, second careers, and benefits isn't glamorous.

It doesn't make headlines on ESPN.

It doesn't get 10,000 likes on Instagram.

But it's **how champions build lifelong wealth and security**.

The game isn't over when the final whistle blows.

The real game — the game of life, of legacy, of leadership — is just beginning.

And the smartest athletes, the true legends, never stop playing to win.

Bonus Expansion: Hidden Pension Strategies Most Athletes Miss

It's not just about knowing you *have* a pension — it's about playing the pension game like a pro.

Here are additional ways to maximize your benefits:

Delay Pension Start (If Possible)

Many pensions allow you to start receiving money at a certain minimum age — but offer bigger monthly payments if you delay.

Example:

- Start at 45 = $3,000/month
- Delay to 50 = $4,000/month
- Delay to 55 = $5,200/month

If you can live off investments, savings, or second career income during your 40s and early 50s, delaying your pension could dramatically increase your lifetime income.

Think of it like strength training for your future paycheck.

Watch for Buyout Windows

Sometimes leagues offer limited-time buyouts for certain retirees — giving you a lump sum instead of monthly payments.

Pros of lump sum:

- You get full control over investing.
- You avoid risk of future pension cuts.

Cons of lump sum:

- You now take on market risk.
- You could accidentally overspend.

Make lump sum vs. monthly decisions with a trusted financial advisor who isn't trying to sell you anything.

Combine Private Savings With Pension Smartly

Think of your pension as your "defensive line" — it's steady, reliable protection.

Your private savings (IRAs, 401(k), brokerage accounts) are your "offense" — flexible, high-potential.

You want both sides playing together:

- Use pensions for essential expenses (housing, food, insurance).
- Use savings for optional or luxury spending (travel, gifts, new ventures).

This way, you always have a safety net — no matter what happens in the economy, your second career, or the world.

Bonus Expansion: Second Career Self-Assessment

Before jumping into life after sports, take an honest inventory of yourself:

Skills Inventory

- What skills did I develop playing sports? (Leadership, time management, pressure decision-making)
- What hobbies or interests have I always loved outside of sports?
- What industries fascinate me?

Financial Inventory

- How many years can I cover living expenses without dipping into pensions?
- Do I need immediate income, or can I take time to retrain or study?
- What's my monthly "burn rate" if I stop living like a baller?

Psychological Inventory

- Am I emotionally ready to be "just a regular person" again?
- What aspects of playing (team camaraderie, competition, structure) do I need to recreate in my second career?

This is not about losing your identity. It's about **expanding your identity** — using the lessons you learned on the field, court, or rink to dominate a new arena.

Bonus Expansion: Tracking CBA Changes Like a Pro

If you're serious about protecting your wealth, make it a habit to track CBA (Collective Bargaining Agreement) changes every 5–7 years.

Here's the playbook:

When a New CBA is Announced

- Read at least the pension and benefits section.
- Ask your financial advisor how any changes affect you.
- Confirm whether your vesting, payout age, or health benefits are impacted.

Questions to Ask

- Did the vesting schedule change for pensions?
- Did the monthly pension payment rates go up?
- Are there new retiree healthcare options?
- Did 401(k) or supplemental retirement contribution limits change?
- Are there bonuses for attending post-career educational programs?

Red Flags

- Any attempts by the league to "freeze" or "terminate" pension plans.
- Shifts from defined benefit pensions (guaranteed monthly checks) to defined contribution (just investment accounts).
- Reductions in retiree health coverage.

Think of a CBA update like a new "playbook" being issued to your team. You owe it to yourself to study it — or risk getting blindsided.

Bonus Expansion: International Players and Taxes

If you earned money playing internationally — even for a short time — taxes get complicated fast.

Key Reminders

- Foreign-earned income still needs to be reported to the IRS.
- You may qualify for the Foreign Earned Income Exclusion (up to a certain limit).
- You must disclose foreign bank accounts if balances exceed $10,000 at any point during the year (FBAR rules).

Mistakes to Avoid

- Thinking "If it's overseas, the IRS won't know." (They will.)
- Letting an overseas team "handle" your taxes without independent review.
- Forgetting to pay estimated U.S. taxes on foreign income during the year.

Hire a CPA who has real international tax experience — not just your old tax guy from your college town.

Bonus Expansion: Protecting Your Retirement in an Uncertain World

The truth is, we don't know what the world will look like in 10, 20, or 40 years.

The economy will change.

Politics will change.

League benefits may change.

You must build your post-career wealth on rock, not sand.

Core Principles

- **Diversify:** Don't put everything in one stock, one property, or one business.
- **Stay Liquid:** Always keep 6–12 months of living expenses in cash or cash-like assets.
- **Delay Big Purchases:** If you're unsure, wait six months before buying houses, cars, or luxury items post-retirement.
- **Invest in Your Mind:** Keep learning. Stay adaptable. You are your best asset.

In sports, the best players adapt when defenses adjust.

Same thing with money.

Appendix A: Sample Rookie Budget

When you sign that first pro contract, it's easy to feel like the money will last forever. But the truth is, even big paychecks can disappear faster than you think if you don't have a game plan.

Your rookie year sets the tone.

It's your foundation year—not your "ball out" year.

Here's a simple, smart, steady sample budget to help you start strong.

Let's break it down.

Sample Rookie Budget

Assumptions:

- Rookie salary (after taxes, agent fees, union dues, etc.): $300,000
- Paid over 12 months: $25,000/month net income

Monthly Rookie Budget (Based on $25,000 Take-Home)

Savings and Investments: 40%

- Emergency Fund Contribution: $5,000
- Investment Accounts (IRAs, brokerage, index funds): $5,000

Fixed Expenses: 30%

- Rent or Mortgage: $4,000
- Car Payment (modest, reliable car—not flashy yet): $800

- Insurance (health, auto, renters, disability, life): $1,000
- Utilities, Internet, Cell Phone: $700
- Personal Trainer/Nutritionist (optional investment in performance): $1,000

Variable Expenses: 20%

- Food and Dining Out: $1,500
- Travel and Flights: $800
- Entertainment (streaming, movies, events): $300
- Gifts and Charity: $300
- Personal Care (barber, grooming, etc.): $500

Buffer/Miscellaneous: 10%

- Unexpected Expenses: $2,400

Key Rules to Stick To

1. **Live Like a Practice Squad Player, Not a Superstar.**
2. **Save at Least 40% of Every Paycheck.**
3. **Cap Housing Costs at 15%-20% of Your Take-Home Pay.**
4. **Drive a Car You Can Afford to Pay Off in Cash in 12 Months.**
5. **Invest Every Month, Automatically.**
6. **Keep a "No Excuses" Emergency Fund Equal to 12 Months of Expenses.**
7. **Avoid Lifestyle Inflation Until You've Completed 3 Full Seasons.**
8. **Budget for Taxes, Even if Withholding Seems Sufficient—Plan for State Differences.**
9. **Set Aside "Family Support" Money Separately—And Limit It.**
10. **Review and Adjust the Budget Every Offseason.**

Real Talk About Big Rookie Mistakes

- **Overbuying Homes:** Renting that first year gives you flexibility.
- **Flashy Cars:** That $150k car might cost you half your rookie salary after taxes.
- **Too Many "Yes's" to Friends and Family:** Set boundaries early.
- **Not Planning for the Offseason:** You might not see a check for months.
- **Assuming the Next Contract Will Be Bigger:** Play smart now; tomorrow isn't promised.

Final Encouragement

You only get one shot at your rookie season.

The habits you set now will either build your wealth or blow it up.

Be the pro who plays smart off the field—not just on it.

Own your budget.

Own your future.

Own your financial life.

This is your launchpad.

Make it count.

[End of Appendix A]

Appendix B: Questions to Ask Before Signing with Any Agent or Advisor

Choosing the right agent or financial advisor is one of the most important decisions you'll ever make.

The wrong hire can cost you millions—or worse, your peace of mind.

You're not just hiring someone to "handle" things. You're choosing a key teammate for the most important game you'll ever play: managing your life, your career, and your wealth.

Never be afraid to ask questions. A real professional will welcome them.

Here's your playbook.

Questions to Ask Any Agent

1. **How many clients do you currently represent?**
2. **What percentage of your clients play in my league or at my position?**
3. **Can you provide references from current or former clients?**
4. **How do you get paid—and what percentage do you take?**
5. **Do you receive any "kickbacks" or fees from endorsement deals?**
6. **Who negotiates contracts—you personally, or someone on your team?**
7. **How will you market me beyond the field/court?**
8. **What relationships do you have with team GMs, coaches, scouts?**

9. **Will you help me with transition planning after my career ends?**
10. **What's your approach to endorsements and off-field opportunities?**
11. **What happens if I get injured—how will you advocate for me?**
12. **Can I meet the entire team that will support me (legal, marketing, PR)?**
13. **How often will we communicate—and through what channels?**
14. **Have you ever had a client file a grievance against you or your firm?**
15. **Are you certified and in good standing with the players' association?**

Questions to Ask Any Financial Advisor

1. **Are you a fiduciary at all times?**
2. **How do you get paid—flat fee, hourly, or percentage of assets?**
3. **Do you receive commissions on products you recommend?**
4. **What licenses, certifications, and credentials do you hold?**
5. **Can you show me a sample financial plan you've created for other athletes?**
6. **What is your investment philosophy?**
7. **Do you have experience working with pro athletes or high-net-worth clients?**
8. **How will you help me plan for taxes, estate planning, and insurance needs?**
9. **Will you coordinate with my agent, CPA, attorney, and other professionals?**
10. **How often will we meet to review my plan and investments?**
11. **What's your approach to budgeting and cash flow management during my career—and after?**
12. **How will you help me protect myself from fraud, scams, and**

bad investments?

13. **Do you custody my assets, or are they held at an independent third-party custodian?**
14. **Have you ever been disciplined or had any customer complaints?**
15. **Can I speak with two or three athlete clients you currently work with?**

Red Flags to Watch Out For

- They avoid answering your questions directly.
- They pressure you to sign quickly.
- They promise "guaranteed" investment returns.
- They suggest risky or complicated investments you don't understand.
- They seem more interested in your fame than your financial future.

Final Encouragement

You are the CEO of your career and your wealth.

Agents and advisors work for *you.*

You deserve answers.

You deserve transparency.

You deserve a team that's committed to protecting your best interests—not just their own payday.

Ask every question.

Trust your gut.

Do your homework.

And remember: hiring the right people isn't a luxury.

It's a necessity.

Own it.

Protect it.

Build it.

Your future depends on it.
[End of Appendix B]

Appendix C: Common Contract Clauses Every Athlete Should Know

When you sign a contract, you're signing more than just a paycheck.

You're signing a legal agreement that can shape your career, your income, your freedom—and your future.

You need to know what you're signing.

No excuses.

No "I didn't know."

Here's a breakdown of the most common clauses every athlete must understand.

Let's walk through them—plain and simple.

1. Term of the Contract

What It Means: How long you are under contract—and when you can renegotiate or become a free agent.

Why It Matters: Longer deals can mean security—but they can also lock you into bad situations.

Real Talk: Shorter contracts = more flexibility. Longer contracts = more guaranteed money (sometimes).

2. Signing Bonus

What It Means: Upfront money paid when you sign—separate from your salary.

Why It Matters: Signing bonuses are often guaranteed even if you're cut later.

Real Talk: Take signing bonus money seriously—it might be the only "guaranteed" cash you ever see.

3. Base Salary

What It Means: The salary you earn over the course of the season.

Why It Matters: Unlike signing bonuses, base salaries are often **not** guaranteed—especially in leagues like the NFL.

Real Talk: Don't count on the full base until it's actually in your bank account.

4. Roster Bonus

What It Means: A bonus paid if you're on the active roster at a certain date.

Why It Matters: Teams sometimes cut players right before roster bonus deadlines to save money.

Real Talk: Stay ready. Stay healthy. Nothing is promised until it's signed and paid.

5. Workout Bonus

What It Means: Money you earn for attending a set number of team workouts in the offseason.

Why It Matters: Extra cash—but tied to your presence and participation.

Real Talk: Every dollar counts. Secure it if you can without jeopardizing health.

6. Incentives

What It Means: Bonuses based on performance milestones (e.g., touchdowns, games played, awards).

Why It Matters: Incentives can add millions—but they're not guaranteed.

Real Talk: Count incentive money as a "nice bonus," not part of your core financial plan.

7. Guaranteed Money

What It Means: Money you receive no matter what—even if you get injured or cut.

Why It Matters: This is the "real" contract value—not the headline numbers.

Real Talk: When negotiating, focus on maximizing guarantees, not just the total deal size.

8. Injury Guarantee

What It Means: If you get injured and can't perform, this clause protects some or all of your pay.

Why It Matters: Without it, one injury could end your earnings overnight.

Real Talk: Injury guarantees are survival tools—demand them if you have leverage.

9. Offset Language

What It Means: If you're cut and sign with a new team, your old team might not owe the full remainder.

Why It Matters: Offset language can reduce how much "double-dipping" you can do.

Real Talk: In some cases, fighting for "no offsets" is worth millions.

10. Trade Clause

What It Means: Limits or prevents the team from trading you without your permission.

Why It Matters: You stay in control of where your career goes.

Real Talk: Getting a no-trade clause is rare and valuable—especially in high-profile leagues.

11. Franchise Tag/Transition Tag Provisions

What It Means: Rules about whether a team can "tag" you after your contract expires, limiting free agency.

Why It Matters: Tags can delay your chance to hit the open market.

Real Talk: Understand your league's tag rules—it can impact your whole financial game plan.

12. Termination Pay

What It Means: Money owed if you're released during the season.

Why It Matters: Protects you from sudden income loss.

Real Talk: Always ask your agent how strong your termination protections are.

13. Conduct Policy Language

What It Means: Defines behavior that could void guarantees or trigger discipline.

Why It Matters: One mistake could cost millions.

Real Talk: Stay clean. Stay smart. Protect your bag.

14. Morals Clause

What It Means: Lets a sponsor cancel deals if you're involved in a scandal.

Why It Matters: Endorsements disappear fast if you're caught up in bad press.

Real Talk: Your personal brand is just as valuable as your on-field brand.

15. Salary Cap Language

What It Means: Clauses that tie your pay to the team's cap situation.

Why It Matters: Restructures, cuts, and bonus conversions can affect your money.

Real Talk: Ask your agent how "cap-friendly" your deal is—and what that really means.

16. Player Options/Team Options

What It Means: Clauses that allow you (or the team) to extend the deal for extra years.

Why It Matters: Who holds the option has the leverage.

Real Talk: Player options = good for you. Team options = more control for them.

17. Offseason Obligations

What It Means: Specifies workouts, appearances, or team activities you must attend.

Why It Matters: Missing obligations could cost you.

Real Talk: Know your responsibilities—don't forfeit money over misunderstandings.

18. Grievance Procedures

What It Means: Outlines how disputes will be handled.

Why It Matters: If things go south, you want a fair process.

Real Talk: Be clear about your rights—before you ever need to use them.

Final Encouragement

Your contract is your foundation.

It's your business deal.

It's your launchpad to wealth, freedom, and legacy.

Understand every word.

Ask every question.

Get everything in writing.

And remember: if it's not in the contract, it doesn't exist.

Own your contract.

Own your career.

Own your financial future.

Read it.

Question it.

Master it.

Your future depends on it.

[End of Appendix C]

Appendix D: Sample Endorsement Deal Checklist

Endorsements can be game-changers for your income, brand, and future opportunities.

But not every endorsement deal is a good deal.

Some can trap you.

Some can hurt your brand.

Some can create legal and financial headaches you don't need.

Before you sign any endorsement deal, slow down, read the fine print, and ask smart questions.

Here's your checklist to make sure the deal fits your game plan—not someone else's.

Sample Endorsement Deal Checklist

1. Who is the company?

- Research their background.
- Check public perception.
- Are they a good fit for your image and values?

2. What product or service will you be endorsing?

- Make sure you believe in it.
- Never promote something you wouldn't personally use or recommend.

3. What are the specific deliverables?

- Appearances?
- Social media posts?
- Commercial shoots?
- Number of posts/appearances required?
- Time commitment expected?

4. What is the payment structure?

- Flat fee?
- Performance-based (e.g., bonuses if sales targets are hit)?
- Paid in cash or product (or both)?
- Upfront payment, milestone payments, or after deliverables?

5. How long is the deal term?

- One-off?
- One year?
- Multi-year?
- Is there an auto-renewal clause?

6. Are there exclusivity clauses?

- Will this prevent you from endorsing other similar products?
- How broad is the "category" covered (e.g., one energy drink or *all* beverages)?

7. What rights are you giving away?

- Use of your name, image, and likeness (NIL)?
- Forever or limited to the term?
- Can they continue to use your image after the deal ends?

8. Is there a morals clause?

- Can they cancel if you're involved in negative publicity?
- Can you cancel if they're involved in a scandal?

9. Who owns the content created?

- If you film a commercial, can they reuse it indefinitely?
- Do you get approval over the final product?

10. How and where will your image be used?

- Digital?
- TV?
- Print?
- International use?

11. Is there a territory limit?

- U.S. only?
- Worldwide?
- This matters for tax and brand reasons.

12. Is there a right to approve materials?

- Do you get to review and approve ads, commercials, or posts before they go live?

13. Who pays for travel, lodging, and other expenses?

- You?
- The company?
- Is there a cap on reimbursed expenses?

14. Are there tax considerations?

- Is the money taxed in another state or country?
- Are you being paid as an employee or an independent contractor?

15. What happens if you get injured or retire?

- Does the deal survive if you're no longer active?
- Is there an exit strategy for both sides?

16. Are there performance benchmarks?

- Do you have to meet certain play milestones to keep the deal?
- Example: "Must play 8 games minimum to receive full payment."

17. Is there a non-disparagement clause?

- Are you restricted from speaking negatively about the product or company?

18. What legal protections are in place?

- Indemnification if something goes wrong?
- Insurance requirements?

19. Who resolves disputes—and where?

- Arbitration?
- Court?
- In what city, state, or country?

20. Has your attorney reviewed the contract?

- Never sign an endorsement deal without legal review.
- Your agent might negotiate—but your attorney protects you.

Red Flags to Watch Out For

- Broad exclusivity clauses that block future deals.
- Low pay relative to deliverables.
- No right to approve content.
- Vague language about expectations or penalties.
- Pressure to sign quickly without time for review.

Final Encouragement

Endorsements are powerful tools—but they're contracts first.

Every post, every commercial, every handshake photo is a business move.

Own your brand.

Own your image.

Own your future.

If the deal elevates your career and fits your values—great.

If not—walk away.

There will always be another opportunity.

Protect yourself.

Play smart.

Build your brand with purpose and power.

You've worked too hard to let anyone else control your story.

You are the brand.

You are the business.

You are the legacy.

Own it.

[End of Appendix D]

Appendix E: Timeline of Key Financial Decisions from Rookie to Retirement

Managing your financial life as a pro athlete isn't about reacting in the moment.

It's about seeing the whole field—planning ahead, anticipating change, and making the right moves at the right times.

This appendix lays out a sample timeline of major financial decisions you'll likely face, from the day you sign your rookie contract to the day you officially hang it up—and beyond.

Use this as your roadmap.

Adjust it based on your career, your goals, and your life.

But always—*always*—be looking ahead.

Let's walk through it.

Rookie Year (Years 1-2)

- Create a simple, sustainable budget.
- Set up direct deposit into multiple accounts (spending, saving, investing).
- Build a 12-month emergency fund immediately.
- Hire a fiduciary financial advisor and CPA.
- Max out contributions to retirement accounts (IRA, 401(k), etc.).
- Set up disability insurance.
- Secure health, renters, auto, and umbrella insurance.
- Start basic estate planning (will, healthcare proxy, powers of attorney).

- Take personal finance courses or hire a financial coach.
- Begin documenting endorsement income and related taxes carefully.

Early Career (Years 2-4)

- Upgrade insurance coverage as wealth grows.
- Purchase modest, reliable housing if settled—avoid luxury "starter homes."
- Evaluate and limit "family financial support" responsibly.
- Diversify investments beyond retirement accounts (brokerage, real estate).
- Formalize a business entity (LLC) for endorsement income.
- Build relationships with estate planning attorneys.
- Review and optimize cash flow planning for in-season and offseason.
- Attend one financial seminar or workshop per year.
- Begin building a professional "Board of Directors" (advisor, CPA, lawyer, mentor).

Prime Years (Years 5-8)

- Renegotiate contracts with clear focus on guaranteed money.
- Expand real estate investments (rental properties, passive income streams).
- Set up family trust structures if starting a family.
- Create a business/investment plan for post-playing opportunities.
- Explore small, low-risk entrepreneurship ventures.
- Refine estate plans with updated wealth levels.
- Insure future earning power (additional disability or loss-of-value insurance).
- Evaluate charitable giving strategies and potential foundations.
- Max out all available tax-advantaged accounts every year.
- Pre-fund future goals (college savings, future home purchases, retirement buckets).

Late Career (Years 8-12+)

- Prioritize liquidity over risky, long-term investments.
- Reassess insurance needs—scale back coverage as needed.
- Solidify legacy planning—wills, trusts, charitable plans.
- Finalize transition strategy (career after sports, businesses, investments).
- Begin building a "Retirement Paycheck" plan: where income will come from after active earnings stop.
- Reduce debt aggressively.
- Formalize mentorship, speaking, or ambassador roles if interested.
- Protect branding and intellectual property (NIL) for post-career licensing.
- Plan for health insurance post-retirement (especially for non-pensioned leagues).

Year of Retirement

- Transition financial advisor from "growth mode" to "income planning mode."
- Review estate plans one final time.
- Adjust investment strategy for reduced risk.
- Create a 10-year "post-career" cash flow and tax plan.
- Decide what lifestyle expenses are sustainable long-term.
- Formalize succession plans for businesses and real estate assets.
- Lock in a healthcare coverage strategy.
- Close out any lingering player-specific insurance policies.
- Build or expand new streams of income: speaking, coaching, consulting, owning businesses.
- Rebrand if needed—shift personal image from "athlete" to "entrepreneur," "coach," "mentor," etc.

Post-Retirement (Years 1-10+)

- Stick to cash flow discipline: protect the "nest egg".
- Reinvest surplus income conservatively.
- Stay engaged with advisors—meet quarterly.
- Update estate plan every 2-3 years.
- Manage Required Minimum Distributions (RMDs) from retirement accounts (after age 73).
- Focus on health—it's your biggest "investment" now.
- Explore new passions and purpose projects.
- Mentor younger athletes about financial literacy and life after sports.
- Travel, enjoy family, stay active—but avoid "lifestyle creep."
- Celebrate milestones—not just on the field, but off it.

Key Financial Milestones and Decision Points

- First Contract Signed
- First Endorsement Deal Signed
- Emergency Fund Fully Funded
- Retirement Accounts Maxed Out 3 Years in a Row
- First Real Estate Purchase
- First Business Investment (carefully vetted)
- Family Trust Established
- Last Playing Contract Signed
- First Major Career Transition Planned
- Sustainable Post-Career Income Plan Completed

Final Encouragement

Your career is a sprint.

Your wealth is a marathon.

You don't build a legacy overnight.

You build it season after season, decision after decision, play after play.

Whether you're a rookie still smelling the new leather of your first contract, a vet managing multimillion-dollar seasons, or a newly retired legend stepping into your next chapter—this timeline is your guide.

Stay patient.

Stay humble.

Stay disciplined.

And remember:

The choices you make when the cameras aren't rolling will determine the story your family tells about you for generations to come.

Own every chapter.

Own every decision.

Own your future.

The ball is still in your hands.

Play smart.

Play long.

Win forever.

[End of Appendix E]

Made in the USA
Monee, IL
05 November 2026

67911532R00420